Active Shooter

Active Shooter
Preparing for and Responding to a Growing Threat

Kevin T. Doss
C. David Shepherd

AMSTERDAM • BOSTON • HEIDELBERG • LONDON
NEW YORK • OXFORD • PARIS • SAN DIEGO
SAN FRANCISCO • SINGAPORE • SYDNEY • TOKYO

Butterworth-Heinemann is an imprint of Elsevier

ELSEVIER

Acquiring Editor: Tom Stover
Editorial Project Manager: Hilary Carr
Project Manager: Punithavathy Govindaradjane
Designer: Mark Rogers

Butterworth-Heinemann is an imprint of Elsevier
The Boulevard, Langford Lane, Kidlington, Oxford OX5 1GB, UK
225 Wyman Street, Waltham, MA 02451, USA

ISBN: 978-0-12-802784-4

British Library Cataloguing-in-Publication Data
A catalogue record for this book is available from the British Library

Library of Congress Cataloging-in-Publication Data
A catalog record for this book is available from the Library of Congress

For Information on all Butterworth-Heinemann publications
visit our website at http://store.elsevier.com/

Working together
to grow libraries in
developing countries

www.elsevier.com • www.bookaid.org

Contents

About the Authors

Kevin T. Doss, MS, CPP, PSP has more than 25 years' experience providing protective services in high-risk environments worldwide. His expertise includes high-risk protection services, risk, vulnerability and threat assessments, emergency planning, security program development and training, and application of physical protection systems. Kevin develops active shooter programs, infrastructure protection programs, and emergency action and recovery plans for government agencies and commercial clients. Mr. Doss regularly teaches courses for many of our nation's top organizations while continuing to take a hands-on approach as a security professional practitioner.

Kevin's credentials include a master's of science in security and risk management from the University of Leicester, UK, and two ASIS board certifications: Physical Security Professional (PSP) and Certified Protection Professional (CPP). In addition to his work-related contributions, Mr. Doss founded the ASIS Foundation's Lines of Hope Program in 2007, which provides monetary and material assistance to wounded soldiers and their families while they recover at the Walter Reed National Military Medical Center in Bethesda, Maryland.

C. David Shepherd, MBA, MPAJA, CHS-III has more than 45 years' experience in security, law enforcement, risk management, and crisis preparedness. Mr. Shepherd retired from the FBI after 24 years in counterterrorism, surveillance, and SWAT. For almost eight years, he was the executive director of security for the Venetian Resort Hotel Casino, the fourth largest hotel in the world. Mr. Shepherd was an adjunct professor of criminal justice at the University of Nevada Las Vegas for six years. He was also the Co-Chairman of Resorts under the Commercial Facilities Sector Coordinating Council (CFSCC), which represented over 100 different associations. Mr. Shepherd  assisted the Department of Homeland Security (DHS) Office of Infrastructure Protection, Science & Technology Directorate, and Office of Bombing Prevention. He is a member of ASIS International and sits on the Gaming and Wagering Subcouncil.

Dave's credentials include a master's of business administration in management and a master's of public administration with an emphasis in justice administration, both from Golden Gate University, a bachelor's of science in marketing from the University of Utah, and a Certification of Homeland Security, Level III, from the American Board for Certification in Homeland Security.

Introduction

Authors Kevin T. Doss and C. David Shepherd have trained thousands of people, organizations, and agencies to help them better prepare for active shooter and workplace violence incidents. In addition, they have planned and developed business preparedness, technology integration, and professional security programs for numerous companies and agencies. From law enforcement tactics to private sector legal issues, the authors have more than seventy-five years' combined experience in matters of high-risk security, law enforcement, and emergency response. This book is a compilation of their experience, education, and wisdom gained during years working in high-risk environments both domestically and around the world.

This book is designed to provide a framework for awareness about active shooters and potential indicators of workplace violence. Incidents involving active shooters are on the rise and are becoming deadlier and more violent. Although there is no way to accurately predict who will become a shooter or when, there are potential indicators that many active shooters exhibit before an attack. This book is distinctive for blending a coordinated mitigation preparedness and response framework between first responder partners and private sector businesses.

The authors' ultimate goal is to help provide information that may help save lives, as well as to provide guidance through all phases for anyone involved in an active shooter incident. It is intended to convey critical knowledge, training, and experiences to help prevent, mitigate, and recover from the disastrous effects of such tragedies. The reader will gain valuable knowledge from the viewpoint of both the first responding community and all operational business departments, as well as front-line employees.

Despite the real threat of active shooters in today's society, many businesses have not properly developed an active shooter program as part of their business planning process; thus the reader will be provided assistance on both the leadership and staff levels in planning for mitigation of, response to, and recovery from active shooter incidents. Moreover, shortcomings of communication have consistently plagued the effectiveness of the response, mitigation, and recovery functions for both the first responder community and private businesses. We live in a communication-based society these days, but no coordinated communication platform is yet standard among most businesses, law enforcement officers, and first responders. Private-sector businesses have a key responsibility to ensure that every employee and guest, regardless of nationality, age, and disability, receives equal notification of an emergency and options for consideration during that emergency.

Both authors stress the importance of recovering from active shooter incidents and provide subject matter that businesses should consider before, during, and after an active shooting event. The questions dealing with recovery, when considered before any incident occurs, can help prepare at-risk businesses for potential legal and employee/human resources issues that could greatly affect the recovery function. In addition, we will examine questions presented by a cross section of interested and concerned parties who look at the actions and decisions made by a business through all phases of an active shooter event.

Not only will the book provide statistical data on the subject, but we will also discuss violence in the workplace, which often precedes active shooter incidents. Identifying the triggers and actors involved in an active shooter incident is critical to understanding risks of and steps for mitigating such events. The book explores various personality traits and behavioral indicators that have been identified by various disciplines as giving clues to active shooters before an event, also exploring the effectiveness of such indicators.

The human resources department is often on the front lines, and how it issues policies and monitors employees is critical in identifying and preventing active shooter events, as indicated by the 33 percent of suspected attacks thwarted by reports of suspicious activity. This book looks at active shooters from an organizational perspective and discusses how policy and standards help expose the underlying issues as preventive measures.

Developing an effective plan is part of a comprehensive approach to preparing for these tragic events. The active shooter planning team process and program is crucial in helping organizations develop, implement, and maintain an effective active shooter program. The identification of key positions and responsibilities that should be in place before an incident will be covered, as will the use of technology to assist law enforcement; first responders will also be defined. From a historical perspective, we discuss some challenges that others have experienced during active shooter incidents and then outline business actions and coordinated efforts that can aid first responders during an active shooting.

The private sector's ability to prepare and communicate with law enforcement and first responders can mean the difference between life and death during an active shooter scenario. Chapter 5 deals with this important collaborative effort, approaching it from a private-sector vantage rather than a tactical methodology. The book will provide details about what to expect when law enforcement and first responders arrive on the scene. The ability to communicate and support the response effort will increase overall effectiveness of neutralizing the threat and set the stage for the recovery phase of an active shooter incident.

An active shooter program is only as good as the training it provides for all individuals who may be involved in an active shooter incident. We examine the process of developing training and awareness programs, both internal and external, specific to active shooters. And because we understand the challenges and costs associated with training, Chapter 9 explores the various training programs that can aid private sector businesses regardless of their size or business philosophy.

It is our sincerest intention to provide readers with the information they may need to better position their organization to protect against, as well as resources to deter, combat, and mitigate active shooter threats. Though no perfect, foolproof technique or preventive measure will ensure that an active shooting will never happen at your organization, we deeply hope that in this book you will find the necessary information to help alleviate trauma and speed recovery while supporting your primary mission: the preservation of human life.

1

Active Shooters and Workplace Violence

Introduction

January 5, 2015, starts as a normal day of school for 223 kids at the Camp Hill Middle School in Camp Hill, Pennsylvania. The children have just returned to school after having several days off to celebrate the holiday season and are busy with their daily routines preparing for first-period homeroom. As they gather their books and supplies and walk to their assigned classrooms, a single police offer directs foot traffic at the main crosswalk adjacent to the school. Camp Hill is a quiet community that seldom experiences any type of violent crime, and the local police department has a visible presence within the community. The students all know each other at school and often engage in community and church activities together after the school day ends.

Bang! Bang! Two shots ring out. Bang! Bang! Bang! Bang! A rapid burst of shots is booming down the downstairs hallway. Outside, the police officer is still directing vehicles and pedestrian traffic. He pauses and looks behind at the main school building—he has heard some sounds but isn't sure what is causing the commotion. Bang! Bang! Bang! More shots ring out. Now the officer freezes, still reluctant to leave his post: The sounds are still somewhat foreign to him, for the building structure and composition is muffling the sounds of gunfire. About ten seconds have elapsed. Bang! Bang! When approximately thirty screaming kids pour out of the main school entrance, the officer realizes that something is very, very wrong.

Ten more seconds have elapsed. The scene is complete chaos. The officer calls in the incident and then forces his way through the chaotic scene. Children are screaming at him that someone has a gun and is shooting. Several teachers now have exited the building, some with visible signs of injuries, including signs of shock. They grab at the officer, trying to get assistance. As the officer rips the students' hands off of his uniform, pushes through the human blockade and yells for everyone to get back. An announcement can be heard throughout the school from a very shaky and stressed voice coming across the public address system: "There is a shooter in the building! This is not a drill! This is not a drill! Follow your protocols and secure your classrooms!" Bang! Bang! Bang! More shots ring out.

Ten more seconds have expired. The officer now is in the main downstairs hallway, looking at several bodies lying bloody on the floor. He steps over the wounded and dying souls to pursue the threat. He sees a dark figure disappear in the west stairwell and sprints down the hall in pursuit. The officer radios back that a suspect has been seen entering the west stairwell and is believed to be heading to the upstairs classrooms. He then enters the stairwell using cover and watching his angles of exposure before heading up the stairs. The officer is now on the second floor—he peers around the hall door threshold, quickly evaluates the situation, and rapidly passes through the doorway to minimize his exposure.

Fifteen more seconds have elapsed. A second, then a third patrol car arrives on the scene. The streets are in pandemonium. Kids are running and wandering through the streets, and abandoned vehicles are blocking traffic and response vehicles. Bloody and wounded victims are looking for any help they can find. EMTs and firefighters have set up a safe perimeter and have started to redirect traffic in the area. They are waiting for the all-clear to enter into the danger zone and start helping the victims. Additional officers quickly move in through the main school entrance to assist the first officer; they move up the east stairwell in an attempt to cut the suspect off. Bang! A lone shot rings out. The first responding officer can be heard yelling, "Drop the weapon! Drop the weapon!" but it is no matter: The lone gunman has committed suicide. The policeman kicks the shotgun away from the shooter's hand, rolls over his limp body, and places the dying suspect in handcuffs. The shooting is now over, but the incident response is still progressing, and the recovery phase has just begun.

The incident described is not a real event, but it could be. It could be any school, business, or organization. It could be in a quiet community with low crime rates. It could happen to you. Most organizations are not prepared for such an event. They have not properly planned for, nor determined, all the potential aspects that an active shooter incident may cause—and, frankly, there is no longer any excuse for a lack of planning when it comes to active shooters. There are many historical incidents and available data to assist organizations in developing both workplace violence and active shooter programs to mitigate loss, improve response, reduce effects, and assist in the recovery phase of such tragic events.

The goal of this book is to provide information to the private sector, as well as to public officials and law enforcement professionals, to help better understand how to prevent, prepare for, respond to, and recover from such incidents. It is our objective to provide facts and methods to better deter, mitigate, train for, and reduce the effects of these catastrophic attacks.

Historical Overview

The world is experiencing one of the most intensive periods of active shooter incidents in history. The latest report issued by the Federal Bureau of Investigation (FBI) in 2014 [1] indicates that active shooter incidents in the United States have more than doubled over the past seven years. During the same period, the amount of casualties from these incidents has more than quadrupled. With over four times the casualties and twice the number of active shooter events over a fourteen-year span, it is anticipated that this expansive trend will continue on an upward spiral in the future.

Events such as the December 13, 2013, shooting at Arapahoe High School in Centennial, Colorado, in which a high school student, Karl Pierson, walked into school and shot another student in the head before committing suicide, are rapidly becoming an all too common occurrence these days. Similar incidents such as the Sandy Hook Elementary School shooting in Newtown, Connecticut, which occurred on December 14, 2012, and in which a single gunman, Adam Lanza, forced his way into the school, killing twenty children and six adults, wounding two others before fatally shooting himself, have put organizations on notice. Such tragic events are becoming commonplace in our society and are evolving and reoccurring— the active shooter threat can no longer be ignored.

Several incidents that have occurred in the United States follow:

- December 13, 2013: Arapahoe High School, Centennial, Colorado: 2 killed
- December 14, 2012: Sandy Hook Elementary School, Newtown, Connecticut: 27 killed and 2 wounded
- July 20, 2012: Cinemark Century Movie Theater, Aurora, Colorado: 12 killed and 58 wounded
- January 8, 2011: Political event outside a grocery store, Tucson, Arizona: 6 killed and 14 wounded
- November 5, 2009: Fort Hood Soldier Readiness Processing Center, Fort Hood, Texas: 13 killed and 32 wounded
- April 16, 2007: Virginia Polytechnic Institute and State University, Blacksburg, Virginia: 32 killed and 17 wounded
- February, 12, 2007: Trolley Square Mall, Salt Lake City, Utah: 6 killed and 4 wounded
- October 2, 2006: Amish School, Nickel Mines, Pennsylvania: 5 killed and 5 wounded

---

This recent period of concentrated violence has seen more than 486 people killed and 557 people wounded by active shooters. This escalation in the frequency and lethality of such attacks carried out by active shooters within the United States is a serious cause for concern.

As well as in the United States, there is a rise in the number of such incidents in many other countries around the world. It is often assumed that active shooters are only a U.S. problem— that if a country allows firearm ownership, it will experience more shootings. This is not true, however; nations that restrict gun ownership are often at a huge disadvantage when a shooting does occur, thanks to the proper preparation and training in that country. Active shooter incidents are a worldwide problem, and all nations must properly develop programs to prevent and mitigate the risk from such threats. International cases involving active shooters are equally deadly and often involve similar indicators and motives. Several notable incidents have occurred internationally that have had similarly tragic results.

Examples of international incidents involving active shooters:

- October 22, 2014: Michael Joseph Hall (later changed his last name to Zehaf-Bibeau), 32 years old, in twin attacks, shooting at a Canadian War Memorial then at Parliament. Zehaf-Bibeau was shot and killed by Kevin Vickers, sergeant-at-arms of Canada's House of Commons.
- July 22, 2011: Anders Behring Breivik, 35 years old, killed 77 in Oslo, Norway, in a double attack: a bombing in downtown Oslo and a shooting massacre at the Workers Youth League Camp on the island of Utoya, outside of Oslo. He was taken into custody on Utoya.
- April 30, 2009: Farda Gadyrov, 29 years old, killed 12 people at the Azerbaijan State Oil Academy in the capital, Baku, armed with a semi-automatic pistol and clips, then killed himself.
- September 23, 2008: Matti Saari, 22 years old, walked into a vocational college in Kauhajoki, Finland, and opened fire, killing 10 people and burning their bodies with firebombs before shooting himself fatally in the head.
- April 26, 2002: Robert Steinhaeuser, 19 years old, who had been expelled from school in Erfurt, Germany, killed 13 teachers, 2 students, and 1 policeman before committing suicide.

Furthermore, in a number of countries, including Afghanistan, Chechnya, Iraq, Kenya, Nigeria, Pakistan, Yemen, and Somalia, shootings and suicide bombings that kill hundreds of people annually are part of full-fledged terrorist insurgencies. Such terrorist attacks often target societies that are loosely governed and ill equipped to combat such attacks.

The Nairobi, Kenya, mall shooting that took place on September 21, 2013, at the Westgate Shopping Mall is a good example of a terrorist incident that has similar characteristics to those of an active shooter event. In this attack, four gunmen began a mass shooting in which at least sixty-seven people were killed and 175 wounded [2]. This attack lasted for approximately four days and is a prime example of how much damage shooters can cause when an organization has not properly planned or coordinated an effective program to mitigate the risk from such attacks.

Active shooter incidents, along with acts of terrorism, demonstrate the various forms of comparable mass casualty violence that threaten every society and challenge those who are responsible for the security and public safety of their citizens.

A 2014 FBI report identified 160 active shooter incidents within the United States from 2000 to 2013, but the report also suggests that the actual number of active shooter events may be much higher owing to limited search criteria, available data, and law enforcement classification of past incidents used during the research effort.

According to the FBI study, 486 people were killed during the fourteen-year period studied, and 557 people wounded (refer to Figure 1–1), by active shooters. Considering the percentage of dead versus wounded people in an active shooter incident, it becomes evident that such terrible incidents are particularly deadly. With a victim death rate of almost 50 percent, active shooters cause an exceptionally high rate of mortality when compared to many other types of deadly crime. It also should be noted that our ability to provide care for the wounded and prevent someone from dying is much better these days. The tactical emergency medicine and care has saved more lives nowadays that would have succumbed to such wounds in the past.

The study does differentiate between a mass killing and active shooter incident, and approximately 40 percent (64 events) of the 160 incidents used in the study could be defined as a mass killing. A mass killing is defined as "three or more killed" under a new federal statute.

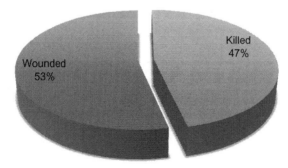

FIGURE 1–1 Number of Killed and Wounded. *Source: FBI 2014 [1].*

In all but two cases included in the study, a single shooter was the perpetrator. Sex does seem to play a big role with the active shooter, as only six of the 160 incidents involved female shooters.

A few other interesting facts were documented in the 2014 FBI report:

- 40% or 64 of the perpetrators committed suicide during or after the shooting.
- 10% or 17 of the perpetrators committed suicide when law enforcement arrived on scene.
- 5% or 9 of the shooters killed family members at home before moving to a populated area.
- 45% or 73 of the shootings occurred in a place related to business and commerce.
- 24% or 39 of shootings occurred at educational institutions.
- Several school shootings involved the highest casualty numbers.
- 60% of the shootings ended before law enforcement arrived on scene.
- Where measurable, most shootings ended within one to five minutes, even with law enforcement present at the site.

One of the greatest concerns involving active shooters is the trend toward ever-increasing numbers of incidents. Using the FBI report as a guideline, the trend of shootings has more than doubled in the past seven years. Another report substantiates the FBI study and documents the growing problem, based on data collected by *Mother Jones* and research performed by the Harvard School of Public Health and Northeastern University; it documents that mass shootings have tripled since 2011 [3].

Although the volume of incidents has more than doubled from 2000 to 2013, another statistic is the most concerning. The amount of casualties over the same period has more than tripled. Figure 1–2 illustrates the drastic rise in incidents from 2000 to 2013.

From 2000 to 2006, there were 247 casualties involved in active shooter incidents, versus 796 causalities from 2007 to 2013. Not only is the frequency of active shooter incidents growing, but nowadays such tragic events are becoming more deadly. Figure 1–3 identifies the

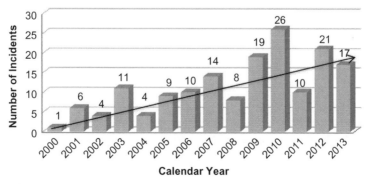

FIGURE 1–2 Active Shooter Incidents by Year 2000–2013. *Source: FBI 2014 [1].*

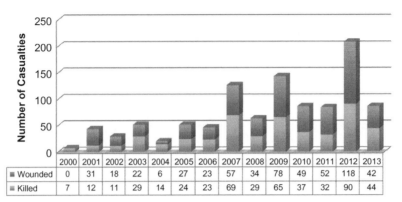

	2000	2001	2002	2003	2004	2005	2006	2007	2008	2009	2010	2011	2012	2013
■ Wounded	0	31	18	22	6	27	23	57	34	78	49	52	118	42
■ Killed	7	12	11	29	14	24	23	69	29	65	37	32	90	44

FIGURE 1–3 Active Shooter Casualty Type by Year 2000–2013. *Source: FBI 2014 [1].*

casualty type and year along with a rising trend in the number of causalities over the past seven years.

Historical incident data provides empirical evidence that is difficult to dismiss no matter how conservative the research gathered and disseminated through various media outlets. Although this is not a perfect predictor of future violence, all indicators are that the active shooter threat is growing and will continue to grow. It would be remiss and foolish to ignore such glaring facts and not make every effort to deter, prevent, respond to, and recover from these violent acts.

Many organizations are searching for proof that their specific type of business is a target for such violence before they will invest in a proactive strategy. Such organizations are choosing to be negligent based on their calculated risk that such an act of violence will not happen at their locations, despite the historical evidence. That being stated, research may suggest that some organizations are at a higher risk for experiencing an active shooter event. Figure 1–4 below identifies the location of attacks based on the latest research.

The greatest number of active shooter incidents occurred in businesses, comprising enterprises such as offices, retail stores, warehouse facilities, and similar operations existing for commercial purposes.

Understandably, the business category has the highest number of attacks, which makes sense from an economic perspective. Economic problems are one of the leading causes of stress among adults, and experiencing problems in the workplace can lead to deadly consequences. In addition to one's livelihood, the lack of interpersonal skills and personal problems in the workplace can be problematic if the early warning signs are not properly diagnosed and intervention accomplished.

Regrettably, the second most frequent category of attacks occurred in schools from pre-kindergarten through twelfth grade. It is easy to understand why schools are easy targets for violent acts involving firearms, but being an easy target does not fully explain the psychology behind why schools are being attacked so frequently. Schools tend to offer a target-rich environment, often very visible to the surrounding communities, and, most important, have various types of issues that many other type of organizations do not.

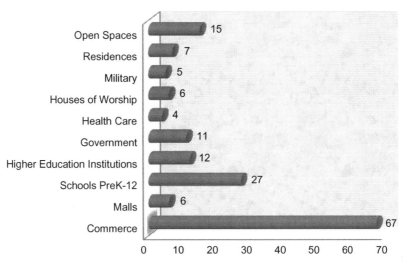

FIGURE 1–4 Active Shooter Attack Locations. *Source: FBI 2014 [1].*

For example, a private business may be able to screen out potentially violent persons by performing pre-employment screening for criminal history and recent drug use. Public school districts tend to accept all registrations, regardless of their mental or criminal problems, unless they have been documented by previous school districts and appear to pose an inherent danger to students or staff.

Bullying is another problem at many schools; the physical and mental abuse of students and/or staff can lead to severe consequences when left unchecked. Many students feel isolated, forsaken, and mistreated, which is easily compounded by verbal or physical abuse by their peers [4].

Although the attack location research identifies several types of organizations that may have a higher probability of occurrence for active shootings, anticipating a shooting is not a perfect science. It has long been established that any type of business or organization is at risk for violence. It would be remiss to believe that such incidents cannot occur any time and anywhere.

Research suggests that emphasis should be placed on prevention, response, and recovery. Most organizations' capability to effectively and swiftly respond to an active shooter threat is marginal at best. To better understand some of the challenges posed, we must define an active shooter.

Active Shooter Definition

The U.S. Department of Homeland Security (DHS), along with the White House, Federal Emergency Management Agency (FEMA), and U.S. Department of Justice (DOJ), among many other federal and state agencies, define an "active shooter" as an individual actively engaged in killing or attempting to kill people in a confined space or populated area [5]. A 2014 FBI report describes an active shooter as a person or group of persons engaged in the killing or attempted killing of people in a populated area. This report eliminated the word "confined" from the definition, for many such shootings occur in open spaces. Furthermore, this definition suggests that the act involves the use of firearms rather than other types of weaponry.

Another term commonly used to refer to this type of threat is "rampage shooting." More and more professionals are using this term in conjunction with the term "active shooter" to describe these tragic events. If we consider the "active" part of the definition, it clearly means that the shooter is still actively engaging targets, on the move locating more victims, or escaping the scene of the crime. After the incident is over, we still refer to the perpetrator as an "active shooter."

Gang-related shootings, along with many other types of classified murder, are excluded from our book and are not considered under the active shooter classification. The motives, indicators, and preventive measures for gang-related shootings and drug violence are very different from those associated with an active shooter. Although murder may occur during an active or rampage shooting, meaning that the shooter has premeditated the killing of specific individuals, typically the shooter is devoid of any specific pattern or selection of victims. Active shootings often are initiated by mental instability, hatred, or a significant life event.

An active shooter typically does not intend to take hostages nor negotiate any terms and often works alone (Figure 1-5). The active shooter wants to decide who lives and dies until he or she stops killing, lose the capability to kill (such as by running out of ammunition), or is stopped by force. Often the shooter will take his or her own life when confronted by law enforcement, though in several documented cases the shooter surrendered before being killed

FIGURE 1–5 Single Gunman. *Courtesy of Level 4 Security LLC.*

or committing suicide. In other cases, the shooter simply walked away from the scene after deciding that he or she was finished or that his or her resources were depleted.

It is extremely difficult to determine the motivation or reason behind many active shooter incidents, especially when the shooter commits suicide or is killed during the act. Without having a proper understanding of the motive behind such violent acts, it becomes very difficult to deter or prevent them.

The difficulty in defining an "active shooter" using a single definition is that many of these shooters can also be classified as "terrorists," their attack being motivated by political or religious objectives. This blurred definition can cause many professionals in academia and law enforcement to argue over an accurate classification of each shooter and event. Our goal is not to argue over the definition, but rather to include those incidents that may fit with or similarly correspond to the active or rampage shooter classifications.

For purposes of this book, and because of the similarities between rampage shooters and some acts of terrorism, we will define an active shooter as "an individual or group actively engaged in killing or the attempted killing of people in an area that is populated or defined by an activity." This definition allows the inclusion of a broad range of weapons and covers incidents whose characteristics involve indiscriminate actions even if there is a premeditated initiating factor. It also provides some inclusion for the cross-classification of some types of terrorist acts, mass murders, and rampage shootings.

Complexity of Violence

Violent incidents are continuing to multiply and increase in frequency, attesting that the active shooter threat is a difficult risk to predict and prevent. A common misconception is that active shooter incidents are impulsive acts by irrational people. A closer examination of many active shooter events suggest that both planning and premeditation evolve over time. The preparatory phase often includes early warning signs and behaviors, which can be identified by those individuals nearest the perpetrator. Security personnel can be another line of defense in the detection and assessment of a potential active shooter threat and can be in a position to respond to indicators, possibly preventing the act from ever occurring.

> Early warning signs associated with active shooter incidents are often ignored or misinterpreted. Many past events have demonstrated numerous early warning signs associated with the attack that should have been recognized, with intervention steps taken. It is not enough just to recognize the early warning signs, for there are many cases of this occurring before a shooting; the assessor must take steps to intervene and prevent the potential shooter from following through with the plan.

There are several notable examples of missed opportunities for early intervention, such as the shootings at Sandy Hook Elementary School (Adam Lanza), Cinemark Century Movie Theater (James Holmes), Virginia Polytechnic Institute and State University (Seung-Hui Cho), an Arizona political event (Jared Loughner), and Fort Hood (Nidal Hassan). In every case, family, friends, coworkers, and counselors of the perpetrators observed irregular and irrational behavior before the attacks. These visible indicators were not effectively acted on nor communicated to the proper authorities for assessment and potential intervention.

In addition to the indicators of potential violence, the complexity of the attacks has also evolved over time. The shooters are often researching previous active shooter incidents and modifying their tactics and behaviors accordingly. In essence, they are doing their "homework" before attacking. The asymmetrical aspect of an active shooter is extremely difficult to defend against, and preventive measures such as detection, assessment, response, and law enforcement tactics are vital parts of the solution.

In part, the press has added to this challenge by the amount of information analyzed and shared with the public after an attack occurs. The openness of our society nowadays adds an often overlooked dynamic when developing preventive and recovery measures. The ability to research past incidents and gain a comprehensive understanding of what works and what doesn't work is available with the simple click of a mouse. When it comes to a planned attack, we are dealing with a thoroughly informed, well-armed adversary who often understands more about the facility or grounds than the responding law enforcement officers.

Prevention

Contrary to popular belief, it is possible to prevent active shooter incidents. In 2012, Blaec Lammers, age 20, had become so obsessed with the Century Theater shooting in Aurora, Colorado, that he was planning an attack of his own. His mother, Tricia Lammers, turned her son over to law enforcement after he purchased two semi-automatic rifles and 400 rounds of ammunition with the intention of attacking a movie theater and Walmart in Bolivar, Missouri [6]. Why did he choose to take the attack to Walmart after the movie theater? Simply because he had planned to resupply his ammunition after the theater shooting so he could continue his killing spree.

Blaec was described by his own mother as being a "loner" and having much difficulty in making friends at school. His psychological profile is similar to those of many other active shooters: being quiet and reclusive, perhaps having feelings of being a failure. Of interest is the report that Lammers had planned to turn himself over to law enforcement officers when they arrived at the scene. Although this is speculative in nature, it helps to understand Lammers's frame of mind during the planning stages of the attack. Often, active shooters plan self-termination or surrender after they are intercepted by law enforcement.

Active shooter incidents are becoming so frequent that it is imperative for law enforcement and security professionals to develop a comprehensive and systematic understanding of these threats and the procedures necessary to prevent, respond, and recover from such tragedies. It is also equally important for organizations to implement effective strategy and protective measures at their facilities. This planning begins long before an anticipated attack and requires a collective effort between security, safety, legal services, and operations within the organization. In addition, a joint collaborative approach between the organization and law enforcement officials is required to develop effective strategy to combat this ever-evolving threat.

Civil litigation against the organization after an attack usually involves claims that the enterprise should have taken additional steps to protect those under their care. This duty to protect employees, vendors, and guests on the property is key. Every aspect of an attack will be scrutinized, from the prevention aspects and response time to tactics, and will include any perceived oversights or failures. Such charges usually arise in our litigious society no matter how reasonable and effective the protective measures and response strategy for proactive intervention.

Development of an effective active shooter program must involve knowledgeable professionals who understand the major aspects of the risk, threat, protective measures, communications, corresponding law enforcement response tactics, and recovery options. This body of knowledge only rarely can be found in a single consultant or advisor and thus may require a team of professionals to participate in the development of a comprehensive plan.

Workplace Violence

Workplace violence can be defined as any act or threat, whether implied, verbal, or physical, intended to intimidate or harm an individual, whether at work or otherwise, that originates in the workplace [7]. Many employees spend as much time in the workplace as they do in their own homes—up to 65 percent of their time may be spent in the workplace. This additional time at work may expose them to acts of violence or threatening behaviors. Factors that can increase risk to the employee often start with choice of career, position within the firm, and location of the workplace.

Violence in the workplace covers a spectrum of threats or violent acts that may cause damage or injury or obstruct normal work conditions. The range of actions covered under the term "workplace violence" can be as simple as abusive and threatening behaviors that intimidate or disrupt business operations or as extreme as physical acts of lethal violence. The active shooter is obviously at the high end of the violence spectrum and can completely destroy the viability and future of the organization. Because a large percentage of active shooter events occur in the workplace, it is vital that every organization properly addresses the potential problem.

Outside facilitators can also influence workplace hostilities. These include financial problems, disturbed family members, unstable relationships, drug and alcohol use, and even agitated customers. Most of us, at some point, will experience an act of violence, intimidating behavior, or verbal aggression during our career. Workplace violence incidents, as an insider threat, have an important role when it comes to active shooters, for they may be a precursor to such violent attacks.

Most of us do not get a choice of colleagues or business partners during our career. Additionally, we often are exposed to clients, customers, and business vendors throughout the business day who can place us in close contact with criminal elements. Although our work-related associates might expose us to violent people, our personal and family relationships can be the most challenging to deal with in the workplace.

Workplace violence may be separated into three major categories:

- Personal relationships
- Employer related
- Property- or commercially motivated

Personal Relationships

Personal relationships can often lead to heightened emotions and unusual behaviors. The workplace is often an extension of our family and can lead to personal relationships, whether healthy or not, as well as problems later on. Some organizations try to limit the type and depth of relationships stemming from workplace exposure, but in a free society, this is a difficult, if not impossible, task. Trouble at home often spills over into the workplace; angry spouses, partners, and immediate family members can all pose a threat to the organization.

Active shooter incidents often involve former lovers and current spouses, as well as a variety of relational issues that can include crimes of passion, drug and alcohol abuse, and various forms of mental illness. Perpetrators often are unhappy in their home life but may not discuss it openly with colleagues or family members—and the internalization of such stressors can help move them past the brink of simply "having bad thoughts" to taking actual destructive actions.

Almost everyone will experience some type of relationship failure, marital divorce, or long-term relationship breakup over his or her lifetime. It is easy to understand how such stressful events can lead to dangerous thoughts and acts of violence, but most people learn to deal with such emotions, overcome them, and move on with life. Yet not everyone is capable of getting past such trauma, which then festers and builds up within him or her. Such incidents are very dangerous to deal with and can lead to serious injury or death.

Employer-Related

Employer-related violence has multiple origins but often is related to personality-related conflicts or other work-related stress. One of the greatest stresses that an employee can face is the fear of losing his or her job. The modern-day business practice of downsizing staff and outsourcing labor is often traumatic to the affected staff, especially when little notice of such changes has been communicated to employees. Other types of employer-related stress may include reprimands for violations of company rules, poor work performance reviews, or trouble with interpersonal relationships and working with others.

Psychologist Abraham Maslow developed a hierarchy of needs theory [8] suggesting that if a person's basic needs are not being met, the resulting climate can include serious criminal behaviors. When a person loses, or fears losing, his or her job, he or she will attempt to satisfy financial needs using any means at his or her disposal. Most people react by searching elsewhere for employment or starting their own business, but a few individuals resort to threatening and criminal behaviors when they feel their job is threatened.

Another reason why employees can be frustrated, angry, or desperate is if they feel that management is being unfair. Many organizations give management a tremendous amount of discretion to run departments using an autocratic management style. These departmental "dictatorships" may be breeding grounds for unfair management practices and abusive management behaviors. Many acts of workplace violence initiated by staff members or former employees are directly related to real or perceived injustices and prejudice. When a worker feels victimized and cannot identify an acceptable recourse through which to resolve the matter, that inability may lead to a surprisingly hostile reaction. Typically, such an employee will try to solicit support from others in the organization and try to undermine management's position.

Many organizations are also attempting to accomplish more tasks using fewer employees. This directly creates additional stress in the work environment. When staff is reduced beyond operational capability, the resulting increase in hours and work effort can create tremendous strain on the remaining workforce. The potential for an outbreak of violence in the workplace or the targeting of management at their residences may increase dramatically.

Employeeonemployee violence is another aspect of employer-related workplace violence. Differences in age, personality, beliefs, cultures, and perceptions can create problems in the workplace. Workplace bullying can lead to resentment, anger, and retaliatory behaviors. However, not every incident will result in physical action, and often these conflicts can be mitigated if caught and resolved quickly.

Most, if not all, of us must work with others to accomplish our core missions. This includes exposure to customers, manufacturers, and suppliers on a regular basis. In addition, many of our businesses rely on other companies to meet their commitments before they can satisfy their own clientele. The workplace provides multiple targets and avenues for staff and exposes them to outsiders who may be intent on harming them. This is especially true for women in the workplace if many men do not control their feelings or emotions and make unwanted advances—or worse.

We are often dismayed and shocked at how openly aggressive men can be in the workplace, whether as customers or otherwise. For example, a female waitress may have to defend against multiple advances during a single shift by male customers. Although some will suggest that this is part of employment in the retail environment, it most certainly is not. People skills are required, but when a simple gesture of appreciation turns into a serious unwanted advance, protective measures should be in place to prevent the action from becoming an incident. No one should have to work in fear of inappropriate sexual advances by individuals who do not control their desires. This is not to say that women themselves never perpetrate personal or sexual workplace violence; indeed, they can often be more aggressive in fighting over a relationship while at work.

Another area of workplace violence that is increasing in frequency is that having to do with employees who provide care services to others. From religious leaders to healthcare workers, this category of worker has become the focus of many prevention programs. Often in these cases, many of the crimes go unreported in consideration of the morality and kindness of many who choose such a profession. Often these workers are targeted because of their gentle and kind spirits and may become repeat victims of violence simply because they do not report the crimes. This attitude is very similar to spousal abuse cases: The victim wants to forgive the perpetrator and hope for behavior to change but often refuses to take the necessary steps to ensure that criminal behavior is corrected. The guiding principle of workers employed in providing care services is to provide services to or care for individuals without doing harm. Although some professions expose employees to acts of violence—such as policing—it is never acceptable to believe that such professionals should accept violence as part of their normal job requirement, even if the conditions under which they operate are stressful.

There is another side to violence in the workplace among service care providers that is far more disturbing: the staff member who commits violence against those who placed in his or her custody or care. Such violent acts can range from verbal abuse to physical abuse. The targets in these cases are often the most vulnerable in society, from young children to the mentally ill and elderly. The media has placed some emphasis on these heinous crimes recently, but there are still many crimes that never receive attention—and unfortunately some such cases are covered up by the organization providing such care to prevent lawsuits and protect the organization's brand or image. Some industries have issued professional codes of ethics and conduct in an effort to combat such violence, and many states have enacted laws governing certain professions.

Property or Commercially Motivated

These violent actions are often directed at the company or organization and their property. Acts such as sabotage, theft, and vandalism can lead to accidents and injury or death. Some such acts may occur during union strike negotiations or other related employee bargaining for rights or income. Although most bargaining negotiations are peaceful and legal, there are several examples of such activities becoming violent and deadly.

Robbery and theft can be placed under the employer related violence category, but it also fits under property-focused violence. During a commission of a crime, such as a robbery, emotions can be stressed and the outcome can lead to a violent encounter. If a criminal is intent on committing a crime to gain property such as money or goods, he or she may view any guardian as a threat and react using violence. There have been countless victims of stabbing or shootings during a robbery just because the employees were working at the time when the crime was committed.

Moreover, if the act is intended to damage or destroy property or negatively affect commerce, the unsuspecting employee can find himself or herself an innocent victim just by being in the wrong place at the wrong time.

Factors that can produce the triggers to initiate such attacks in the workplace are varied but usually involve life-altering events such as divorce or the loss of a job and can be as simple as a perceived wrong when an employee is disciplined. The workplace also exposes many individuals to people or situations they may not otherwise encounter.

Not every country provides the same level of freedom for all its citizens. However, most, if not all, countries do protect the rights of their citizens by designing laws to protect them against criminal acts. Frequently laws are developed to protect the community, culture, and commercial interests of the nation. The workplace is no exception, and individuals should be provided protection from acts of violence or aggression.

Large business is often indistinguishable from its government, and in some cases they are one entity, often referred to as a quasi-government agency. This exacerbates the challenge of detecting a potential active shooter just due to the sheer numbers of potential threats. When one considerers the numerous potential adversaries that a government must account for, it is a daunting task just to detect impending danger among the staff, contractors and guests, not too mention all of the outside groups and enemies intent on causing them harm.

According to the U.S. Bureau of Labor Statistics of Fatal Occupational Injuries (CFOI) and the U.S. Bureau of Justice Statistics National Crime Victimization Survey [9], government employees represented about one of every five victims of workplace violence homicides, and the rate of assaults against government employees is as high as three times higher than that of private sector employees. However, serious violent crime is approximately 10 percent greater in the private sector than in the government. These reports also highlighted that shootings were the cause of death in 78 percent of workplace homicides. A few other findings of interest were reported as well:

- Shootings were the most frequent manner of death in both homicides (80 percent) and suicides (47 percent).
- Workplace violence is the primary cause of fatalities in the workplace for females. Female employees are most likely to be attacked in the workplace by someone with whom they have a work relationship. Of the 302 fatal work injuries involving female workers, 22 percent involved homicides, compared to 8 percent for men.
- Male employees are most likely to encounter an incident of violence with a stranger in the workplace. Men represented approximately 85 percent of deaths in the workplace.
- The highest number of fatalities in the workplace is experienced in sales, retail work, law enforcement and corrections, management, and security.

When it comes to workplace violence, an active shooting is one incident that no one wants to experience, but it is prudent for every employee to consider such acts of violence and prepare for them should they ever become a reality.

Four Levels of Violence in the Workplace

Violence in the workplace can be characterized into four levels:

Level 1 involves the types of behaviors or incidents that often don't require disciplinary actions by the organization but that may require documentation, awareness training, and verbal reprimands. Included in this type of violence are actions that in involve low-level use of profanity, difficult behaviors that are not violent in nature, rumormongering, and uncooperative attitudes toward colleagues and management.

Level 2 may involve actions and behaviors that involve obstinate or perverse comments, inappropriate comments of a sexual nature, and outbursts of anger, shouting, and low-level verbal threats. This level involves documentation of the incident and may require disciplinary actions that range from additional awareness training to a written warning.

Level 3 offenses are the type of events that warrant intervention and disciplinary actions. In some cases, professional help may need to be solicited to assist with the problem. This level includes actions such as inappropriate touching, verbal and physical threats, and minor violence, such as fights, punching walls or tables, and throwing objects.

Level 4 is the level of violence and involves the most inappropriate and dangerous behaviors and actions. This level includes robbery, severe beating, active shooting, violent attack, crime, murder and manslaughter, sexual assault (including rape), and nonviolent incidents such as of arson and sabotage.

The level of violence perpetrated should determine the response and corrective disciplinary action. A Level 1 response may be a simple verbal reminder that the workplace is a professional environment and an instruction to stop the behavior or be disciplined. Level 2 and 3 behaviors should be well documented and should result in some type of corrective discipline. These incidents should be corrected quickly and disciplinary actions enacted before the events escalate into dangerous situations. The final level, Level 4, is the most serious level and should involve a team approach to address. Along with the human resources department and the management supervisor, the organization should involve legal and security personnel in the incident. If the act is a crime or is illegal, then the law enforcement agency having jurisdiction should be contacted immediately, and the organization should fully support the investigation.

The cost of doing nothing and ignoring the problem can be very costly to an organization, as these types of problems seldom go away on their own. Intervention, training, and disciplinary action is often required, but the cost of doing nothing and letting the atmosphere of violence fester and grow is often more expensive in the end.

Costs to the Organization

It is always difficult to determine the overall costs of workplace violence to an organization. It is even more complicated to calculate the losses of a single active shooter incident when it occurs at the location of business. Direct loss to the organization may involve any of the following:

- *Lost productivity.* In some cases of workplace violence, the entire staff resigned after the incident. The location can be closed or relocated, and such changes costs time and money. Employees who return after an incident often are not the same, and productivity can be greatly altered. In addition, the entire site may remain a crime scene for days or weeks, with staff unable to return to work until the on-site investigation is complete.
- *Property damage.* Although property damages may be minimal at times for some types of incidents, when it comes to active shooters, this may not be the case. From driving vehicles through entrances and breaking in doors to bullet damage and blood left by those who were wounded or killed, damage to both personal and organizational assets can be extremely expensive to repair and replace after an incident.
- *Lost sales.* Although difficult to ascertain, lost sales is another aspect of direct loss to the organization. Not every company offers direct sales of products, but this category also

includes any loss of service that the department or company produces. No matter the organization, if the mission is affected in a negative manner that can be measured, it equates to the loss of sales.

- *Medical costs.* Active shooter events often involve numerous killed and wounded. When dealing with multiple injuries and fatalities, the ambulance and hospital fees alone will be immense. In addition, the long-term medical rehabilitation and therapy can also be a tremendous cost to the organization even with insurance coverage.
- *Legal fees.* Any serious workplace violence event will involve litigation by the injured parties. Such cases may range from easy out-of-court settlements to multi-million-dollar decisions. The attorney fees alone can bankrupt organizations; such lawsuits can take years to reach a settlement or decision, and all the while, attorney fees continue to grow. Furthermore, disregard for preventive and preparatory measures can also lead to gross negligence claims and increase the legal payouts to the injured by millions of dollars. Unfortunately, if you do not invest in a proper workplace violence/active shooter program along with a proper security plan and emergency action plan, you may expose the company to addition litigation.
- *Physical security measures.* Many organizations choose to wait until after a serious incident to improve their security posture. Although this is a foolish status quo to maintain, it is common in the real world. The additional costs to develop proper action plans and security programs, along with physical security countermeasures such as barriers, access controls, video surveillance, and intrusion alarm systems, may all be part of the costly investment required after an incident.
- *Counseling.* The costs of providing counseling to all affected employees and guests can be a tremendous expense, especially considering all the other costs involved in recovery from an active shooter event. Counseling may continue for weeks, if not months, after an incident and is tied closely with the loss of productivity by the affected staff members.

Indirect costs to the organization may include the following:

- *Reputation.* It is hard to measure the effect an active shooter may have on a company's reputation. However, it is easy to recognize that it certainly will psychologically affect employees, clients, neighbors, and partners. Reputation is often a closely guarded attribute for successful organizations—many will sacrifice profit to maintain their standing in the eyes of their investors and the public. A single incident could shake the foundations of trust in an organization, especially if the response and recovery phases are not well planned and executed.
- *Business relationships.* It is easily inferred that many companies choose business partners based on their trustworthiness, deliverables, and financial sustainability. Typically it is a two-way street for both partners. An active shooter incident may affect the relationship for several reasons. First, such threats could be a risk for businesses doing business with the affected company, especially when one's operation could endanger the other's by exposing it to such threats. Second, if the affected business cannot deliver on its commitments, the business may be quickly moved to a competitor. Another aspect involves the risk of reputation loss by doing business with a company that is being portrayed in a negative light by the press.

- *People/experience.* As already mentioned, a company should expect that some of its best and brightest employees might not return to work after a serious incident. This can cause the organization to lose a tremendous amount of experience in a very short time. Most professionals take years to master their trade, and such losses can be traumatic to the company. The loss of senior people may also negatively affect the organization's stock value, causing serious shareholder and investor losses at a time when the company can least afford it.
- *Business location.* In the event of a deadly attack in the workplace, the company may choose to find another location to do business. As the old saying has it, location is everything in business—meaning that a large part of the value of a company may be based on its physical geographic location. The cost of a move can cost business, diminish productivity, and lose sales opportunities. If a business closes its doors because of an active shooter incident, the costs to relocate and establish the business can be another excessive expense to incur at a time when such changes and expenses can be extremely detrimental to the company.

The organization has a duty of care to protect its guests and employees while they are on the premises—and even off the premises at times. The ability of the organization to protect all employees and guests from acts of violence is challenging even for the most secure operations. Depending on your organizational mission, it can be quite simple to secure the site from outside interference, but for those working in the medical field or at educational and religious institutions, it can be quite a challenge to protect everyone from such a wide range of threats. It is harder still to protect against those who are trusted colleagues.

The insider threat is a very difficult problem for many organizations to address, for often such personnel are provided open access to the site and can document security procedures and countermeasures. Such information provides valuable data during the planning stage of an attack by an insider. Often, these employees do not have previous criminal records and may be "good" employees for many years before deciding to commit an act of violence. Not surprisingly, the insider threat may be the most difficult threat to identify and mitigate prior to an active shooter event.

On October 14, 2014, Abdulaziz Fahad Abdulaziz Alrashid, an American–Saudi national working in Riyadh, Saudi Arabia, shot and killed a former coworker at an off-site gas station [10]. Allegedly, Abdulaziz shot his former colleague because he believed that he had turned him in to his bosses for using drugs, causing his termination by his employer. Although many of the details in this case have not been released to the public, if the reported facts are true, this example illustrates the level of violence that many people face daily in the workplace. Furthermore, perceived wrongs in the workplace—or, in this case, reporting illegal activity to superiors—can lead to ferocious retaliation by colleagues who are not mentally stable.

References

[1] Blair JP, Schweit KW. A Study of Active Shooter Incidents, 2000–2013. Washington D.C.: Texas State University and Federal Bureau of Investigation, U.S. Department of Justice; 2014.

[2] <www.aljazeera.com/indepth/opinion/2014/09/mysteries-linger-over-westgate--201492171737803205.html>.

[3] <www.motherjones.com/politics/2014/10/mass-shootings-increasing-harvard-research>.

[4] <www.stopbullying.gov/prevention/at-school/>.

[5] U.S. Department of Homeland Security Active Shooter: How To Respond. Washington DC: U.S. Department of Homeland Security; 2010.

[6] <www.washingtonpost.com/business/economy/no-good-option-parents-called-policeonmentally-ill-son-but-he-got-prison-not-help/2014/05/28/d15e6fba-e6a7-11e3-a86b-362fd5443d19_story.html>.

[7] <https://www.osha.gov/OshDoc/data_General_Facts/factsheet-workplace-violence.pdf>.

[8] Doss KT. Physical Security Professional (PSP) Study Guide, 2nd ed. Alexandria, VA: ASIS International Press; 2011.

[9] <www.bls.gov/news.release/pdf/cfoi.pdf>.

[10] <www.thenational.ae/world/middle-east/americans-shot-in-saudi-arabia-work-for-us-defence-contractor>.

2 Motivations and Triggers

As soon as the active shooter begins his or her deadly rampage, people watching the nightly news instinctively want to know what the shooter was thinking. They also want to know why the shooter did what he or she did. Unfortunately, when a person is shooting randomly through a business or stabbing anyone who gets in the way, the last thing a law enforcement officer is concerned about is what the person is thinking right then. To the first responders, it doesn't matter what the shooter is thinking, what caused the shooter to commit this barbaric act, or what in the shooter's life has caused the active shooter to lash out in such a violent manner. The first responder's primary mission is to neutralize the threat and stop this cycle of death. Nothing is more important in the minds of the victims, the business management, or the first responders than stopping the active shooter as soon as possible.

After the threat has been eliminated, victims treated, and employees, guests, or students reunited with their families, only then will attention be directed toward the shooter's psychological classification, sociological category, and behavioral indicators. Psychiatry, forensic psychologists, sociologists, behavioral analysis, criminal investigators, federal law enforcement agencies, psychologists, therapists, and academics can analyze every detail in the active shooters life at their leisure. They can accumulate and collate data, interview family members or friends or coworkers, and pore over mounds of investigative files and review social media sites, all in hopes of preventing another active shooting by finding the missing links in the chain that would have or should have been replaced before any violent act occurred. For these professionals, this process is painstakingly slow. There is no silver bullet nor single psychological or personality trait that clearly and undeniably pinpoints who will or who will not become an active shooter. For the sake of society, victims' families, and society it is imperative to try. If one active shooting can be prevented by isolating traits and deficiencies, then the pain and suffering of the victim families will not have fallen on deaf ears. However, it should be pointed out that unlike with the laws of physics, there are no absolutes in psychology. A person may possess all distinguishable traits found in 90 percent of the classifiable characteristics, but that doesn't mean that that person will become an active shooter. There is a distinction between a person who seriously considers doing a dangerous act and a person who actually carries out the action.

Because active shootings can occur in almost any setting, from a crowded mall to the confines of a supervisor's office, from high-rise office buildings to the openness of city streets, articles and studies have attempted to determine the mindset of active shooters in a specific setting, such as a school, hospital, or the workplace. These works attempt to aid first responders and help workplaces mitigate and prepare for these events. Only time will tell whether the accuracy of these articles and studies has helped. One underlying fact cannot be disputed: that the active shooter is not a business problem or a first responder issue, but rather a community and societal problem that must be tackled by all disciplines and professions to find solutions together.

Profiling or Behavioral Profiling

Countless warning signs and a long trail of issues may be observed by nearly everyone who has had contact with the shooter—often these same traits and indicators have been observed for years. Threatening communications, both verbal and written, have been seen by relatives, friends, administrators, and bosses but have been ignored or never documented. Many attackers formulate a plan, and even when others knew about the attackers plan, the information was never passed along to the appropriate agency or department to mitigate.

There is no demographic profile of an active shooter or other traits had in common by a set of perpetrators of active shootings. There are significant differences in active shooters' thought processes, target selection, and desired goals when considering the broader areas of schools, hospitals, workplaces, religious facilities, malls, and open areas where shootings have occurred. If every active shooter case were reviewed in uncompromising detail and not merely a representative sample, it might be possible for active shooter and workplace violence homicides to be classified and categorized. But if we can characterize a certain profile, then there is a considerable risk of false positives being produced by stereotyping individuals. There is a significant difference between thought and action. Many people may possess all traits and indicators listed in Figure 2–3, but these individuals never turn those thoughts or even plans into the action.

There are two significant points that cannot be overstated: First, many of the active shooters have a history, sometimes even a long history, of disturbing thoughts, actions, verbalizations, and other warning signs. These warning signs may be overlooked or ignored, with an attempt at resolution made in the short term, but they are almost never fully resolved by medical professionals. As an example, does a person automatically jump into extremes of road rage when one person cuts him or her off, or does it take numerous incidents, often publicly communicated to a friend or relative? Second, is there some type of trigger event that sets the active shooter into action mode? If so, what is it? The trigger event and the intensity of this event are usually only known to the active shooter. What one person can tolerate is often very different from what another person can. We each have a filtering mechanism that should draw us up short of doing something stupid, insane, and deadly. Whether we choose to stop or are mentally capable of listening to this filtering mechanism is up to us.

When reviewing numerous recent active shooters articles, reports, research findings, white papers, and studies concerning active shooters, the following investigative action indicators were absent when identifying personality traits and behaviors. Consider the following when planning a study of active shooters:

- It is important to point out that no single shooter nor type of shooter possessed all or even a portion of these indicators. One shooter can be an honor student, and another can struggle in school. One shooter may be an ideal employee, another constantly written up for policy infractions. One shooter may be popular and outgoing, another disliked and a loner.

- The personal intensity of an indicator as regards the active shooter isn't known, so there isn't a method for determining which indicator is dominant or whether a select group of indicators take an active shooter beyond his or her normal stopping point.
- Because active shooters are also classified as active threats based on their weapon selection—e.g., knives, boxcutters, hammers, swords, vehicles—a determination of the relevancy of the below indicators is not known to those classified as active threat individuals.
- Approximately 2 percent of the active shooters conduct the killings together with another person, whether male or female; it is unknown whether another relevant indicator may apply to this category.
- Many people who have mental illnesses and who abuse alcohol or drugs never become active shooters.
- One aspect not fully understood is how age may play a part in an active shooter. People are quick to conclude that active shooters in schools are aged 16–21, but the New York City Police Department report "Active Shooter: Recommendations and Analysis for Risk Mitigation" [1] lists active shooters in several different age categories, aged 10–44 and aged 50–64. The overwhelming majority of school active shooters are in the 15–19 age group, but one must remember there are at least seven different levels of schools—elementary, middle school, and so forth.
- A number of individuals have secured weapons, explosives, and ammunition, have planned extensive details of an attack, and have even identified the exact date and time for the attack, but have stopped short of carrying out the active shooting for a variety of reasons. What common elements do they possess, and which trait curtailed their action?
- It is important to consider that if the active shooter is trying to be a copycat, fascinated by another active shooter event, this person has often exhibited similarly extreme personal action for self-gratification or notoriety in other parts of life.
- The differences in active shooting may also be subdivided by location of the shooting, such as school, business, religious, or mobile environment, and whether the shooter is affiliated with the shooting location in some manner. The real question is whether active shooters can be statistically categorized as a current employee, a former employee, a spouse, or an ex-spouse or whether they been passed over for promotion or because of unsatisfactory work performance or the like, creating a financial catalyst triggering the active shooting.
- Personality traits and behaviors may be dormant and suppressed in the active shooter for months or even years without any indication of their existence or may be passed off as an adolescent phase and not taken seriously.
- Another aspect concerns active shooters who are women. Even though the number of active shooters who are women is very low, it still does not negate the fact that they may also possess the same personality traits and behaviors as their male counterparts.

What are They Thinking?

The best possible source to determine what an active shooter is thinking is to interview a surviving shooter. The U.S. Department of Justice Federal Bureau of Investigation report "A Study of Active Shooter Incidents in the United States between 2000 and 2013" [2] indicates that in commercial areas, a total of seventeen shooters out of forty-four were apprehended at the scene or later by law enforcement. The report further indicated that these shooters potentially provide seventeen research opportunities for analysis. However, even this logical process has its own set of barriers:

- The shooter must be willing to talk to the researchers, and there is no guarantee that the information provided will be truthful or accurate; it may be delusional or mask the shooter's true feelings and motivations.
- The interview process cannot start until all legal proceedings have concluded, but the challenge is ongoing, for the shooter may be declared mentally incapable of trial, which may allow the researchers access to medical findings at a later date, or may be sentenced to death and await execution on death row. Again, the appeals process may prevent access to the active shooter for years.
- Defense attorneys generally will not allow their clients to be interviewed under any circumstances if there is still a chance the verdict can be changed.

Another source of information about the active shooter may be the relatives of a shooter. The relatives will have intimate knowledge, current information, and a prolonged history that can document significant events and mood swings and that often can outline dramatic turning points in the active shooter's life. However, this process also poses barriers:

- The parents may be so distraught, dismayed, and in shock themselves at what their loved one has done as to be in no condition to provide information. The parents realize that they are also under a microscope because of what their loved one has done. Their entire world, as they knew it, has gone. People point their fingers at the relatives and criticize their ineffectiveness at preventing such hideous acts. Relatives often experience public ridicule in every aspect of their life regardless of whether they have legitimately attempted to parent their loved one over years of emotional challenges or completely emotionally disowned the active shooter long ago.
- Defense attorneys generally will also not allow relatives of their client to be interviewed under any circumstance.
- Relatives may also allow an interview for the sole purpose of distancing themselves from the active shooter by possibly providing false information, recounting events that are significantly different from what actually occurred, or shifting blame toward the school system, medical doctors, or anyone who comes to mind.

Assumptions

- DNA or genetics may offer some insight into the shooter, such as whether the shooter's father or mother had a history of mental illness and took prescription medication for years or whether the parents were known alcoholics or lifelong drug addicts.
- Perhaps the mother or father, or both, almost daily resorted to physical or psychological abuse, which permeated the active shooter's entire life.

- Perhaps in the school environment, the active shooter stood out as being physically or psychologically weak, perhaps having a disability that prompted other students to bully the active shooter to the point of fearing for his or her safety almost daily. Perhaps the active shooter was actually victimized by a bully, not a bully himself or herself.
- Just because a person is much younger than another active shooter does not mean that he or she does not share commonalities, complaints of similar injustices, or a similar troubled past.
- Even though there are few female active shooters, this does not mean that they do not share the same personality traits and behaviors as their male counterparts. When attempting to find a commonality among active shooters, it is illogical to dismiss this category.

Mental Illness

An active shooter's mental and physical health issues, as well as dependence on psychiatric medications such as Prozac, Ritalin, or other antidepressants, may significantly alter or magnify aspects of the individual's rational thinking process and judgment. Each individual who take medications may experience unwanted and unexpected side effects that can exacerbate and compound issues even further. Virginia Tech shooter Seung-Hui Cho was declared mentally ill and ordered to attend treatment for severe anxiety disorder. Columbine High School shooter Eric Harris was on psychiatric medication. Is it possible that all other active shooters have been undiagnosed mental cases who slipped under the radar?

The identified individual may need help understanding that the path he or she is taking may lead to medical and clinical treatment and can divert their thoughts from turning into actions. To begin treatment or counseling, someone must report a concern with the individual. Unfortunately, people often don't report questionable individuals. If it's a relative that is acting strange or out of character, the family will often dismiss the emotional or mental display as just a sign of a bad day. The relative may empathize with how someone because of all the problems the person has experienced. It is very typical for relatives to seldom report on other family members.

For an individual to pick up a firearm or another dangerous weapon, then meticulously plan to kill a specific person or as many people as possible, must mean the person is mentally ill or at least not in a normal state of mind. Surely the active shooter cannot possess a conscience and must lack compassion. But such a shooter is likely to provide warning signs of a deteriorating psychological balance or a shift in behavior, especially if the individual is a student in school or a coworker. Observations by coworkers and fellow students, both daily and over the course of weeks, can isolate provocative actions and comments. Fundamentally, the benefits of such observations sound appropriate and consist with a safe and secure work or school environment, but unfortunately, regardless of what nefarious act is observed, any of the following may be true:

- People have no desire to report any unusual behavior or action, not wanting be involved themselves in any way.
- Because the individual is a loner, it is a difficult to discern his or her good or bad tendencies.

- People have no desire to cause friction between the individual and themselves.
- People believe that the person is having a bad day (or streak), which will pass without incident.
- People share the same beliefs as the individual in question but are unwilling to take their radical idealism to the next level.
- Even if the person communicates intended actions of physical harm, observers believe that he or she is just blowing off steam—that a verbal threat will not be acted on.

These fundamental fault lines are tantamount to giving ruthless active shooters free passes, and they essentially, though unknowingly, endorse murder. We must consider criminal or civil legal action against individuals who minimize, trivialize, and conceal potential life-threatening comments or actions by another if the other actually carries out such ruthless and barbaric actions against innocent victims.

Mental illness and violent aggression have been researched by a cross-section of professionals for many years now. From analyzing overcrowded prison populations and mental health facilities to cubing adolescent behavior, mental illness, and violent aggression, studies have mutually exhausted most perspectives of human behaviors. So it seems logical to approach active shooters in the same analytical manner. The U.S. Secret Service (USSS) and Department of Education (DOE) report "The Final Report and Findings of the Safe School Initiative: Implications for the Prevention of School Attacks in the United States," released in May 2002 [3], indicated that "fewer than 20% had been diagnosed with a mental health or behavior disorder prior to the attack and 34% of the attackers had ever received a mental health evaluation." It is also important to note that "78% of the attackers exhibited a history of suicide attempts or suicidal thoughts at some time prior to the attack." Because almost 50 percent of active shooters commit suicide before law enforcement intervention, a partial link can be implied with a history of mental illness.

If mental illness is to be considered the common link between all active shooters, then it is logical to identify how many people are classified as having a mental illnesses. The National Institute of Mental Health (NIMH) indicates that "[r]esearch on mental health epidemiology shows that mental disorders are common throughout the United States, affecting tens of millions of people each year, and that, overall, only about half of those affected receive treatment." [4] Because millions of people experience mental disorders, and because there are more than 60 million students in the United States, attempting to correlate and classify only active shooters is unfeasible.

Even if loose correlation can be drawn between mental illness and violent aggression, what percentage of these mentally ill individuals, regardless of age or any other common factor, could conceivably commit such murderous acts? The Treatment Advocacy Center, in its article "Violent Behavior: One of the Consequences of Failing to Treat Individuals with Severe Mental Illness," indicated "that a small number of individuals with serious mental illnesses commit acts of violence including 5% to 10% of homicides" [5]. Almost all these acts of violence are committed "by individuals who are not being medically treated, and many such individuals are also abusing alcohol or drugs." Ultimately no one personality trait or behavior stands alone to identify an active shooter before he or she carries out a deadly rampage. Conversely, the study of genetics or specific DNA holds little clues to active shooters, for there are no documented active shootings, outside of wartime engagements, in which a father or mother and/or siblings have orchestrated an active shooting.

Medications

Each day, radio and television stations provide commercials espousing the remarkable benefits of medications to alleviate chronic pain, discomfort, or specific ailments. The commercials try to persuade and entice the viewers into believing that their suffering can remarkably disappear or be controlled by the simple use of the medication advertised. Each commercial always provides a legal disclaimer encouraging the viewer to seek out medical advice from the medical professional before using the medication. This disclaimer statement is generally followed by a laundry list of side effects and warnings about negative effects on preexisting ailments that the viewer may possess. Surprisingly, some of the side effects may include hallucinations, depression, suicidal thoughts, strokes, heart attack, and death. If the medications have such a wide variety of side effects and warnings, it is conceivable that the medications may also produce violent tendencies that can be the catalyst that ultimately is manifested as an active shooting.

Alcohol and illegal narcotics have been a catalyst prompting action in some people to act violently. After enough drinks, all fears, impediments, and anxiety barriers can evaporate. It is through alcohol and drugs that the individual masks the dangerousness of confrontational situations and ignores all internal warnings of his or her conscience. "Courage in a bottle" or in a plastic baggie has been observed in many various incidents and is one catalyst that is almost impossible to calculate. Nevertheless, history has demonstrated the negative interdynamics of these ingredients but simultaneously includes prescription medications in this mix of influencing a person's behavior and actions to a new level of unpredictability that cannot be evaluated effectively.

Can combining these two variables be the missing link? The USSS and DOE Safe School Initiative Report indicates that approximately 24 percent of active shooters had a history of alcohol or substance abuse. The figures are somewhat affected because even a smaller number, possibly only 4 percent, of these active shooters took medications or alcohol on the day of the school shooting. Furthermore, Peter Langman, Ph.D., in his article "Psychiatric Medications and School Shooters," [6] indicates that "[j]ust because a shooter took a medication at some point in his life, however, doesn't mean there was any connection between the drug and the attack." Because millions of adolescents and young adults take medications daily, arguably an association between aggression, violence, and medications may be classified only as a contributing factor to, but not a common link between, active shootings.

Bullying

When attempting to determine what aspect of an individual's life became so overwhelming, persuasive, and unrelenting that the person would decide to start shooting, every stone should be turned over in the individual's life afterward in the attempt to prevent additional senseless murders. But in active shooters who are younger, the condensed version of their life may offer more clues, which is why a school setting may highlight more specifics as documented by the school administrators. One area that has been the center of attention in extensive research reports and the corresponding preventive measures by school administrators and teachers is the act of bullying. What is bullying? The U.S. Department of Health and Human Services (DHHS) defined bullying as "intentionally aggressive, usually repeated, verbal, social, or physical behavior aimed at a specific person or group of people." [7] The categories of bullying may be identified as follow:

Physical violence or actions include hitting, kicking, pushing, tripping, spitting in a person's face, throwing items at the presumed target, pouring drinks over the person's head, destroying a person's property, tossing a person into a locker, pointing a finger at the person as if it were a gun and "pulling the trigger," physically intimidating a person by standing atop him or her, or hitting a locker and saying, "The next time, it will be your face."

Verbal or written communications include a variety of verbal threats, offensive comments, and writing or marking comments on lockers or books or on the person.

Indirect actions or comments include abusive untrue rumors, exclusion of a person from social events, and telling fictitious offensive stories about the person.

Cyberbullying includes email, social media, and text messaging that is designed to intimidate, harm, or harass another person or group. In many instances, cyberbullying is perceived to be more harmful than the physical bullying.

One looming question is how significant a problem bullying is in our school systems. Some people believe that bullying isn't a real problem—that encountering bullying is part of growing up, something that people experience throughout their entire life. Others believe that if bullying is experienced at school, teachers will intervene and take care of any problem. Unfortunately, some children never tell their parents about bullying at school, because the parents never talk to their children or do not have a relationship allowing open dialogue. This section will shed some light on the extent of the bullying problem in schools.

The USSS and DOE Safe School Initiative Report, released in 2002, indicated that 60 million students attend 119,000+ schools in the United States. The total enrollment is for schools up to and including high school but excludes colleges and universities.

On October 8, 2012, the National Education Association published the article "Nation's Educators Continue to Push for Safe, Bully-Free Environments," which estimated that nearly 160,000 miss school each day out of fear of bullying by fellow students, and especially of being physically attacked or intimidated [8]. A student must have a safe and secure educational environment to learn, but unfortunately 62 percent of educators and teachers surveyed indicated that they had witnessed bullying two or more times in the last month. So if such a large percentage of teachers witnesses bullying on almost a weekly basis, why is the problem not effectively addressed in our school systems?

The National Center for Education Statistics found that approximately 3 percent of the school-age population was homeschooled [9]. The figures did not indicate the reason for the homeschooling or what percentage of the students left a public school system because of bullying, but 91 percent of the parents indicated the school environment was their biggest concern. Although there could be many reasons why parents may choose not to send their children to a public school, this research may suggest that the parents who were part of this study have no faith in the school administrators and/or teachers to effectively intervene and resolve bullying issues at their school. If this lack of faith were justified, it might partly explain why bullying is so prevalent in our schools.

The National Voice for Equality, Education and Enlightenment indicated that every seven minutes a child is bullied, but adult intervention only occurred in 4 percent, peer intervention in 11 percent, and no intervention in 85 percent of events [10]. Building on the foregoing and assuming that each time the educator or teacher witnessed a bullying event he or she intervened, the problem of bullying in schools is an enormous problem seemingly unchecked by school administrators.

A report by the Institute of Education Sciences titled "Indicators of School Crime and Safety: 2013," indicated that 27.8 percent of the 12- to 18-year-old students reported being bullied at school during the school year. The report further indicated by race that 31 percent of white students, 27 percent of black students, 22 percent of Hispanic students, and 15 percent of Asian students reported being bullied. In addition, 31.4 percent of female students reported bullying at school, more than their male counterparts [11].

Now that the problem of bullying has been identified in the school system, how does this issue intersect with active shooters, and what is the significance of bullying when considering the personality traits and behavior of the active school shooter? The 2002 USSS and DOE Safe School Initiative Report also indicates that "many attackers felt bullied, persecuted or injured by others prior to the attack." Later in the report it states that "[m]ost attackers, 73%, had a grievance against at least one of their targets prior to the attack" and "[a]lmost three-quarters, 71%, of the attackers felt persecuted, bullied, threatened, attacked or injured by others prior to the incident."

Could bullying be the common link between all active shooters? Unfortunately not, for to proclaim bullying the universal element, it must be found in all active shootings. The report by the USSS and DOE identified that 29 percent of shooters did not feel persecuted, bullied, threatened, attacked, or injured by others before the active shooting. Look at the assumption from a different perspective. Darmawan published a report titled "Bullying in School: A Study of Forms and Motives of Aggression in Two Secondary Schools in the City of Palu, Indonesia" [12] indicating that girls are victims of bullying at a higher rate than boys. However, less than 4 percent of all active shootings are perpetrated by females, and no women were identified by the USSS in the thirty-seven targeted school attacks over the twenty-five-year study from 1974 until June 2000.

Violent Video Games, Movies, and Television Programs

Invariably after every school shooting in which the active shooter was younger than 18, people wonder whether violent video games, movies, or television programs played a significant part in forming the shooter's mindset before he or she carried out this horrendous act. Almost daily the public is exposed to television commercials that promote violent video games, shocked at the subject matter and graphic nature of the game, as well as its apparent realism and pushing of boundaries. Each violent video game, movie, or television program has avoided censorship under the umbrella of free speech: "It's only a game; it isn't real," echo gamers to their parents, but some smoldering questions need asking:

- Why didn't the parents monitor the children's entertainment intake?
- Do studies or reports support violent video games as transferring aggressive behavior to their users?
- Did the active shooter learn skills in these games that were later used during the shooting rampage?
- Did the active shooter use violent video games to shape his or her behavior?

Of course some parents do take an active part in their child's life by monitoring and scrutinizing their entertainment activities as well as by restricting violent programs and activating parental controls on computer websites. Other parents pay little attention to their children and are happy when they aren't being bothered by chit-chat or distracted from their football game or favorite reality program. For these parents, so long as the child is out of sight or in his or her room, life is good. But what is the child doing in that room? What video games is he or she playing? These questions are rarely asked by parents who desire only peace and quiet from the perils of life.

One approach in determining whether violent video games, movies, and television programs have a casual or significant (or no) effect on active shooters is to turn to the quantifiable research field. Academics may, through survey modeling, establish a database broad enough to identify relationships or similarities in active shooters and their participation in violent video games. A search across available research may provide persuasive data that may tilt the scales one way or the other.

One report titled "Effects of Violent Video Games on Aggressive Behavior, Aggressive Cognition, Aggressive Affect, Physiological Arousal, and Prosocial Behavior: A Meta-analytic Review of the Scientific Literature," by Craig A. Anderson and Brad J. Bushman, of Iowa State University [13], indicates that violent video games increase aggressive behavior in children and young adults. The research also concluded that "[e]xposure to violent video games increase[s] physiological arousal and aggression-related thoughts and feelings" as well as "decreases prosocial behavior." As an example, Eric Harris and Dylan Klebold, the active shooters in the Columbine High School massacre, were habitual players of violent video games. The report also indicated that 89 percent of parents never limit time spent playing video games, and 90 percent of parents never check the ratings of videos. Last, research has shown over five decades of analyzing the effects of violent television programs and movies that viewers display significant increases in aggression, continuing from transcends adolescence into young adulthood.

In the paper "The School Shooting/Violent Video Game Link: Causal Relationship or Moral Panic?" by Christopher J. Ferguson, Behavioral, Applied Sciences and Criminal Justice Department, Texas A&M International University, Laredo, Texas [14], indicates that "scholars who attempted to draw links between laboratory and correlational research on video game playing and school shooting incidents are faulty." For example, Seung-Hui Cho the Virginia Tech active shooter had little or no exposure to violent video games. Sulejman Talovic, the

Trolley Square Mall shooter, did not own a computer or video games. No evidence suggested that Steven Phillip Kazmierczak, the Northern Illinois University shooter, was an avid violent video game player. The paper concluded that any empirical link between violent video games and acts of aggression or violent behavior is slim.

An article titled "Do Violent Video Games Contribute to Youth Violence?" [15] indicates that 97 percent of 12- to 17-year-olds in the United States played video games in 2008 and also lists twenty-nine different pros and cons for the article's title topic that may further potentially identify and support increased aggression or nullify any relationship between aggression and potential aggression. It should be noted that the video game industry is a multi-billion-dollar industry evolved well beyond anything resembling Pac Man or Pong; today's games are more realistic, violent, and bloodier, but this is the same industry that contributes to military flight simulators and battlefield tactical technologies within the United States military today for protection. Thus video games are designed to increase hand–eye coordination, improve tactical thinking, and foster the ability to think rationally under perceived stressful conditions in varying scenarios. They also may develop a basic understanding of shooting skills, from reloading and aiming various weapon platforms to choosing the appropriate weapon for a scenario. Unlike video games, in an active shooter incident, when someone is killed, there is no reload button, no superpowers card that can be turned in: In the real world, you only get one life to live.

Violent video games, movies, and television programs may increase aggressive behavior and aggressive thoughts and possibly decrease humanitarian instincts or the feeling of empathy toward fellow humans, but these entertainment outlets may instead help safely release pent-up emotions and aggression through games rather than against live people. Video games may provide a level of interaction that cannot be experienced in a movie or television program as well as a complete body–mind coordination experience, which again may help release feelings internalized and collected in response to being bullying, relationship rejection, or a sense of inferiority instilled by peers and classmates.

Another point to consider in violent video games is that one player can interact with another player anywhere in the world as a partner. Each player encourages and directs partners through the battlefield. The players communicate about obvious threats and challenges based on a long history of trial and error found when attempting to advance from one level to an increasing harder level. Conversely, in real life there is only one level, and fewer than 2 percent active shootings occur with more than one shooter involved.

Last, there are more than 190 million video gamers in the United States, as well as, according to the U.S. Census Bureau in 2009, more than 77 million students from pre-K to twelfth grade [16] and, according to CNN.com, who in a June 19, 2014, story titled "A Closer Look: How Many Newtown-like School Shootings since Sandy Hook?" identified that there have been seventy-four school shootings since the December 2012 Sandy Hook Elementary shooting [17]. The possibility of pre-identifying a potential school active shooter based on his or her violent video gaming is statistically practically impossible. To further complicate the matrix, consider that the gamer may not even be skilled at video gaming, might not have achieved the highest level, or might even only remain on an entry level to maintain an internal balance of self-worth. Now consider that prolonged gaming or recreational gaming is not measured by hours played, but by intensity, effect, and perception. Each gamer sees, feels, and absorbs what he or she accumulates and envisions. One gamer may feel euphoric when reaching level 2, but another gamer is distressed because level 25 wasn't achieved. The length of gaming and the internal emotional dynamics of the player are only another piece of the puzzle. Continued research in violent video gaming is a worthwhile endeavor, especially if it prevents the potential active shooter from acting on his or her ideas.

Classifications

From haves and have-nots to overachievers and underachievers, individuals are placed into areas or even fields to structure how people accept or reject a person. This is also true in the world of criminality. Every classification of murderer, active shooter, or serial killer has unique traits, beliefs, rational, and so forth. These classifications are also important for background investigators charged to select the ideal employee for an emerging business, or a human resources interviewer who must swiftly process thousands of applicants while trying to fill open company positions. We are a society are obsessed with categorizing and stereotyping people. Let's begin by looking at one fact: There is no specific age for an active shooter. How can an active shooter be classified and categorized with personality and behavioral traits if the age range is from 12 to 88? The 12-year-old has just begun his life, while the 88-year-old has lived well past the national average of an adult male's lifespan. Let's look at another area: Can violent video games or movies be the defining factor that starts the shooter in his or her deadly rampage? Did the 12-year-old or 88-year-old watch violent movies or play violent video games? Most 88-year-olds don't own a computer, nor understand how to use a smartphone—they may have difficulty even seeing a television screen. Scholars often refer to a few cases, such as two or three cases that are not within the normal range of a study, as an anomaly. Regardless of whether this is an anomaly, people still died in these incidents.

The classification of certain murders has taken decades to document and multiple clinical and academic studies to validate. The active shooter designation is a relatively new term and may have originated from the Columbine High School shooting in Columbine, Colorado, on April 20, 1999. Investigators, psychiatrics, and academics attempted to piece together every detail, clue, emotion, life choice, family influence, nationality, and education under their microscopes. To make matters worse, not every active shooter event can be classified by reason for the shooting—take, for example, Sulejman Talovic's active shooting in Trolley Square, Salt Lake City, Utah, on February 12, 2007. Investigators and researchers can only theorize about why he began shooting: The reason has not been clearly identified and is still unknown.

Figure 2–1 has been extracted from a plethora of report findings, research papers, white papers, and studies that all attempt to identify a few psychological traits or behaviors of active shooters. Each helps us try to find a common denominator that can be used by the appropriate officials to thwart an active shooter before an attack. Many researchers and professionals attempt to isolate some smoldering, dormant, or intertwined cluster of characteristics that have not been previously vigorously studied before. Some of the data leans toward the possibility of school active shootings, while other data could point toward a disgruntled employee or even an estranged lover. The most important considerations from Figure 2-1 are for businesses, educators, therapists, and investigators to determine how to establish warning signs, preventive measures, and procedures after these identified personality traits and behaviors have been displayed. Unfortunately, educators and administrators must follow an identified process in the school environment, but this process is not limited to the school, as medical professionals, therapists, and parents are all partners in outlining the proper care for these identified students. In addition, school shooters may be adults, not attending school at all.

Individuals in the real world do not have the same structured mechanism after becoming an adult. The most obvious question still remains: What common characteristics, behaviors and psychological traits can found in active shooters for school shootings, disgruntle employees, religious settings, government agencies, random targets, and business environments?

The USSS and DOE Safe School Initiative Report in 2002 examined thirty-seven school related shootings between 1974 and 2000 in hopes of identifying similarities that could be used to prevent future school place violence. The report further wanted to educate and prepare first responders and school administrators regarding preventive measures, pre-indicators of potential troubled students, and appropriate responses to this deadly violence. Figure 2-1 identifies several indicators or traits derived from the research. It should be noted that not all active

Alcohol and drug abuse	Anger	Anxiety	Bullied	Classroom or work disruptions	Conflict with peers
Conflict with management	Conflict with religion	Conflict with social contacts	Conspiracy thinking	Demanding	Depression
Disturbing writings	Empowered	Fear	Frightened of world	Frustration	Hallucinogen use
Hanging out with outcast group	Harassed	Hatred of almost anything	History of issues reported	History of issues not reported, yet people were aware	Hostility
Ignored conversation attempts	Isolated	Lacks compassion and empathy	Laughed at	Low self-esteem	Mental illness, possibly undiagnosed
Mood swings	Nonconformist	Obsessed with lucid dreaming	Paranoid	Prejudice	Personality change
Pressure	Psychological reward	Resentment	Retaliation	Revenge	Self-centered
Severe anger reactions	Severe social anxiety	Suicidal	Trapped, feeling no way out	Thrill	Unsuccessful
Vengeance	Victimization	Volatility			

FIGURE 2–1 Indicators, Traits or Actions.

shooters possessed all indicators. Additionally, numerous seriously troubled students who have considered committing a school shooting or other act of violence possess many of the same traits listed, and even made plans for an attack, but did not carry out the attack. Please note that the percentages identified in Figure 2–2 do not pinpoint a single common denominator that will positively identify an active shooter before an attack. Furthermore, the statistical data represent only school shootings, with no clear indication whether these same percentages will remain consistent for nonschool active shootings. Finally, even though the report was prepared in 2002, no recent empirical studies have changed or altered the data provided in this report.

Society attempts to classify and categorize incidents to help cope with the deadly effects of an event. It is much easier to understand and rationalize a murder to protect ourselves if the individual is provided with a classification and category. Researchers classify multiple murderers and assign particular characteristics and labels to such individuals. After a classification has been established, any future incident can be clearly identified. Unfortunately, labels don't always work, nor does neatly placing an incident into one box or classification because there

Middle-School and High-School Active Shooters: Thirty-seven School Shootings Committed by Forty-one Attackers				
Current student 95%	Male 100%	Sole attacker 81%	Single weapon 76%	Handgun 61% Rifle/shotgun 49%
Targeted school admin/teacher 54%	Targeted more than one person 44%	Grievance against the person targeted 73%	Targeted before the attack 46%	Shooter race: White 76% Black 12% Hispanic 5%
Two-parent family 63%	Doing well in school (Bs or higher) 41%	Social mainstream of school 41%	No close friends 12%	Characterized as a loner 34%
Participated in social activities 44%	Never been, or rarely been, in trouble at school 63%	No change in grades 56% Friendship 73%	Felt bullied, threatened, or attacked 71%	Mental health evaluation 34%
History of alcohol or drugs 24%	Failure to take medications 10%	Violent movies, games, books 59%	Violent writing 37%	Prior history of arrests 27%
Difficulty in coping with loss 83%	Developed idea to harm beforehand 95%	Planned attack in advance 93%	Revenge 61%	Multiple motives 54%
Threatened target before attack 17%	Other people knew about attack beforehand 81%	More than one other person aware of attack 59%	Engaged in behavior causing concern 93%	Encouraged/dared by others to attack 44%

FIGURE 2–2 The Final Report and Findings of the Safe School Initiative. *Source: USSS and DOE.*

are similarities. Second, researchers often base classifications on the criminal offense itself without fully understanding all variables behind the act. Third, as new classifications are identified, some of these incidents conflict with one another and may fall into multiple categories. Fourth, some murders are misclassified because they fail to meet certain law enforcement definitions or media-generated stereotypes. Fifth, some of the variations within the classifications are descriptions of causation, whereas others are diagnostic in nature.

Researchers and professional organizations have indicated a wide variety of ways that murders can be classified, and the discussion concerning the correctness of these classifications has been going on for decades. The method of death, thought process, simultaneous murders or extended period of time, location, association with target location and victims are only a few points of consideration when determining classifications. When a category is identified, researchers often attempt to ensure that the category is correct; if not, a new category may be identified. Furthermore, as new disciplines contribute to the murder classifications, they approach the topic from a different perspective, for the incident may not be an isolated event. The new perspective may further verify the traits within the classification or further expand the indicators to aide professional organizations and law enforcement.

Indicators

From first responders and school administrators to therapists and academics, all hope that if pre-indicators of active shooters' mentality and mindset can be identified there will be a greater likelihood of defusing and treat such individuals before a shooting occurs in an effort to avoid bloodshed. The FBI report "The School Shooter: A Threat Assessment Perspective" [18] identified a four-pronged assessment model that can "assess someone who has made a threat and evaluate the likelihood that the threat will actually be carried out." The four prongs include (1) personality of the student, (2) family dynamics, (3) school dynamics and the student's role in those dynamics, and (4) social dynamics. The FBI's National Center for the Analysis of Violent Crime has spent decades assessing, documenting, cataloging, and verifying personality traits and behavior to aid the prevention and investigation of violent crimes.

- Figure 2–3 provides descriptions of each item.
- When looking at Figure 2–3, remember the data source are students, not individuals in society. Students provide a condensed version of society without decades of influences and life lessons to dilute or mask the underlying precursors leading to violence.
- The data source is not specific to only students who were active shooters, but an analysis of students who made a threat.
- Just because a student makes a threat doesn't mean that the student really intends, has the skills, or has previously planned to carry out a threat or has the weapons or equipment to be successful.
- The report focuses on adolescent students, which may produce slightly more traits and behaviors for young adults attending a college or university. It may be important to consider that the traits that college students display may have been fostered during their adolescent education and so still be valid.

THE SCHOOL SHOOTER: A THREAT ASSESSMENT PERSPECTIVE (FBI)				
PERSONALITY TRAITS AND BEHAVIOR: STUDENTS				
Leakage (giving prior knowledge of impending event	Low tolerance for frustration	Poor coping skills	Lack of resiliency	Failed love relationship
"Injustice collector"	Signs of depression	Narcissism	Alienation	Dehumanizes others
Lack of empathy	Exaggerated sense of entitlement	Attitude of superiority	Exaggerated or pathological need for attention	Externalizes blame
Masks low self-esteem	Anger management problems Lack of trust	Intolerance	Inappropriate humor	Seeks to manipulate others
Closed social group	Negative role models	Rigid and opinionated	Change of behavior	Unusual interest in sensational violence
Fascination with violence-filled entertainment	Behavior appears relevant to carrying out a threat			
It is important to note three important cautions highlighted in the report, which be considered whenever lists are provided: • No one or two traits or characteristics should be considered in isolation or given more weight than the others. • Behavior is an expression of personality, but one bad day may not reflect a student's real personality or an unusual behavior pattern. • The four-pronged threat assessment model cannot be a substitute for a clinical diagnosis of mental illness.				

FIGURE 2–3 The School Shooter: A Threat Assessment Perspective. *Source FBI Personality Traits And Behaviors-Students.*

After reviewing the foregoing personality traits and behaviors, it is extremely difficult—in fact, impossible—to predict which student will become an active shooter. A student may possess or demonstrate all twenty-seven traits but still with no indication that the student will become a shooter. Just as frustrating and perplexing, there is no secret formula to isolate which trait or behavior may be the catalyst that drives the student from verbal threats to premeditated actions. Furthermore, there are recent examples of students' entered schools with weapons to carry out their barbaric act but stopping just short of performing their lethal act without any intervention from the school staff or law enforcement officials.

When looking at the personality traits and behaviors not found above, one may consider the following drivers or catalysts when forming personality traits and behaviors:

• Today's social fabric is constantly changing and forcing adolescents into the competitive job market. Employment is another prong that may be a catalyst for good or evil, based, again, on the student. For some students, the choice of working or not is not an option, but a necessity for survival. With broken family units and dwindling incomes, many students are effectively forced into the job market. This phenomenon is not new, but it is more pronounced nowadays. But then throw into the mix an economic downturn and the reduction of staffing levels, new pressures, rejection, and fluctuating coworker personalities, and a student's building negative personality and behaviors may produce actions in place of words.

- Technological and entertainment influences might be another thorn magnifying and channeling the student's personality traits and behavior. As an example, there have been more than eighty studies on the effects of violent movies and television shows, but only a handful of these studies considered violent video games and aggression. Is it possible that if a student plays violent video games, he or she will become a more effective killer and gain tactical skills based on the conceptualizations of potential battle zones learned in the games? Is it possible that younger active shooters are not combat-hardened veterans, just individuals who confuse a game with reality?

- Another consideration may include type and level of school, such as elementary, middle, high school, university, college, graduate school, trade school, private or public, and alternative schooling. Consider the affiliation of the active shooter with the school, such as a student, a former student who left or was expelled, a student who graduated, a teacher, an administrator, or an school employee. On June 19, 2014, in the CNN story "A Closer Look: How Many Newtown-like School Shootings since Sandy Hook?" [19] indicated that there have been seventy-four school shootings since the December 2012 Sandy Hook Elementary shooting. It may be interesting to categorize the most recent seventy-four school shootings and then expand to school shootings over the past twenty years to help identify and isolate potential active shooters.

Triggers

A common phrase used by many people to describe active shooters is that they just "snapped." Active shooters do not just snap in the purest sense of the word; the horrific act is not an instantaneous, kneejerk reaction to an event that just occurred. Rather, it is the culmination of something that can no longer be tolerated, condoned, accepted, or dismissed. Look at this point from another nationally recognized aggressive act—road rage—by asking one question: Does the road rage shooter decide to pull the trigger on the first motorist who disrespects or angers the individual, or is the trigger pulled on the third or eighth or twenty-fifth motorist? The answer is that typically in a road-rage incident it is the latter. Thus the active shooter in almost all cases does not just snap. As a matter of fact, often they plan well ahead of their attack. The USSS and DOE Safe School Initiative Report of 2002 also indicates that "93% of the attackers planned out their attack and 51% developed the idea for the attack at least one month prior." There are no recent reports that would alter these findings: Most active shooters plan their deadly rampage prior to the attack.

When attempting to determine the motivations and triggers behind an active shooter, researchers and academics begin by looking at the shooter from the day they were born to better isolate foundational or consistent personality traits and behaviors. The purpose is to develop over the course of time an entire history of abnormalities, frequency of occurrence, life-shattering personal tragedy, inconsistencies in treatment or discipline, and injustices that may have befallen the individual.

A reoccurring problem for researchers is securing relevant information about the shooter. One would think that using today's information and communications resources it would be easy to assemble a plethora of knowledge about the shooter, but with Protected Critical Infrastructure Information (PCII), Personally Identifiable Information (PII), the Family Educational Rights and Privacy Act (FERPA), the Individuals with Disabilities Education Act (IDEA), and the Health Insurance Portability and Accountability Act (HIPAA), roadblocks and hurdles unfortunately stand in the way of those attempting to identify personality traits and behaviors of active shooters. So alternate methods and processes are necessary to achieve reliable findings.

For a researcher, it is problematic to ask neighbors to describe the active shooter in terms of his or her behavior and psychological traits immediately after a shooting. The neighbor's response may fall within three distinct silos:

- Immediately condemning the active shooter as a "psycho" who was always doing strange things in the neighborhood: "He always looked at me in a strange way," or "He was a loner, and I knew he was up to no good."
- Many neighbors really don't know their neighbors, cannot remember their names, and have had no interaction with the shooter or even know the shooter's daily routine.
- Depending on the length of time the neighbor associated with the shooter and the shooter's family, there may be some information and intelligence to be gleaned during the interview.

A triggering event in one person does not carry the same significance for another person. What is personal, devastating, and destabilizing in the active shooter's life is symbolic and forceful to him or her alone. Another person may not even be phased by the event or find it of little impact in his or her life. Each person, almost weekly, is presented with options and challenges based on his or her own personal actions, accidents, unexpected actions by others, choices and decisions made by others, and individual successes and failures based on hopes, wishes, and hard work. Sometimes no matter how hard we work toward an objective and plan to achieve prosperity and accomplish our goal, we fall short. A coach or teacher may say that we are measured only by our successes, but also by our failures. How we handle failure and rejection will define you as a person. Unfortunately, for many people who possess a false sense of reality or who are in denial, the experience is life-transforming. However, the triggering event that started the planning process is often based on much more than failure and rejection; it may also be based on a sensation of loss, disrespect, depression, frustration, or revenge. The bottom line? No single common denominator triggers an active shooter, regardless of age, social status, and education—just as there are no common triggering denominators that can be isolated for mental illness.

References

[1] New York City Police Department Active Shooter: Recommendations and Analysis for Risk Mitigation. New York: New York City Police Department; 2012.

[2] Blair JP, Schweit KW. A Study of Active Shooter Incidents, 2000–2013. Washington, D.C.: Texas State University and Federal Bureau of Investigation, U.S. Department of Justice; 2014.

[3] Vossekuil B, Fein R, Reddy M, Borum R, Modzeleski W. The Final Report and Findings of the Safe School Initiative: Implications for the Prevention of School Attacks in the United States. Washington, D.C.: U.S. Department of Education, Office of Elementary and Secondary Education, Safe and Drug-Free Schools Program and U.S. Secret Service, National Threat Assessment Center; 2002.

[4] The National Institute of Mental Health <www.nimh.nih.gov/health/statistics/index.shtml>; 2015.

[5] Treatment Advocacy Center <www.treatmentadvocacycenter.org/resources/consequences-of-lack-of-treatment/violence/1381>; 2015.

[6] Langman, P. Psychiatric Medications and School Shooters. <https://schoolshooters.info/sites/default/files/Psychiatric_Medications.pdf>; 2013.

[7] U.S. Department of Health and Human Services <www.stopbullying.gov/what-is-bullying/definition/index.html>; 2014.

[8] National Education Association Nation's Educators Continue to Push for Safe, Bully-free Environments. <www.nea.org/home/53298.htm>; 2012.

[9] National Center for Education Statistics. See at <http://nces.ed.gov>, under Parent and Family Involvement in Education, from the National Household Education Surveys Program of 2012.

[10] National Voice for Equality, Education and Enlightenment. <www.nveee.org/facts-statistics/>.

[11] Institute of Education Sciences Indicators of School Crime and Safety. <http://nces.ed.gov/pubsearch/pubsinfo.asp?pubid=2014042>; 2014.

[12] Darmawan Bullying in School: A Study of Forms and Motives of Aggression in Two Secondary Schools in the city of Palu, Indonesia. <http://munin.uit.no/bitstream/handle/10037/2670/thesis.pdf?sequence=2&isAllowed=y>; 2010.

[13] Anderson and Bushman Iowa State University, Effects of Violent Video Games on Aggressive Behavior, Aggressive Cognition, Aggressive Affect, Physiological Arousal, and Prosocial Behavior: A Meta-Analytic Review of the Scientific Literature. <http://pss.sagepub.com/content/12/5/353.abstract>; 2001.

[14] Ferguson Texas A&M International University, The School Shooting/Violent Video Game Link: Causal Relationship or Moral Panic? Texas A&M International University: College Station, TX; 2008.

[15] ProCon.Org. "Do Violent Video Games Contribute to Youth Violence?" <http://videogames.procon.org>.

[16] U.S. Census Bureau <www.census.gov/hhes/www/poverty/data/incpovhlth/2009/index.html>; 2009.

[17] Fantz, K., Wang A Closer Look: How Many Newtown-like School Shootings since Sandy Hook? <www.cnn.com/2014/06/11/us/school-shootings-cnn-number/index.html>; 2014.

[18] Toole, Critical Incident Response Group (CIRG) and the National Center for the Analysis of Violent Crime (NCAVC), FBI Academy, Quantico, VA. "The School Shooter: A Threat Assessment Perspective." <www.fbi.gov/stats-services/publications/school-shooter>.

[19] Fantz, K., Wang A Closer Look: How Many Newtown-like School Shootings since Sandy Hook? <www.cnn.com/2014/06/11/us/school-shootings-cnn-number/>; 2014.

3

Effective Planning

The recent increase in active shooter incidents has caused organizations to rethink their strategies for protecting their most critical assets, their people. Both individuals and companies must think beyond the simple strategy of having a gun readily available and being proficient with it to defend against an active shooter. The reality of being involved in an active shooting goes well beyond such a simple strategy because both sides of the fight may have firearms along with the ability to shoot them accurately. The difference between surviving the attack or becoming a statistic may come down to how well you have planned and prepared.

The first step in any program is to properly plan. No one would dare construct a building without first laying the facility out, hiring an architect, and properly managing the project to completion. Yet when it comes to security matters, many organizations choose a reactive stance rather than being proactive. Planning is often the most critical step in preventing, preparing for, and responding to a crisis [1]. This is especially the case when it comes to active shooters.

These unthinkable situations go beyond the ability of a simple emergency action plan (EAP) to require a more proactive approach. The active shooter is a threat very few people are prepared to effectively deal with. Just arming oneself is not by itself a viable solution for an active shooter, especially if one has never been involved in a serious conflict or such life-threatening violence. The asymmetrical qualities of an active shooter complicate the planning process and require a more comprehensive approach to planning.

In addition, split-second decisions about whether to render aid to the dying and wounded and how to best care for them while under fire without getting yourself injured or killed is a skill of its own. It is easy to think that we would not render medical assistance and would run from the area, but often people we care about are the ones who have been shot, and we should at least think about and plan what to do. For example, suppose a shooter seriously injures two of your colleagues and leaves the building: Have you considered what you would do after calling police? Would you start to initiate first aid and try to stop the massive hemorrhaging and try to prevent the wounded from going into shock? Do you even know the basics of providing such medical care? Do you have a first aid kit containing items helpful for stabilizing the victims? Would you render care to stop the bleeding, then try to move the injured to a safer location? What happens if the shooter returns while you are assisting the wounded? This is just one small aspect of planning for such violence, yet it can be the difference between life and death.

It is essential that every organization develop a plan for security and potential crises. No matter how your company or business is structured, it is important that violence in the workplace be considered and be part of the overall comprehensive protection program. Active shooter planning differs from the basic emergency plan in that the active shooter is challenging to predict, difficult to prevent, and costly to recover from. This is especially true if the shooter is an employee or contractor who is given access to the site, is trusted by staff, and has no past history of violence.

The development, implementation, and maintenance of an effective active shooter program is paramount to the organization's preparedness when it comes to acts involving gun violence. It is through awareness and training that each employee will be better prepared mentally to make quick decisions and determine his or her best option for survival. In an active shooter incident, quick thinking and the related parallel actions often become the difference between surviving the incident or becoming a casualty. Planning, awareness, and mental preparation are the best defenses against the active shooter.

ASIS International, a leading global security professional association, describes the Comprehensive Emergency Management program, which includes the entire process of managing such incidents [2]. A comprehensive process includes a three-pronged approach involving three types of planning:

- Emergency action planning
- Response and recovery planning
- Business continuity planning

Emergency Action Planning

An EAP should identify potential emergency conditions and specific actions to minimize loss of life and property damage. An EAP may include topics such as natural disasters, life safety issues, terrorism, health, manmade threats, accidents, and cyber threats. When it comes to an active shooter, the organization should develop a separate plan for these types of incidents or incorporate the active shooter plan as an addendum into the comprehensive EAP. It may be preferable to incorporate the active shooter plan into the EAP, for it may be easier to communicate and develop awareness across the organizational structure. No matter which option is chosen, it is imperative that as you develop your active shooter plan, the organization align the program with the overall mission and protection needs.

It is vital that staff and contractors should be able to easily understand the plan. A plan that is too complicated, that is impossible to implement, or that is not effectively communicated is worthless. The plan should contain relevant information and be written in a concise manner that minimizes use of acronyms, code words, and jargon to prevent confusion or misunderstandings. The plan should be realistic and actionable and must contain accurate and current contact information. It should document the actions that will be taken to mitigate the risks and coordinate the plan with first responders and law enforcement.

In addition the plan should include cooperative agreements and support agreements and may include an alternate site for operations until the recovery process is complete. It should identify key roles and the delineation of duties of the personnel responsible for implementing and managing the incident. It should include early warning notifications that can be issued when a potential threat is actionable.

An incident command structure should be developed and well defined to standardize an incident management approach to integrate procedures, personnel, facilities, equipment, and communications among different agencies. Coordination with the various jurisdictions and emergency management authorities is essential for ensuring the safety of personnel and the general public. It also allows for discussions about planning issues such as personnel, available equipment, and communications.

The plan should consider the use of facility, building population, and special needs. This includes protective measures, warning systems, and planning. Having procedures to detect and monitor the situation should help first responders and law enforcement get to the fight quickly and neutralize the attack. Procedures should be tested before an actual incident occurs to determine any issues or special accommodations required to best protect all people on the property during the incident.

Response and Recovery Planning

One aspect that is often overlooked during the development of a plan dealing with active shooters is the focus on what to do after the attack begins. Although the average attack often lasts only a few minutes, the effects that follow can last for months or even years. Rapid response and recovery from incidents, such as those involving an active shooter, may determine whether a business can continue its operations.

Response is the ability for the organization to coordinate an effective reply and reclaim the site during an attack. Recovery, on the other hand, is the organization's ability to return operations to a normal state. Response and recovery go hand in hand when it comes to an active shooter, but both must be approached separately. Although Chapter 5 of this book provides more detail on the response function as regards an active shooter and Chapter 10 provides more specific information regarding the recovery aspects, we will approach the topic here from a planning perspective.

Active shooters are one of the most dangerous types of threats most organizations can experience. The random and vicious actions of an armed individual make the response function in planning a significant factor in reducing injury and death. The ability for the organization to inform and coordinate an effective response with law enforcement and other first responders is a fundamental aspect of any plan. The sooner first responders can get to the threat and neutralize it, the sooner the organization can begin trying to return to normal operation. Information and communication are the cornerstones of the response plan and must be coordinated and tested before an actual event.

Recovery is the second function that is an important part of any crisis management program. Unfortunately, most crisis management programs stop at response function and never consider recovery as a critical part of the plan. An organization doesn't just automatically recover from an active shooter incident; it takes appropriate planning and suitable conditions to minimize potential exposure to the associated risks after the attack has been neutralized. The long-term effect is what the recovery aspect of the plan is designed to address.

Moreover, the effects of an active shooter can affect the community, other industries, and even regional or national resources. The ability to recover quickly from these effects and repair the damage can minimize such adverse effects. Recovery planning should include the ability to recover using a short-term response, that begins immediately after the incident to restore critical functions and a long-term recovery that brings the entire operation back to normal. Because it is impossible to know every type of damage or incident that may occur, response and recovery planning should be general enough to provide relief from any type of event, regardless of cause.

Reconstruction will require coordination with local authorities and often code enforcement agencies. The ability to facilitate a quick response might be necessary to streamline both internal and external authority for procurement or contracting. Recovery also requires rapid access to key information, such as architectural drawings, specifications, and maps.

> Recovery includes the ability to clean up, to repair, and to provide professional counseling to staff and guests who may require it. There is a huge psychological advantage to getting things back to normal and removing all signs of violence after a shooting. The ability to recover quickly after an incident takes proper planning, coordination with law enforcement officers/first responders, and having the proper support in place before a shooting occurs.

Business Continuity Planning

Business continuity ensures the continuation of core processes and operations before, during, and after a major incident. Unfortunately, not every company has a plan in place to ensure continuity of operations after an incident and so is often dependent on the EAP to provide enough information and processes to protect the core mission of the organization.

An active shooter can severely affect an organization's continuity of operations. Depending on the number of casualties, the operation may not be able to continue. If a department of ten employees has four killed and four wounded, it will be extremely difficult to operate relying only on the two remaining staff—not even considering that those two may choose not to return to work after the incident! The company may lose the entire department because of one dreadful event. Business continuity planning helps prepare an organization for such a scenario, among many other potential situations.

The first step in planning for continuity of operations is the ability to be ready for anything that could affect operations. This usually involves performing a risk assessment to identify and analyze essential operations and personnel for potential threats and risk. A strategy must then be determined for how to best approach continuity by the management team, which includes backup plans and strategies for essential operations and public safety. Moreover, the plan must include the coordination with community emergency response teams to develop interoperable communications and site familiarity. The ability to avoid, deter, or detect hostile environments is part of business continuity. This includes the development of protective measures and procedures that best mitigate such threats.

It is imperative that someone be assigned responsibility to declare that a crisis exists after one is recognized. This task usually is assigned to a senior member of executive management before a crisis. After it is declared, the response and recovery portion should be implemented immediately. The goal is to get operations restored to normal as quickly as possible. The use of available resources to keep employees and the public safe is critical during this process. It also is important to consider the environment as part of the overall plan. Items such as temporary personnel, alternate facilities, equipment, and hazardous material handling must be prioritized and managed.

Last, it is important to implement, train in, and maintain the continuity plan. All applicable personnel should be part of the maintenance and review of the plan to keep it current. It is the responsibility of the organization to develop a senior leadership team responsible for creating, maintaining, testing, and implementing the site continuity plan. Tasking senior leaders to manage the plan should ensure that all levels of management and staff adhere to and properly support the program. Business continuity plans should be maintained at least annually, or as conditions change. All employees should receive training for security and preparedness, including updates to the plan and lessons learned from exercises, training programs, and previous incidents.

Planning Stages

An idea without a plan is just a thought; and when it comes to a crisis, planning is everything. Organizations without a plan are certainly at a disadvantage when an active shooter incident occurs. Planning should consider all threats and hazards and take into account the various threats that could affect the organization. This includes thinking about the security and safety needs before, during, and after an incident.

Another often overlooked aspect of planning is the organization's responsibility to provide access and functional needs to anyone at the site. This includes people who have disabilities, the elderly, children, people who have limited mobility, people who have language considerations, and people who have any of a host of other limitations. Such challenges are demanding during times of crisis and require special attention during the planning process. Another aspect that should be considered during the planning and distribution phases is part-time employees, volunteers, contractors, and tenants.

Moreover, the planning process must consider the various times and settings that could involve a crisis. Active shooter threats can begin at company-sponsored events, during a sales call, or even at a neighboring business. Unfortunately, these shootings can and do happen everywhere, which complicates the preparation and design of such a plan. Another aspect that may affect the development process, is how the global economy exposes the organization to different religious, racial, and cultural backgrounds. Diversity is beneficial in many ways, but it also presents the possibility of additional stressors into relationships that can result in acts of violence and that thus should be taken into account during the plan's composition.

The Federal Emergency Management Agency (FEMA) [3] provides information and support on crisis management planning, and the process described herein uses this foundation as the cornerstone of the development process. Although there are many different approaches to planning, follow a defined process to obtain the best results.

Furthermore, the business should consider developing an actionable plan for the various departments and working groups. The plan is designed to assist supervisors, managers, and department or team leads and often includes two approaches to the program. The first is to plan for the entire the entire organization, the second to segment the plan by department or working group.

For an active shooter, planning should consider events before the incident, actions during the attack, and after-attack recovery aspects.

There are five main stages to consider during the planning process:

1. Developing the crisis management team
2. Assessing the situation
3. Determining objectives and goals
4. Developing, preparing, reviewing, and approving the plan
5. Implementing and maintaining the plan

Stage 1. Many organizations form a crisis management team (CMT) that, among things, determines what planning and programs will be implemented to best protect organizational assets, improve response, and speed recovery of operations in the event of a crisis. This is the first step in the planning process and should not be minimized, being a crucial step in the planning process.

Coordination, communications, and collaboration for the CMT should be assigned to one key member of staff. This person can be designated the emergency coordinator and is responsible for ensuring that departmental boundaries and conflicts do not hinder the development of a comprehensive plan and process. Typically this role is assigned to the head of security, safety, or engineering, but it can be assigned to anyone having the position and interpersonal and technical skills to accomplish the goals of the program. An alternate coordinator should also be assigned to support the program in the event that the primary coordinator is not available during an emergency. Furthermore, senior leaders must fully support the program and the coordinator along supplying the necessary requirements to ensure that all departments and managers comply and assist in the development process.

The CMT is comprised of key stakeholders in the organization from departments such as safety, security, information technology, human resources, legal, operations, facilities, corporate communications, executive management, and compliance. Although this list is not a comprehensive listing of potential stakeholders, it provides a general understanding of the key players involved in the crisis management process for many organizations. The key stakeholders from the various departments should be assigned to support the emergency coordinator in establishing and organizing the program.

The final plan should consider the mission of the organization as a whole and each operational department and functional team. If one department is overlooked or excluded, the plan will fall short of protecting everyone in the organization. In addition, the organization might need to coordinate with outside resources, such as a landlord and other tenants or neighboring businesses. Such relationships can prove invaluable during the planning process.

The team members should be knowledgeable, forward-thinking professionals who can participate in and bring value to the crisis management process, refer to Figure 3-1 which illustrates a planning team at work. These sponsors will need to strategize, manage, coordinate, and communicate anything that could interrupt business. These incidents could range from accidents to manmade attacks to natural disasters. The team needs to be structured to handle anything that could potentially happen to adversely affect the mission of the organization. It is the CMT that assigns responsibilities to the team stakeholders and ensures that each team member is accountable for their involvement in the planning process. The CMT also provides the plan framework and determines the meeting and maintenance schedule for the plan, including the determination to test the plan and coordinate with outside resources.

Another aspect during the initial development process is the formation of the incident command system (ICS). The ICS often is composed of a command structure, operations, planning, and logistics, along with the appropriate administration and finance components used to manage the various agencies and responders during an emergency. The ICS may include assigned staff positions for security/safety, public affairs, legal counsel, liaison, operations, and logistics, among several others, depending on the organization.

It is important to note that both private industry and the government share responsibility for prevention, response, and recovery. No organization is an island, and active shooter incidents can shake an entire community, state, or region. It is paramount that the organization coordinate with law enforcement and other responsible agencies to best prevent and respond to an active shooter incident. The U.S. Department of Homeland Security has instituted the National Incident Management System (NIMS) to provide guidance and seamless integration for government agencies to work with private companies and nongovernmental organizations in times of emergency.

FIGURE 3–1 Planning Team at Work. *Courtesy of Level 4 Security LLC.*

Stage 2. The second step in the process is to assess the situation. The establishment of baseline conditions helps to establish the state at which the organization should operate. One must know the baseline conditions before truly assessing the plan to estimate its effectiveness. The assessment includes identification of assets, critical operations, and consequences that could be realized if the incident occurs. Identification of the realistic threats and risks that could affect the organization must take place during this step.

Notwithstanding, the assessment process includes the identification of the individuals or departments mostly likely to be attacked by an active shooter. For example, executive management may have a greater risk of experiencing an active shooter incident after deciding to lay off hundreds of employees to pay for their annual bonuses. Or a human resources manager may reprimand a hostile employee, who may retaliate by shooting everyone in the department. Unfortunately, when someone snaps and chooses a gun as his or her tool to resolve the issue, innocent bystanders are often caught in the line of fire.

Another aspect of assessment process is to understand the process that law enforcement and first responders use when responding to an active shooter threat. If an organization does not fully understand requirements and tactics, it will be at a huge disadvantage, its response function less effective. Most security measures are designed to keep people out of the facility; if a shooter has compromised such measures, special accommodations may need to be considered for law enforcement officers and first responders. Moreover, the ability to communicate effectively with first responders and provide them with the facility information they require is vital to a successful response. It may be the difference between life and death.

Stage 3. The third step is to determine the overall objectives and goals of the plan. In developing the active shooter plan, the establishment of the program's goals must be measured and well though out before development. The order and priority may depend on the organizational mission, but here are a few goals to consider:

- Deter or prevent a shooting event.
- Protect human life and stop the shooter from killing.
- Provide direction to employees, contractors, and guests during the incident.
- Help law enforcement officers get to the shooter quickly.
- Assist emergency medical technicians, and provide care to the injured.
- Provide timely and effective internal and external communications.
- Get operations back to normal.

It is prudent to understand your goals before you begin to develop active shooter procedures and policy. The first goal of any active shooter plan should be to prevent such violence from happening in the first place. The second objective is to prevent the loss of human life; the third, to assist employees, contractors, and guests by providing clear directions and awareness training. The fourth objective might be to mitigate the effects of a shooter by supporting first responders and law enforcement. A fifth objective might be to protect the organizational mission or critical operations. These are just a few examples of the types of goals and objectives that need to be developed before actually writing your plan.

Stage 4. Now comes development and review. It includes the who, what, when, where, how, and why. This is where the each course of action is properly documented and written procedures assigned to personnel that must be accomplished, including in what order to implement them. Organizations must consider integration and compatibility with state and federal agencies and should use terminology that is easy to understand and standardized with outside agencies. Not only must outside groups be considered during this process, but each internal department should receive consideration.

Though common in government, acronyms should be avoided, as should slang, jargon, and abbreviations. Another aspect of minimizing confusion is using a structure that improves concepts and readability and logical flow of materials. Visual aids often improve the plan and should be added when appropriate. The addition of appropriate tools and aides to communicate the program effectively should be part of this process. Technology may help with this process through use of websites, text messages, visual and audio instruction, translators, and so forth.

A properly developed plan involves a summary of the key points and actionable information with enough detail that the average person can understand and follow, along with a structure that provides for easy reference and rapid identification of the procedures and solutions to be implemented.

After the initial draft is complete, the plan review must be started. First, the plan must comply with any applicable laws and regulations, assessed for level of effectiveness before final approvals. The plan should be reviewed against the goals and needs of the organization and its employees, outside contractors, and the agencies that may be involved in the response and recovery aspects. The CMT should be the on the approval team, actively involved in any edits or modifications. Often the plan must pass through the organization's legal department before final approval is received. This process can include several rewrites and modifications before the plan is complete, so timelines and milestones should be developed and managed during this process. After the plan has been developed and approved, it must be disseminated to those on the distribution list.

After all approvals are received and the final plan is accepted, it must be distributed. Sharing the plan with internal and external partners is critical. First responders need to understand the plan and should have the latest contact information to prevent delays during a incident. The plan also needs to be shared with internal stakeholders and anyone responsible for performing any of the tasks. The plan also needs to be protected from anyone who does not have a need to know—including in any electronic forms of the program.

Stage 5. The last step may be the most crucial in the entire process: implementing, testing, and maintenance of the plan. It doesn't matter how great the written plan is if when the shooting starts it has not been properly tested or is not followed. Training personnel in the plan and then testing it for gaps or flaws is critical and cannot be overvalued. The cost and time involved to perform this crucial step are where most organizations fail in their preparation. It takes total commitment from senior and mid-level management to make this final step successful.

Training should involve all stakeholders and people involved in the process. Their responsibilities and roles should be reviewed and instructed. The training meeting should involve a tour of the muster points, medical stations, and media areas. Information such as evacuation routes and shelter-in-place locations should be considered. Many companies like to post the muster points in the event of an emergency; though doing so is okay for fire and bomb threats, please note that in an active shooter scenario, posting this information could be counterproductive, providing valuable information to the shooter. It is, however, a good idea to print brochures or send electronic media for distribution to help with awareness and training.

Exercising the active shooter plan to make sure that it takes into account all aspects of the process and hasn't missed any critical steps is paramount to effectively dealing with threats such as an active shooter. A regularly scheduled tabletop or functional exercise should be conducted. These exercises should include first responders and law enforcement personnel whenever possible, helping the organization support and communicate more effectively. By understanding how to assist and support, the organization is improving response time and effectiveness, which should save lives during a crisis.

The final steps involve reviews, revisions, and maintenance of the plan. Most plans are designed to be continuous in nature. It is easy to lose interest after the initial plan has been developed, so it takes a concerted effort to review and revise the plan, keeping it up to date.

Figure 3-2 illustrates the 5-step process of the planning stages. The U.S. Department of Homeland Security (https://www.dhs.gov) and the Federal Emergency Management Agency (https://www.fema.gov) provide a tremendous amount of resources on incident management, emergency operations, and crisis management. The Federal Bureau of Investigation (https://www.fbi.gov) also offers information.

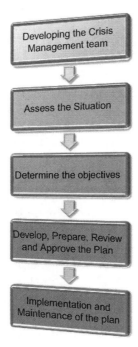

FIGURE 3–2 Five Main Stages of Planning.

The dynamic nature of the numerous threats that may affect an enterprise makes proper planning a tremendous challenge for any organization. This is especially true when considering an asymmetrical threat such as an active shooter. The preparation and response for a fire should differ greatly from that of a bomb threat, and a bomb threat is very different from an active shooting. Each threat must be evaluated and prepared for in a specific manner to best prevent or reduce the amount of loss.

The plan must consider employees, volunteers, contractors, and tenants in all plan phases, for guests will not know, understand, or appreciate the differences if they do not receive equal training and information.

Active Shooter Planning

The organization should take into consideration an active shooter threat within its crisis management and security planning process. Too often security stands alone and does not interact effectively in the emergency planning process, including when it comes to violent threats and response. Proper emergency planning cannot occur without security in mind. This is especially true when the threat is terrorism, or in our case, an active shooter.

Some organizations engage in wishful thinking and don't want to discuss the possibility of a shooting or violent crime. They pretend that if the problem isn't addressed or discussed, it will go away. We know that this is not the case—that shooting violence is growing, and it is your responsibility to provide a safe environment for anyone on your property, as well as for staff while in the performance of company activities, whether on site or not. That last statement should grab your attention: How does one prevent shootings when employees travel off site? This is where awareness and training is critical. It's not necessarily the company's duty to protect employee off site, but it is the company's responsibility to prepare and educate employees if they could be exposed to acts of violence. The active shooter plan drives the requirement for such training and education. Of all the planning an organization can do, this is often the most difficult to provide for fear of scaring employees, but companies can no longer ignore this threat.

Moreover, the active shooter plan requires a particular set of skills when developing the program. It is unadvisable to try to develop a plan without proper skills and experience. The industry is filled with employees and consultants who imitate and reproduce the plans developed by others, expecting that they will be effective in time of need. Doing so is dangerous; it is advisable to seek out someone who has the proper credentials and experience to ensure that the plan is comprehensive in scope, specific to the site being protected. If the trainer is not educated and experienced in active shooter issues, he or she will be an ineffective trainer. This is especially true if the company just has the employee or contractor read presentation slides and does not provide an interactive education media. One cannot become proficient in matters such as active shooting by reading a few slides.

Another flawed approach when developing an active shooter plan is to attend a training session on the subject matter in hopes of becoming an expert in such matters. It is difficult to properly understand all the dynamics of such an asymmetrical threat in a few hours or days. Training courses do have their place, but typically they are more effective at the individual level rather than for program development. This is because the individual must develop the ability to detect indicators and plan for personal decisions—it being easier to decide what to do on a personal level—rather than develop procedures and plans for an organization that could involve liability and legal responsibility for all employees, contractors, and guests.

Active shooter planning, like all crisis management plans, requires in-depth planning and is best developed using a team approach. Appendix C provides a list of questions that an organization should consider as it develops its business continuity plans regarding an active shooter. Although every organization is different, this list of questions can help the team identify areas often overlooked during the planning process.

It goes without saying that all the planning in the world is ineffective without the ability to develop protocols and procedures and communicate them to those who will be responsible to implement and execute the plan. For most organizations, this involves development of policy and procedures, awareness and training programs, and performing tests on the plan's effectiveness. The active shooter plan begins with the development of thorough policy and procedures.

Policies and Procedures

In an organization, policy differs from procedures as policies establish the priorities for the company. Procedures, on the other hand, provide detailed instructions for the day-to-day work activities. It is important that we establish this contrast before delving into the process of determining what to do or develop in preparation of an active shooter event. Unfortunately, many companies integrate their procedures into their policies and convolute the process. First of all, when developing policy and procedures for an active shooter, both should be written concisely and approach the issue generally. One of the greatest mistakes an organization can make is to be overly specific with its active shooter programs.

As stated before, active shooters are unpredictable and can change their tactics or targets in a matter of seconds, making it virtually impossible to provide direction and guidance for every possible scenario that could be encountered. A policy that is written in the attempt to cover every potential scenario would be extremely lengthy, and it would be unreasonable to expect employees to memorize and implement such a plan. Indeed, it would be impossible to write an active shooter policy to address every possible scenario—so our goal is not to deal with every situation, but rather to provide guidance and direction to those who are exposed to such threats. It is to provide information that can be retained and used when necessary.

For example, many programs instruct that during an active shooter incident the department managers lock down the area, hide staff, and switch off the lights. Although the intention of this approach is to save lives, this may not be an effective tactic, especially if the shooter is another employee who has access to the site and understanding of where employees are located. In this scenario, the shooter will also know the procedures and will use such knowledge to attack more people. In fact, in this example, you would be endangering the lives of your staff instead of protecting them by requiring such actions. It can't be stressed enough that lives have been saved or lost because of split-second decisions—so make the right one.

So is developing a written plan unnecessary? Absolutely not! The written plan doesn't force a person to react a certain way, but rather provides the procedures and awareness that may mean the difference between life and death. The plan also provides contacts and protocols to assist law enforcement officers who are key to stopping the threat. In the most basic terms, the plan provides the framework to help make quick and informed decisions during a shooting, and this is often the difference between survival and injury or death.

When you assess your preparedness for an active shooter or similar attack, you should focus on four main areas or missions:

- Prevention: Prevent or deter an active shooter or mass casualty event.
- Protection: Is the site secure against attacks using violence or other hazards?
- Mitigation: Eliminate or reduce the loss of life and property damage.
- Response and Recovery: Provides the capability to stabilize a crisis, secure the environment, provide medical care to save lives and property, and restore the site operations back to normal.

The plan should consider the four mission areas as it is developed. It is a basic roadmap to help outline the focus of policies and procedures for the company. Procedures will provide the actions or nonactions for implementing and carrying out the policy's objectives. Procedures provide more detail and specific actions that should be carried out during an incident. These include, but are not limited to, the following:

- Communications to staff and guests
- Reporting procedures to law enforcement and/or security
- Locate the threat (look, listen, move, communicate)
- Responses to the shooting (evacuate, hide, fight)
- Plans to assist and communicate with law enforcement/first responders
- Preparation for law enforcement screening
- Medical support and transport
- Recovery (cleanup, repairs, counseling, etc.)

The bottom line is that procedures are designed to protect human life, contain the incident, support the response function, and help the organization recover as quickly as possible, and they should be customized to the specific organization and site being protected. Policy and procedures have a side benefit of developing more awareness throughout the organization, especially at its top. It is our leaders who are often exposed to implied, verbal, and physical threats as they make the difficult decisions about how the company is run. Losing employment, or even being reprimanded, can cause the affected party to snap and lash out against the management team. Policies and procedures help illuminate the issues and communicate them to everyone in the company.

Dissemination

After the plan, policy, and procedures are developed, it is critical that these be communicated properly throughout the entire organization. As mentioned earlier, the actual plan will not be shared with everyone, but rather just the key stakeholders, who are responsible for implementing the plan. Company policy and procedures should be communicated in some manner to all staff and contractors. Even guests to the site should have an understanding as to what to do in the event of an emergency. There are several ways to accomplish the dissemination of this critical life-saving information:

- In-person training courses
- Webinars or Internet-based learning modules
- Manuals and written training modules
- Awareness pamphlets and handouts
- Training videos/media

Every organization is different and must determine the most effective means of delivering the information to those who need it. We have developed and trained using each of these delivery methods but prefer the in-person training sessions to the rest, because the topic can be customized to the business, because they allow for interaction between the instructor and participants, and because there is just something to be said about developing a connection from human to human. That said, many companies operate on a global basis and may prefer a web-based instructional program using webinars or videos. No matter your choice of instruction, it is always a good idea to provide handouts or a "takeaway" for participants to review later on.

Another of the many benefits to developing these programs is that your employees can take this knowledge home and share with their friends and families. Most of the information in an active shooter plan can be used to protect against other types of violent crimes. Furthermore, the ability to share this information to others is a great benefit because it could save lives. The dissemination of such information is truly a great service to those with whom we come in contact and about whom we care.

References

[1] U.S. Department of Homeland Security National Infrastructure Protection Plan (NIPP): Partnering for Critical Infrastructure Security and Resilience. Washington, DC: U.S. Department of Homeland Security; 2013.

[2] ASIS International The Protection of Assets Manual: Crisis Management. Alexandria, VA: ASIS International; 2011.

[3] U.S. Department of Homeland Security, Federal Emergency Management Agency Developing and Maintaining Emergency Operations Plans: Comprehensive Preparedness Guide 101, Version 2.0. Washington, DC: FEMA; 2010. <www.fema.gov/pdf/about/divisions/npd/CPG_101_V2.pdf>.

4

First Responders and the Private Sector

Roles, Responsibilities, and Action

The primary mission of first responders is to protect and serve the public under all threat conditions and environments that may affect the public. Regardless of whether an emergency is frequent, unique, or seasonal, first responders train for the worst and pray for the best regardless of the magnitude or sophistication of the emergency. These professionals must consider a full range of potential threats and hazards when protecting individuals, business, and communities. The following list gives only a few examples of the many threats and emergency situations for which first responders must prepare and to which they must respond to protect and serve the community:

- Natural hazards, such as avalanche, drought, earthquakes, flash floods, severe weather, wildfires, natural gas explosions, and mud slides
- Threats to health, such as anthrax, avian influenza, ricin, West Nile virus, and norovirus
- Manmade hazards, such as air pollution, water pollution, aircraft crashes, dam failure, utility failure, structural fire, pipeline ruptures, and radiological low or high events
- Accidents, such as railroad train derailments causing chemical release, petroleum tank explosions, and bridge collapses
- Terrorism, such as plane hijackings, bombings, kidnappings, and ecoterrorism
- Human events, such as bomb threats, civil disturbances, traffic accidents, food poisoning, and a complete list of criminal activity, including active shooters

First responders are a unique breed, often cut from a different cloth. Unique how? Instead of running away from a roaring fire, they run into it. Instead of fleeing a deadly chemical spill, they put on a suit and enter to contain the release. Instead of escaping gunfire, they seek out the shooter to stop his or her path of destruction. We all know people who would go back into a fire to save their daughter or son, a cherished one for whom they would risk their own life. But first responders generally do not know the victims in an emergency, yet they believe that these people need their help merely because they are part of the human race. Preservation of life and rescuing people from harm are only two elements of an entire portfolio of traits that can be attributed to these exceptional people we call first responders.

To establish a baseline, first responders comprise law enforcement officers, firefighters, paramedics, emergency service providers, and public health professionals. Each department has its own mission statement, roles, functions, responsibilities, and duties during an emergency. Each agency and department has secured and trained in using equipment essential to

FIGURE 4–1 Resiliency Components.

its respective roles and will facilitate, accelerate, and revitalize the safe and secure environment at the emergency location.

To accomplish this, the role of first responders begins well in advance of any emergency through a national overarching directive found in Presidential Policy Directive/PPD 8 [1]. The purpose of the directive attempts to strengthen the resiliency and security of the United States through a series of capabilities, such as prevention, protection, mitigation, response, and recovery, refer to Figure 4-1. Note that each area is essential for a sustainable and comprehensive resiliency plan for any emergency, disaster, or crisis. The active shooter emergency is no different, so all first responding agencies and departments should follow an established national preparedness model. Furthermore, three key components bind each functional area; they are the Incident Command System (ICS), a common communications platform, and coordinated training among first responding agencies and departments. The business, community, and individuals caught up in the reality of an active shooting emergency expect nothing less from the first responder community.

It should be noted of all the identified elements in PPD 8 that first responders will not participate in the recovery element or reconstitution of business services. Unlike a natural disaster that affects numerous businesses and communities, such as earthquakes or floods, the active shooting emergency is generally limited to one business or location, so the recovery component falls directly on the shoulder of the business to navigate and assess the damages associated with the active shooting. First responders will mobilize resources to treat and aid the victims, but only during the emergency. However, first responders cannot assist with certain key recovery areas:

- Customer base restoration
- Inventory destroyed
- Lost revenue
- Shipping delays
- Union negotiations
- Employee conflicts
- Advertising and promotions
- Restoring utilities
- IT computer databases

Remember that first responders' primary missions are to neutralize the threat, treat the injured, and investigate the emergency for potential criminal legal action. In an active shooter incident, first responders will frequently hold press conferences with the local and national media outlets to provide an overview of what happened during the shooting and assure the public that the threat has been resolved.

Requirements and Assistance

Every first responder knows that any department or agency charged to protect and serving the community cannot rely on tools, equipment, tactics, and training from the past, but must incorporate into a new era lessons learned and best practices for responding to and resolving a threat or emergency. The active shooting emergency is no different; each shooting exposes strengths and weaknesses in the overall response, which generally are found in after-action reports. A number of after-action reports have been written regarding active shooters' barbaric acts, such as those at Virginia Tech and Columbine, and these have circulated throughout the first responder community. The following after action-reports (AAR) present new lessons that should be considered, discussed, and incorporated by each first responder agency and department. In the aftermath of an active shooting, review each after action-report in its entirety to incorporate the lessons learned into each respective first responder agency and department. It is important not to fall prey to two extremely tragic words: "If only." *If only I had read the reports and applied the lessons learned. If only we had taken the necessary steps to develop or procure effective training solutions.*

- The Los Angeles World Airport's "Active Shooter Incident and Resulting Airport Disruption: A Review or Response Operations" [2] provided some key lessons learned:
  - Response to armed threats at LAX must consider a range of scenarios and provide for training and tactical integration of public safety partners as well as the readiness of the airport's civilian residents.
  - The right systems, clear lines of responsibility, and well-documented processes for alert notifications are critical to avoiding delay in mobilizing a response team during the early stages of any emergency.
  - Unity of command and effective coordination of interdependent response operations rely greatly on a well-integrated and rehearsed communications plan, along with having interoperable communications equipment.
- Some key lessons gleaned from the "Fort Hood Army Internal Review Team: Final Report," Department of the Army, August 4, 2010 [3], include the following:
  - There was no process or procedure to share real-time event information among commands, installations, and components.
  - Services are not fully interoperable with all military and civilian emergency management stakeholders.
  - Information sharing agreements with federal, state, and local law enforcement and criminal investigation organizations do not mandate guidelines nor actions, nor do they provide a clear standard.

- The "Active Shooter/Suicide After Action Report," Police Department, University of Texas–Austin, September 28, 2010 [4], provided some key lessons learned, including the following:
  - The primary responding officers understood the Incident Command System (ICS), implemented it effectively, and complied with its provisions.
  - Many aspects of the command communications proved problematic, for not everyone switched to the selected channel, nor was able to dispatch, transmit, or even monitor the selected channel—along with issues stemming from inconsistent uniformity when using definitions and terminology, such as "shelter in place" and "lockdown."
  - On the day of the shooting, the officers were secure in the knowledge that they were well equipped and had previously rehearsed for such an incident.
- The 2010 "Lessons Learned in Response and Recovery: Northern Illinois University," [5] by the Northern Illinois University (NIU) Police and Public Safety Department, provided several key lessons learned:
  - Planning together within the responder organizations contributed to a good working relationship, trust, and rapid triage, treatment, and the transport of victims.
  - The NIU emergency medical technicians (EMTs) first on scene used their emergency medical training to good advantage.
  - The NIU emergency communication plan provided clear messages, described the situation, and told people what to do.
- The "Internal Review of the Washington Navy Yard Shooting: A Report to the Secretary of Defence," November 20, 2013 [6], also provided some key lessons learned:
  - The structure, layout, and environment of Building 197 posed a substantial tactical challenge for the responding officers.
  - Almost every agency and installation/facility at the site had its own emergency plans, but not the necessary stakeholders (local first responders in particular) were familiar with those plans.
  - During the initial response, while the crisis was evolving and the gunman was still clearly active, a full incident command was not clearly established, but the vital ICS objectives were already in place and a unified command was soon established. Unfortunately, not all agencies and critical functions had representation within the unified command.

Consider an active shooting in your respective jurisdiction from the viewpoint of a panel of experts who will assess the first responders and review their actions. The panel would focus on every aspect listed in the after-action reports identified from previous shootings. What will your response be if some of the same challenges, issues, and discrepancies occurred despite having historical data available? Before answering this question, consider that many of the above lessons learned and recommendations may be ignored within your department or community because "it will never happen here." To successfully harness these lessons learned takes cooperation, coordination, education, and synchronized training that transcends historical and traditional boundaries between first responders within the same jurisdiction.

First responders may respond to the active shooting emergency from all directions and in a variety of transportation modes, including the possibility of aerial support, when available. Officers will arrive in regular department uniforms, tactical uniforms, and plainclothes. Unfortunately, active shooting emergencies produce an unexpected threat to these plainclothes responders that is experienced only rarely during law enforcement training. The possibility of law enforcement officers' being mistaken for the shooter is an aspect is commonly referred to as "blue on blue," or "friendly fire." How does the law enforcement community identify officers not in uniform as friendly, not as the active shooter? To initially counter this problem, in some cases only one department or task force is allowed to enter a danger zone while all others remain outside, forming a secure perimeter around the area. This is an age-old problem for the law enforcement community, now more compounded by a surge in active shooting messages' being broadcast across multiple agencies and departments at the same time, each of which wants to intervene to neutralize the threat. Law enforcement officers are trained to identify their target, assess the background behind the threat, and think before using their weapons. Every pull on the trigger should be carefully calculated by the officer and based on the threat posed and the likelihood of protecting human life. Unfortunately there are times of uncertainty that each officer faces, because the active shooter is looking for more victims: The faster the response by law enforcement, the fewer injuries and the less loss of life. The entry officers will be rapidly searching for the shooter, and on seeing a person carrying a gun who is not in uniform or who does not have any identifiable markings distinguishing him or her as a first responder, they are very likely to mistake that individual for the active shooter.

Consider the possibility of providing a universal method to identify law enforcement and other first responders (or authorized individuals) within your community who may be encountered during an active shooting. What universal method of identification could be considered? Figure 4–2 provides nine different options that may be considered, along with possible advantages and disadvantages.

Whatever option is selected, it is important to coordinate the choice with all first responder associations and unions, then with federal, state and local agencies both inside the community and outside, who, predictably, may respond to the active shooting. Before implementing a choice also (1) consider where and how it will be manufactured, (2) restrict the use of the chosen option to authorized first responders, (3) find out how and where it will be distributed, (4) choose a common color scheme or pattern, (5) the words to be placed on the chosen option (if required), (6) promulgate the rules and restrictions for use, and (7) observe how visible is it in low-light conditions and at night.

Gaps and Challenges

First responders are thrust into life-threatening emergency situations because of the type of work they do and the environments in which they operate. This is their profession, the life they have chosen.

Each person should prepare himself or herself both mentally and physically for how to respond to an active shooter emergency; yet most businesses have never seen an active shooting

VISIBILITY	ADVANTAGES	DISADVANTAGES
Badge on the belt around the waist		
Primarily from front	• Identifies as law enforcement • Carried on person at all times • Can reflect light • Universally understood	• Visible only from front and possibly side • Visibility depends on angle of view • Visibility depends on whether officer wearing a coat • Can be stolen or faked • Could be private security
Badge dangling on a lanyard around the neck		
Primarily from front	• Identifies as law enforcement • Carried on person at all times • Can reflect light • Universally understood	• Visible only from the front • Visibility depends on whether officer is wearing a coat • Not all officers have lanyards including a badge holder
Windbreaker		
All directions	• Identifies as law enforcement • Unique and not available to general public • Commonly used across departments • Universally understood	• Not standard across all agencies and departments • Generally only visible from two directions—front and back • Some have words on sleeves • Difficult for plainclothes officer to carry on person
Sash extending from waistband to shoulder		
Primarily from the front	• Identifies as law enforcement • Unique and not available to general public • Carried on person at all times	• May catch or snag during various entry positions • Not visible from all angles and viewpoints • If worn on belt at all times, will be viewed the same as a badge
Custom wristband		
All angles except from behind	• Custom to armed officers	• Difficult to see because may be covered by weapons or clothing • May be confused with nightclub wristband or charity wristband • If worn at all times, alerts criminals what to look for to detect surveillance and law enforcement officers • May be difficult to see because of size or color
Armband on one arm		
Front, back, and side of arm band, as well as from above	• Carried on person at all times • Can be placed over any clothing • Unique and custom-made	• May be difficult to see if not large enough • May compress with use and become more difficult to see • One size may not fit all • If too small, may constrict officer movements
Armbands on both arms		
All directions, including from above	• Carried on person at all times • Can be given to another officer who is without • Can be placed over any clothing • Unique and custom-made	• May be difficult to see if too small • May compress with use and become more difficult to see • One size may not fit all • If too small may constrict officer movements
Baseball cap		
All directions including, from above	• Can identify law enforcement department • Universally known and currently used by law enforcement	• Cannot be carried on person at all times, because hard brim cannot fit in pocket • Generally identifying marks on front only • Standard law enforcement hats cannot be worn by private security
Custom flexible hat		
All directions, including from above	• Carried on person at all times • Unique, custom, restricted, and made locally • Can adjust to larger or smaller sizes • Larger than armbands	• Takes time to implement for all departments

FIGURE 4–2 Advantages and Disadvantages of Armed Individual.

nor even experienced a serious incident involving firearms. A direct by-product or consequence of this fact creates a large gap between first responders and businesses; these challenges begin well before the first call to report a shooter or to request assistance when a credible threat is made.

First responders may believe that there are no gaps or challenges, because an emergency response is second nature to these professional. In addition, these professionals may only look at the problem from the totality of the emergency itself, not from the overall mission perspective. But an active shooting emergency is sudden and ferocious, yet the same can be said for a refinery tank explosion or a railroad train derailment that spills deadly chemicals into the air and across the ground. So what are the gaps and challenges to an active shooting emergency? First, unless first responders are invited to businesses to reshape expectations and open a dialogue on how to remove these gaps and challenges from the slate of accounts, then misstep after misstep may occur on both sides. Second, unless first responders and businesses train together in a cooperative environment, then gaps and challenges are destined to dominate the overall response to a shooting. The company should review the following list and determine what it can control and coordinate with the first responders. The first responders should do the same thing from through collaboration with the business.

Look at gaps and challenges from a different viewpoint. What if someone told you that you would box against a world champion boxer in five minutes and gave you a book about boxing: What gaps and challenges would you see? You would undoubtedly say to yourself that such a thing would never happen; but everyday in businesses, cities, and communities, we experience similar challenges because of our belief that an active shooter will never come knocking at our door. Listed here are a few gaps and challenges experienced during active shooting. The list is not an exhaustive culmination of after-action reporting or Senate subcommittee hearings, but rather compiled from two significant perspectives—first responders' and businesses'. From the first responder perspective, the following gaps and challenges may present themselves:

- First responders may know part of the business structure because of past calls but may not know the facility past public-access areas.
- First responders may have been to the business before, but unless there was a previous shooting, the first responders will look at the business from an entirely new threat analysis perspective.
- People may have evacuated before law enforcement officers' arrival—among them, perhaps, the active shooter, or key witnesses who may have relevant information.
- Until law enforcement arrives at the site, in most cases, no one will have established barricades or access points around the business perimeter.
- First responders cannot determine observation platforms if they never been inside the building.
- First responders will attempt to determine the interior layout of the facility, such as open work environment, cubicles, number of departments, number of floors, location of elevators or escalators or stairs, locations of deadly chemicals, how many people are still inside the business, and so forth. Each element must be visibly reviewed and mentally analyzed, which takes time and significantly lengthens the response time to get to the shooter.

- First responders do not understand the sights and sounds within the facility or location; each business has its own sounds and feel.
- If first responders have not been inside the business or know nothing about the business, then there is no way to eliminate emerging problems and impediments before the emergency.
- Many people think it easy to understand the nature of a business, but until they see a business, they can only make assumptions about what the business actually does.
- First responders heading to the active shooting structure may encounter hazardous and dangerous elements that need to be negotiated or avoided.
- Unless first responders have been inside the business previously, the first responder communications network inside building may fail to provide adequate coverage because of dead spots in communication signals or networks.
- Firefighters and paramedics may not be allowed to enter an active shooter location before the all-clear signal is broadcast by law enforcement.
- Coordinated training between first responders is often missing and overlooked.
- Training does not always include the mental and physical training aspects for all potential first responders.
- Joint training by the different responding agencies, including a unified tactical entry, such as a four-person team, is practically nonexistent.
- Effective training on the Incident Command System (ICS) between all first responding agencies and departments is often still problematic.
- Effective training may not be afforded to surrounding agencies that may be required to respond during major emergencies.
- A communications platform that allows numerous agencies, departments, and response disciplines to communicate over a common communications network is often lacking in many parts of the country.
- First responders may lack access to specialized equipment that they may need, such as entry and close-quarter weapons, bolt cutters, ballistic shields and helmets, gas masks, and torches.
- A coordinated response network often does not promote the cross-pollination of agencies and departments, such as fire and police, reinforcing a "silo" mentality.
- Departments may not allow solo officers to enter active shooter location, even while victims are being systematically killed. Additionally, departments may not allow a law enforcement response team to enter the business unless all responders are from the same department.
- First responders will be receiving reports of the active shooting that often provide incorrect details and assumptions—and add into the equation that eyewitness accounts during or after the shooting are frequently inaccurate, incomplete, misleading, or even completely false, preventing first responders from determining the full extent of the emergency before they experience it first-hand.

Before determining the effectiveness of the response and how seriously a business takes its duty to protect employees and guests while providing a safe and secure environment in coordination with the first responders, consider the coordination of assets. The coordination process will experience gaps and challenges from the business's perspective under the following circumstances:

- No active shooter plan
- No emergency plan
- No primary or secondary common communication platform
- No prescripted emergency message for active shooting
- No emergency command center (ECC) or emergency operations center (EOC)
- No emergency evacuation assembly area (EEAA)
- No video surveillance or security control room
- No prior coordination between the business and first responders
- No trauma medicine training or supplies for staff and contractors
- No expectation that the business knows how to coordinate with the first responders on any level
- No prior training of employees, tenants, contractors, or volunteers in active shooting
- No coordination between tenant properties, contractors, vendors, and volunteers

Insider Threat

An active shooting is a barbaric and insidious act that is difficult to absorb by the average person on any level, but when the shooter is someone the victims have worked with and even shared a laugh with, the tragic event cannot be reconciled easily. The spectrum of emotional discourse when the shooter is seen or known to be a trusted coworker crushes every sense of the employee family unity and dissolves trust in mankind. It is one thing to see an active shooter on the national news, but when the shooter is an employee or former employee, the boundaries of loyalty and camaraderie evaporate with the first shot. This has been the case all too frequently, as seen by the following insider threat active shootings:

- Ft. Hood, Ft. Hood, TX
- Columbine High School, Littleton, CO
- Washington Navy Yard, Washington, D.C.
- Maryville–Pilchuck High School, Maryville, WA
- United Parcel Service, Inglenook, AL

For the first responders running code (lights and sirens) to the active shooting location, knowing that the active shooter is an employee or former employee of the business is invaluable information that should not treated lightly. Information about the shooter, including his or her prior association with the business, should be transmitted immediately. However, there are significant differences that segregate insider threats depending upon the latitude, clearances, and functionality of a current or former employee:

- If the business requires access cards to restricted or sensitive areas, this may limit the locations and movement of the shooting rampage.
- The shooter may know the security officers and whether they are armed or not but may not know the security protocols or each element of the active shooter response plan.

- The shooter may not understand that security technology, such as access cards and biometrics, can be canceled to restrict the active shooter's movement.
- The shooter may not realize that elevators can be overridden and may trap the shooter in the elevator.
- The business may have the ability to seal exterior doors and floors without warning or prior communication.
- The shooter may be familiar with the primary communications platform, but not secondary platforms.
- Altering and pre-empting the shooter's movements by using preventive measures may frustrate or overextend the shooter. A security command center or control room operation may be able to monitor and limit the shooter's movement throughout the facility or site.
- After the shooter's identify is known, the business may broadcast over the communications platform the shooter's name and physical description, as well as a description of what the shooter is wearing.
- If the active shooter is known, coworkers will be able to point out the shooter if he or she attempts to escape during the emergency evacuation process.
- Pictures of the shooter can be handed out to first responders and disseminated to all first responder checkpoints and entry teams.

Conversely, the mere fact that the active shooter is familiar with the business gives the shooter a greater advantage and hampers the response. Each detail about the shooter is important to the first responders and warrants a complete cumulative picture of the threat environment that must be negotiated. For the first responder, knowledge and intelligence when engaging the active shooter is paramount for the survival of the potential victims and protection of first responders entering the hostile environment. From the outset, the insider knows, though the first responders may not, the following:

- Interior floor plan. First responders generally know common areas.
- Length of hallways, and whether first responder movement is visible from a higher floor.
- The interior design of the business, such as office cubicles, open area operations, and individual offices.
- Location of elevators, stairwells, and escalators.
- Location of offices or departments, such as human resources, cafeteria, and managers' offices.
- The shooter knows his or her intended victims, such as managers, supervisors, specific coworkers, and CEOs, and may allow potential "nontarget" coworkers to escape. First responders must consider that any employee or person within the business can be a victim or could be the shooter masquerading as a panicked employee.
- The shooter knows obscure, less traveled exits for use escaping before first responders arrive. In the September 16, 2013, the FBI report "A Study of Active Shooter Incidents in the United States between 2000 and 2013" [7] indicated that nearly 18.125% of active shooters, after done shooting their intended victims, merely walked away afterward.

The first step in countering and preventing an insider active shooter begins with the active shooter plan. Acknowledging the possibility of an insider active shooter by including a specific section on insider threat begins the process of developing preventive measures and counter-measures. From this perspective, countermeasures can be built into the internal response protocols, active shooter movements channeled and restricted, systems and technology restructured to block off physical sections of the building (compartmentalization), and possible safe routes developed for employees trapped in this nightmare. However, it should be noted that if the active shooter is prevented from exiting from a specific section of the building, this option may unilaterally prevent employees from evacuating as well or even expose their attempt to escape when they find their egress point blocked.

The second step may be to remove potential casualties from the equation by eliminating the emergency evacuation assembly area (EEAA). If the shooter missed one or two of his or her intended victims, the shooter may think them located at the EEAA. If there is no EEAA—or if it is eliminated by allowing employees to evacuate and disperse to locations well outside the business property—additional potential victims may be avoided.

Third, remotely reversing escalators to maximize the first responders' tactical mission is one of several different technology actions the business can exert in effecting the response to an active shooting. The plan should articulate these options and actions before any active shooting emergency. The time to test this procedure is during training and when trained, then replicating it during the actual emergency.

Before, During, and After

Before

After first responders receive the emergency call, their minds and bodies begin to mobilize and prepare for any abnormality that may face them. Each responder shifts from his or her previous function, such as conducting a traffic stop, completing burglary reports, or conducting training, into a focused professional who mentally runs through a checklist and categorizes each piece of equipment that may be required for this type of emergency. Their minds run through lessons learned from previous active shooting emergencies and may embrace the value of their last coordinated active shooting training exercise. Unfortunately, if there has been no coordinated training between first responders or if lessons learned from previous active shootings were dismissed as something that would never take place in the community and the first responders never toured the business beforehand, the response is unavoidably hampered. Figure 4–3 identifies a couple of business assets that may be coordinated prior to an incident.

Some of the most relevant and value-added considerations for first responders may be accomplished by a simple visit to the business before any emergency. The purpose of the visit will simply be to conduct a fact-finding and coordination mission. First responders are as overworked as any agency, but the significance of this visit cannot be understated. The tour is a reasonable and prudent measure that may do the following:

- Save lives and reduce casualties
- Reduce misunderstandings about what first responder will do or need
- Maximize coordination efforts between the business and responders

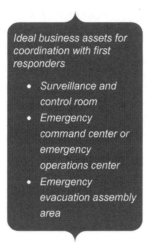

Ideal business assets for coordination with first responders

- Surveillance and control room
- Emergency command center or emergency operations center
- Emergency evacuation assembly area

FIGURE 4–3 Coordination Assets.

- Mitigate challenges by identifying corrective measures beforehand, such as by identifying communication dead spots
- Possibly improve agency response time
- Discuss equipment needs and specific resources, identifying their locations

Each of the above points is just an example of the compelling attributes of a single simple visit.

First responders may routinely travel in the vicinity of the business each day without any concept of the challenges that the structure may pose. Without touring the business beforehand, first responders cannot know, see, or feel the property first-hand. Each business has its own distinct feel and environment, and each property has its own unique noises and smells. The first responders will also need to identify the where, when, how, who, and why for each of the following items:

- Determine the differences between each business shift and the hours of operation.
- Preview floor plans.
- Determine the number of floors, subfloors, and landings.
- Understand the departments on each floor.
- View the signage used to identify significant business features, such as human resources, executive offices, and the cafeteria.
- Understand the room setup, including furniture, dividers, and plants.
- Locate exits, entrances, stairwells, escalators, and elevators.
- Identify any open balconies or railings.
- Understand atrium, planters, and sitting areas.
- Identify the type of lighting and skylights.

- View any areas of glass that may expose entry teams.
- Identify what areas will provide both cover and concealment for entry teams while also determining the same for a shooter.
- Noises and sounds of the business are important, such as machinery and water fountains, as well as to what extent sound echoes and travels.
- Understand the type of flooring, such as carpeting or tile, noting how it may affect the entry team.
- Identify any blind hallways that may present challenges for first responders.
- Understand the length of the hallways, which will expose first responders as potential victims.
- Identify any areas that will expose the response team to danger from above, including from higher floors.
- Determine whether the doors are glass or hardwood or contain windows.
- Identify areas that have added security features, such as an access card system, advanced locks, or biometric credentials, that may need to be circumvented.
- Understand which areas are open and closed to the public.
- Identify the composition of walls, such as glass, block, brick, or drywall.
- Determine how many people work inside the building during each shift and which areas have the highest concentrations of employees.
- Can the response team make a rooftop entry?
- What other areas are important? This is an excellent question for your first responders to answer.

During

As soon as first responders are notified of the active shooting, an internal stopwatch is activated in each responder. In their minds there can be no distractions, no hurdle too big to be surpassed, no barrier to the complex that cannot be breached. The first responder must tactically and systematically overcome every obstacle in his or her path without hesitation—but safely. First responders know what they must do to neutralize the shooter and rescue any people in harm's way. However, people often forget the challenges of the situation from the viewpoint of the first responders. Consider a few points from the first responder's perspective that must be overcome during the response:

- Responders must fight traffic delays en route to the incident, which could include rush hour traffic, preexisting accidents, or road construction.
- Responders may attempt to navigate through routine traffic whose drivers have seen their normal share of emergency vehicles, meaning that other drivers may not attempt to clear a path for the responders.
- Weather conditions can hinder a fast response as flooded roads or snowy conditions make the journey more treacherous.

- Even when the responders are close to the business, traffic may come to a complete standstill and the responders be forced to pursue the emergency on foot.
- Pedestrians may dart across streets, and people in panic mode won't follow traffic laws or pedestrian crosswalks—they often run in any direction.
- After the first responders arrive at the business, generally no one is stopping to help provide any real information or intelligence, so the responder may only have the information received from the dispatcher.
- No one in charge at the site contacts the first responder.
- No one at the site provides a point of entry, only vague directions and hurried responses.
- Even when people are found, they may provide the same information over and over again, with nothing new to aid the first responders.
- People are hiding behind barriers, cars, and walls, some of which offer cover and some only concealment.
- People at the scene are panicking, yelling, screaming, and crying; some are seen running away.
- Some people may be injured—not just by the active shooter, but by having incurred injuries during their escape from the building.
- First responders must determine from this mass of humanity exiting the structure which person may be the shooter, filtering through all the individuals exiting the shooting area.
- First responders must determine whether there is more than one shooter.
- Responders must determine whether there are any improvised explosive devices (IEDs) as people retreat past the responders, knocking over items and dropping personal belongings to the ground.
- First responders seldom have reliable, complete, accurate, or even sufficient intelligence before entering the active shooting location.
- After the property has been breached, the interior layout of the building becomes a challenge impeding the response, especially if the responders are totally unfamiliar with the internal dynamics of the business.
- Firefighters, EMS personnel, and paramedics will work their way to the emergency evacuation assembly area to treat any injured or wounded.
- Firefighters, EMS personnel, and paramedics will be treating any injured person whom they encounter during the emergency—for injured people may have escaped the shooter—regardless of the person's injury.

After

After the active shooter has been located and neutralized, arrested, or found to have committed suicide, the active shooting emergency is still not over. There are still many facets unresolved, and dangers may be lurking behind each down or hallway. Consider the following from both the responders and individuals' perspectives:

- First responders must clear all offices, rooms, closets, storage areas, departments, and areas within the business, because they cannot rely on there being only one shooter.
- During the clearing phase, all offices, rooms, and departments must be searched.

- When doors are found to be locked, they still need to be breached, because the door may have been locked to secure the area from the active shooter. In addition, the shooter may lock himself or herself in a room or area to slow law enforcement officers' approach.
- Even when a door is found unlocked, it does not mean that the room can be easily entered; the individuals inside the room may have barricaded the door with heavy furniture.
- When a shooting begins, many potential victims may run in any direction but may not be able to escape the building and instead hide a variety of places for a variety of reasons:
  - People may hide under desks, in closets, or in supply rooms.
  - Those injured during the escape or by the shooter may only be able to hide.
  - Individuals that are disabled may be forced to hide.
  - The disabled may have lifelong, early onset, progressive, recent, fluctuating, or episodic conditions that may affect their abilities to acknowledge first responders' presence, such as limited hearing or deafness.
  - Individuals who are hiding out may choose not to exit for any reason, causing further challenges for first responders.
  - Some individuals are so scared that they freeze up, their muscles or brain unable to accept any first responder requests to come out, with every noise considered a threat or danger to their hiding place.
- The clearing phase is still a dangerous time for first responders and for individuals hiding out within the property. Please note every action found in DHS pamphlets, booklets, and videos, such as the city of Houston's video "Run, Hide and Fight" [8] and the Department of Homeland Security's video "Options for Consideration" [9].
- As a last resort, individuals may fight with all their might, and using all means available, to defend themselves against unwanted intruders—force that may also be directed toward the responding officers. These individuals may
  - throw items, such as lamps, laptops, staplers, books, vases, or pictures
  - stab with scissors, knives, letter openers, or even umbrellas
  - hit with furniture, including chairs and fire extinguishers
- The individuals inside a dark room do not know who is at the door and often really don't believe who is at the door, even if the word "police" is used.
- First responders must protect themselves from an attack by individuals who are hiding out in case a responder is mistaken for the attacker.
- During the law enforcement response, officers may have stepped over or walked past injured or dying victims of the shooter. Law enforcement will not take any time to assess their medical condition or the seriousness of their injuries, so paramedics, firefighters, or EMS personnel should be called inside the property to assist. In many areas, law enforcement officers are now being trained to triage victims by using tourniquets and combat gauzes or are working with tactical EMTs trained to work alongside law enforcement during the response.
- Firefighters and EMS personnel should be escorted inside the business by armed law enforcement officers.
- Law enforcement officers will be assembling witnesses and contacting business management for their investigation.

- Because of this unfortunate emergency, the business is now a crime scene, so the business is turned over to the appropriate law enforcement agency during the investigation. The length of time the business will be considered a crime scene depends solely on the law enforcement agency. The business management staff is expected to cooperate fully with any request from law enforcement during the investigation.

Effective Coordination

The business should understand that the moment the active shooter fires his or her first shot, the business must begin coordinating the response efforts with the first responders. Every resource and asset available at the business should now be a tool for the first responders to neutralize the active shooter. There should be no reservations or exemptions to what a business can supply during the active shooter response. The momentum of the response cannot be thwarted by incremental or contradicting coordination efforts from the business. The ideal way to effectively coordinate response efforts between the business and the first responder community is to invite the first responders over to the business before any emergency. Ask the responders what they desire the business to provide, and identify functional areas such as the security surveillance and control room, emergency command center, and emergency evacuation assembly area. Ask what the first responders' role would be in each area identified. Once this is completed, the first responders can write these actions into their response program to cover the entire spectrum of assets and services the business possesses to advance the emergency coordination between the responders.

Security Surveillance and Control Room

The security surveillance and control room is an invaluable business resource that can be used to maximize response efforts and direct entry teams. It is imperative to let the first responder know of the existence of, and to escort first responders to, this room. First responders need information and intelligence about the building and operations as they are entering to neutralize the active shooter. A well-positioned first responder inside the surveillance or control room will help guide responders through the maze of obstacles found within the business. A seemingly harmless floral planter may provide concealment for the shooter and an obstruction for the responders, but when assessment is provided in real time from the control room, such intelligence can escalate the response around every corner, on every floor, and when traversing each department. This room is undeniably a tremendous advantage to any response effort, and one that an active shooter cannot easily overcome or exploit.

Emergency Command Center or Emergency Operations Center

The emergency command center (ECC) or emergency operations center (EOC) is an extremely important asset for any business confronted with an emergency. For many businesses, the

ECC/EOC is a very elaborate and technology proficient room, but for other businesses the ECC/EOC may be the executive conference room or even just the CEO's cell phone. The primary purpose of the ECC/EOC is to direct, command, and control the emergency through preparedness, response, and recovery. Businesses view an emergency from one perspective, whereas first responders view the same emergency from an altogether different one. First responders should be allowed to enter the ECC/EOC to aid in the response to the active shooting. A representative of the business should direct or escort first responders to the ECC/EOC to maximize response times and unify coordination between the business and responders.

Emergency Evacuation Assembly Area

The emergency evacuation assembly area (EEAA) is a function of the business and cannot be delegated to the first responders. The activation process of the EEAA falls directly on the business. Although this task may be seemingly overwhelming for some organizations, the first responders are not responsible to account for each individual who was inside the business during the active shooting emergency. They rely on the company to know who was inside and each individual's possible location. Mistakenly, many businesses believe this essential function to be a component of the first responder community.

Regardless of the size of the business, the EEAA is a progression of a safe and secure environment that the business is mandated to perform. This is not a new revelation or a distraction from the emergency itself, but rather a legitimate duty. To maximize the effectiveness of the EEAA, the business should understand the mechanics of the key employee roles, responsibilities, and requirements for succeeding throughout the process. Without an effective EEAA, the business may tarnish its reputation and frustrate employees, guests, and relatives of those individuals. Synchronizing and propositioning the appropriate personnel and equipment, choosing the right location(s) and leveraging the business's resources all can contribute to an effective calculated response. The EEAA is the significant conduit in the road to recovery.

When a business is engulfed in the active shooting emergency, that is not the time to figure out how best to aid employees and guests—it is an injustice to those individuals who have successfully escaped the active shooter. A gradual approach to the EEAA devalues the mission of the business. Providing a fully operational and effective EEAA enriches and embraces the business's response to an active shooting emergency. Many businesses have no clue where to start or have no ability to acknowledge the key functions, because, just as with the active shooting emergency, the business has never needed to implement an EEAA before. Following are numerous aspects of the EEAA that should be considered to facilitate an effective EEAA:

- Outsourcing
  Because of the dramatic nature of the active shooting emergency, outsourcing is often not feasible. Any company that may be contracted as an outsourcing EEAA partner may not be able to assemble in sufficient time to travel the distance to the business, which will hinder its effectiveness. Additionally, because of possible traffic congestion experienced en route to the business, such a party might be prevented altogether from entering through the first responder protection lines.

- Inside Location
  With employees and guests evacuating the business, the EEAA cannot be positioned inside the location of the active shooting. That said, if the business has multiple buildings or structures, then the EEAA may be sustainable on the business property or campus. Another option is to contract or establish a voluntary commitment with a nearby business through a cooperative agreement making its property accessible in sufficient size to accommodate neighboring employees, guests, and the various functions of the EEAA. This concept is not commonly in use but was used successfully in the 2013 Washington Navy Yard shooting.

- Outside Location
  Traditionally, the location of most EEAAs that have been associated with fire emergencies is generally adjacent to the building, such as the employees' parking garage or lot, a designated street corner, or a distinctive park. For most emergencies, this may be appropriate, but during an active shooting, being just outside the building may expose employees and guests to indiscriminate gunfire. Select an EEAA that provides both cover and concealment from the active shooter. If feasible, design the EEAA with a roof to protect people from the elements. It is important to realize that the location may be used for a prolonged period of time, so it should be designed accordingly. Furthermore, remember to allow for persons with disabilities: The location should be accessible by wheelchair and be tolerant of individuals who cannot travel long distances. Optimal locations should be discussed and identified before any emergency.

- Staffing
  The size of the business will determine how the EEAA will be staffed. Despite the number of positions that are identified, the organization may not be able to staff every position as a standalone function. If that is the case, then employees may be empowered to wear more than one hat within the EEAA. It is important to remember when selecting employees for each position to identify primary and secondary individuals who can function equally in the EEAA. Some EEAA staff might be a casualty of the active shooter or might be out of town on assignment or on medical leave that day—or still be hiding out inside the business.

- EEAA Management
  The EEAA cannot be effective without solid leadership. The business has a responsibility to fill this position with a person who can methodically direct, guide, and communicate to the EEAA staff and its occupants under adverse conditions. This leader must inspire action, be mindful of unrelenting chaos, leverage the cooperative spirit in each employee, and minimize misunderstandings through effective communications. The leader must also eliminate emotions and not be so overwhelmed by the tragedy or decisions that may be detrimental to the mission of the EEAA. The leader nurtures support but demands swift action from the EEAA's staff. The business should consider two strong leaders—one as a primary and one as a secondary—because one may be on leave, be out of town, or be a victim of the active shooter. Take care that the EEAA plan does not go without updating to choose a replacement for a former employee. No matter who is chosen for this function, the leader must be functionally familiar with all operational sections within the EEAA and understand each section's functions, needs, and requirements. The EEAA leader

is the stabilizing force that preserves functionality and operational integrity regardless of the formidable challenges, emotional instability, and shock or disbelief experienced throughout the emergency. It should be noted that sometimes the most effective leader for the EEAA is not always an executive manager, but perhaps a line manager who has the skills, experience, and leadership abilities to fill the leadership position.

- Human Resources
  Some businesses have selected the human resources manager as the employee in charge of the EEAA, for the function encompasses numerous legitimate human resources functions. After the first responders enter the business to neutralize the active shooter, the business must determine the human resources verification of employees. Each employee must be accounted for, regardless of whether he or she is off site or merely on leave. Until each employee is located, he or she may be considered still trapped inside, either hiding in some obscure office or a victim of the active shooter. Accounting for employees is an OSHA emergency function for each business under 29 CFR 1910.38(c)(4) [10]. The following areas are only some of the human resources functions relating to an EEAA; please consult with your human resources department to discuss other functional aspects as required:
  - Daily attendance sheets—employee verification
    - Confirmation of which employees are working and their current location
    - Unaccounted-for employees perhaps still inside the business
    - Contractors working inside the business
    - Volunteers working inside the business
  - Accounting for guests inside the business or, if a victim, outside the structure
  - Monitoring individuals at the EEAA to determine how they are coping with the emergency by walking through each section and ensuring that people do not just wonder off or attempt to go back inside the building
  - Counselors who can provide some immediate services on site to help individuals cope with the loss of a coworker or a coworker not yet accounted for
  - Reunification coordination, especially when reuniting families and children and ensuring that children are not given to the wrong person
  - Use of trusted employees to aid in performing EEAA tasks, with each functional area is scalable based on need and the number of individuals requiring service
  - Assistance teams to hand out food, blankets and water.
- Communications Coordinator
  One of the most important elements of any response or recovery is effective timely and accurate communications throughout all areas of the business and within each operational function. When a communications coordinator is assigned to the EEAA, this employee should monitor all communications platforms, coordinate with each business department, and provide information to the EEAA executive in charge. The communications coordinator will also ensure that both the primary and secondary communications platforms are operational and will communicate, as needed, relevant information to any of the EEAA functional coordinators.

- Note Takers
  During chaos people often forget what happened, when something happened, and who told them to react a certain way. When an employee is assigned as a note taker, he or she will document the actions of the executive in charge of the EEAA and its operations, as well as keeping the EEAA on track by following the EEAA operational plan. If the business does not have an EEAA operational plan, and has never trained people in this important function, then the success of the EEAA is left to chance, memory, and instinct.

- Emergency Medical Technician (EMT)
  Many businesses do not have an emergency medical technician in house, but if they do, then this employee can assist disabled guests and injured individuals and coordinate with the first responder medical response. The EMT will coordinate the medical function within the EEAA until the first responders arrive and the injured are either treated at the EEAA or transported to a local hospital. There have been numerous examples during active shootings when medical responders have been bogged down by traffic congestion and forced to traverse extra miles to reach the scene of the emergency. The in-house EMT may provide life-saving care long before the first responders arrive.

- Security
  Be mindful that regardless of whether the EEAA is located inside or outside the building and whether the active shooter is a former or current employee, the shooter may be fully aware of the location of the EEAA, so you must plan accordingly by adding a security component. Security may be a law enforcement officer, an in-house security employee, or a contract security force. Security points to consider at the EEAA include the following:

- If the security officer is a contract service, remember to check with the security contractor to determine whether the officer is armed with a weapon and what are the rules of engagement with a active shooter threat or the protection roles they will fulfill at the EEAA.

- A section of the EEAA should be dedicated for law enforcement interviews of witnesses. When witnesses are located who possess valuable information, these individuals should undergo timely interview by law enforcement. This same information can and should be relayed to the first responders as soon as it is known.

- Security functions within the EEAA are essential to preserving a safe and secure environment. As families are reunited, individuals will reprocess the active shooting nightmare in their own minds, and hysteria gives way to gradual self-assurance. A security presence is a priority for those who have escaped from this life-threatening emergency, to help them feel safer.

- Media Coordinator
  As is normally the case in emergencies, multiple representatives of the various media outlets will endeavor to determine every aspect of the active shooting for their viewers and reading public. A well-positioned and professional media coordinator can simultaneously balance the needs of the media and those of business through professional communications while also interacting with the business's executive staff and the first responder community. The media coordinator is keenly aware of the sensitivities of victims

and their families and is the face of the business as everyone attempts to make sense of this emergency while moving forward as a company.

• Equipment and Supply Coordinator

  After employees, contractors, and guests arrive to the EEAA, they will need more than bandages; they will require some of the necessities of life. People cannot be expected to stand for hours or go without food or water. They may need blankets to stay warm or prevent shock, among other items:

  ● Food and water
  ● Basic medicines (aspirin, antacid, etc.)
  ● Blankets
  ● Chairs and tables
  ● Signage for each section within EEAA
  ● Clipboards, pens, and paper

References

[1] Presidential Policy Directive/PPD-8. National Preparedness on the Department of Homeland Security. <www.dhs.gov/presidential-policy-directive-8-national-preparedness>; 2011.

[2] Los Angeles World Airports. Active Shooter Incident and Resulting Airport Disruption: A Review or Response Operations. <www.lawa.aero/uploadedFiles/LAX/LAWA%20T3%20After%20Action%20Report%20March%2018%202014.pdf>; 2014.

[3] Department of the Army. Fort Hood, Army Internal Review Team: Final Report, Protecting the Force. <www.defense.gov/pubs/pdfs/DOD-ProtectingTheForce-Web_Security_HR_13Jan10.pdf>; 2010.

[4] University of Texas at Austin Police Department. Active Shooter/Suicide After Action Report; 2010.

[5] Northern Illinois University, Police & Public Safety Department, DeKalb, Illinois. Lessons Learned in Response and Recovery: Northern Illinois University; 2010.

[6] Metropolitan Police Department After Action Report, Washington Navy Yard. <www.defense.gov/pubs/DoD-Internal-Review-of-the-WNY-Shooting-20-Nov-2013.pdf>; 2013.

[7] Blair JP, Schweit KW. A Study of Active Shooter Incidents, 2000–2013. Washington D.C.: Texas State University and Federal Bureau of Investigation, U.S. Department of Justice; 2014.

[8] City of Houston, video, Run, Hide, Fight. <www.readyhoustontx.gov/videos.html>.

[9] U.S. Department of Homeland Security, Options for Consideration. <www.dhs.gov/video/options-consideration-active-shooter-preparedness-video>.

[10] U.S. Department of Labor, Occupational Safety & Health Administration, Emergency Action Plans. <https://www.osha.gov/pls/oshaweb/owadisp.show_document?p_table=STANDARDS&p_id=9726>.

5

Coordinated Response, Expectations, and Goals

When do the business and those individuals who are under attack during an active shooting want first responders to arrive? Ideally, the very second when the first shot is fired—but, realistically, as quickly as humanly possible. The first responders have lights and sirens for a reason, and those experiencing a shooting expect them to respond quickly to stop the threat. For a person locked down in an office behind stacks of furniture with heavy items blocking the door, whose heart pounds in his or her chest and throat and eardrums, every second seems like an eternity—his or her only hope and prayer is for rescue. Every noise heard outside the office is magnified in intensity and filters through the brain as a potential threat. Subconsciously, people are afraid to breathe for fear of being detected—the smallest of sounds emancipating from within the room could expose the secret location to the shooter. This scenario is repeated over and over again and will continue until the first responders arrive and each person has been rescued. Who will rescue them, and who will arrive? Will the people hiding respond when the officers tell them to come out or open the door?

Who Will Arrive?

Thrust into the grips of an active shooting crisis, the management of a business immediately knows the crisis is something it cannot resolve on its own. Someone at the business instinctively calls 911 or the local emergency dispatch number, just as many individuals will do as they try to escape the area. Which responding agency will arrive to save the company and neutralize the threat? The answer is everyone who can help and who, it is to be hoped, has been specifically trained to collectively handle an active shooter emergency. The call for assistance will be broadcast across the airways and will receive an immediate response. However, which agencies and departments will arrive depends on pre-established notification protocols. In a normal law enforcement agency or department, officers and agents may be on routine patrols, special operations teams may be investigating significant criminal cases, surveillance teams may be deployed on key drug or gang houses, and detectives could be interviewing witnesses or suspects of some felony act—all when the active shooter alert is broadcast.

Many responding agencies, departments, and resources may not arrive immediately, for they will be performing their regular duties. Additionally, first responders must prepare for secondary active shooter attacks in different parts of the city or community. The lessons learned from the Mumbai, India, attack in 2008 [1] and the 2013 Westgate Mall attack in

Nairobi, Kenya [2] have prewarned first responders to the potential of multiple attack locations, so not every available officer will rush to the scene.

Federal, state, and local law enforcement agencies will arrive with weapons and specialized equipment to attempt to dominate the active shooter. Responding law enforcement agencies and departments may include state highway patrol, city police, sheriff's departments and deputies, constables, marshals, park police, school police, conservation officers, and reserve officers, etc. The federal response may include any of the three-letter alphabet agencies—the Federal Bureau of Investigation; Drug Enforcement Agency; Bureau of Alcohol, Tobacco, Firearms, and Explosives; Internal Revenue Service; Transportation Security Administration; Department of Homeland Security; Federal Protective Service; Department of Interior; and Department of Prisons, among many others. The business may also consider an armed private security company to aid individuals and secure the command center to help resolve the threat.

Now add to the response fire departments, emergency medical services, and paramedics. The Department of Emergency Management and public health will also play a part in the response, for victims may need counseling or assistance with their disabilities. Consider also that individuals responding as described could be full-time, part-time, or volunteer personnel. Responders may also arrive from surrounding cities, counties, and even states as the call goes out about the active shooting.

If a group of foreign visitors is present during the active shooting, translators might be required for language assistance. Religious leaders often volunteer to offer assistance to victims from various denominations, for some victims will turn to their faith for solace. Other people simply show up to volunteer as members of the community or as members of the Federal Emergency Management Agency (FEMA) Community Emergency Response Team (CERT) emergency preparedness program [3].

Friends, relatives, and coworkers of individuals believed to be caught in this brutal emergency will arrive to support and greet their loved ones or friends instead of watching the emergency unfold on television. This is never more evident than in the case of a school shooting, when parents of students want to be reunited as soon as possible. They want to know that their children are safe; they want to see their children in person, not sit by their phones waiting for a call. If it is good news, they want to be there; if it is bad news, they still want to be there. Nothing is more important to them than their children, and no power will disrupt their unwavering desire to be on scene.

Media outlets, including radio and television stations and newspapers, will arrive to record and report on the emergency. Media will open up live feeds to capture the active shooting emergency unfold and will translate to the audience the effects on and painful experiences of victims, colleagues, and families. The media will interview people who have escaped the horrors of this dramatic emergency and strive to capture all information possible about the shooter, the number of casualties and injured, and sound bites from first responders who may provide an overview of the emergency.

Unfortunately, there is a dark side in the social fabric of who will arrive at an active shooting. People who have no connection to the response or to the individuals inside, who merely want to watch the horror unfold, may arrive on scene. They want to be the first to post video of the incident on YouTube or to broadcast on-the-scene commentary on Twitter. Is it a sense of history, a nefarious purpose, or just an adrenaline rush that drives these people to clog over-stressed roadways? They are often a hindrance and distraction to the professional responders and those involved in the shooting. The first responders still need to anticipate the entire spectrum of onlookers who are just outside barricades of separation from the emergency. First responders must be mindful of hostile individuals who desire to exploit the active shooter's perceived cause or belief system. They may desire to offer their approval of the shooter's actions perpetrated against specific victims, such as law enforcement or military, or against the type of business attacked.

When Will First Responders Arrive?

An aspect of an active shooting emergency that haunts each potential victim, undermines the first responders' effectiveness, and attacks the vigorousness of the active shooter response is "response time." No matter how the time is calculated, every response time is too slow in the minds of each casualty or potential victim who are experiencing this nightmare. In addition, the victim's families are emotionally drained, and the community as a whole will desire answers about how long it took for a response to arrive. That said, the victims and the business want a rapid response, but the community also demands a coordinated response from first responders. People demand that first responders drop their routine tasks and less significant cases to respond to the active shooting emergency. First responders typically have been afforded lights, sirens, and high-speed driving courses for this type of event, so they are expected to arrive quickly. However, the speed at which they should drive is based on considerations of personal safety and the obstacles that lie before them during the response. And response time must also take into account the weather and road conditions impeding first responders as they converge on the active shooter's location.

When does the clock start? For the victims living through this life-threatening emergency, the first shot starts the clock, but for the first responders, the clock starts with the first 911 call or a radio transmission to the dispatcher from a first responder who received information about the emergency. Unfortunately, many people do not immediately call 911 at the first sign of danger or will not call until they can safely do so—perhaps three, four, or five minutes into the emergency. A first responder might see an individual running toward a patrol vehicle and receive information about the emergency. This individual might have been running for blocks, or for only a few yards, and might not have started the frantic escape until he or she felt it safe to do so—so, again, the emergency might have started several minutes before. Generally a victim's first instinct is to protect or remove himself or herself from danger no matter how long that takes or how far away he or she must go to do so. After it is safe to get out, and if the person is capable, he or she calls 911. Response time also is affected by how close the first responder is to the scene and whether he or she has been trained in response actions.

A response is based on an array of time-sensitive variables, and if these variables are explored, the issue of response time can further be calculated. Commonly, a response is accompanied by lights flashing back and forth, sirens blaring, and radio traffic increasing as first responders negotiate their route to the active shooting. However, for secondary responders who have never driven on code (i.e., lights and sirens on), it is extremely disconcerting to witness how people react to lights and sirens. The following examples add precious seconds to the response:

- People may never hear the siren because of hearing problems, loud music, air conditioning or heaters blowing at full blast, or an ear firmly placed against a cell phone. They can be surprised or frightened when they first see the emergency vehicle, and they may react accordingly.
- Many people do not move to the right to allow first responders to pass, simply because they are not paying attention.
- People may be stuck in traffic themselves, with no room to pull over.
- People may believe that first responders have enough room and so not move.
- People see so many emergency vehicles that they consider them normal, feeling that there is no reason to do anything.

The FBI-sponsored report "Active Shooter Events from 2000 to 2012" [4] indicates that of the fifty-one cases for which data was extracted, the median response time was 3 minutes. It should be noted that the response time is based on data fields, so other reports having larger or broader data fields may have a slightly different response time average. First responders are keenly aware that response time translates into statistics—i.e., the longer the response time, the greater potential number of victims. Faster is better, but blind disregard for the personal safety of the first responders, as well as individuals driving on the roadways, isn't acceptable, either.

How is response time calculated?

- When the first officer arrives on scene?
- When the first responder arrives at the building of the shooting, not just within the complex or campus?
- When the first responders are allowed to enter the structure or location of the shooting?
- When the first responders locate the active shooter?
- When the first responders engage the active shooter, either arresting or neutralizing him or her?
- When all active shooters and victims are located?
- When the active shooting is declared over by first responders?

If response time is merely based on arriving at the active shooting emergency, then if the responding officer is alone and the department does not authorize the solo officer to enter, response time is inconsequential to the victims inside the building. Similarly, if the business hires an armed security contractor for the building but the contractor prohibits the armed security officer from engaging the active shooter for insurance or safety reasons, then the purpose behind the armed security contractor's staffing has been negated in an active shooting emergency.

Thus response times are relative and are based on straightforward events experienced by either the victims or the responders in the active shooting. When considering when the response ends, look at the shooting from the perspective of the victims who are hiding out in a dark closet or the casualties who lie unconscious on the floor. The business must consider every individual within the active shooting emergency, as well as their family members waiting to know the fate of a loved one. What does response time mean to you?

First Responders

During an active shooting emergency, the primary mission of first responders is to resolve the threat by disrupting the shooter's cycle of brutality using whatever means and force needed to neutralize the shooter. First responders commonly post lessons learned from previous active shootings and other emergencies, then incorporate them into their response framework. The response should be coordinated and practiced on all levels, including those of technology, communications, applications and systems, functions, roles, and responsibilities. The responsible or lead agency and management structure in most cases has been predetermined based on the type of emergency. Each emergency response consists of such aspects as a multi-jurisdictional hazard mitigation plan, incident command system (ICS) structure, and concept of operation, with all functional components scalable based on the level of the emergency. See, for example, the following emergency and lead agency correspondence, remembering that this may not be representative of all communities and cities:

Fires	Fire department
Floods	Department of emergency management
Disease	Public health
Active Shooter	Law enforcement (local, state, or federal, depending on location)
Terrorism	Federal Bureau of Investigation
Earthquake	Public works

For first responders, an effective response consists of various components, units, and departments based on both immediate and short-term needs, while also planning for long-term requirements. The coordination of response units is based on a solid foundation of training and of resolving any reoccurring conditions that degrade the response. A fragmented, distracted, and strained response will delay the trustworthiness and reliability of the responders, so realistic training reignites readiness, invigorating and maximizing the cooperative spirit of the responding agencies and instilling professionalism in responders. In the eyes of members of the public, who evaluate and critique every wasted moment or decision, such training is invaluable. An active shooting emergency is not the place and time to be meeting all first responders' and departments' for the first time.

First responders have displayed exceptional skills as individual units, but many times these same units resemble silos when thrust into an emergency. Each unit has its own unique functions and skillsets, and each unit has demonstrated its talents in emergencies over and over. However, an active shooting emergency, such as in the cases of Aurora, Colorado, or Virginia Tech, will stretch responding units beyond their limits. The on-scene unit commander should immediately recognize the requirement for additional resources, summoning supplemental units from surrounding communities. Law enforcement officers, firefighters, and paramedics will all see their resources stretched to their limits during an active shooting emergency but can be reassured—thanks to mutual aid agreements—by receiving assistance scalable to the need. Finally, silos are slowly disappearing across the country as departments and agencies train together in active shooter response, understanding and outlining their roles, and transcending fundamental fault lines to fulfill their mission.

Response

When the public attempts to define an emergency response, people envision a synchronized mobilization of manpower and equipment that can expeditiously traverse backed-up traffic by manipulating traffic signals and deploying sirens and lights en route to their final destination. This is as true as it has been for decades, but the response to an active shooting has not remained constant with time. Figure 5–1 shows six factors that response time may be dependent on.

Metamorphosis best describes the transition of first responders—from receiving no training for an active shooter emergency (they being so rare) to a cross-section of training programs specifically designed for active shootings. The training offered to first responders is reengineered to adapt to various types of structures and business settings, including schools, hospitals, office buildings, government facilities, and places of worship, among many others. It is advisable to check with your local and state law enforcement departments to determine which program is ideal for a coordinated response by the first response partner agencies. As already stated, many different public and private models are in use today, including the following:

- ALERRT: Advanced Law Enforcement Rapid Response Training (Texas State University, San Marcos, Texas) [5]
- A.L.I.C.E: alert, lock down, inform, counter, and escape (ALICE Training Institute, Medina, Ohio) [6]
- MACTAC: Multiple Attack Counter Terror Action Capabilities (Los Angeles Police Department, Orange County, California, and Las Vegas Metropolitan Police Department, Las Vegas, Nevada) [7]

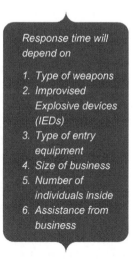

Response time will depend on

1. Type of weapons
2. Improvised Explosive devices (IEDs)
3. Type of entry equipment
4. Size of business
5. Number of individuals inside
6. Assistance from business

FIGURE 5–1 Response Time.

We are not going recommend a particular program to use, for each training program may have both advantages or disadvantages for different types of organizations and operations. In addition, we have not listed all the active shooter training programs available—so search out all your options before moving forward with such training. You and your company must determine which program is right for you and which best suits your specific organization.

Active shootings have been occurring for decades, regardless of whether this barbaric act was defined as an active shooting or using another term. And the law enforcement response has changed in terms of tactics, technology, and equipment, now including ballistic helmets and shields. Moreover, multiple-department coordination and redefinition of who are the real first responders in an active shooting emergency have also evolved to become more collaborative in recent years. From revolvers and shotguns to sniper rifles and fully automatic entry rifles, first responders are changing to meet the demands of the recurring active threats they encounter. However, equipment and weapons are only part of the equation. Entry and response tactics have been reprioritized and reshaped based on careful analysis and in response to outcry from the public. Unfortunately, not every law enforcement department has a SWAT (Special Weapons and Tactics) team, and unless such a team is already assembled, it will take time to prepare for deployment. If it takes time to assemble a SWAT team and get its members to the scene, who will typically be the first law enforcement officer on scene? Unless the active shooter location has a law enforcement officer assigned to the business, the first responder to arrive at the active shooting is usually the patrol or beat officer. This officer might be on foot, on a bicycle or motorcycle, or in a patrol vehicle. The officer might be working alone or as part of a team depending on the size of the department, the time of day, and his or her specific assignment.

If only one officer first arrives at the site of the active shooting, will that officer immediately enter the structure to engage the shooter? The answer is not consistent across the United States; some police departments do not believe in a "solo officer" response and may even prohibit officers from entering the building with fewer than a predetermined number of officers from the same department or agency to form an entry team. Moreover, there is a significant difference between military and law enforcement tactics when confronting armed individuals. In the U.S. National Archives article "Teaching with Documents: D-Day Message from General Eisenhower to General Marshal," [8] the number of casualties the U.S. 101st Airborne would suffer in the invasion of Normandy, France, on June 6, 1944, was projected at 80 percent. But the projected casualty percentage for law enforcement officers who are attempting to neutralize an active shooter is zero (0%). There are no acceptable losses of first responders in any emergency situation. Second, in the FBI report "A Study of Active Shooter Incidents in the United States between 2000 and 2013" [9] data indicated that in twenty-one, or 46.7 percent of, incidents in which law enforcement officers engaged the active shooter, nine officers were killed and twenty-eight wounded. These statistics illustrate how dangerous an active shooter is and how important it is for responder officers to take the necessary precautions and safety measures when responding to this threat.

The response will also depend on the active shooter or shooters, including on types of weapons, presence or suspected presence of improvised explosive devices (IEDs), type of equipment needed to negotiate the shooting site, facility size, and number of individuals inside. Many officers are inserted into a shooting situation without knowing all the information about the challenges that lay ahead. The responders, especially if they have never been inside the structure before, will be faced with an obstacle course of barriers, challenging floor plans, varying security measures to overcome, and a lack of accurate timely information. The individuals trapped in this emergency only want the active shooter neutralized—and to be rescued. Unfortunately, many individuals will never understand or appreciate the relentless challenges that must be overcome by first responders, and they will only emphasize how long it took to be rescued.

Tactical configuration type (diamond, wedge, T formation, or solo), philosophy about when law enforcement officers can enter an active shooter location, joint training opportunities, and coordinated response all must be discussed, defined and understood across all first responder and interagency partners before an emergency situation. The tactical considerations and communications platforms enacted by the first responding community are expected to function properly under all threat environments that an active shooter may present, because experience, preparedness training, and lessons learned have forged the correct path forward. The individuals trapped in this nightmare expect nothing less than a coordinated, trained, and reactionary team who will interrupt the active shooter's deadly rampage and rescue potential victims from harm.

Tactical considerations, lessons learned, and doctrine shifts in deployment are not solely left to law enforcement responders but rather are unilaterally expected in all first responding elements when it comes to preserving the lives of those individuals living a real-life nightmare. The integrated response eliminates silos, with element incentivized when it comes to saving lives. Today, first responders across the country are debating when to allow fire department and EMS personnel to enter into the active shooting building. This shift, once based on a clearly defined agency response model and selective professional skillsets, now incentivizes fire department and EMS personnel to treat critically injured persons sooner, without waiting until the entire building is secure. Fire department and EMS personnel can treat, triage, retrieve, and transport victims of the active shooter more quickly than in past years—when they are allowed entry to do so. The time to enter the active shooting building is decided by the law enforcement response agencies charged to neutralize the threat. Only they can provide the direction in such a threat environment. During the response, law enforcement should transform once potentially lethal rooms and hallways into more secure locations. Fire department and EMS personnel do not enter a hostile shooting location to become casualties, though neither do they expect the site to be free of conflicts; they merely wish to leverage their professional talents to treat victims in need without standing outside, waiting, for hours. It is difficult for these professionals to watch as people exit the active shooting location while dragging and carrying victims outside—minutes and even hours later—knowing that they could have assisted. Last, it must be clearly understood that fire department and EMS personnel do not typically carry firearms and are not expected to neutralize the shooter; that is the role of law enforcement.

One important consideration that fosters a closer alliance within the first responder community is the unintentional similarity between an active shooting and military triage principles that statistically improves survival percentages. Just as law enforcement equates response times with potential casualties, so do fire department and EMS personnel when treating victims. The sooner the triage response and casualty transport can begin, the greater victim's chances of survival. For this very reason, fire department and EMS personnel are moving closer to the shooting location. And in some cities across the United States, such as Las Vegas, Nevada, fire department and EMS personnel are provided ballistic helmets and vests and are allowed to enter a clearly identified "warm," or semi-safe, zone inside the building. These first responders are expeditiously escorted by armed law enforcement officers to help victims. This potentially life-saving tactic undeniably reprioritizes the response roles to active shooting emergencies. Additionally, to synchronize the entry into an active shooting location, each action should be choreographed, yet flexible enough to avoid formidable obstacles, through proper training involving all partner agencies.

Expectations

The first responding community does not expect businesses to be so embroiled in an active shooting emergency that they are completely unfamiliar with first responders' expectations or are dysfunctional within their own organization. First responders expect businesses to see to their own properties before any emergency by training employees, implementing effective technology, and mitigating many of the disruptive acts that are precursors to a delayed response within the property. A business must know before an incident what first responders will need, not during the active shooting.

As the first responders are entering the business in pursuit of an active shooter, first responders will expect employees to have received some type of rudimentary training instructing them what actions and choices to use to protect themselves, their coworkers, and guests. First responders cannot train employees while they are entering the property or take time to rationalize the shooting with each person they meet. The organization can provide fundamental employee choices and actions by accelerating the recommended actions found in such training videos as a video developed by the city of Houston's Mayor's Office of Public Safety and Homeland Security, "Run, Hide, Fight," [10] or the Department of Homeland Security's video "Options for Consideration," [11] which presents options for individuals to consider during an active shooting. Such videos provide various options for individuals who must remain flexible while deliberating on real life-threatening circumstances that only they can see, feel, and hear. The Department of Homeland Security and the city of Houston identify three aspects that each individual person should consider:

- Evacuate, escape, run
- Hide, hide out, take shelter
- Fight, take action, resist

The active shooting emergency forces law enforcement departments and concerned citizens to simultaneously develop additional programs for businesses and employees responding to an active shooting. The descriptive words outlining individual's actions and choices may be different, but the intent is still the same—to empower people to act, reacting to this senseless

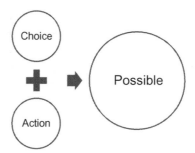

FIGURE 5–2 First Responder's Actions When Encountering Employees.

emergency well in advance of the first responder's arrival. Figure 5-2 illustrates the choice and related action that will result in possible outcomes for first responders who encounter employees. Examples of some additional programs and concepts follow but are by no means an exhaustive review of all active shooter programs. Check in your area, contacting first responders, to determine which program will work best for your business and employees.

- A.L.I.C.E.: **Alert, lock down, inform, counter, and escape**. Developed by the ALICE Training Institute, Medina, Ohio.
- The Four A's: **Accept, assess, act, and alert**. Discussed by the International Association for Healthcare Security Safety (IAHSS) in a Security Information Watch [12].
- The Four E's: **Educate, evade, escape, and engage**. Developed by Tier One Tactical Solutions, LLC, St. Charles, Missouri [13].

These choices and actions provide guidelines to help individuals who find themselves in this life-threatening emergency, providing meaningful options and common-sense advice that will resonate throughout the entire property after training. These videos and programs further incorporate and illustrate the first responder's actions when they encounter employees and reassert their primary mission in neutralizing the active shooter.

Each person must first mentally associate a triggering event, noise, or visual observation with a specific choice and culminating action. An option that works for one individual may not be possible for another for a kaleidoscope of reasons, emotions, and physical abilities. Moreover, some people are followers, but others are individualistic, marching to the beat of their own drum. Remember that the above videos offer choices but do not attempt to cover all business settings or potential victims.

- Individuals in the public health setting, such as in hospitals, retirement homes, nursing homes, and treatment centers, take a professional oath to provide care for people who cannot care for themselves. Many of these professionals cannot in good conscience abandon their patients regardless of threats or dangers to themselves. For these employees, professional responsibility epitomizes their human compassion and unwavering commitment to humanity throughout all aspects of care. Running and escaping the active shooter is not typically the first option, or even an option, that most will consider.

- There are numerous articles and reports written on school shootings because of Columbine and Sandy Hook. Schools can initiate either a "lockdown" or a "lockout" procedure to protect the students. A lockout is when a threat is off campus and the schools completely lock gates and doors and post employees to prevent the threat from infiltrating the campus. A lockdown is when the threat is already on the campus and each classroom locks and blocks doors to prevent entry into classrooms. For a school, the three options of run, hide, and fight are not always feasible. In an elementary school, 5- to 12-year-old students cannot be expected to run in a safe direction nor be expected to fight. Conversely, a high school teacher, if he or she knows the location of the shooter and the shooter is a considerable distance away, may believe it best to run rather than waiting inside a classroom. Additionally, high school students may desire to run but be prohibited because of the lockdown. Parents only want one thing: Their children must be safe and secure regardless of the environment, just as they would be if they were home.
- People who have disabilities may not understand the message, comprehend the danger, or have the physical ability to run, hide, or fight. The Economics and Statistics Administration, in "Americans with Disabilities: 2010 Household Economic Studies," by Matthew W. Brault, July 2012 [14], indicated that 56.7 million people, or 18.7 percent of the civilian non-institutionalized population, had a disability in 2010; 38.3 million people, or 12.6 percent, had a severe disability; and 12.3 million people aged 6 years or older, or 4.4 percent, needed assistance with one or more activities of daily living. Consider the following questions:
  - Can the disabled navigate through the property without assistance?
  - Can the disabled assemble and forge an adequate barricaded hiding location or hide out for a prolonged period of time?
  - Can these same disabled individuals mobilize a formidable persuasive attack against the active shooter?

Thus, without the assistance of a "buddy" or an employee to make efforts on behalf of these individuals for their safety and security while inside the business, they may be at great risk of harm during an incident.

Employee Actions

Businesses usually consist of dedicated employees who can guide a business toward prosperity and apply their unyielding determination to inspire growth and progress in all business units. These same employees are often experts in their chosen field, but expertness does not always translate into good leadership during an emergency. For a guest of the business who is only on site briefly, the employee may be the last resource for survival. It is well known that guests pay little attention to exits and emergency procedures. However, employees and tenants are looked to by guests and contractors for assistance and guidance during emergency situations, no matter whether they have been trained for this role. Conversely, these same employees look to their supervisors and management for guidance. How do employees apply a standard of care and acknowledge that such responsibility is part of their duties, even if they have never been trained how to react and act during emergencies? Employees are to aid all guests and to help coworkers away from harm during an emergency—but how? What can the employee even think about doing when a shooter is active? Consider the following for each employee during an active shooting emergency:

- Employees know the building and shortcuts out of the area.
  The guests do not know all the areas in the building that can offer protection, nor the corresponding escape routes from an active shooting. The employee knows these shortcuts, which often are not found on any emergency map or on overhead signage. The employees also know the distance to the street and may be able to steer away from corridors that may lead back toward the shooter.
- Employees can guide and direct away from danger areas those who are willing to go.
  It takes little or no effort for an employee to tell or signal a guest to follow him or her to safety. Saying, "Please follow me this way to safety" is virtually effortless for a caring employee. Whether the employee escorts the guest to the back office to avoid visual observation by the shooter or through the employee back hallway, the employee may have just saved a guest's life by such action. The guest will remember and appreciate the employee's response to the emergency—or may reflect on an employee's uninspired and inconsiderate disregard for the guest's safety.
- Employees can pull down gates and lock doors.
  The employee will know which gates can be pulled down to create a barrier between the shooter. The same is true for doors. The employee knows how to lock doors as well as which doors can be locked, something not always evident in a business setting. During an active shooting in a mall, tenants may direct innocent bystanders outside their stores to come in for protection and may direct customers already within the store to remain inside. An employee may pull down the security gate and lock it, then directing individuals to move to the rear of the store. Other tenants operating kiosks in the mall may direct people to follow them as they retreat from the active shooter.
- Employees can communicate to coworkers, guests, contractors, and visitors the nature of the threat and location.
  Communication is extremely important during and after emergencies. If the company opts to use coded terminology, such as "Code Silver in D" or "Code Purple on 3," to warn employees about a life-threatening emergency, only the employees—not customers, vendors, volunteers and contractors—will know the significance and urgency of the message. To safeguard nonemployees, the employee must translate the message into action based on the approximate location of the shooter in relation to guests.
- Employees know what is behind exits and know the nearest areas of safety.
  Knowing the layout behind an exit, such as an enclosed stairwell or a long corridor, is important to the uninformed guest mentally preparing to evacuate. Depending on the floor plan of the business, including whether it uses cubicles or portable walls, the nearest safe exit may not be visible from all locations. The nearest safe exit doesn't always mean the closest exit, especially if the closest exit exposes the evacuee to the shooter.
- Employees have access cards, codes, and passkeys.
  Some businesses use specialized security technology to restrict entry into sensitive areas or departments, such as access cards and codes, fingerprint or palm readers, and passkeys. If

the safest and quickest exit requires use of an employee's security card, then the employee should render assistance for safety reasons. However, depending on the nature of the restricted location, employees may be prohibited from allowing access into the area regardless of the severity of the emergency.

- Employees know established security measures.
  Knowledge of security measures involving individual employee functions will improve responsiveness and prompt optimal actions. The employee should make a hasty exit from the area of the shooter while keeping all security measures in mind. Without knowing the basic security measures installed within a business, the employee is at the same disadvantage as a guest.
- Employees can facilitate an orderly exit.
  A supervisor is responsible for individuals within his or her respective working group or department, and if the supervisor is not present, then the employee should render the same level of support. When an employee can explain the nature of the threat and communicate exit points, then direct an orderly evacuation using words or gestures, he or she has systematically removed potential victims from danger.
- Employees can prevent guests and employees from entering the shooting area.
  The employee knows the property and the location of the shooting and thus can prevent potential victims from approaching the shooter's location within the building. Instructing guests and coworkers to immediately follow a course of action without hesitation, dynamically and unarguably, may save lives.
- Employees can communicate to employees and guests in multiple languages.
  Many employees speak multiple languages; when an emergency occurs, these same employees can communicate to guests and coworkers who speak different languages. To ascertain which languages are spoken by employees, the human resources department can conduct a survey. After the various languages spoken by employees are identified, the entire communications notification process has been enriched at no cost to the business.
- Employees can help disabled guests away from shooting area or help them hide if they need mobility assistance.
  When an active shooter begins his or her deadly rampage and people run to avoid becoming victims, what will disabled guests do? Many cannot run—or even hear the warning message over the public address system. Some cannot negotiate stairs; others cannot process the seriousness of the emergency or are frozen in sheer panic. Each guest of a business should receive the same level of protection regardless of age and mental or physical condition. How does a business prepare to aid disabled guests and employees swept up in a tragic event? The company must anticipate the actions to be taken, discuss alternatives in the event that the primary process doesn't work, and train employees to help with these special needs.
- Employees can prevent additional vehicles from entering the business.
  Just as employees prevent individuals from walking into the area of the active shooter, employees can detour vehicles away from the property. Employees can also separate first responders and allow them entry. This is not a function of the first responders, but it is something that the business can do as the emergency unfolds.

- Employees know the active shooter contingency plan and the location of the evacuation assembly area.

  Employee knowledge of the active shooter contingency plan and the location of the evacuation assembly area, acquired through execution and training, is just that much more value added. Each identified function and duty in the employee plan will improve responsiveness and be a force multiplier in a time-sensitive emergency. Exceptional employees will rise to the task to enact the keys to survival, but the real overarching power of the plan is accomplished when all components come together for a common cause—the preservation of life. Without planning, the result could be an uncoordinated, restricted, and unfocused response. The employee actions should not be alien and unresponsive to the emergency, but credible and second nature.

- Employees can communicate to guests to tell them whether the shooter is getting closer or moving away.

  Not every active shooter will remain in one location; a shooter may well mobilize in search of a specific victim or groups of individuals. During the evacuation, if someone yells out, "The shooter is in Accounting!" it means nothing to those unfamiliar with the floor plan of the business. An employee will know the significance of that statement and can change route accordingly. Guests will rely on employee leadership for assistance and guidance to safety.

- Guests believe that all contractors, volunteers, and tenants know what to do (because they are working on property), so such persons should receive the same active shooter contingency plan or a suitably modified version.

  When a guest arrives on property and enjoys the entire spectrum of activities that the business may offer, he or she has no idea whether the person standing behind the counter is a part-time employee, contractor, or volunteer. Of course, many businesses clearly identify individuals as volunteers by using nametags, but regardless, guests expect all such persons to know all emergency plans—and expect them to help guests reach safety regardless of their employment status. The guests also expect the same of contractors, who generally do not wear a badge specifying their status within the business. A tenant may or may not have a name tag for his or er respective property, but because the tenant is situated inside a larger property, guests also expect tenants to know all emergency procedures and to assist guests. The responsibility falls on the property management to ensure that all tenants are familiar with their duties during an emergency. Unfortunately, many tenants experience a high turnover in staff—and many tenants' employees may be in their late teens. Yet what better time to instill in employees, and at such an early age, their duties and responsibilities to preserve life?

- Contractors and tenants should understand what to do during an emergency.

  Each contractor and tenant is viewed by guests as someone who will physically protect them and guide them. The contractors and tenants should be capable of adjusting preventive measures and imposing predictable prompt actions to minimize the consequences of the emergency. The business is the driving force in defining emergency response expectations, not the tenants or contractors.

- Contractors and tenants should receive active shooter training, just like they would for emergency evaluation fire procedures.

  If contractors and tenants are not trained, then a tremendous opportunity has been lost in fostering a coordinated propertywide response to an active shooter emergency. It is irresponsible for a business to assume that any individual working on property does not have the potential to prepare for, prevent, respond to, mitigate, communicate to guests about, and recover from such an emergency. Again, guests believe that anyone working on property is current in and knowledgeable about all emergency actions and procedures.

- Contractors and tenants should receive be trained in and understand emergency communications.

  When a business chooses to broadcast an emergency code, such as "Code Silver" or "Code Purple," contractors and tenants should know each code's meaning. When a guest asks the contractor or tenant what Code Silver means after it is broadcast over the public address system, the answer cannot be "I don't know." Such a response will not instill confidence, project a sense of reassurance, nor reinforce an integrated action plan, and it may jeopardize the safety of guests as well as employees.

- Contractors and tenants should know the procedures pertaining to their tenant space or contractor location.

  In a business, each department and working group is one piece of the overall puzzle. Each piece connects with one another and isn't an isolated island. The contractor and tenant should know the procedures exclusive to their space, allowing them to help guests as needed.

- In contract and working agreements, require contractors to know the active shooter contingency plan and emergency procedures.

  Contractors working on the property do so pursuant to a contract; within the contract agreement should be a provision requiring each contractor to review, understand, and accept certain duties to perform per the plan. The contractor and tenants will appreciate the knowledge and will accept such responsibility as part of the contract—these actions are self-explanatory to any safety-conscious business. Some contractors and tenants may object to shouldering an additional cost to their company when it comes to billed hours, but when the concept is clearly stated in the contract, contractors or tenants can always say no, and other companies can take their place. This approach to emergencies is forward-thinking and is new to many businesses. Unfortunately, guests already believe that contractors and tenants are already trained to deal with, and have planned for, all emergencies. The first time they find out otherwise is often when an incident occurs.

- Employees, contractors, and tenants can hide in and barricade rooms.

  It is much easier for an employee or tenant, rather than a guest, to barricade rooms using such items such as tables, chairs, filing cabinets, printers, copy machines, and other heavy furniture. A guest typically will not begin grabbing such items until the employees, tenants, and contractors make the first move. After the employee starts moving items and asks for help moving items, the guest will join in the same actions. Second, the guest will not move thing out of a fear of being held liable if something is broken or damaged. This may sound strange under such circumstances, but it is human nature not to touch someone else's property. Third, if the guest begins moving furniture to barricade the door and the employee does not move anything, the guest may believe he or she has made a poor decision, leading to a feeling of remorse, not security.

Business Actions

During an active shooting emergency, the business cannot presuppose that it has only an insignificant and incremental role in the emergency just because 911 has been called. The business has a responsibility to alert all individuals on the property to dangers that exist. When floors are being cleaned, place signs strategically around the work area. When construction has commenced in a portion of the property, place signs and caution tape; in some cases a security officer may be placed to isolate the area from unauthorized pedestrian traffic. In the case of a train accident, perhaps with cars carrying chemicals and a deadly cloud of chlorine gas slowly approaching the business, the business has a duty of care to protect individuals inside the building and to prevent them from exiting to certain death. In each scenario the business has previously outlined duties, roles, and assignments for staff to guide, direct, and protect employees, guests, and contractors. The same is true of an active shooting emergency. Consider the following areas to incorporate into the active shooter plan:

- Assign someone to meet first responders and direct them to the closest entrance to the threat.
  If the business consists of several million square feet of space, includes several entrances—both pedestrian and vehicle—and contains more than 100 exterior doors leading out of the building, which door will lead the first responders most directly to the active shooter? Traditionally, first responders are only aware of the main pedestrian and vehicle entrances and have no useful knowledge of the effectiveness of other entrances. The business should consider assigning one or two employees to direct first responders to the nearest entrance to the active shooting. Without this information, the first responders may greatly increase their response time.
- Describe the weapons and the number of shots fired.
  The type of weapons being used at the business is extremely important information. Knowledge of the weapons employed by the active shooter helps prepare the responding units, both mentally and tactically, as they penetrate the building envelope. Knowing whether the weapon used is a semi-automatic rifle or a revolver helps in formulating entrance strategies. The number of bullets fired by the active shooter provides intelligence about weapon type, as well as whether the weapon is fully automatic, semi-automatic, or pump/lever action. This information gives a hint about what the first responders will experience when the shooter is located.
- Describe the shooter's sex, race, hair color, facial hair, height, and weight.
  When law enforcement personnel arrive on the property, they are met by people running, screaming, crying, and in shock, yet at this same moment, law enforcement officers are

scanning, analyzing, and evaluating each person as either a victim or a threat. The most useful information is sex, race, hair color, facial hair, height, and weight of the active shooter. With this information, or as much of it as is known, law enforcement is better prepared to validate and discriminate among individuals while proceeding toward the shooting location. The FBI report "A Study of Active Shooter Incidents in the United States between 2000 and 2013" states that nearly 18.125 percent of active shooters, having finished their attack, merely walked away and tried to blend into the panicking crowd fleeing the shooter. Without timely accurate and descriptions of the shooter, the shooter could elude capture by vanishing into the evacuation.

- Describe the shooter's clothing color, clothing style, and headgear.
  Describing the shooter's clothing, including its color and style and such accessories as hats, gas masks, and ammunition belts, may help in identifying a potential shooter from greater distances when law enforcement officers are responding to and encountering individuals at the business location. Each distinguishing feature may allow for detection and neutralization of the shooter. However, law enforcement teams will not rely on clothing description alone, for articles of clothing may be discarded or changed during the deadly rampage.

- Describe how many shooters are known or suspected to be present.
  Tell the first responders how many shooters are on the property. When a shooting occurs, the number of shooters is not always apparent, especially when several shots are fired and from different types of weapons. When the active shooter fires two different weapons, the noise may make it seem as if more than one person is engaged in the attack. The number of shooters is also complicated if the shooter is mobile, shooting while running from building to building, floor to floor, and room to room. Witnesses may believe there is more than one shooter, as happened in the case of the October 22, 2014, shooting in Ottawa, Canada, when shots were reported at the Canadian National War Memorial, the Parliament of Canada, a shopping mall, and a hotel. When the active shooter was neutralized, it was determined that there was only one shooter, not multiple shooters as originally believed.

- Describe the number of victims and their location.
  When the first responders arrive, they need to know the victims' location and number. Some victims will walk or stumble out of the shooting zone; others may be incapable of even that. After the number is known, first responders will be summoned and deployed from nearby stations. The number of the victims and the severity of their injuries may prompt requests for assistance from organizations or agencies outside the city or community. The spectrum of victim injuries may range from gunshots and knife wounds to injuries incurred during the evacuation, such as sprained ankles, broken legs, and cuts; some victims may experience shock and posttraumatic stress disorder (PTSD). People may be without prescription medications, special apparatus, or a buddy on whom they lean for support.

- Provide open vehicle access for first responders.
  Getting access to the business may be extremely difficult as people and vehicles flee the business even while first responders arrive simultaneously from all directions. Ambulances, fire trucks, police cars, motorcycles, unmarked police vehicles, and personal vehicles

of off-duty officers will engulf the property. The business should provide any available access to the area closest to the shooting, which may not be the main entrance. It is also important that the company prevent nonemergency vehicles and the general public from entering the site. On many occasions, first responders have been forced to park almost a mile away from the business because they cannot negotiate the traffic nightmare. However, many businesses do not have an outside security force, or the business may be located in a mall or a high-rise complex, making it impossible to preserve a clear access route for first responders.

- Find out whether anyone knows the shooter's name.
  Not every active shooter is unfamiliar to the business. The FBI report "A Study of Active Shooter Incidents in the United States between 2000 and 2013" says that nearly 95.65 percent of shooters were employees when a business was closed to pedestrian traffic, whereas 47.7 percent of shooters were employees or had a relationship with an employee when a business was open to foot traffic. The shooter may be a current or former employee, a relative of a current or former employee, or a customer. If the name of the shooter is known, then first responders can extract receive information and intelligence from dispatchers. A photograph of the shooter may prove invaluable. The shooter's home address and cell phone number are also vital pieces of information for first responders.

- Indicate the shooter's last known location.
  If shooting is occurring in the cafeteria or the human resources department, let the first responders know the shooter's last known location. However, location is an indicator only. The last known location of the shooter may date to five minutes ago. Each second can translate into distance during the shooting. The first report may have the shooter on the second floor, but the shooter may relocate to a different floor or department in just a few seconds. Because many business use signs to direct employees and visitors to areas within the business, first responders can use the same indicators to minimize delays during their response.

- List the of exits, stairwells, and elevators nearest the shooting that first responders can use or by which the shooter can escape.
  Only the business's employees are completely familiar with all locations on the property. Regardless of how many times law enforcement officers or the fire department have been on property, they have usually not been to all areas within the business. It is important to provide the number of exits, stairwells, and elevators nearest the shooting—not only for first responders to use, but also by which the shooter might escape. Escape routes may be clogged with people, so the nearest escape route may not provide the quickest access to the shooter.

- Describe the area of the shooting.
  For first responders, every area within a business is a potential obstacle course, with items often knocked to the floor while people scramble to leave, and with each work setting a potential ambush zone. First responders will move through the building as quickly as possible to neutralize the threat, but their safety must be considered. The FBI report "A Study of Active Shooter Incidents in the United States between 2000 and 2013" says that in 46.7 percent of incidents, law enforcement officers responding to an active shooting

themselves became casualties. Nine officers were killed and twenty-eight officers wounded engaging active shooters.

- Provide information about surveillance cameras in the area and about whether the shooting is under video surveillance.

  Many businesses deploy surveillance cameras. Knowing the location of these cameras relative to the shooting, and whether the active shooter can be observed, is a tremendous advantage to first responders. The cameras may also allow a visual observation of the number of casualties in or near the shooter. It is important to relay this information to first responders as soon as possible.

- Allow first responders to enter the surveillance control room.

  Give first responders access to the surveillance control room during an active shooting. The law enforcement officer may be able to guide response teams past inconsequential large areas, help discriminate questionable zones, and warn responders as they approach the active shooter's location. The officer can help block off exits, identify potential escape routes, and provide approximate distances before the entry teams reach these areas.

- Provide a picture of the shooter to first responders.

  This may seem like an odd request during an active shooting, but because many shooters are current or former employees, this can help discriminate individuals who are leaving the area of the shooting. This picture will alert all officers to the identity of the shooter and eliminate unnecessary emphasis on similar individuals. Providing a picture of the shooter will save valuable time locating the identified shooter.

- Describe backpacks or other items the shooter is carrying.

  First responders need to know what the shooter is carrying. When a shooter brings such items as a backpack, bag, or a briefcase, he or she does so for a reason. Whether the shooter is concealing an IED, extra ammunition, or extra weapons, the shooter has planned ahead and is carrying something with which to aggravate the threat he or she poses. If the shooter has left a backpack in a particular section of the business and relocated to another area, let the first responders know this as well. Just because the shooter is not carrying the item any longer does not make it any less dangerous to first responders.

- Did the shooter say anything to anyone?

  Anything the shooter may have said during the shooting or before it is important information for first responders. When a shooter says, "I am going to die here today," it may mean that he or she has no escape plan and he that or she will fight until killed. If the shooter says, "I told you I would be back," it may indicate a prior history with, and grudge against, the organization. If the shooter asks for directions before the shooting, there is an intended target in the indicated location, and the shooter may not have previously had any physical contact with that location within the business. Any comment made by the active shooter can be a gold nugget of information for first responders.

- How many people are in the area?

  First responders need to know how many people are in the location of the shooting. During the midnight showing of *The Dark Knight Rises* on July 20, 2012, first responders encountered almost 1,400 moviegoers exiting a theater in Aurora, Colorado. As emergency exits became jammed with people running in all directions, the stampede blocked police access to the shooter's location. The people evacuating this deadly scene must be visually scanned by first responders to ensure that the active shooter is not trying to escape in the mass of humanity. Furthermore, first responders may want to know how many employees and guests are in an area or in a department.

- Prevent people from entering the shooting area.

  One would think that observing people running screaming from an area would prevent other people from wandering into an active shooting location, but remember that during a fire alarm many people do not immediately leave on hearing the alarm. The company needs to prevent people from entering the active shooting location but must first allow responders to enter. Remember that not all first responders who are attempting to neutralize the active shooter are in uniform; some might have responded from home, and others may be plainclothes officers or federal agents.

- Provide "Go Bags" for first responders and strategically place medical kits throughout the site or facility.

  Every business is different in the preventive measures and target hardening it employs to protect employees and guests. Businesses often use specialized security technology to restrict entry into sensitive areas or departments, such as access cards/codes, surveillance cameras, metal detectors, fingerprint or palm readers, and passkeys. And these are just some of the technologies that may be encountered during a response. But these security measures will slow first responders down unless a "go bag" is deliberately developed and strategically placed to help responders bypass security measures. This bag may contain such items as passkeys, access cards, elevator keys, doorstops, hard keys, flashlights, property maps, and passcodes. (The doorstops are used to keep the doors open for all following first responders as they move through the business. The map of the property should be a single page, not folded or overcomplicated.) Refer to Figure 5–3 for examples of GoBag/Kit contents. Two questions always come up when discussing go bags: First, how many bags are needed? The number of bags depends on the size of the property and the number of buildings. If there are five buildings, then perhaps five bags. If only one building, but it is extremely large,

Go Bag/Kit Contents
Access keys/cards
Elevator keys
Door stops
Passkeys
Flashlights
Radios
Map of property

FIGURE 5–3 Go Bags/Go Kits.

then more than one bag. Second, to whom does the business give the go bag? Generally the first and second law enforcement officers focus on the active shooter and try to use an unobstructed path made by people evacuating who are leaving doors open. The third group of officers may grab a go bag to help the first group of officers if they are delayed or stopped by security measures. The strategically placed medical kits include items such as tourniquets, blood clotting bandages, airway tubes and other emergency medical supplies can help to save lives. Often someone may only have a few minutes to live after being shot and these items can be the difference between life and death. Also consider offering training courses for staff on emergency medical care for injuries that result from an active shooting.

- Make anyone who was in the area available for interviews by law enforcement. Law enforcement officers need information and intelligence to help safeguard people from harm. They cannot be deprived of any asset or aid that will resolve the danger by leveraging any piece of information or detail. Individuals evacuating the building possess near real-time knowledge that is still fresh in their minds. Law enforcement must extract this knowledge before the shooter can claim more lives. The business can ask people who are evacuating the building whether they saw the shooter. After individuals are located who did, their information must be extracted and relayed to the first responders.

- Provide information about construction issues and obstacles to a response. Invite first responders from every business shift to tour the business. Meeting first responders for the very first time during a shooting emergency is not ideal: Every second counts. However, for first responders who are charged to neutralize the threat, each business is an obstacle course and a precursor to indecision and delays. Thus notifying first responders about which portion of the property is under construction may avoid delaying the response. Inoperable elevators and escalators, as well as construction carts, hanging wires, and unfinished lighting all present both physical and mental distractions to be negotiated. Of course, alternate routes can and should be provided to hasten the response. It is nevertheless important to communicate information about construction to first responders, because any area is a path that an active shooter may use to avoid capture.

- Describe any dangerous chemicals in the area of the shooting. When first responders are entering a building to neutralize an active shooter, their adrenalin is off the chart, all senses integrated to mentally prepare for every possible scenario they may encounter within the business. For this reason, it is important to advise the first responders of dangerous chemicals that may be stored in or around the area of the shooting. First responders will certainly want to know whether propane tanks, liquid chlorine, and other dangerous chemicals may be encountered. Bullets and dangerous chemicals do not mix well, so it is important to account for these locations. In addition, a business may consider providing or prepositioning chemical masks for first responders as a precautionary measure. First responders know that a gas mask works on gas, but not on chemicals, so providing the proper personal protective equipment (PPE) to first responders will increase response time in case of a dangerous chemical release.

- Provide clear access route to the area of shooting and indicate any blockages caused by people jamming stairs and elevators.

One of the most challenging problems is when first responders endeavor to reach the affected areas but must negotiate a sea of evacuees blocking their path. The first responder traditionally begins communicating to make a path to allow passage, but it is a struggle at best. The faster people pass, the better, but slower, disabled, or extremely stressed individuals may be overcome by so much emotion and physical stress that they may just sit down, exacerbating the problem. Employees can help guests and employees stay to the right. EMTs and firefighters will help individuals who are sitting on steps and who cannot move any further to safety.

- Let first responders know whether the business has armed security, as well as what such guards are wearing.
  Not every business has a security department or contracts with private security companies, but businesses that do should provide information about security officers' uniforms as well as the number of officers on duty and whether they are armed. Also describe the company's position on whether employees are allowed to carry weapons to work. If so, identify who might have a firearm on the property. With an increase in active shootings, some companies have given employees more freedom to carry firearms at their place of business. This information is vital to first responders who are entering the building in search of the active shooter.

- If possible, contain and seal off areas so the shooter cannot expand the scope of the rampage. Businesses have the ability to override many security technologies from the security control room. Opening doors, releasing magnetic locks, and deactivating access card systems are only some of the many options available to the business in aiding the response effort. Changing the direction of an escalator to allow more people to safely exit the active shooter's area may fall within the authority of the business. Restricting access to other areas may keep the shooter from injuring or killing additional victims and deny the shooter free rein inside the building. However, if the restrictions are too tight, individuals trying to escape may be subject to the same upheavals intended for the shooter. Timely restrictive actions may be coordinated with first responders when they are near the active shooter.

- List areas that may provide a visual of the shooter.
  Because employees within the business have intimate knowledge of the property, they can direct first responders to positions that may provide a good visual of the shooter. Law enforcement officers are trained with a variety of weapons, allowing them to ascertain the practicality of neutralizing the active shooter from greater distances and to visually provide immediate tactical direction to entry officers.

- Relay information communicated from anyone hiding in the shooting area.
  Because of the operational complexity of the business and the proximity of the shooter to potential victims, and because many individuals will not leave a hiding place, the business may receive telephone calls from individuals who are hiding. These individuals can provide updated intelligence on the location of the shooter, on what is being said during the shooting, and on their own locations. This information must be relayed to first responders without hesitation. With this information, first responders can cover conceptually greater distances to close in on the shooter.

- Convey first responders to secondary entry and exit points.
  Law enforcement officers desire to approach the active shooter from a position of strength, so knowing all primary and secondary entry and exit points in the facility will give law enforcement officers an advantage by allowing them to cover all escape routes. Just because initial indications are that only one active shooter is involved does not mean that there is not a second shooter. Anyone exiting the shooting area should be challenged and investigated.
- Give the location of any vehicle the shooter drove.
  The active shooter arrived on the property somehow, and if the shooter is an employee, he or she may have driven a vehicle. This may be significant, especially because approximately 1.875 percent of active shooters, according to the 2013 FBI report "A Study of Active Shooter Incidents in the United States between 2000 and 2013," brought an IED to the shooting location. Thus the shooter's vehicle may contain an IED. Determining the shooter's method of transportation may prevent further casualties.
- Provide any equipment that first responders previously requested for this emergency.
  When the first responders toured the business, they may have identified some items and equipment that would aid a response. Because the first responders took the time to visit the business and provided the organization with input into how the company can aid their response to an active shooter emergency, the business should have available precisely what the first responders requested, if feasible. During outreach between the first responders and the business, the reasonableness of any requested item can be debated. But when a business takes that one last step to empower first responders, it speaks volumes about the philosophy and leadership of the company.
- Monitor threats.
  The business is in the unprecedented position to monitor the threat as it unfolds through surveillance cameras, sensor monitoring, and life safety systems, as well as coordinated interaction with first responders. No one knows the business and its formidable challenges better than the employees. Surveillance cameras may provide real-time intelligence on the active shooter's location, movements, and actions while also revealing whether the shooter is taking hostages, laying explosives, or barricading hallways and whether the shooter is stationary or mobile. Door sensors and entry alarm notifications can help indicate direction and location. Additionally, operators may receive information from individuals trapped inside or information about additional threats directed toward the business during the incident.
- Train select employees in trauma medical care.
  Unfortunately, hospitals have been the site of several different active shooter emergencies, but for a potential victim, this location provides the optimal trauma medical care response. Various school systems have implemented or are in process of implementing trauma medical care training for school district employees as well as of installing medical kits throughout the campus. These kits may contain instructions and necessary supplies for treating open chest wounds along with hemostatic tourniquets and dressings. If fire department and EMS personnel are prohibited from entering the active shooting location,

trained employees could deny the shooter another victim by providing medical assistance. This is only the first step in stabilizing a victim, but in its absence chances for survival are greatly reduced. The ultimate trauma step, of course, is treatment in a hospital setting.

Goals

In an active shooter emergency, the business has one overriding goal—preserving life. There is no higher calling, no higher mission—nothing more important. This goal is not murky or elusive; it should be indelibly etched on each business license. After an emergency, what will a visitor or an employee remember about how the business faced adversity and the leadership displayed to protect life? A business must always look to the safety and security of its guests, employees, and contractors in every threat situation, as must every city, community and state.

References

[1] The Police Chief, Learning from the Lessons of the 2008 Mumbai Terrorist Attacks, <www.policechiefmagazine.org/magazine/index.cfm?fuseaction=print_display&article_id=2309&issue_id=22011>.

[2] U.S. Army, Case Study: Terrorist Attack on Westgate Mall, Nairobi, Kenya 21-24 September 2013, <http://isdacenter.org/wp-content/uploads/2014/03/1-FY14_2Q_Final-Westgate-Mall-Attack-Case-Study-31-Jan-14-1.pdf>.

[3] Federal Emergency Management Agency, <https://www.fema.gov/community-emergency-response-teams>.

[4] Blair, J.P., Martaindale, M.H., and Nichols, T., Active Shooter Events from 2000 to 2012, <http://leb.fbi.gov/2014/january/active-shooter-events-from-2000-to-2012>; 2014.

[5] Texas State University, San Marcos, Texas, <http://alerrt.org>.

[6] ALICE Training Institute, Medina, Ohio, <www.alicetraining.com>.

[7] MACTAC—Los Angeles Police Department, Orange County, California, and Las Vegas Metropolitan Police Department, Las Vegas, Nevada, <www.hendonpub.com/resources/article_archive/results/details?id=1384>.

[8] National Archives of the United States, <www.archives.gov/education/lessons/d-day-memo/>.

[9] Blair JP, Schweit KW. A Study of Active Shooter Incidents, 2000–2013. Washington, D.C.: Texas State University and Federal Bureau of Investigation, U.S. Department of Justice; 2014.

[10] City of Houston's Mayor's Office of Public Safety and U.S. Department of Homeland Security, Run, Hide, Fight, <www.readyhoustontx.gov/videos.html>.

[11] U.S. Department of Homeland Security, Options for Consideration, <www.dhs.gov/video/options-consideration-active-shooter-preparedness-video>.

[12] Security Information Watch, <www.securityinfowatch.com/article/10653373/iahss-president-elect-lisa-pryse-discusses-industry-best-practices-in-siw-webinar>; 2012.

[13] Tier One Tactical Solutions, LLC, St. Charles, Missouri, <http://tieronetacticalsolutions.com>.

[14] Brault, M. W., Americans with Disabilities: 2010 Household Economic Studies, <www.census.gov/prod/2012pubs/p70-131.pdf>; 2012.

6

Internal and External Communications

Systems and Platforms

From a very young age, each person knows the importance of communications. Teachers, when asking students their opinion about the topic of the day, are teaching skills that will be used throughout students' lives. Attorneys hope to present a persuasive argument for their client before the jury and judge using both visual and verbal communication. Lecturers, through their communications skills, want their audience to embrace the theories and points of view they are presenting. However, during emergency situations, communications aren't designed to solicit debatable dialogue or a presentation, but rather are designed to provide direction for everyone to take the appropriate actions.

Unless recent news broadcasts pique an individual's attention or ab individual is traveling away from home, security and safety rest with the business. Tourists traveling to exotic locations just want to have fun and do not want to be dissuaded from their vacation by entertaining the notion of an emergency event's ruining their trip. Practicing lifeboat drills on luxury liners is a requirement on most commercial ships that sail the high seas. However, asking a hotel guest who has just arrived after two business meetings and a four-hour plane flight to participate in a fire drill would not go over well. So emergency practices and procedures fall squarely on the shoulders of the organization and its employees. Employees, on the other hand, who are working on a business deadline or performing customer service do not routinely deliberate on emergencies or the consequences of their actions or inactions. So how do the employees and each guest under the care of the business react during an emergency? The answer is by communicating the appropriate message, in the right format, over a recognizable platform, covering all areas of the property, to all people regardless of age, disabilities, or station of life. Let's ask another question to set the stage: During an emergency situation when you are with your significant other and two small children, and your lives potentially rest with that message, what message would you like to receive?

People are generally reactionary to a threat, with the compelling need of the individual to remove himself or herself from personal injury being a primary driving force after the threat is known. Unfortunately, people do not heed some warnings and signs that there is a problem, nor do they approach the threat with the same level of urgency urged by the message. When a fire alarm sounds, people do not immediately evacuate, being they are accustomed to an associated message, such as "We are investigating the cause of the alarm and will advise as soon as possible." People will wait and continue their normal course of business until a clarifying message is received. A second internal qualifier that people encounter is a false alarm. Because this event happens so frequently, it nullifies immediate emergency reactions by people to expend any effort other than waiting in anticipation for an all clear message. These internal actions are counterproductive to what the sender of the message expects to happen.

Looking at the active shooter emergency from an alarm notification process, such as a fire alarm or a tornado siren, there is no nationally recognized alarm, siren, or audible noise for an active shooting. If there were a national alarm or siren for an active shooter, would people even know what it meant or the location of the active shooter? A fire alarm provides a visual and audio alarm to all individuals within the area regardless of country of origin, age, or disability. However, remember there some people who have disabilities will not understand the message or problem, be able to react physically or mentally to the alarm, or be able to acknowledge that they received the alarm warning. The same challenges are also true of tornado sirens or any outdoor warning system that essentially expects people to take actions such as sheltering indoors because of the high winds outside.

During an active shooting emergency there is no platform tantamount to a false alarm that is being investigated and resolved. Prematurely or inappropriately communicating an active shooting is only possible in verbal message form at time of writing, not by a siren or pull alarm. Thus any communication platform warning beyond that to the immediate affected area or department rests on the shoulders of the message sender.

Platforms of Communication

When considering platforms of communication during an active shooting emergency, businesses should contemplate what is available at the time of the crisis, especially if they have not designed or planned for communications. If available, the person in charge may turn to the public address (PA) system as their medium of communications without considering any other alternatives. This action is quite common, and the organization may believe that it has fulfilled its duty without giving any other thought on the effectiveness of the chosen communication system in reaching potential victims in a time-sensitive emergency. The dynamics quickly change when the manager realizes that the company does not have a PA and that placing a call to 911 will not raise the consciousness of employees and other potential victims under attack by the active shooter.

Each business realizes that the world consists of choices based on needs, abilities, and budgets, and typically a single platform of communication will not reach the entire population intended or affected audience. The implication of a single communications system limits effective communications. Unfortunately, many businesses have not invested in a PA system, or any system, as the main communication platform. Even if a business uses a PA system, you must ask whether the system will reach all areas, departments, exterior buildings, tenant spaces, rooms, and parking areas of the business? Active shootings have occurred in every area just listed, so the method of communicating to potential victims in these areas should translate into an action item for the business. Furthermore, the platform must imagine how each person on property will receive the communications, where the person is located on the property, and how the recipient will be able to understand the message and its urgency.

Following is a list of potential options for a communications platform. There is no perfect system, for each business is unique in its combination of marketing offerings, size, operational design, and configuration. Think of the solution from the following perspective: What system or platform should the company use if you are located in one end of the building, your spouse is located on the third floor with a group of foreign visitors, and your two infant children are located in the nursery on the first floor? Though this example may seem extreme, this type of situation can occur, and that it can brings home the need to account for everyone at the site and consider all aspects of communications. The following methods of communications may be available at a business:

- Fire alarm: Pulled or initiated whenever a fire emergency occurs or when a full evacuation is required. Fire alarm also provides both audible sound and visual notification.
- Public address (PA) announcement: Specific directions or information can be issued to all individuals on the property. Each situation will require specific directions and can consist of its own unique prescripted message.
- Emergency text alert: A short message service (SMS) text message used when specific directions or information must be issued to only registered recipients. Because individuals must subscribe to this system, only subscribers will receive the alerts and messages. It may be used in conjunction with an alarm or PA announcement.
- Mass notification systems: Mass notification across multiple platforms and in multiple languages.
- Cell phones.
- Tablets and laptop computers.
- Social media (e.g., Twitter, Facebook, MySpace).
- Online conferencing programs, such as Skype.
- Two-way cell phones and text messaging.
- Walkie-talkies or business handheld radios.
- Private warning subscription providers.
- PBX phone tree patterned and call-down system.
- Nationalization or local news coverage.
- Visual images and information monitors to use text for the hearing-impaired.
- GPS for alert and notification.
- Teleprompter or closed caption on monitors.
- Hardline telephones.
- Television: Hotel/resort home channel or property television network.

After the solution has been selected for the business, consider the individuals on property who have a disability. These individuals may have certain limitations that interfere with the receipt of and response to emergency communications and will need information provided via methods they can understand and use. They may not be able to hear verbal announcements, see directional signs, or understand how to get assistance due to hearing, vision, speech, cognitive, or intellectual limitations, and/or limited language proficiency. Such consider-ations need to be part of the planning process, and the company must determine and provide communications in alternate formats (e.g., Braille, audio recording, large-type, text message, e-mail, multilingual) to meet the needs of all disabled employees and guests.

Social Media

Fifteen years ago, if someone had suggested or even hinted that social media would transform into a vibrant and innovative communication platform, people would have laughed. At one time, it was inconceivable that we would rely on social media during times of emergencies. First responding agencies and federal partners believed that social media was unreliable, that the information could not be trusted and problematic, and that the sources of the messages were self-serving. However, today social media has reshaped the communication environment like nothing ever before. If a person is hiding out in a dark office with the lights out and furniture blocking the door, he or she cannot keep dialing 911 over and over again and so may turn to social media for help, reassurance, and information. Social media can provide information on news reports and timely pictures of the emergency that may offer some comfort to individuals who are trapped by an active shooter. Social media may also provide contact with loved ones, who can provide information, intelligence, guidance, and a perspective on the problem.

Naturally, social media should not be the primary or secondary communications platform for a business or an emergency response, but it can provide information and intelligence that may otherwise be missed. When first responders are actively engaging in social media platforms and even exploring tracking systems, these technologies may allow them to locate the individuals that are hiding out. The problem with social media is that the same it increases the volume of messages that must be read, filtered, and responded to, much like the many telephone calls received by 911 and PBX operators. Each dispatcher must painstakingly filter through these calls to concentrate on people trapped in the life-threatening emergency rather than those individuals who have safely escaped the danger and want to hear a familiar soothing voice. The process takes time—and time is at a premium for first responders who are charged to neutralize the threat.

Now add into the communication solution the following questions:

- What method of communication is designated for areas of refuge or assistance? These areas are designed for individuals who have disabilities or other limitations or who may need assistance from first responders. Areas of refuge or assistance are generally located in emergency stairwells and should be large enough to receive wheelchairs. It is also important to check to see whether your company has any communications platforms in such areas.
- Did the method of communication take into consideration primary and secondary platforms, considering that one system may be overloaded or malfunction?
- Did the method(s) of communication consider what happens when the power goes out? Are there backup power sources or batteries?

The ideal time to construct a solid communications platform is before any emergency and under all threat conditions, not just active shootings. Walking the property and testing the communications systems, soliciting the aid of employee, tenants, and contractors to help in the process, will ingrain in each group that the business is a well-organized and well-disciplined organization that holds the safety and security of its people as a high priority.

Alarm, Employee Notification, Verbal Warning, or Observation

A business may be confronted by incidents and events daily or weekly that may pose a potentially serious threat to the business. Protocols and procedures direct the business staff to investigate the incident to best prevent premature activation of an emergency evacuation alarm or warning message. However, owing to a threat's nature, seriousness, magnitude, and type, such as an active shooting emergency, a business cannot assume the company will be the first notification source that guests and employees receive. In addition, the business may not have the ability to investigate the source of the problem, as expected for fires and/or water leaks. For many guests and employees on property, the first indication that a business is experiencing an emergency is when

- an audible alarm (internal to business or external) sounds
- a verbal warning over PA system is broadcast
- verbal warning comes from an employee, guest, or emergency first responder
- he or she personally observes the threat

In the business's emergency communication planning process, after the types of notifications have been identified, the active shooter plan should be activated. Another consideration is whether the business uses the same notification alarms or sounds for more than one type of emergency. The following points should be considered in the planning, training, and education process for employees and the business to consider during emergency situations:

- A fire alarm may be the only source of emergency notification system that the business uses. Additional notification methods should be considered to ensure that all guests, employees, or visitors are duly warned of the threat.
- The business may use the fire alarm system as an emergency evacuation system for several different types of emergencies and threats.
- Without an additional verbal warning message, guests may not understand that the fire alarm is being used by the business for more than one type of emergency and threat.
- An audible fire alarm system without strobe lights will not accommodate the needs of deaf guests and employees.
- A verbal warning message over the PA system will not accommodate the needs of deaf guests and employees.
- Employees and contractors working in the business are responsible for communicating the verbal warning when received from a guest or emergency first responder and/or conveying personal observations of the threat according to business policies and procedures.
- Each employee and contractor working in the business should be instructed and trained in the proper protocols for crisis communications.

- Employees and contractors working in the business are responsible for knowing the type of emergency alarm sounds so that they can be communicated to guests, visitors, and new employees.
- All emergency plans should include any community warning alarm sounds (tornado, nuclear emergency, etc.) to avoid any confusion and to properly inform employees and guests of the purpose of the warning alarm sound.

Messages During an Active Shooting

As a society, we expect immediate communications to help stabilize the challenges of the active shooting, support personal issues and needs, direct relief efforts, remove anxiety, and demonstrate leadership in a chaotic environment. Each individual hopes that he or she will not be forgotten or minimized during and after the shooting. The individuals involved in an active shooting will undoubtedly hope for reassuring words, timely direction, and professionalism from the business in each aspect of this brutal emergency.

The issue of broadcasting a message during an active shooting isn't always simple. Companies, or even buildings containing multiple businesses, do not always have a common communication platform. Secondly, there may not be sufficient time to warn anyone inside the building because it is such a rapidly developing emergency, or because the business is not a large facility, engulfing each employee and guest in every terrorizing sound. Last, even if there is time, the business may not know the proper concise warning message to provide the appropriate directions without becoming a catalyst for panic and hysteria, refer to Figure 6–1. Panic need not be the direct result of a message broadcast, so long as the author of the message provides a clear, concise, accurate and informative message. Panic and hysteria will not help resolve the emergency, nor will such unproductive actions allow potential victims to focus on their options. Ineffective emotional responses that dominate actions are indeed counterintuitive. We have already seen that people want accurate information, demanding details, options, and timeframes within which to operate.

FIGURE 6–1 What is Your Message.

During the Shooting, What Message Should Be Sent over the Communication Platform?

Unlike a fire, in the case of which an employee or guest can activate the alarm pull station from almost any location in the building, typically on any floor, there is no known identifiable alarm or siren that can be transmitted to sound an emergency for an active shooter. Active shooters, according to the FBI Law Enforcement Bulletin "Active Shooter Events from 2000 to 2012" [1] states that in 93 percent of incidents, shooters used a gun to dispense death to the innocent victims. The weapons used over this timespan included pistols (59%), shotguns (8%), and rifles (26%). The first sound victims and witnesses may hear will be a gunshot, which may or may not be understood as an actual gunshot. Some witnesses have reported gunshots' sounding like a *pop pop pop*, not a *bang bang bang*, whereas others have thought the noise a car backfiring. In either case, unless a witness sees the shooting, he or she will need further confirmation of it being an actual shooting before being able to issue an alert. The sight of people running away, wounded and/or bleeding may prompt the witnesses to communicate an emergency message. So what message would you communicate over your communications system to alert everyone?

- An active shooting is a very violent, shocking, and harsh event, but it is also one that ends fairly quickly. According to the U.S. Department of Justice FBI report of September 16, 2013, titled "A Study of Active Shooter Incidents in the United States between 2000 and 2013," [2] approximately 56.3 percent of the time, the active shooting ends before law enforcement officers arrive on the scene. This means that in a majority of active shootings, the business or witnesses never had an opportunity to deliver any message other than to those in close proximity to the shooter. The only warning may be provided by people running and yelling or, according to that same report, 13 percent of the time, innocent bystanders who took immediate action to stop the shooter.
- If the security control room receives a call from an employee providing details about an active shooter, what message should the security control room issue?
- The health care industry often uses an alert of "Code Silver" to warn staff in the building that an active shooting is occurring. The code alerts employees to an active shooter but does not necessarily help patients, visitors of patients, or visiting medical teams or even therapists of the direction of the threat, the nature of the threat, or even on which floor, in which wing, or in which building the active shooter is located.
- Many schools train for an active shooter and use a lockdown process as their method of choice to protect the staff and students. A sample message may be: "This is an emergency. Go to lockdown. This is not a drill." Two thoughts must be considered as regard a school lockdown procedure. First, a lockdown of students may be an appropriate measure for elementary students who are too small to run or fight. This also establishes a barrier between the shooter and potential targets. Second, if the teacher and students can safely evacuate the school because of the distance between the shooter and students, then it seems very appropriate to get away, not to wait to become a statistic.
- Some business may decide to deliver a message such as "Shelter in place. We have an active shooter." There is a difference between a lockdown and sheltering in place. A shelter-in-

place message, as defined by FEMA [3] for an emergency involving a dangerous chemical spill may sound something like "Emergency officials would likely advise individuals to shelter in place when the chemical is expected to dissipate in a short time period, and there is not time to evacuate." Sheltering in place is not the appropriate instruction in an active shooter emergency.

- Some businesses may decide to deliver a message such as "We have an active shooter on property. Hide out now." Because active shooters use more than guns, such as knives, axes, scalpels, hammers, and swords, "active shooter" does not necessary describe the formidable threat. Second, legal departments are debating both sides of the argument: What if a business tells a customer or employee to hide when he or she has a clear chance of safely evacuating? If the person obeys and decides to hide, then becomes a casualty, is the company responsible for that person's death? A business safeguards individuals and directs individuals according to facilitywide information sources, presumably away from the threat. If the victim solely bases his or her decision on the business to protect or direct them, is the company liable?
- Consider the message "Attention! Attention! This is not a drill. There is a man with a gun, wearing a red shirt, shooting at people on the first floor in the main lobby. Take appropriate actions to protect yourself." This short emergency message provided seven different important points for any potential victims to consider.
- The last point to consider is to develop your own message using an advisory committee, and be sure to involve your legal department in this process, lest whatever message delivered be left in the hands of the person sitting in front of the communications platform.
- What is your message?

Prescripted Message

Many people debate whether an active shooter message can be prescripted. One side indicates there are too many variables and unknown facts that cannot possibly be identified to validate the message beforehand. The other side of the argument indicates that an accurate and timely message, designed to help preserve life, can be developed before an incident to aid individuals. A second debate centers on how if there is not a prescripted message on which to rely, then whatever message is broadcast over the entire communications platform was abruptly scripted at that moment. Right or wrong, good or bad, it becomes the business's authoritative guidance.

The active shooter message is not a standard message that will conform to all threats, disasters, crises, or emergencies. There are different types of options for consideration, as well as different locations that employees and guests may be caught in during the active shooter emergency. The initial message and any update messages broadcast during an active shooter crisis are quite different from those in a natural disaster or an industrial accident. If the author of the message places himself or herself in the shoes of the individual engulfed in the emergency, then an instructive message may be the result of his or her efforts.

If there is time, the business must decide what protective action(s) or options are appropriate for employees and guests to take before an active shooter message is issued. The recommended protective action(s) or options must be fully identified and described in the message, then broadcast over all communications media, formats, and platforms. The message content may consider what specific areas are at risk, as well as where the safest areas are and what choices may be available to all individuals in the emergency.

If the business chooses to prescript messages in different platforms, media, and formats for employees and guests, it is advisable to develop these messages ahead of time. A preapproved message or series of messages, based on the nature of the threat, can be developed, approved by management, prepositioned on all methods of communication platforms, and tested during training exercises. The best time to prepare a clear, concise message accessible to all categories of employees and guests is well in advance of any potential emergency.

The active shooter message and updated messages may be a lifeline securing the safety of each employee and guest. Each message can be customized for each group, including a disability category, thereby increasing the ability of individuals to plan and survive in the event of an emergency. Considerations should be afforded to the various prescripted messages as part of every emergency plan, incorporated in false alarms, test messages, and training exercises.

Content of Warning Messages

Regardless of whether the message is prescripted or developed at the time of the emergency, the warning message should tell individuals the basics of what, where, when, how, and who of the active shooting, identifying options for people to avoid harm. The message should be specific, clear, concise, accurate, consistent, and timely. The active shooter warning message and follow-up messages should contain the following aspects:

- What are the options and guidance?
  During any emergency, people will want to understand their options and will desire guidance on what to do. Any guests, whether with or without disabilities, who are not completely familiar with the business will want to know what they should do to protect themselves, as well as where they will be safe. Thus the safest option in their mind is to remain where they are at the moment of the message. The message sender should understand that people may not know what constitutes an appropriate protective or safe action or where they will be safe.
- What is the location?
  It is important to communicate the location of the threat to the people at risk as well as to people not at risk so that they, too, may consider their options and actions. Describe the area, department, or location of the active shooting, which may be described by landmarks inside or outside of the building. Alerting people where to go and where not to go during the incident should potentially place individuals in a safer location. It is important to avoid giving cardinal directions, especially because many people do not know where is north or south is located after they enter a building, let alone when they are in a life-threatening emergency. Cardinal directions have almost zero value to the average person. Furthermore, remember that trapped individuals may include an entire spectrum of disabled individuals and international guests who have language challenges.

- How much time?
  It is important to communicate how much time employees and guests have to respond or react to this emergency. Communicate any known time before an active shooter may affect the building so that employees and guests may consider their actions based on physical abilities and time constraints.
- What is the hazard?
  Describe the emergency hazard and the exact threat to employees and guests so that they know what they are facing to identify and remove misconceptions of the threat. If an active shooter situation is under way, describe the type of weapon, also giving a physical description of the shooter(s) and his or her (or their) clothing if possible. However, an active shooter designation will not help people who do not know or understand what an active shooter is: A possible message could instead say "a man with a gun." Also remember that not all active shooters use guns. Several murderers have used knives, swords, or razors, so consider using the words "active threat" to help describe the emergency.
- Who is the source?
  If the warning message is authorized by the business, indicate such authorization accordingly. The source of the message is important because it has a consequential effect on whether people believe the warning and may override the negative effects of not having a credible source issue the warning.

Should You Send a Second Message Out to Individuals inside the Business?

Whatever message was delivered throughout the business, people will be hiding out from the active shooter or trying to escape. If they are evacuating, people want to know whether they are running in the right direction. If they are hiding out, they may not have the capacity to move their frightened legs or the physical ability to move owing to their health or disability—or the ability to see the shooter heading their way and their escape route blocked. Regardless of why people choose to hide, it is important to provide them with as much warning as possible. Hiding out may mean hiding under a desk and locking the door to the office or having sufficient time to move filing cabinets, desks, and tables to block entrances. These individuals will generally stay in this position until they know they are completely safe. There are two different schools of thought when sending messages to individuals who are hiding out.

- Some believe that no second message should be sent across any platform for fear of the active shooter's hearing the message, which may provoke the shooter to look behind every door and in every room.
- Conversely, according to the FBI Study of Active Shooter Incidents in the United States Between 2000 and 2013, approximately 23.1 percent of the active shooters committed suicide before law enforcement intercepted them. If the shooter hears a message that law enforcement is searching the building, he or she may commit suicide.
- If a business were to deliver a message across the communications platform, it may consider adding a message similar to "Attention! Attention! Law enforcement officers are in the building right now! Take appropriate actions to protect yourself."

- Some people may believe that if the message indicates the location of the shooter or the shooters last known location, then individuals hiding out may decide to leave their concealed positions to seek safety. This may be the case, but also consider that these people are there for a reason and may have been hiding out for a period of time without being detected.

What Update Message Will the Business Send to Employees and Guests Hiding out from the Shooter?

Let's assume the business had the ability to send out message initially, but as the active shooting emergency endlessly continues, the people hiding out are not feeling any safer, but rather more stressed. In active shooter situations, law enforcement will clear the entire business in search of additional shooters, casualties, and victims. They cannot rely on the fact that, according to the FBI report "A Study of Active Shooter Incidents in the United States between 2000 and 2013," approximately 98.7 percent of the active shooters act alone. Law enforcement will not provide any communication that indicates that the one active shooter has been neutralized; they are searching for another possible shooter. Thus people hiding out will continue to wait until they receive a trusted communication or officers come and get them.

- Some properties may deliver the same message listed above, just to reassure these people that they have not been forgotten or ignored. It should be noted that depending on the size of the business, the law enforcement search may take hours.
- Some businesses may still believe that no message should be provided. So a question within a question: If businesses provides messages on fire alarms, why not active shootings?

What Is Your Message to the Entire Building When the Shooter Has Been Neutralized?

With tensions and fear running high, neutralizing the active shooter is the predominant action on everyone's minds. Law enforcement response teams want nothing less than to stop the shooter using any means possible and as quickly as possible. After the shooter is neutralized as confirmed by the first responders, dies as a result of committing suicide or surrender, is subdued by individuals at the scene, or is killed by non–law enforcement officers, what message should be broadcast throughout the building?

If the shooter is neutralized by one of the above actions, how does the company decide whether to broadcast a message over the property's communications system?

Some believe that law enforcement should be the only party to approve a message broadcast throughout the business. We know that first responders will continue to search the business during the clearing process to determine whether there is a second shooter and to communicate with each room or area where individuals are hiding out. This may not be as easy as one would think, especially when these individuals have no idea whether the law enforcement officers are really police officers or just the shooter pretending to be one. The process of clearing rooms in which people are hiding out is a slow process and one that reinforces safety for all parties involved. Historically, verbal commands issued by law enforcement officers have been effective at clearing rooms. If a room is barricaded and the occupants are still resisting such commands by refusing to open the door, consider a coordinated approach and have the business contact these individuals over a landline telephone located inside the office.

A second way of thinking believes that a familiar voice over the same communications platform will add value and reassurance to those hiding out. The message is not an "all clear" message, but rather one of support and encouragement.

Not matter your school of thought, it is important to note that all messages should be coordinated with the first responders, for response and search teams are actively working to neutralize the shooter. Messages such as "Law enforcement teams are currently clearing the second floor" or "The shooter has been arrested—come out" will jeopardize the safety of first responders and those individuals hiding out in the business. What message would you want to hear if you were the one hiding out?

Who Prepares All the Messages, and Who Communicates Them?

As noted, the proper message, carefully scripted, may spark immediate action, offer encouragement, and stabilize overwhelming fear. Conversely, the wrong unscripted message may do just the opposite. The dialogue presented will be remembered by those who are living this unprecedented nightmare and may be the subject of witness testimonies that attempt to paint a less than favorable picture of the business's leadership. A prescripted message can be offered up as proof of what was exactly expressed, without relying on fragmented memory and overextended emotions.

Last, the message sender may instill trust and confidence or, conversely, skepticism and insecurity, refer to Figure 6-2. Choosing wisely who will communicate the message will not marginalize and diminish the importance of the message. In schools, students hear the same familiar voice relaying important school functions, and in businesses the same familiar voice may be heard after fire alarms have been activated. However, that the same familiar voice is only familiar to those individuals working on property, such as employees, tenants, and contractors. Any voice that communicates will be new to the guests. Preplanning who will be the message sender during all emergency situations is a wise decision, and a appropriate backup communicator should be selected in the event that the primary person is unavailable.

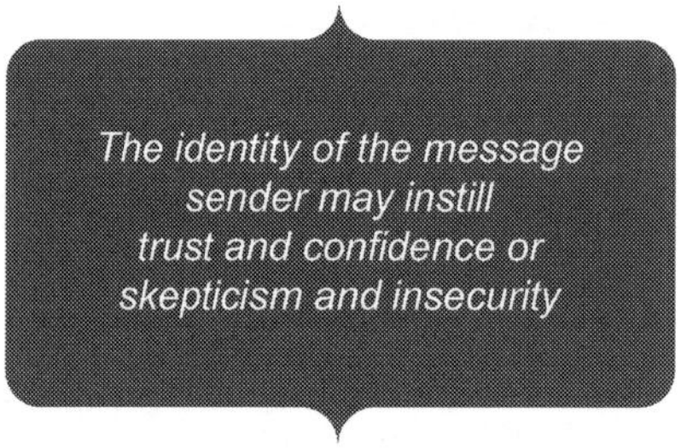

> The identity of the message sender may instill trust and confidence or skepticism and insecurity

FIGURE 6–2 The Message Sender.

Internal and External Communication

Communications, both internal and external, during and after the active shooting resonate across employees, contractors, tenants, vendors, customers, neighboring businesses, victim's families, and law enforcement immediately and for months to come. **Appendix C** outlines only a few communication areas that must be addressed by the business in negotiating the destabilizing events of an active shooting. Reconciling potential communication pitfalls and anticipating fundamental gaps in the social fabric will go a long way in reducing rumors and gossip while also dissuading toxic peaks from unnecessary obstacles in supporting the response and recovery efforts.

First responders also need timely communication and assistance throughout all areas of the building. Because the business knows what communication systems work, as well as any areas that lack signals, it will know what communication gaps are present and can be a valuable partner in resolving the active shooting. An open line of communications is a necessity between both first responders and the business. In an emergency, the business cannot be silent, but is expected to support the first responders. The business is not exempt just because someone called 911: In the end, the business is responsible for the safety and care of its people and guests.

During an active shooting, first responders will need to synchronize the response inside the business to aid individuals who are hiding out or injured. As an example, let's assume that individuals are hiding out in the human resources department, room 235, and will not open the door to the first responders for fear the active shooter is trying to trick them into opening the door. In this example, the business could use the landline or computer network or text message to contact the occupants, especially because most emails and all text messages go directly their cell phones. In addition, the business's command center or security control room might be able to text the individuals believed to be in the room by comparing employee cell phone contact numbers, then sending a text. The text can be a simple message: "This is Mr. Smith. Law enforcement officers are outside room 235. Listen to their commands." Additionally, the business may receive information from individuals hiding out and then direct first responders to their location. The business can maintain contact with these people until rescued. It should be noted that first responders will not race to these locations, but will methodically advance, even after the active shooter has been neutralized.

The telephone calls that are received into the private branch exchange (PBX) can allow the operators to get information that only the business will know. The business understands the internal dynamics and the direct byproducts of these discriminating facts, which could ultimately result in the protection of people. This information should not be retained but should be shared with first responders for tactical considerations. As an example, relatives of any employees who are hiding out within the property may be in direct contact with the loved one; neighboring properties may see individuals waving their arms out the window, or a guest may relay hearing screams and shots directly above them that could identify the exact location of the active shooter.

What Message Should Be Communicated to Tenants?

Not every business has tenants, but if a business does, tenant employees may face the same upheavals as the rest of the property during an active shooting. However, not all tenants are tied into the business's main communication platform, so a notification method should be established in monthly tenant meetings, or individually, before any emergency. Tenants may also request that their particular business receive emergency messages over one platform, such as a text message or cell phone call, whereas another tenant may desire emails. This factor alone will suggest that simultaneously messages should be sent across multiple communication platforms.

Ideally, the same message should be sent unilaterally across all methods of communication, regardless of the location within the business. The initial messages can be misconstrued, cause confusion, and hinder a timely individual's response when facing an active shooting emergency. During a fire, a business may consider a phased evacuation, partial evacuation, or full evacuation depending on the location of the fire. Because active shooters can be mobile and can move rapidly between floors, departments, and even buildings within the same complex, a universal message is one appropriate method to warn individuals throughout the entire property and complex.

What Message Should Be Communicated to Employees Reporting to Work?

Not every business has three shifts to interact with guests and customers, or twenty-four hour operations for such aspects as information technology, facility maintenance, or customer service call, but if a business is open longer than an eight-hour shift, employees will arrive to work without knowing there is a problem, or they may call in to see whether they are still needed—or just call off.

If the employee, contractor, or volunteer physically arrive at the business, he or she definitely will not be allowed to enter the company premises. He or she will, however, either be told to go home and wait to be recalled to work or be recruited to assist in the emergency evacuation assembly area function. As the active shooting escalates and the effects of the emergency are realized, trusted employees may fortify and stimulate the business's response and recovery functions.

If the employee, contractor, or volunteer calls into the PBX, they will be told not to report to work or to report and assist with the emergency evacuation function. Naturally, the individual will not be allowed to enter the building; and because the business will be a crime scene, the work shift will most likely be canceled. However, if the employee function falls under the U.S. Department of Labor Office of Safety, Health Administration (OSHA) OSHA 29 CFR 1910.38 (c) for Evacuation Plans and Procedures section 1910.38 (c) (3) procedures are to be followed by employees who remain to operate critical plant operations before they evacuate [4]. If the employee position is involved with the critical plant operations, that employee may be needed to work their shift even though the business is considered a crime scene. Once the crime scene is cleared by law enforcement, employees may be allowed to re-enter the site to get their personal belongings. The organization's leadership will determine the next steps as far as business operations are concerned.

Should a Message Be Provided to Your PBX Department for When People Call?

During emergency situations, the business will receive approximately nineteen different types of telephone calls into the PBX department. If the type of telephone call can be anticipated and plotted before the emergency, then the process for effectively administrating a favorable outcome is the byproduct. When the type of business concerns customer service effectiveness, each misstep will automatically translate into a gap in efficiency, replicated many times over. By identifying the compendium of likely calls and predetermining transfer extensions, some problems may be avoided. Second, many people who call have no prior knowledge that there is an active shooter emergency occurring at the time of their call. Third, the PBX operator may be the lifeline and the only outside contact for individuals hiding out in the active shooting zone. The types of phone calls that the PBX operators may receive include the following:

- First responders (law enforcement, fire, emergency management, EMT, federal agencies)
- 911 Operators
- Individuals hiding out
- Disabled guests employees
- Injured guests and employees
- Customers making reservations
- Vendors delivering supplies
- People asking about business services and show times
- Relatives of employees
- Relatives of guests
- Relatives of contractors
- Relatives of volunteers
- Employees for the next shift
- Neighboring properties
- Tenant properties
- Inquisitive people trying to find out what is happening
- Volunteers, religious organizations, American Red Cross
- News media
- People who agree with the shooting or dislike for the organization that was attacked

The operator desires to forward and clear non–life-threatening calls as soon as possible to allow the affected people the attention they deserve. These individuals may have timely information on the exact location of the active shooter or be able to relay information about their location and about how many other individuals are in the same location. This information will be extremely useful to first responders and the emergency evacuation assembly area as they attempt to account for all individuals who were inside the business when the shooting began.

Persons Who Have a Disability

From preservation of life and safety initiatives to damage limitation and reconstitution, a business is charged with the awesome responsibility of understanding the perceived risks, threats, and hazards that may befall employees, guests, vendors, or volunteers at the business. Unfortunately for many businesses, the active shooter or emergency action plans do not take into consideration guests who are international travelers, individuals who fall under the Americans with Disabilities Act (ADA), visitors who have special needs or physical condition limitations, or senior citizens and minors.

When a message is broadcast concerning an active shooter, the message will automatically generate panic, fear, and a sense of urgency for guests and employees alike. During an active shooter emergency, consider that for even the physically fit and sound of mind, the sheer message will be a challenge to considering their options and potential actions. For ADA employees and guests, the sheer thought of an active shooter creates a monumental and menacing scenario that they know will require additional support to overcome. How the business anticipates, mitigates, responds to, and supports all ADA employees and guests is a foundational element of the planning cycle. Regardless of the intent and expectations of the active shooter plan, the actions and choices for consideration will be left to the discretion of each ADA employee or guest after the active shooter message is broadcast. Undeniably, for persons who have disabilities, their options are reduced based on their needs, assistance, and equipment requirements. Second, unless the disabled individual is an employee, many businesses do not know how many ADA guests are on property, or where they are, at the time of the active shooting.

It is also important to understand the options available to ADA guests and employees during an active shooting emergency that may not require the immediate evacuation of the building. The ADA guest and employee may be safer within the building as opposed to in a complete evacuation of the building. In the case of an employee or guest who has a disability, or an individual who is in a less than normal state, the entire active shooting emergency experience can be a marketing and social media nightmare for the business if such a person is completely discounted and ignored.

An individual who has a disability is defined by the U.S. Department of Justice, Civil Rights Division, Disability Rights Section, in the Guide to Disability Rights Law [5], as "a person who has a physical or mental impairment that substantially limits one or more major life activities, a person who has a history or record of such an impairment or a person who is perceived by others as having such an impairment." ADA does not specifically name all the impairments that may be encountered during the active shooter emergency, but the ADA ensures that individuals who have disabilities enjoy equal rights and opportunities to be afforded the same protections as those who do not have disabilities.

Many businesses believe that ADA guests and employees will be easy to spot and that a person who has a disability during an active shooter emergency is easily identified, but actually this is not the case. Will an individual who has mental retardation or who is deaf be obvious by his or her physical appearance? Will an individual who as a respiratory condition or a recent medical operation be visible to the casual observer? Approximately three-quarters of ADA employees

Type	Description
Communicative	Inability to speak, slurred and stuttering speech or difficulty in forming sentences or words, and Tourette syndrome
Cognitive	A learning disability that affects communication and remembering which can be a development delay
Hearing	A sensory disability which can result in a complete loss of hearing (deafness) or result in various stages of hearing levels below
Mobility	Ambulatory ability to move, but may require the assistance of special equipment, e.g. canes, walkers, doesn't specify the speed of the person walking or distances that must be walked, nor the ability to walk down stairs or over obstacles, or the speed or rate the person can walk. Non-ambulatory will not be able to move from one location to another without assistance of another and without a motorized wheelchair
Multiple	Disabilities are not limited to only one type or form, but a person may possess more than one, such a person who is Deaf-blind or resulting from an accident
Physical	From missing limbs, obesity, dwarf or little people, and accident related to internal disorders or conditions such as cardiac, respiratory, internal organs and chemical dependency. Cerebral palsy, Epilepsy or seizure disorders, orthopedic impairment and general weakness and fatigue, plus equipment assistance dependency
Psychological Psychiatric	Emotional or mental illness, which could be identified in autism, Alzheimer, an emotional disturbance, and a brain injury due to accidents
Visual	A sensory disability which can result in complete blindness or limited vision

FIGURE 6–3 Categories of Disability Impairment.

and guests have nonobvious disabilities that in many cases will not be known until the emergency occurs. Initial, updated, and postcommunication messages should consider the categories of disabilities impairments, which may include the impairments as illustrated in Figure 6–3.

Communications Considerations for Persons Who Have a Disability

During an active shooter emergency, each individual will initiate an action and choice process both physically and mentally that begins with the first verbal or nonverbal notification communicating that there is a problem, which may affect his or her safety and security. For an individual who has a disability, this process is more elaborate and detailed. Before even considering moving from a location, regardless of whether it is secure, the person who has a disability may require special equipment to meet his or her unique needs and may need reassurance that there really is a threat and assistance to move. Unlike a disabled employee who is familiar with the property, alarm notification system, areas of refuge, and emergency evacuation assembly area, the disabled guest does not have the same knowledge and experience.

After the terrorist attacks the United States on September 11, 2001, if a fire alarm sounded, in many instances individuals evacuated buildings before listening to the first audio message that provided information on the alarm. It should also be noted that a fire alarm signal may be used for more than one type of emergency in some buildings. This fact may be known to employees but perhaps not to individuals who have disabilities. It should be noted that during an active shooting, the fire alarm can present an active shooter with additional potential targets as people are encouraged to evacuate from their secure locations or hiding places. The active shooter may push the fire alarm just to continue his or her relentless attack on the occupants of the business. Consideration should be given to developing a message over the designed communication platform to clarify that there is no fire and possibly nullify the active shooter's intentions.

Based on the disability, a person who has a mental disability may not respond to any alarm or desire to leave the comfort of his or her room or current location within the business. The person who has the disability may not be able to proceed to the area of refuge or assistance or the emergency evacuation assembly area or to understand the active shooter emergency in the same manner, or even respond with the same actions, as those who do not have his or her physical, cognitive, or emotional disabilities.

The Americans with Disabilities Act Accessibility Guidelines (ADAAG), 4.1.3(14), 4.28 [6], provide specifications for emergency alarms so that they are accessible to persons with disabilities, including those who have sensory impairments or psychological or psychiatric challenges. When emergency alarm systems are provided, they must meet criteria and specifications of audibility and visibility. For additional guidance and requirement, check each category in the ADAAG. Some examples found in the ADAAG include the following items. In reviewing these bullet points, consider how they will be addressed in the active shooter response plan or, indeed, any business emergency plan.

- Visual strobes notify people who are deaf or hard of hearing that an alarm has sounded.
- Visual alarms are required in hallways, lobbies, restrooms, and any other general usage and common use areas, such as meeting and conference rooms, cafeterias, lobbies, dressing rooms, theaters, and bowling alleys, to name a few.
- ADAAG specifications for visual appliances address intensity, flash rate, and mounting location, among other characteristics.
- It is not sufficient to install visual signals only at audible alarm locations.
- Audible alarms installed in corridors and lobbies can be heard in adjacent rooms or hallways and over long distances, but a visual signal can be observed only within the space it is located due to the configuration of the building.

Employee or guests who have a disability who will need assistance during an active shooter emergency should be encouraged to notify the business operator at their location. Knowing their location will allow emergency personnel additional situational awareness for an effective evacuation.

Employees who might occupy the building after regular work hours, or at other times when staff are not usually present, should be encouraged to notify the department/building manager of their location and provide the building, floor, room, and time of their arrival and departure. Knowing their location will allow emergency personnel situational awareness for an effective communication and the ability to plan for real-time assistance.

A business may establish ADA hotlines during an emergency. If so, a hotline should include TTY/TDD (text telephone, also known as telecommunication device for the deaf) numbers, when available, along with instructions on how to use the TTY caller's relay. For those employees and guests who have cognitive disabilities, frequent repetition of the most essential active shooter emergency information in a simple message format can help them understand and follow instructions.

When multiple methods of communications are broadcast, each will compete for an individual's attention. For many individuals, including a person who has a disability, this can also be a distraction, problematic especially in a fast-moving active shooter emergency. A misconception has circulated for years that emergency communication messages must be short, because it is difficult to hold a person's attention, but actually the reverse is true. People are information junkies and want more and more information, not less. Active shooter emergency messages resemble an ongoing dialogue with an individual caught up in the emergency. Persons with a disability need a lot of information, and they need to have it communicated to them often.

When a person who has a disability is positioned in the area of refuge or assistance, communications should be considered in fifteen-minute intervals or more frequently for repeated or update messages in an active shooter emergency. No single factor affects what a person who has a disability thinks and does in response to an active shooter emergency more than is said in the emergency evacuation message.

Signage

Another form of communication is signage. During an emergency situation, each employee, guest, and person who has a disability looks for guidance in the form of signs to aid in safe evacuation to an area of security. People demand quick and unimpeded paths, if appropriate, to exit a business during emergency situations. Exit signs are required by law in most buildings, illuminated and at a proper height to allow visibility from a distance. Emergency exit route signs are often posted in conspicuous locations throughout the business and include such signs as primary exit routes, alternate exit routes, fire safety equipment, areas of refuge or assistance, emergency evacuation assembly areas, and particular departments or safe rooms. However, an illuminated exit sign, regardless of the height or purpose of the sign, may not be seen by a person who is blind, who has limited vision, or who has cognitive, psychological, psychic, or numerous other types of disabilities.

Persons who have disabilities are not the only individuals who may have difficulty with emergency signs; as mentioned, many international guests may not be able to decipher what such signs mean. If they cannot interpret the business's emergency signs, the international guest's quick evacuation from the business will mean simply following other people. If the international guest is also a person who has a disability, the challenges are magnified. The International Organization for Standards (ISO) provides international accepted graphics for signage at www.iso.org/iso/graphical-sympbols.booklet.pdf. Please refer to Figure 6–4 for examples of the ISO signage [7]. However, the person must have an understanding of these signs and graphics if they are to be effective during an emergency.

FIGURE 6–4 Various ISO Emergency Signs.

When an individual is provided with a message during an active shooting emergency advising people to consider their options, the individual begins to assess his or her location while contemplating the old adage: "Fight or flight." Because it is a predictable human instinct for many people to evacuate, escape, or run away from danger regardless of their station of life, the individual will not be tolerant of a business that does not embrace expected guidance, especially if signage is absent and people run blindly down seemingly never-ending corridors. If the shooting is occurring, say, in the human resources department and there are no signs to aid people, then they become immersed even deeper in disaster as they run directly into the human resources department. No business is expected to know in which department or location an active shooting emergency will take place, but giving potential victims and first responders assistance through signage is attainable and should be addressed properly during the planning phases.

International Guests

A business cannot assume that international guests will understand the nature of the emergency, such as an active shooter, just because a message was broadcast in English. And just because a guest is in an English-speaking country does not mean that he or she speaks or understands English. To an international guest, there is no difference among messages that are mundane, autocratic, harsh, mediocre, or inspirational if the guest does not know the language. Words are only chatter. The international guest's interpretation of the message is based on the actions of people observed, the sounds of panic and shock, and a sense of danger. The fastest method to alleviate the challenges of international guests who do not understand English is to consider using a multicommunication platform to broadcast several common languages across the previously identified business's communication systems.

Many businesses have a marketing strategy that attracts international guests, so the sales and marketing department already are versed in the most common languages, and their members may be on property at the time of the active shooting. Depending on the business model of the property, such as a mall, restaurant, hotel, casino, theme park, sports arena, or convention space, each model may contain dozens of individuals who communicate in different languages. One business cannot be expected to verbally communicate in every language, but there are technical communication systems that can broadcast prescribed message across several languages. This innovation definitely envisions and concentrates on a gap in the communication framework that is, as a general rule, completely overlooked.

International guests may be experiencing challenges that we may take for granted, such as different languages, signage, currency, traffic patterns, customs, and beliefs and popular culture based perceptions. Now add to the stress, the equation an active shooter, and experience for the international guest has just become distorted and overwhelming. To compensate the compendium of security and safety, the individual searches for nonverbal communication clues, such as facial expressions, eye contact, hand gestures, and the intensity of any words spoken. The guest may not fully understand the meaning of what is being communicated, but he or she can certainly sense anger, hostility, or urgency in a person's voice. When it comes to emergency communications remember the famous quote that states, "We don't see things as they are; we see things as we are".

An employee is familiar with the business's internal dynamics, including any shortcuts to specific locations, and understands an emergency message, but for the international guest, frustration and indecision hinder a meaningful response to an active shooter message without the assistance of the business's employees. Thus, for a business that deals with international guests, effective communications, understanding of differences, diplomacy, and response expectations cannot be an afterthought but should be a carefully coordinated strategy based on safety and security.

Communication Gaps

When considering what communication platform that will be used, two certainties must be addressed: First, regardless of the sophistication of the system and deliberate efforts to contact each individual in the business, people will still never hear the message, because the system cannot effectively reach all areas of the property, which creates gaps. These gaps could be the result of the building design, construction materials, and the size of the structure. Second, gaps do not automatically and miraculously fix themselves at the exact time when communication is needed. If the business has a known dead zone, regardless of the emergency and the limitations of the communications platform, these areas will still be significant impediment for employees and first responders. The business can either convert these dead zones into a zone of coverage through capital expenditures and a collaborative effort of potential users or immediately communicate the dead zones to first responders as they enter the property. It is important not to deprive first responders of valuable information that may affect their response in neutralizing the active shooter. If the business has special radios that optimize communications within the building, these should be provided to first responders in a "go bag/go kit" or directly handed to first responders when they arrive on the scene. Another excellent option to determine dead zones for first responders is to invite them to tour the business or conduct a training exercise. Either option is an enormous learning experience that can transform a chronic problem into a lesson learned and provide the proper support needed during an emergency response.

Primary and secondary communication platforms should be considered for all areas of the property. By operating parallel communication systems, the organization encompasses the concepts of redundancy and survivability, of disruption and alienation. During an emergency, there is no assurance that the primary platform will operate for the entire duration of the emergency, nor that it will not be overloaded and fail. If communication conflicts are rationalized and chartered before an incident, then the likelihood of inoperable communication is lessened. The emergency communications platform is based on foresight and demonstrating a concerted effort in eradicating these cancerous dead spots, all to safeguard people.

Communications After

Anticipating the needs and desires of employees, contractors, and/or guests has ramifications well beyond the initial interaction, for social networking and media sites can paint an extremely ugly picture of the businesses response to the emergency. What was communicated, how it was communicated, when it was communicated, and using what means will set the tone, good or bad, as the corporate response to the emergency will be replayed over and over again on news broadcasts and social media sites.

For the business, the experience doesn't stop after the people evacuate the building; many of the employees, contractors, or guests will still have bags or personal belongings on property, such as airplane tickets, passports, personal, and business documents inside the building. Relatives may still be unaccounted for, and business associates or partners may be missing as well. The after-effects of an active shooting, and the attendant communication requirements, do not stop when the shooter is neutralized but should be considered for days, weeks, and months after the emergency.

Internal Self-Assessment Process During and After an Active Shooting

The self-assessment process is designed to consider how each area was processed, understood, questioned, or acted on by the people involved in an active shooting scenario. First, how would you act under any emergency? A process should be developed and followed to reach your conclusions and subsequent actions.

Consider whether the person receiving the communication was alone or in a group. Consider whether a person is in a position of authority, such as an employee, or a person perceived to be in authority, such as a contractor or volunteer.

After you have identified who is involved and how they will interact during an emergency, review your communication platforms and the contents of each message.

Last, the assessment process should list any aspects that may occur over the course of minutes or even seconds depending upon the situation and the information received. Refer to Figure 6–5 for an internal self-assessment that may be used during an active shooter incident.

	Process	Questions	Action
1	Warning alarm sounds, message or first responders notify of an active shooter emergency.	What is happening? Is this real or training? Where is the shooter? How severe is threat? How far away is the shooter? Do I see anyone in authority reacting to the alarm or message? If a verbal message will the message be repeated to see if I heard it correctly?	Listen to see if alarm will continue or just an accident or a drill and if the message will be repeated again. See how other people are responding.
2	Identification of the active shooter emergency, attempt to confirm by sight, hearing or smell.	Is the nature of the emergency and active shooter? What is an active shooter?	Look out the window, down the hall or how other people are reacting. Use all your senses to confirm or negate.
3	Credible and accurate threat, it is real.	Continue to question if the active shooting is real or not? Do I need to evacuation or hide? How far away is the shooter? How far away is safety or am I safe here	Employ all senses while attempting to contain emotions. Think and process options for consideration and protection.
4	Verbal message is broadcast again for a second time.	Do I believe the threat to be so significant that I need to leave my location? Are any details provided? What has changed from the first message or it is the same?	Listen to the message and listen to see if message is repeated or changed. Any difference may prompt an action to avoid harm.
5	Understanding the contents of the warning message	Did I understand everything that was in the message? Did the second message make the emergency any clearer?	Mentally and physically process the message.
6	Personalizing the warning to oneself	What does the message mean to me and those around me? What affect will message have on my disability?	Mentally and physically process the message
7	Follow up message	Is the message the same or is there new information? What are the new details and will these details change my response to the active shooter emergency?	Mentally and physically process the message
8	Self-assessment and risk	How severe? What can I do to protect myself before considering to move?	Mentally and physically process the message
9	In fashion or method confirming the warning and message is true	Is anyone actually evacuating? Are people moving? Are people panicking?	Physically observe people evacuating. Continue to evaluate the threat and options
10	Risk and threat reduction	What are my options to reduce the threat on my own? How do I protect myself where I am or must I move? If I do move will the shooter see me? How far away is a safe location with first responders?	Talk and listen to others. Call for assistance or aid. Collect any specialized equipment and medication needed to evacuate or stay. Mentally prepare.
11	Initiate a protective response	What option will I select? How much time do I have to select? Can I wait until the last moment or should I evacuate now? Again processing all sensory clues, does it change my option?	Fight or flight? Make a choice Evacuate or not to evacuate. Initiate the evacuation looking for assistance and confirmation doing the right thing or continue to stay.
12	Follow others during evacuation or remain in place and hide out	Even though evacuating, alarm may turn off at any time? Will another message be broadcast? How are other people acting?	Physical and mental reinforcement, but still cautious to determine if going in the right direction. Continue using all senses for survival.

FIGURE 6–5 Internal Self-Assessment Process during an Active Shooting.

References

[1] Blair JP, Martaindale MH, Nichols T. Active shooter events from 2000 to 2012. 2014. <http://leb.fbi.gov/2014/january/active-shooter-events-from-2000-to-2012>.

[2] Blair JP, Schweit KW. A Study of active shooter incidents, 2000–2013. Washington, DC: Texas State University and Federal Bureau of Investigation, U.S. Department of Justice; 2014.

[3] Federal Emergency Management Agency, <www.fema.gov/faq-details/When-to-prepare-for-shelter-in-place-1370032119700>.

[4] U.S. Department of Labor, Occupational Safety & Health Administration. <https://www.osha.gov/pls/oshaweb/owadisp.show_document?p_table=STANDARDS&p_id=9726>.

[5] U.S. Department of Justice, Civil Rights Division, Disability Rights Section (2009). "Guide to Disability Rights Law," July 2009.

[6] United States Access Board, ADA Accessibility Guidelines. <www.access-board.gov/guidelines-and-standards/buildings-and-sites/about-the-ada-standards/background/adaag>.

[7] The International Organization for Standards. <www.iso.org/iso/graphical-sympbols.booklet.pdf>.

7 ⠿

Human Resources

Every good security program begins with the human resources department. The ability to screen out potential threats during the hiring process, or the identification of risky behaviors in existing employees, is vital to protecting the organization.

Human Resources

The ability to screen out potential threats during the hiring process, or the identification of risky behaviors in existing employees is vital to protecting the organization. Depending on the organizational structure, human resources may be responsible for conducting the background screening, drug testing, and interviews of potential employees. Moreover, it is often the human resources professional that must deal with disciplinary actions and employee separations. Such high-stress environments may lead to verbal hostility and threats along with acts of violence and retaliation. Furthermore, certain types of employment may expose one to additional risk of violence while at work. Law enforcement officers, security personnel, and medical staff are exposed to additional acts of violence just because of the nature of their profession.

With this in mind, it is logical to declare *that every security program should begin with the human resources department.* The human resources department is the cornerstone in developing policies and standards for prospective employees, staff, and contractors and is a major participant when dealing with separations. How it issues policies and monitors staff is critical to the identification and prevention of active shooter events. The prevention of violence begins by not employing those individuals who have a history of violence. For prospective employees, the organization may choose to perform psychological and honesty testing before an offer of employment to reduce the potential for loss from theft or violence. Such tests may help identify a potential problem with an applicant and often can used to indicate an issue. However, such tests should not be used alone and should only be part of the overall assessment of an applicant's suitability for employment. It is quite a challenge to determine whether someone may perpetrate an act of workplace violence during employment; indeed, there is no foolproof method to predict such destructive actions.

When evaluating a prospective employee, considering his or her entire background—including application, résumé, and pre-employment screening—the organization can get a better look into his or her suitability for employment. Notwithstanding, when it comes to active shooters in the workplace, preventive measures can be inconclusive, as many of these actors have no prior history of violent actions. This complicates the challenge of the human resource professional in being the first line of defense for the organization.

Bad Hire Statistics [1]

- Up to 30% of business failures result from employee theft and dishonesty
- 48% of shrinkage results from employee theft
- Employee dishonesty costs organizations more than $50 billion annually
- More than 60% of résumés, applications, and references contain inaccurate information
- More than 10% of applicants have a criminal history
- The average cost of employee turnover is approximately 150% of the employee's annual salary

---

The human resources department should be the lead for performing background checks and pre-employment screening for prospective employees and contractors. When the employer secures criminal records, it should be very cautious of the sources used to ensure that they are thorough and accurate. If your organization does not have a human resources department, or if it outsources it, it is vital that the company interact and provide guidance to ensure that the employer's needs are addressed uniformly while considering each individual's special needs and conditions.

The use of a national criminal database to determine suitability for employment may not be enough to satisfy this requirement, and any decision to use Internet-based searches should be properly researched beforehand to verify the completeness and accuracy of these searches based on the needs of the organization. Screening should be performed for both prospective employees and contractors. Employers may be liable for the actions of the contractors they hire, so they should exercise caution and require screening actions for contractors similar to what they require for their employees.

The company may also be found negligent if the company retains or promotes employees who have problems or who cease to be fit for employment during the course of their employment. When employers know or should have known about such changes yet fail to take appropriate actions, they could be found negligent in a court of law. Additionally, the organization has a duty to warn those under its care when terminating an employee or contractor who has a propensity to be violent.

It is the human resources professional who reviews and assesses personnel files before disciplinary action, terminations, and/or promotions. He or she becomes the cornerstone for detection of abnormalities, issues, and problematic behavior in the workplace. Such professionals must work closely with the management team to be proactive in their approach to the detection and prevention of workplace violence.

Lester S. Rosen, in his book *The Safe Hiring Manual*, provides a S.A.F.E. system of hiring practices that consists of the following elements:

Set up programs using written policies, procedures, and practices to achieve a safe workplace.
Acclimate and train all staff with hiring responsibilities to use safe hiring practices.
Facilitate and implement the safe hiring program throughout the organization.
Evaluate and audit the program to ensure compliance and understanding.

The system provides for the application stage, the interview process, checking references, and pre-employment screening, along with final analysis of the information.

Internal Threats

The insider threat is often the most difficult threat to protect against, and the human resources department is the first line of defense against such risk. Disgruntled employees, contractors, volunteers, and service providers who currently work with or have formerly worked within the business can use their knowledge of operations and personnel to their advantage to perpetrate acts of violence. They often have intimate details about the site design and layout and security and access procedures, as well as gaps in protection that can be used in an active shooter scenario. In addition, often spouses or significant others have been to the place of business and may also have an understanding of security protocols and layouts.

If the person is still employed by the organization, he or she often has authorized access to the facility and, in some cases, to multiple facilities or sites. It complicates the protection scheme when the enemy has legitimate access to his or her targets.

There are several ways to minimize some risk for acts of violence from internal sources in the workplace. First, as already stated, performing criminal background checks and reference checks may identify any history of violence in potential employees, contractors, and volunteers. The organization should develop policies and procedures to ensure that this process is followed. This includes past residence addresses, previous employer, and work references for all permanent and temporary employees, contractors, and volunteers. In addition, there should be a requirement for all service providers to meet minimum standards of screening and verification/certification from the service provider for any employee that performs work at a facility.

In our many years of performing risk vulnerability and threat assessments for agencies and companies, we have identified several areas that often receive little attention when it comes to violent actors in the workplace. One example is the delivery driver who is allowed into the facility without verification of background or criminal history. Loading docks and bays areas often leave their doors open for convenience, and these areas can lead to many other areas within the facility. Moreover, some companies allow delivery drivers to use their facilities with no supervision or controls to prevent them from meandering throughout the facility. A truck driver intent on shooting would have almost nothing in place to stop him or her if the site perimeter is not properly secured or delivery gates and bay doors are left open—there is little deterrent and no delay in the way of the potential shooter, offering easy access to outsiders.

In this scenario, a few options to assist the overall protection program may be to require all trucking and delivery companies to provide verification of background screening for their drivers and to require all drivers to be easily identifiable and have visible company ID displayed while at your facility. The physical security program could be enhanced by the installation of perimeter fencing and motorized vehicle gates that remain closed and locked when not in use. Additional controls and barriers could be installed to restrict unauthorized movement throughout the facility and segregate the driver waiting area and restroom from the rest of operations. It is always a good idea to limit the number of access points to a facility and to ensure that all access points are properly secured. However, as already stated, the internal threat normally has access or can acquire it through deception, tailgating through an access point, or using brute force.

When it comes to the employee and contractor, whether current or former, it becomes even more difficult to properly prevent access to the site. When an employee is removed from his or her position, it is crucial that all access rights be immediately terminated and all keys, badges, and credentials collected. An unwitting employee may not be aware that another employee was just released from his or her position and may allow him or her to tailgate into the workplace. This is a case in which policies and procedures can help.

For those employees who are being disciplined or put under probation, the manager must work closely with the human resources representative to monitor potential issues with behavior and threatening actions. Such awareness can help intercept a potential threat and mitigate the situation. It is vital that unaddressed issues in the workplace involving those employees receive attention and communication. Such perceived wrongs can have disastrous consequences, especially in the case of an employee who is mentally unstable, financially stressed, having relational problems, or under the influence of drugs.

What day of the week is best to terminate or release employees from the company? Determining the best day of the week for company separations or terminations may be based on such variables as the size of the company, number of employees, type of business, reason for the termination, and employee's history of violence or aggressive behavior. The company wants to be compassionate and sensitive to the employee's feelings, but at the same time the company must look after the safety and security of its employees who interact with the employee before, during, and after the termination. Safety is paramount for all parties involved.

The hours of operation for the business and how many days a week the company is open may also play a part in determining the best day of the week for termination. If a company is open seven days per week and 24 hours per day, then Friday may be the first day of the employee's work week. Thus consideration should be given to the employee's work schedule before selecting a date and time.

Traditionally, late Friday afternoon has been "D-Day" for terminating employees, but this common knowledge also allows for the employee to make plans before a possible termination, such as devising a vengeful plan, bringing weapons to work, and preselecting potential targets who may have contributed to the termination or part of the termination process. A Friday termination will also allow the employ to fume over the weekend, but this doesn't mean that the person will not return on Monday morning at 8:00 a.m. with a firearm. If the employee is escorted out of the building, this should be done in such a way as to avoid embarrassment in front of friends and coworkers who may be watching the entire event.

If the termination takes place late Friday afternoon, then the majority of the business's staff has no idea that the person has been let go and thus may unwittingly allow the person access back into the building or into former departments.

Terminations performed earlier in the month may allow the person additional time to secure unemployment insurance for himself or herself and his or her family and may also give better chances to apply for a new job at another business.

Regardless of the day of the week when the termination occurs, the act of terminating an employee may itself be the catalyst that begins the planning process for revenge. The length of the planning process is up to the person: Some people have returned one or two years later to take out their retribution against the company and select individuals. The first anniversary of an employee's termination should receive special attention, especially if the former employee has not yet secured a new position with another firm.

A basic course of many human resources departments is to train on the termination process itself and the actions of the HR staff. The process, at minimum, should involve not being alone during the exit interview, having all documentation prepared in advance, keeping the exit interview short, keeping the interaction professional, and not apologizing for the termination or making excuses. Yet remember that the person sitting on the other side of the table was a former employee who may have helped the company for years—he or she is still a human being.

Who is usually notified, and what departments should be involved, in the termination process?

The lead behind any termination is the human resources department. However, the termination should not be common knowledge for everyone within this department—or should it be? The human resources department is responsible for all employees as well as for the work environment and openness in sharing both positive and negative issues. Resolving problems, mitigating challenges, and preparing for potential issues that affect employees all take place in the human resources department. Common knowledge may be afforded the human resources staff after the termination—but not before, unless there are extenuating circumstances warranting such an action.

The security department should be notified of all terminations and may need to even be present during the termination process to ensure the safety of the human resources staff, as well as to escort the individual off company property.

If the company has a security department that watches live surveillance feeds and controls access, its members are an important component in the process, for they control access systems, cameras, biometric systems, and parking access systems and can monitor and record all actions or reactions by the terminated employee. The security department can deactivate access cards and other control systems the employee may have been afforded. It is critical that all access cards and keys be recovered at the beginning of the termination process.

The information technology (IT) department will need to deny access to computer systems and networks, thereby preventing the employee from sabotaging or stealing files or computers, forwarding sensitive files, and so forth. In most cases the IT department has already been informed and has denied the employee access to the computer system before the termination.

What is the process for terminating employees? There should be a clearly defined process for terminating employees that is concise, consistent, and identical regardless of the reason of the termination. Even if an employee voluntarily resigns, the process should not vary too greatly from that afforded a terminated employee. The process should take into consideration hypothetical scenarios and potential actions.

Eventually all full-time employees, part-time employees, contractors working on property, and tenants will find out that the employee is no longer with the company. Several important questions should be considered in the termination process:

- When are keys, access cards, uniforms, cell phones, laptop computers, vehicles, and the like collected from the employee?
- What is the process for collecting uniforms and other company property that the employee has at his or her home?

- Should the employee be prohibited from returning to the property for any reason for at least 60 days? How about 90 days?
- How will the employee be allowed—or should the employee be allowed—to clean out his or her work desk to gather his or her private, personal belongings?

Each step within the termination process may set the stage in determining how the employee or, for that matter, the employer will accept the entire termination process. It is important to note three viewpoints in the employee mind during the termination—what is right, what is wrong, and what is fair. When the employee feels as if he or she has been fairly treated in the process, considering the totality of the circumstances, the person is less likely to react rashly. However, remember that some people will feel that nothing about the termination is fair or level.

Another aspect of human resources is in understanding the differences between a contract human resources department, on call as needed, versus in-house staff, especially when it comes to the activities assigned and associated with the human resources department during the recovery portion of an active shooting. This also may include how quickly an outsourced human resources staff can react to the active shooting. One problem is that an outsourced human resources staff may not be able to respond to the scene in a timely manner because of police barricades, the distance they live from the business, and the day of the week when the shooting occurs. Many outsourced human resources companies offer their services via the Internet and may be located in a different city or even a different state.

Another big challenge that organizations face today is the continual expansion of the global marketplace. Companies may find it challenging to properly screen employees, contractors, and service providers in other countries because of privacy laws, lack of information, and even corruption within the government and private sectors. Obstacles such as inconsistent screening practices and determining one's identity can leave the company exposed and vulnerable to violent acts. Furthermore, several potential motivators may lead to shooting incidents. The potential for real or perceived wrongs can lead to a violent act of retribution. Religious, ideological, and cultural differences can also lead to a radical response by the actor(s) and place the organization at risk. Even crimes such as armed robbery can go awry and lead to shootings in the workplace. Although the latter is not characterized as an active shooter, there is little difference between the two crimes, except for possibly the motivation for the criminal act. Being shot at sucks, no matter how you define the shooter and the reasons behind the act.

An active shooter may have no legitimate relationship to the victims or the workplace itself. The outside threat must be considered and can develop quickly and without notice. Sometimes people and businesses are just in the wrong place at the wrong time. This is why planning and preparation are key in developing a protection program: There are not guarantees that you will avoid such violence, so it is always best to be prepared.

Considerations

There are many things that the human resources role must consider before and after an active shooting. Some of these areas are sensitive to discuss, especially for those who have dealt with such tragedies, but they are a critical part of the process. Human resources is often one aspect of a shooting that is overlooked by planners, and yet it is one of the most critical components of an organization's survival.

Active shooting events are some of the most traumatic crimes to experience because of the senselessness of the act and the degree of carnage caused in a short time. The effect of seeing your colleagues dead and dying while fearing for your own life is a terrifying ordeal. The human resources professional will need to determine the best way to handle the fallout from such violence. The business must consider the loss of key employees as a result of the violence and the attrition caused by the resulting trauma.

Staff and Contractors

An organization cannot exist without people, and often this component determines the future and viability of the organization. The organization must prepare for employees' quitting or taking long periods of time off after a shooting. This includes providing professional counseling services and any other mental health–related services that may be required because of the shooting. Arrangements for counselors should be in place before an incident, involving enough professionals to deal with the potential numbers of staff affected. Attrition is another issue that can be an ongoing problem owing to flashbacks and fear of the incident, and the human resources department must be prepared to have a strategy in place to keep valuable staff members from leaving the organization.

In addition, the business may need to ask employees to work from their homes or in an alternate location, which can lower productivity and cause communication issues. Even if employees can and do return to work, there could be an emotional shift affecting their performance, especially in the departments that experienced loss or injury during the incident. The ability for the company to enforce basic rules such as tardiness or unauthorized sick leave after a shooting incident may be challenging for human resources and should be considered as part of the planning process.

Simple items such as reassigning offices, telephone extensions, and parking spaces, as well as updates to the company directory, should all receive consideration to minimize the effects on the remaining staff. Furthermore, because recovery is paramount to the organization's survival, the timing for replacing injured or killed staff members, as well as how these positions are advertised, can all have affect the employee population. This issue includes outsourcing or temporary employee placements after a shooting incident, as well as how to reintegrate injured staff into the organization. Another decision that will need to be made is determining whether to keep employees on company payroll rather than having them make workman's compensation claims. Many people are on tight budgets these days, and even a week's delay in payroll can have negative connotations for the organization. Suppliers will also be nervous about the accounts payable and may require additional communication considerations to ensure timely payment.

Another aspect is dealing with the families of those killed or wounded. Attending funerals and dealing with grieving and angry family members and their posttraumatic stress are part of the role the human resources department must fulfill on behalf of the organization. The grieving process is a major aspect of active shooter incident planning, and plans should involve the stages of grieving, including whether to allow faith-based organizations to be involved, and helping families and employees deal with the press.

Both internal and external communications play a major part in the human resources role after an active shooter incident. Despite having someone in charge of corporate communications, the human resources department and the legal department are still actively involved in what is disseminated to outside organizations and the press—and how. It is important to remember that whenever an active shooter incident occurs, the area will be considered a crime scene, and any supporting information about the shooter or their actions should be discussed with the presiding law enforcement agency and your legal department before any discussions with the press. This is essential if the shooter(s) have not been killed or arrested during the incident, remaining still at large as the investigation process begins. All information should be considered evidence and protected as such until you are authorized to discuss it.

Additional concerns such as unauthorized interviews or books and articles can be damaging to the company and the families of the injured or deceased and could lead to additional legal challenges. It is important to develop communication procedures and policy that refer to each employee's responsibilities and limitations as regard communications during and after a crisis.

The human resources department should be prepared to discuss several other issues:

- Human resources staff levels during and after the incident
- Requests for additional security staff and protective measures
- Self-defense weapons, with employees asking to bring guns to work
- Requests for additional input from employees on company matters
- Whether people can leave items left at the crime scene (teddy bears, flowers, etc.) and, if so, for how long
- Providing a company representative at the hospital for recovering staff
- Timing for allowing employees back to the site

There are many facets for the human resources professional to think about regarding the active shooter threat. One of the best defenses in the prevention of an active shooter is to ensure that every employee feels part of the team, treated in a fair and just manner. Although there is no perfect defense against active shooters, any proactive measure that helps reduce the risk of these acts' occurring should be implemented. The organization should develop standards and guidelines to which all employee and contractors are required to adhere.

Standards of Behavior

When it comes to developing a workplace violence program, it is critical that all employee or contractor actions be within acceptable standards of behavior to the organization. The study of aggression is complicated but seems to best fall into two different categories of behavioral theory, the *rational choice theory* and the *frustration–aggressive hypothesis* [2]. In the rational choice theory, aggression and violence are based on the perception or realization of a reward or specific desired outcome as compared to total costs of achieving such goals. Even though the essence of this theory is based on risk versus reward, it doesn't necessarily mean that an act of violence will include the identification and calculation of risk before initiating it. Rather, the choice involving aggression and violence may only consist of the aspect involving the reward without any consideration of the risk involved. This is especially true in cases involving mental illness or crimes of passion. The frustration–aggression theory, however, suggests that violence and aggression are responses to certain provocations, initiating an expressive or reactive response. This theory asserts that people tend to respond in an aggressive or violent manner when provoked by stress, failure, pain, or suffering. No matter to which theory you subscribe, it is evident that aggressive acts and violence are part of every organization and must be properly addressed.

Because every organization is different, such standards should be customized to meet the needs required to best protect the interests of the mission. For example, a police officer may be exposed to verbal abuse often throughout his or her career, and accordingly acceptable workplace actions might provide some accommodations for their position. A police officer is unlike a banker, who is seldom exposed to injurious verbal abuse while at work. The use of damaging language and threats in the bank may cause a bank employee serious emotional distress and negatively affect their ability to work. In this dichotomy, it is easy to see why organizations must develop their workplace violence policy around standards of behavior.

In addition, different cultural backgrounds and acceptable behaviors may vary based on the geographic location of the business. The globalization of the workforce exposes the workforce to varying levels of acceptable behavior in the workplace. Behaviors that are acceptable in one country may vary quite substantially from acceptable practices in another. Acceptable traditions and cultural perceptions can include grievous offenses such as rape, sexual harassment, and physical abuse. Special attention should be paid in developing countries and other countries having a history of human rights violations, for these conditions are breeding grounds for acts of violence.

Standards of behavior are the foundation of the program and set the parameters for the entire organization. Standards are the rules that all employees and contractors are expected to follow to help ensure that the work environment operates safely and efficiently. The organization must treat those entrusted to its care fairly and consistently.

One of the great rules of life is to always treat others the same way you want to be treated. If we all lived our lives according to the great rules of life, there would be no need to develop policy or standards to govern our conduct. Unfortunately, some individuals choose to perpetrate acts of evil and disregard the rights of others. Frankly, we all are susceptible to abusing power—taking advantage of people and/or belittling others to promote our own interests, as it has been since the dawn of time. This is why setting fair and consistent rules and standards of behavior are critical to the success of the company mission.

Human nature is often extremely challenging to predict, changing with time and location. In some cases, these changes involve a disease or illness; for others, it can be an alteration of circumstances such as a lost job, failed relationship, or other effects on one's safety and security.

People change. If you think about who you were ten years ago and, if old enough, thirty years ago, you should note definite change in your personal growth as a human. These changes are natural and involve a myriad of situational experiences, influences, and environmental conditions that either improve you as a human or make you worse—or, in some cases, both. Your colleagues also experience many of these changes, and when the changes are for the worse, many choose to ignore the signs and reflect on the good. This is where the development of acceptable and prohibited behaviors is crucial to protect the organization and those under their care. Companies need to prepare for such changes and help their staff both identify and report negative behaviors when they could affect the workplace environment. Generational gaps, though often positive, can also result in conflicts that can lead to deeply rooted resentment.

The decision to engage in an act of violence may involve rapid decisions involving intense emotions, as well as drugs or alcohol. This is one reason why organizations should implement policy and procedures that reduce the company's exposure to such elements. Virtually every company policy should help reduce the effects of aggression or violence and promote the organizational mission to provide structure. When implemented properly, it can provide a culture of fairness and a team environment. The ideology of a fair and balanced culture may also help to reduce workplace stressors and provide awareness about acceptable behaviors that all employees must adhere to.

Another aspect to consider is what your weapons policy is for the company. The ability to access a gun or other deadly weapon during an argument or disagreement can result in deadly violence. The organization must determine what is acceptable as far as weapons, noting that almost every state and country has different regulations and requirements for the possession and transportation of firearms. This can be complicated depending on whether the employee, contractor, or visitor has been issued a concealed carry permit providing him or her with the ability to carry a concealed firearm in their specific state or any state that has a reciprocal agreement with the issuing authority. In some states, laws provide protection for employees to store loaded firearms in their vehicles no matter what company policy dictates. It becomes even more convoluted when a visitor or contractor has a concealed weapon in his or her possession. Off-duty police officers often moonlight as security officers for private companies, and the weapons policy should also document the requirements for such personnel while on company premises and acting under the direction of the company.

A few policies and procedures that should be considered to help reduce acts of aggression and violence in the workplace are as follow:

- Workplace harassment and violence policy (including active shooter)
- Weapons policy
- Physical security policy and procedures
- Travel policy and procedures
- Emergency action/crisis management policy and procedures
- Pre-employment and selection policy
- Acceptable conduct policy
- Equity and diversity policy

- Fraud and corruption policy
- Mental health policy
- Salary, benefits, and leave policy
- Reward and recognition policy
- Grievance procedures
- Performance development, appraisal, and promotion procedures
- Reward and recognition policy

This list is not a comprehensive catalog of all of the policies and procedures an organization should implement to protect its assets, but it is a good starting point for those companies that are behind in developing a solid strategy for preventing and mitigating violence in the workplace.

It is important to consider the downside of not developing comprehensive human resource programs and policies. Every employer has the responsibility to exercise due diligence for those under their direction and care. If the organization fails in its duty of care and doesn't meet minimum industry standards, it can—and usually will—be sued in a court of law if a preventable incident occurs. This accusation is often one of "negligent hiring" and asserts that the company should have known or been able to determine that a prospective employee or contractor was a foreseeable risk. These lawsuits can expose the organization to expensive litigation and very costly verdicts. "Let the master answer," or the doctrine of *respondeat superior*, is a legal concept that means that employers may be responsible for an employee's actions taken under the direction of the employer or in the scope of their duties. Even when the employee is acting out of self-interest, the company may be responsible for the employee's actions under the *respondeat superior* theorem, if there has not been an established program in place to mitigate the potential risks for anything that could have been foreseeable by proper hiring practices, screening, and any corresponding policies and procedures.

Discrimination

Discriminatory behaviors are unacceptable in the workplace and can destroy the organization that allows them to exist and fester. Many laws and statutes prohibit such behaviors and even provide legal recourse for those who experience such unfair treatment, but there still are individuals and companies who engage in discriminatory practices. Discriminatory business practices may lead to numerous types of retaliatory and violence- even acts of sabotage, or worse, murder in the workplace.

The human resources department is the overseer of fair and balanced practices in the work environment and should take the lead in making sure such practices are eliminated from the organization. Notwithstanding, companies in the United States cannot legally discriminate based on religion, race, color, national origin, medical condition, age, sex, or marital status. Complying with discrimination laws is a must for all companies. All jobs and hires should be based on performance and potential, not on items not relevant to the position or career. Unfair treatment and prejudice in the past have caused internal turmoil, riots, and led to the civil rights movement in the United States.

Nowadays, prejudice and discriminatory practices are often well hidden from the public eye, but still exist in individuals and organizations. Often claims of discriminatory hiring practices begins at the selection process for applicants and may come by selectively screening out certain groups of people who are fully qualified to be employed in that role. Even a claim of discriminatory practices can create problems for the employer, so it is important that any sign of discrimination be resolved and corrected as quickly as possible to prevent future issues.

Often it is out of financial need that an applicant decides to apply for a job. Being turned down or ignored can incense a person, especially when the applicant or employee feels he or she is being treated in a discriminatory manner, enough to lash out at the individuals whom he or she feels are perpetrating the prejudice. And the resulting violence can end in hail of bullets.

One law that has direct relevance to active shooter incidents in the United States is the American with Disabilities Act (ADA). This act has broad implications for organizations that fall under its regulations. This is especially important in active shooter planning, because if your organization falls under the requirements of the ADA, you will need to make special provisions for those employees, contractors, or guests for the many covered disabilities. This includes such considerations as communications for the disabled, access and egress to and from the facility, along with any needs for assigned personnel to assist with the disabled in the event of a crisis.

Workers' Rights

Historically, the rights of workers can be a stimulus for initiating acts of violence in the workplace. Collective bargaining rights can be an explosive topic for many organizations and, based on historical evidence, may lead to acts of violence perpetrated by both sides. Many among us think that long gone are the days of the Molly Maguires and the Pinkertons [3], but a remnant of their struggles continues today. This false belief that workers, collective bargaining personnel, and employers no longer use intimidation and violence to impose their will on the other party is misleading. Such incidents still occur and can result in deadly violence when they escalate past the boiling point.

No matter what your personal beliefs are when it comes to the rights of the employer versus the rights of the workers, the potential for highly charged emotions and physical violence is high, especially if workers strike. The human resources professional must be prepared to deal with managing conflict and the corresponding escalating emotions, intimidation, and verbal or physical threats. Left unchecked, the problems only get bigger until there is an outlash of violence between the parties.

There are several areas that can lead to escalating violence when it comes to workers' rights, often beginning at the bargaining table and/or picketing lines. Labor strikes are often not an individual effort but rather a concerted effort to get the other side to concede to demands. This collective approach can increase the level of aggression and violence, for some people are emboldened in a group setting. Picket lines are a unique venue, especially when some union members choose to side with the employer and cross the picket line. In addition, replacement workers who cross picket lines may have to endure verbal and physical abuse initiated by the strikers. Often the violence results in acts of sabotage and vandalism to their vehicles and homes. The violence may also be directed at family members of the company's management or its workers. Moreover, if violence erupts at the picket line, it can endanger any member of the general public who happens to be in the vicinity. Conversely, the strikers can also be in danger of violence directed at them by the security force, replacement workers, or the various law enforcement agencies sent to keep order during a strike.

Strikes may offer the opportunity for legitimate directed violence at individuals or the organization, as many U.S. laws are ineffective at restraining and preventing labor-related violence during the strike process and in fact may support such activities [4]. If true, this means that violence on the picket line is expected and is viewed by the courts differently from other forms of violence in the workplace. This legal gray area along with the emotionally charged actors can have the potential to escalate into a shooting incident. No matter how you spin it, the resulting atmosphere during a strike along with any perceived injustices may lead to acts of violence involving a shooting.

Does this mean that every strike or time workers come to the bargaining table that there will be violence? Absolutely not; in fact, most of the time there are no problems during a strike that result in an outbreak of violence. However, because it is always a possibility, human resources must work closely in a collaborative effort to stem any issues that could lead to violence. As the organization develops its program for shooting violence in the workplace, these issues should be discussed and addressed in the plan. Strike- and labor-related disputes are one aspect to consider, but how does the human resources professional mitigate the risk of hiring potentially violence workers in the first place? It all begins with the employment application and the capability to screen out higher-risk employees. This is where pre-employment screening can be worth its weight in gold.

Pre-employment Screening

Pre-employment screening is different from a background investigation. A background investigation is focused on one individual to determine his or her suitability for a particular position, whereas pre-employment screening is a set of procedures and checks to ensure fairness and thoroughness for every applicant during the hiring assessment process. Moreover, pre-employment screening is a generalized and less in-depth study of the applicant versus the more intense background investigation. Simply put, pre-employment screening saves time and money.

Several types of screening can be used depending on the position and its associated responsibilities:

- Work history/past employment references
- Criminal history
- Education and credential verification
- Motor vehicle reports
- Credit history, bankruptcies, and judgments and/or liens
- Worker's compensation record and civil lawsuits

Every organization is different when it comes to pre-employment screening. Some employers perform the checks internally; others may outsource the process. The decision may depend on whether the organization has the experience to perform a thorough check or, in some cases, enough personnel to accomplish the task. These days, it is common for a company to use a hybrid model of performing some checks in-house and hiring outside firms for those services that may require specialty skills and abilities.

Additionally, there may be legal advantages to outsourcing some of these services. A good example of this is when you are screening using a consumer report. A consumer report provides data on the applicant's creditworthiness, credit capacity, and credit standing, along with his or her character and other personal characteristics, which may be used to assess personal suitability.

The Fair Credit Reporting Act (FCRA) is designed to protect the applicant ("consumer") when a consumer report is used by the organization and may expose the organization to legal issues if an internal employee performs the screening process incorrectly. Although the FCRA is intended to provide guidance to third-party vendors, a company may be required to comply with the FCRA rules because of company actions and how they deal with third-party vendors. By outsourcing consumer report checks, an employer may mitigate some exposure to potential compliance issues and legal actions, but often cannot transfer the responsibility to a third-party in its entirety.

Procedures and Process

The human resources department is the starting point for building security awareness throughout the organization. By close partnerships with the security and legal departments, human resource professionals can collaborate in building an effective security awareness at the individual level as well as the organizational level. Part of the security orientation process should include information pertaining to each employee's responsibility and obligations in helping make the workplace safer and more secure.

Part of this process should include an overview of acceptable and unacceptable workplace behaviors as well as an overview of potential indicators of workplace violence and the reporting process. It is strongly advisable that organizations also provide information regarding violence in the form of active shooters and educate the employee or contractor about the options he or she should consider if this threat ever is realized. As stated before, the organization has a duty to provide a safe environment for its employees, contractors, and guests, and part of this duty involves providing information that could help to save their lives.

Knowing the procedures and muster (gathering) points for violent incidents could be the difference that means survival. For example, if the muster point for a building fire is in the employee parking lot, it is most assuredly not the best choice if the threat is an active shooter or bomb threat. Sending employees into the zone of fire or a place where secondary explosives may be detonated will cause more carnage, fatalities, and injuries. Through proper planning and awareness, employee procedures can, and do, help save lives and prevent injury.

One of the greatest assets a person can have during a violent encounter is the ability to think clearly despite of the stress and chaos. The capacity to think and react quickly may be the best defense against an armed attacker; in some cases, it may be the only defense.

Reporting Process

It is important to think about the reporting process when it comes to workplace violence and active shooters. Many employees spend the better part of their lives committed to their work, and often this involves being at your place of work. Spending time with others often results in the building of professional and personal relationships, and often we get to know coworkers very well. Severe changes in a person's demeanor, attitude, or appearance can indicate stress or other issue in their life. Illegal drug use, alcohol abuse, family issues, financial problems, relationship failures, and the like can mount up and contribute to such changes. In addition, bullying, sexual harassment, verbal, and physical abuse, among many other factors, can add up to bring a person to the breaking point.

So when should a colleague get involved and report unusual changes within a coworker— and how does he or she report them? Many of us do not want to get involved in other people's business, especially if it involves personal issues that occur outside of the workplace. Moreover, many employees will not report any issues at work unless they can do so anonymously. This is especially true if they work closely together with the subject of their complaint and are from the same community. The importance of reporting along with the information sharing process is a vital part of mitigating the risk of an active shooter.

The reporting process will take some forethought for design and implementation. Which department will be assigned to handle the reporting? Can they keep the information confidential and not expose their sources? Do they have the ability to determine whether a report is valid or whether the reporting employee has a vendetta against the person he or she is reporting? The list of questions could go on, but for purposes of relating this to an active shooter incident, we will look at a few aspects of the reporting process.

First, the organization should consider having a toll-free anonymous hotline that all employees and contractors can use to report issues or request assistance. Although some reports will be false, this provides a safe manner of reporting unusual activity and types of crime affecting the company. Providing awareness training for the hotline is critical, and the organization should ensure that all employees and contractors are aware of the reporting process and the number to call. A great way to do this is through the use of small business card–style hotline cards that explain the process and provide the number to call.

In additional to the awareness training and establishment of a hotline, all company management should receive a form for use in reporting suspicious activity and/or potentially harmful activity to senior leadership. Often the human resources department is the conduit to make this happen. As often is the case, management can often bear the brunt of directed violence in the workplace for its role as disciplinarian and goal setter. It also can be great at detecting when something doesn't feel right at the individual employee level. Providing the network for management to report incidents and suspicious behaviors within staff, other employees, or suppliers can be vital to stemming the potential for acts of violence in the workplace.

After reports are received, verification of the facts and people involved must begin. The organization must determine how best to handle the allegations and, if valid, determine their course of action. Again, process and procedures are needed to make sure that no information or reports slip through the cracks; every allegation must be taken seriously until proven otherwise.

If the investigation identifies the need to move forward with action, then consider the following:

- If it involves a crime, contact law enforcement immediately.
- Personal issues may require counseling or medical assistance.
- Violent behaviors may require assistance from security or law enforcement.
- Verbal abuse and bullying should not be ignored.
- Develop organizational disciplinary procedures and violence escalation charts.
- Repeat offenders may require special attention.

It is important to remember that even if the perpetrators are first-time offenders, the issue must be taken seriously. Often excuses are offered for individuals with no known prior history of violence; however, people change, and ignoring a problem can lead to bigger issues down the road. Each case should be reviewed and investigated using a documented process to eliminate any issues involving prejudice or personal opinions. Many organizations are implementing a zero-tolerance policy when it comes to acts of violence in the workplace, and such a policy requires a solid awareness program to make sure that every employee, contractor, and guest is fully aware of the rules and corresponding disciplinary actions.

Zero Tolerance

The organization is responsible for policing its own ranks for issues involving workplace violence. Many companies have stated through comprehensive policies that no form of harassment or intimidation is acceptable while at work or after hours when related to work relationships. Zero tolerance has quickly become the standard for many workplace violence programs for many organizations for many reasons. First, it sets the bar for acceptable workplace interactions and limits the gray area for those individuals who choose to engage in such negative behaviors. By not allowing initiation of violent actions, it also protects the organization's most critical asset—its people—from potentially damaging behaviors.

Often, abusive and demeaning people test the limits when it comes to negative behaviors in the workplace, and zero-tolerance is designed to stop such destructive influences from psychologically damaging or physically damaging those exposed to these behaviors. When implemented effectively, such a policy has the ability to prevent verbal abuse and intimidation from becoming a physically violent episode. Moreover, it helps maintain a safe work environment where staff and contractors can be productive.

The trouble with organizations that choose not implement a zero-tolerance policy is the perception of injustice and favoritism. Fairness, or the perception of equality in the workplace, is paramount to developing a great organizational culture. Conversely, allowing the poison of abuse and violence to corrupt the company's culture can lead to the destruction of the entire management structure and possibly even lead to retributory acts of serious physical violence.

Another aspect, and one difficult for most organizations to understand and identify, is the difference between nonphysical aggression and physical violence. Acts of physical violence in the workplace are low when compared to acts of nonphysical aggression. Notwithstanding, many companies focus on physical acts of aggression rather than the more common harassments such as sexual advances, verbal abuse, and bullying. Such psychological aggressors can be and often are just as damaging to the organization and the overall mission. Threatening, harassing, and humiliating behaviors can seriously damage the victims of such violence and virtually undermine the entire organization's operations.

The organization's policy should address all forms of harassment and violent behavior, including those initiated by use of drugs or alcohol. The policy should be easy to understand and should be communicated at all levels and to every employee, contractor, and supplier. This is often accomplished during the orientation process and through development and implementation of awareness programs. Those businesses that have customers who visit the premises should also develop and post an explanation of the policy, explaining that any violations may result in the removal of the perpetrator from the premise and could involve legal or criminal action.

As important as involvement by the human resources department can be, it is equally important to properly prepare the organization for an active shooter incident, including through protective measures and procedures, as well as by performing risk assessments and ongoing surveys. Preparedness begins with the human resources department, but it doesn't end there.

References

[1] Rosen LS. The safe hiring manual: the complete guide to keeping criminals, imposters and terrorists out of the workplace. Tempe, AZ: Facts on Demand Press; 2004.

[2] Kelloway EK, Barling J, Hurrell JJ. Handbook of workplace violence. Thousand Oaks, CA: Sage Publications, Inc; 2006.

[3] <http://explorepahistory.com/hmarker.php?markerId=1-A-3B9>.

[4] Francis Crossing the line: violence on the picket line Handbook of workplace violence. Thousand Oaks, CA: Sage Publications, Inc; 2006. pp. 231–260.

Preparedness

Preparing for an incident that involves an active shooter is paramount to the prevention, detection, response, and recovery functions. Preparedness is mitigation to reduce or eliminate the active shooter threat. It involves making a case for risk management to reduce both the exposure and effects of an active shooter may have on the organization and its people, which involves the psychological, emotional, and physical aspects of an attack. When it comes to preparedness, it takes a solid strategy from the organizational level, department level, and the personal level. Being prepared and taking the proper actions begins with a full understanding of the issues. It is important to remember the areas of prevention, protection, mitigation, response, and recovery, as shown in Figure 8–1, while developing a program and preparing for worst-case scenarios.

The ability to be prepared for an active shooter attack begins with proactive thinking. This involves myriad aspects, from being aware of your surroundings to reporting suspicious activity. In addition to forethought about the active shooter, preparedness involves several characteristics that should be part of the process.

Prevention: Whenever possible, including as you develop your program, the best option is always to prevent an active shooter. Prevention involves proactive programs that should evolve with the organization, such as workplace violence policy, awareness programs, community watch programs, early detection, and any other measure providing protection before an attack. This can also include physical security detection systems and barriers.

Protection: An active shooter threat can be difficult to protect against, especially if the shooter originates from within the organization. However, protective measures that can be deployed to mitigate the risk and reduce the effects of such a tragic event. Such measures include intrusion detection and surveillance systems, protective barriers, electronic access controls, armed security officers, and policies and procedures, among other things designed to protect organization assets. The protection of employees begins by empowering each individual to take action to decide whether to should run, hide, or fight the attacker(s). The simple, yet effective process of deciding whether to run, hide, or fight is easy to remember and offers the employee a fundamental methodology when under the extreme stress of shots' being fired at, or in close proximity to, him or her.

Mitigation: Mitigation begins after prevention and protection have been compromised. These are features that are designed to minimize loss and lessen the effects of an attack. This includes procedures involved in sheltering in place and lockdowns, evacuation, and staging, as well as any other feature that will help reduce the effects of an attack.

Response: The ability to respond quickly and neutralize the attack is a crucial step in every successful active shooter program. Response includes preparing and supporting law enforcement and in getting to the fight and in helping first responders in providing medical aide to the

FIGURE 8–1 The Five Core Areas of Active Shooter Program Development. *Source: DHS.*

wounded and dying. Providing a "go bag" that includes keys or badges, maps, door stops, and other special equipment to help police overcome existing security measures is another example of the response function, including supporting the medical response by having trauma medical kits with tourniquets, airway tubing, blood clotting bandages and other emergency medical items placed strategically around the site. Training is another key aspect of preparing for the response and should help employees to practice their actions while under simulated conditions. Training also provides each person with the ability to plan on where they might hide or take cover, potential evacuation routes, and the potential makeshift tools or items that can be used for fending off or stopping an attacker.

Recovery: Organizations often overlook the recovery function when it comes to active shootings. The ability to recover quickly from an active shooter may reduce the psychological effects on employees and the community. Getting the business back to normal conditions is paramount to the organization's survival after such violence.

Understanding one's own organization and personnel is key when preparing for acts of violence and other risks to the organization. Having a good understanding of the organizational mission, employees, products and services, suppliers, and contractors, the organization may be able to better identify critical operations, as well as potential vulnerabilities and gaps that might otherwise go unnoticed.

Preparedness is more than a state of mind when it comes to the organizational and department levels; procedures must be developed to protect groups of people. At the individual level, mental preparation is extremely important: Your life is literally in your own hands. A wrong decision can lead to serious injury or death, whereas a quick and appropriate decision may save your life and the lives of those around you.

Roles and Responsibilities

Each employee, regardless of position or status, should have a specific role and clear responsibilities during any crisis. Employees should know what is expected of them in each phase of an incident. They must know what critical support services they may be called on to provide under the most difficult of circumstances.

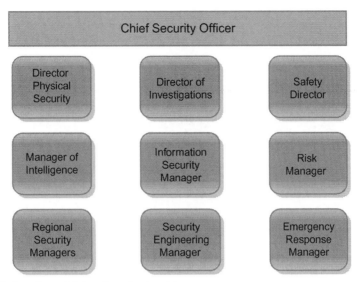

FIGURE 8–2 Sample Security and Safety Organizational Structure.

Preparedness should consider the roles and responsibilities in how best to communicate and track employees, guests, ADA special needs individuals, volunteers, contractors, and tenants. The planning should identify actions, procedures, and resources required to carry out assigned roles and responsibilities. When appropriate, such actions may require the prepositioning of resources and equipment to assist those responsible for this process.

Each department should be considered by itself first, then from the organizational perspective. This ensures that some redundancy occurs between the departmental and company levels. When it comes to security preparedness, several positions are necessary for planning security measures. The chief security officer (CSO), the highest-ranking company official for matters of protection, typically has the overall responsibility for securing and protecting organizational assets. The CSO will usually delegate specific responsibilities, depending on the structure of the organization, such as a manager of investigations or physical security director, to manage the day-to-day business operations. Figure 8–2 provides an illustration of several potential subordinate positions that may report to the CSO.

The security department is often underfunded, viewed as a cost rather than a profit center within many organizations—that is, until something bad happens, when it seems that everyone wants to hide behind security professionals. Part of this issue lies within the security industry, for some security leaders do not fully understand the business side of their operations and thus do not receive the funding or respect of senior company officials.

Usually the task and responsibilities of protecting the organization against such threats as the active shooter falls to the physical security director (PSD). The PSD is the main point of contact and interface when it comes to emergency notifications and protection measures at a site. The PSD is often in daily contact with the CSO, keeping him or her apprised of threat and security conditions throughout the company. Both the CSO and the PSD keep in communication with human resources department, along with the various business unit managers, to better understand the threat picture as it relates to employees, contractors, and operations.

The PSD is also responsible to implement physical security protective measures, also known as preventive measures, to keep organizational assets from harm or compromise. They are the professionals who often plan, design, and develop the equipment, personnel, and procedures used to deter, prevent, detect, and mitigate threats. They are a critical part of an active shooter prevention program.

Preventive Measures

Preventive measures are designed with one goal in mind: to protect. They comprise polices and procedures, facility design and layout, equipment and technology, along with the people who are responsible for the program. Preventive measures include anticipating the effects of the active shooter incident on employees from the perspective of both physical and emotional response.

It requires development of a strategy from the business, functional department, and employee perspectives. Site entry points and access controls and physical and psychological deterrents, along with other protective measures, such as site monitoring, on-site staffing, law enforcement involvement, notification methods, and response times, are all part of preventive measures [1].

Physical Measures	Administrative Measures
• Barriers and locks	• Security policies and procedures
• Electronic access controls	• Security awareness programs
• Intrusion detection systems	• Employee and contractor screening
• Surveillance cameras	• Business continuity and contingency plans
• Protective lighting	• Emergency action plans
• Blast mitigation	• Drills and exercises

The prevention of violence begins during the planning and design phases of a facility or site. By taking a proactive stance, the company can mitigate various risks to the company. Crime prevention through environmental design (CPTED) [2] is a design-based risk mitigation solution considered by most security professionals to be a proactive security measure designed to prevent crime. CPTED based on three major concepts: natural surveillance, territorial reinforcement, and natural access control.

- *Natural surveillance* is directed primarily at keeping potential adversaries easily observable. Natural surveillance uses features that maximize the visibility of people and any approach to project, parking areas, and building entrances, as well as adequate protective lighting schemes.

- *Territorial reinforcement* can create or extend a sphere of influence. Authorized users develop a sense of territorial control, while potential offenders perceive this control and are discouraged. Promoted by features that define property lines and distinguish private spaces from public spaces using landscape plantings, roadway designs, gates and fenced boundary perimeter protection.
- *Natural access control* is directed primarily at decreasing crime opportunity by limiting access to critical assets and creating a perception of risk to potential adversaries. This includes designing streets, sidewalks, building entrances and gateways to clearly indicate public routes and discouraging access to private or restricted areas.

CPTED is often designed into new construction and renovation projects nowadays, but many existing buildings do not have these features incorporated into their design. In addition to CPTED principles, every organization should evaluate facilities and operations using five primary functions for security effectiveness: deterrence, detection with assessment, delay, response, and integration.

Protective measures are often best designed using a layered approach. The system should be organized in layers and contain supporting elements connected together to prevent gaps in protection or system performance. This is known as a layered protection strategy, or simply as protection in depth. In addition to developing layers of protection, the system should be balanced to prevent weaker areas from being easily compromised. For example, you should not implement all your security features at the front of the building, leaving the back portion of the facility exposed.

No matter how you approach the protective strategy, it is important that all components of protective elements be integrated into one comprehensive system having procedural security measures, physical protective measures, and effective communications. There is no silver bullet when it comes to protecting the organization against a violent person wielding a gun, but some strategies may minimize exposure to such threats. The following are some general options to consider when developing the site's physical security countermeasures:

- Limit access to authorized personnel at facilities, and harden entry points.
- Use an intrusion detection system around the site perimeter, entry control points, and critical areas, taking a layered approach.
- Install an integrated video surveillance system having automated assessment capabilities around the site perimeter, at entry control points, and in critical areas of the facility.
- Access to sensitive or high-risk areas should be managed using access controls and a video surveillance system to monitor all access points.
- Panic buttons should be installed in security officer buildings, human resources, and reception and delivery areas, and remote panic devices should be carried by security officers during patrols for speedy communication in high-risk emergency situations.
- Increase illumination levels for low-light areas, installing protective lighting where necessary.
- Develop comprehensive policies and procedures to deter, detect, assess, delay, and respond to all known and potential threats.

- Conduct frequent security awareness training programs for staff, contractors, and guests.
- Ensure that comprehensive, integrated and redundant means of communications exist.
- Develop written procedures restricting or prohibiting public or unauthorized access.
- Develop a site emergency response and recovery plan.

The measures will not be as effective until they are integrated into the organization, for integration of different protective measures, personnel, and technologies is a crucial part of developing and managing an effective protection program. Integration includes all emergency communication equipment and systems, critical communication redundancies, and the convergence of physical security and information technology systems.

Physical Security Policy and Procedures

Security technology has grown considerably in recent years, but proper security is more than just technology. Procedures and training of security staff may be more critical to protect people and assets. Operational security measures are typically the first line of defense for the business or operator. They are the least expensive, typically are the easiest and quickest to implement, are the least intrusive, and often provide the highest return on investment. Examples of operational security procedures are adopting security plans, increasing patrols, and conducting periodic security awareness training for project staff, contractors, visitors, and the general public.

Physical security enhancements should support operational security processes whenever possible. Often there is a tendency to overprotect when implementing physical security devices, but personnel and operational efficiency must be considered when developing layers of security at the site. Developing a robust security system with multiple layers of barriers and access points can unduly burden employees. For example, multiple barriers and secured access points could negatively affect operational efficiency at the site for the employee who must traverse these barriers many times each day.

When it comes to security and workplace violence, proper development and implementation of policies and procedures is vital to keeping everyone safe. Too often, organizations spend millions of dollars on the latest technology and equipment and never design effective protocols and procedures to use its capabilities. The human side of protective technology is often the most critical component of the overall security program. Effective physical security begins when people, equipment, and procedures can be properly integrated, measured, and tested.

True integration begins during the planning phase and involves a solid understanding of what the program should accomplish and protect. Policies and procedures drive the technology to realize the potential of the equipment and the corresponding limitations. If we assume that every protective technology can be defeated, then the only remaining variable is the human element. As we know, humans make mistakes and often do in matters of security; this is where technology can assist.

As already stated, policies are legal documents to whose stipulations every employee should adhere. They are designed for complete compliance by all employees and contractors and give little room for deviation. Security policies are especially important: One violation can endanger the entire organization. Because policies provide the strategic goals of the organization, they need to be considered when planning and designing a protective system.

Moreover, the daily procedural activities to manage the protective system should provide the guidelines for the people who must implement them. Every employee and contractor should be aware of his or her responsibility in following security policies and procedures. One door held open out of kindness that allows an adversary to enter the building unhindered can endanger everyone.

Preparedness for the organization involves every employee at every level. One gap or vulnerability, when overlooked, can compromise an entire system that may have taken years to develop.

Technology and Equipment

Technology without a good program to manage it is a waste of time, money, and other resources. The human aspect of any system is often the most critical component when it comes to technology. Purchasing the latest and greatest in security technologies can offer streamlined efficiencies and advanced capabilities, but technology still needs managing. Often such systems are complex and require substantial training to fully use their features and capabilities. A physical protection system always begins and ends with the people who manage it.

A properly developed protection system will integrate various subcomponents into one comprehensive system. These subsystems are normally what most people see as security measures:

- Protective lighting
- Perimeter fencing and gates
- Barriers and locking devices
- Intrusion detection and early warning systems
- Electronic access controls
- Video surveillance systems

Protective lighting. Protective lighting is designed to expose illicit activities during low-light conditions or to enable surveillance capabilities in an area. Another critical aspect of protective lighting is to create a psychological deterrent for potential adversaries. Lighting is a critical part of any protection scheme and should be assessed to determine that minimum lighting standards are being met. Lighting is a critical part of surveillance during night conditions and must be considered as part of the overall protection system. If an active shooter incident occurs at night, special considerations should be analyzed for law enforcement control of the protective lighting system—they may need to turn the lights off to capitalize on the element of surprise and to make use of night-vision technologies to give them an advantage over the shooter.

Perimeter fencing and gates: Securing the site perimeter using fencing and gates will keep foot traffic at the site to a minimum. Chain-link fencing offers little delay, for a motivated aggressor can circumvent it easily. However, it does keep the average person from simply walking onto your site and should help reduce some exposure to criminal acts. If perimeter gates are automated, special considerations should be made during the planning process to get law enforcement officers and first responders access to the site.

Barriers and locking devices: Vehicle and pedestrian barriers are designed to deter or to delay access to the site and building when properly designed. They allow for "control points" and can help eliminate unauthorized access to the protected area. These items include vehicle barriers, doors, turnstiles, windows, roofs, floors, and so forth. Locks are typically used in conjunction with barriers and can often be the weakest part of the barrier system. It is important to consider locking devices and key control when you assess your protective system. For example, an adversary who has a key can circumvent the barrier protective system. A lock should never be used alone but should be layered with other security measures to protect people and assets. An important point to remember is that any type of fencing or barrier creates additional obstacles for law enforcement and first responders, and special accommodations should be planned before an attack to speed up response in an active shooter scenario.

Intrusion detection and early warning systems: Intrusion detection systems (IDS), when correctly designed, should provide advanced notice of an issue in an area or specific asset, monitoring of equipment or facilities, detection of fire, and emergency notifications. The major functions should deter, detect, and provide notifications for a response. The IDS capabilities should be quantified using the probability of detection, nuisance alarm rate, and vulnerability to defeat. In addition, the IDS must consider the confidence level of the system, which includes response force communications and the time it takes to communicate.

Electronic access controls: The use of electronic access control (EAC) systems is becoming more common these days. The issuance of a badge or key fob or the use of biometrics is commonplace in many organizations. An EAC system is used to define and restrict and control the movement of people or vehicles, and it includes the process of managing and tracking such movements. The software usually will determine who or what will be granted access, as well as when and where it can occur. There are several ways an active shooter can circumvent an EAC system, including by stealing a badge, counterfeiting credentials, or even socially engineering a way into a secured site. Often employees will hold the door open for others who are approaching the building as they pass through the access point—in this case a door. This, known as tailgating, is one of the greatest vulnerabilities in the EAC system.

Video surveillance systems: There are three main reasons why video surveillance systems are used in most applications. First, they may be used to witness what is occurring, which involves someone physically monitoring the video images or the use of automated video analytics. Second, it can be used to record what has already occurred, which means that it is intended as more an investigatory tool than a proactive measure. Third, it can be used as a deterrent. Unfortunately, security cameras do not stop crime, and the use of cameras as a deterrent is not a proven strategy. For example, if the active shooter is not in a "normal" state of mind, they he or she not care whether camera is present (and actually may prefer to be recorded) while he or she commits the heinous crime. Because the majority of active shooters have no exit strategy or escape plan, whether their actions are under video surveillance does little to curb the attack.

Identification of Gaps

Gaps, otherwise known as vulnerabilities, exist in every protection scheme. Both the security practitioner and the adversary will look to identify weak points in the system—security looking to fix the gaps and the adversary to circumvent them. This is why security professionals who perform risk and vulnerability studies must have experience, knowledge, and skills to effectively identify and understand various threats, security technologies, and procedures, as well as the environment in which they operate.

Gaps often occur where least expected and usually are most apparent when you experience them first-hand, during an incident. All layers of in-depth protection should be checked against the vulnerability in danger of being penetrated [3]. Vulnerabilities in an active shooting may prove very deadly: With active shooters, seconds count.

Penetration testing is another consideration that many businesses overlook or choose not to perform. Penetration testing is the evaluation of existing security measures by physically attacking them or through cyberattacks to simulate a real-life incident. Some organizations choose not to physically test their systems because of the cost and resources required to do it right. In case of high-security facilities, skilled third-party operators who have experience attacking security countermeasures often perform such penetration testing. In addition, operators can determine cover and concealment along with shooting angles, gleaning valuable information for law enforcement responders. Figure 8–3 shows a sniper team zeroing their rifle indoors at a facility.

FIGURE 8–3 Sniper Team Zeros Rifle.

The process of performing a comprehensive study and analysis of all risks and their probable effects on an organization, along with the measures implemented to mitigate and reduce the risk, is known as risk management. Risk management begins with an understanding of all aspects of the organization, including assets, site, facilities, operations, processes, existing protective measures, threats, and vulnerabilities, along with potential consequences. The risk management process often begins with a risk assessment [4].

Risk Assessment

There are multiple security risk assessment methodologies available for a company to choose from. It is not the purpose of this book to suggest any specific risk assessment methodology for use an organization, but rather to log common elements that most methodologies typically incorporate to effectively assess risk.

The risk assessment process is a comprehensive process that involves identification of assets, calculation of consequence values, vulnerabilities, likelihood of attack, threats, and security effectiveness calculations. All sites and facilities have some level of risk inherent in their design, method of construction, or lack of protective measures.

Security professionals and engineers normally perform the risk assessment process to assess the vulnerability of various assets and critical operations and to make professional judgments about appropriate actions for preempting or responding to potential threats. This includes identifying the likelihood that an event may occur and the potential consequences should the event occur. Such measurements are essential for calculation of the effects of an event.

In addition, the process of a risk assessment can provide a vehicle for the organization to effectively communicate the quantification of risk and the corresponding support requirements to internal and external stakeholders. The risk assessment process should help the company maximize expenditures and optimize security countermeasure performance by providing the necessary details to analyze and solicit program funding.

When it comes to the active shooter, performing a risk assessment is not as simple as some professionals assert; rather, it may require a more comprehensive approach to fully examine all of the potential ways a motivated shooter may choose to attack a person or company. To understand the probability or likelihood of attack is difficult at best when it comes to an active shooter. Moreover, the research needed to understand the full scope of potential consequences that could be experienced from an active shooter threat is not an easy process to complete. Part of the risk assessment process involves having a good understanding of the threat picture for all aspects of the organization, including individuals, specific departments, and the company as a whole.

Threat Assessment

Threats and adversarial capabilities continue to evolve, becoming more sophisticated and asymmetrical, making protecting critical assets increasingly more difficult. The effectiveness of each countermeasure should be evaluated against a specific vulnerability, or against multiple vulnerabilities depending on threat. The active shooter is a dynamic threat that is very difficult to protect against. No matter what anyone says, protection against this type of threat takes a lot of planning, awareness, detection skills, and physical security measures, as well as an effective response to prevent. There are two types of threat assessments that the professional should analyze to try to understand the threat environment: *internal* threats and *external* threats.

Internal threats. Internal threats can be classified as either intentional or accidental events. Although the focus of a threat assessment may be on intentional acts, it is equally important that the internal threat assessment take into account accidents, as well as any natural events that may equally harm critical operations. As stated previously, the planned insider attack is one of the most difficult to protect against because of the authorized access that employees are given to the site and associated operations. The internal portion of a threat assessment must take into account the facility's staff, including all contractors and guests who have access to critical assets and operations.

External threats. When performing the external threat assessment, local, state, and federal law enforcement agencies should be involved, because such agencies can provide historical data and information on groups or individuals living or operating in the vicinity. Such information is often not readily available to businesses because of its sensitivity, but many law enforcement agencies will provide security related intelligence when appropriate to those organizations that may be affected by it. The Internet is another source of threat information readily available to anyone with access to a computer and network. Often blogs or other social media (e.g. Facebook) may expose individuals or groups that express negative sentiments toward a specific organization, industry, or person. Historical information may also be found on the Internet that may expose an adversary and their likely tactics and techniques.

When it comes to a threat assessment, some professionals prefer to use a threat vector approach and others prefer to use a design basis threat approach when estimating security effectiveness. A design basis threat approach will assess the security system against a specific type of threat or adversarial group and base the data on the greatest possible threat to each specific asset. The threat vector approach assesses the path an adversary takes, along with the necessary tools and delivery method to attack the target or assets. By classifying threat vectors during the threat assessment process, the organization can focus on specific adversarial numbers and capabilities, range of tactics, and access to weapons or other malevolent attack tools and any techniques they adversaries use.

It doesn't matter which approach you choose; what is important is that it follow a documented, thorough process that identifies the most vital data in protecting people and the organization. A threat assessment is only as good as the information it is based on, and it only captures the threats that exist at a specific point in time. Threat assessments need to be re-evaluated frequently to effectively determine or detect threats. As asymmetrical threats like active shooters continue to evolve, it has become increasingly crucial to rapidly adjust security countermeasures accordingly. It is important to be aware that the information documented during a threat assessment information is highly sensitive and must be properly handled and secured.

Vulnerability Assessment

A vulnerability assessment is part of the risk management process and is often based on features that if compromised could result in damages to, or otherwise threaten, the organization. The vulnerability of these features is evaluated based on attractiveness to the adversary, existing or potential threats, and how security countermeasures have been implemented and integrated in an effective manner.

It is known that certain organizations and people attract negative attention and may be more prone to experience acts of violence. When it comes to determining vulnerability from a traditional perspective, this is important to know, but when it comes to the active shooter, this may not be the case. Any business or person can experience an active shooter, because many times the shooter has no previous criminal record, and the decision to attack in such a violent manner is often very personal. The active shooter does not necessarily follow a thought process that fits into normal criminal activity patterns or criminological theories.

This is where a vulnerability assessment can make a difference. Some professionals use the term "vulnerability assessment" interchangeably with "risk assessment" and that is okay. Semantics doesn't matter in this case so long as you use a comprehensive process that covers all of the basics functions that a thorough assessment process should contain. Figure 8–4 shows an actual vulnerability assessment in process.

FIGURE 8–4 Author Kevin Doss Performs a Vulnerability Assessment in Lagos, Nigeria. *Courtesy of Level 4 Security LLC.*

There are six basic functions that should be calculated and analyzed when performing an assessment:

Step 1: Identify the consequences of a loss (usually in terms of monetary value—and yes, human life is measured in monetary terms for assessment purposes). One way to identify the critical assets is by estimating the effects of an incident based on two quantitative measures, loss of life and economic effects. There are two additional components that may also be estimated: psychological effects and mission effects. By adding these two additional components, which are more qualitative in nature, the consequence calculations become more comprehensive and provides additional information on which to base risk decisions.

Step 2: Identify the critical assets and operations that could achieve the estimated consequences. Critical assets are the features or operations that if compromised or destroyed would result in the damage or disruption of the organizational mission. They comprise human assets, physical features, and information technology assets, along with operations and processes that operate interdependently to support the company mission. Such assets may be intangible (e.g., reputation, brand image, staff experience) or tangible (e.g., life, buildings, operations, equipment, data).

Step 3: Document the list of critical assets and prioritize them based on criticality to the organization. The identification and prioritization of critical assets along with any calculated risk factors will help the organization prioritize decisions and determine the appropriate levels of mitigation measures. This is an important part of the process, because it provides the data needed to determine the best options for short-term, medium-term, and long-term security program improvements. Most companies cannot afford to improve all aspects of their security measures in a single step, and this provides the foundation on which to develop mitigation strategies while still making sensible business decisions.

Step 4: Assess the most likely attack scenarios and/or attack vectors and define the threats. First, it is important to determine what constitutes the threat by understanding the adversary and his or her skills. Is it an employee or contractor, or is he or she working in collusion with an outsider? The goal in determining attack scenarios should involve a determination of (1) the type of weapons, equipment, or materials used; (2) adversarial capabilities and numbers; (3) the adversary's planning process; and (4) the steps that might be used to initiate an attack. Often the assessment team must make assumptions to properly evaluate a threat. By determining elements of the threat, such as what constitutes the threat, tactics and capabilities, potential access to equipment and resources, intent, motivation, and history, the organization can better plan security measures and response along with recovery options for each threat.

Step 5: Document and calculate the vulnerability of the critical assets, and evaluate comparative risk. The vulnerability of each critical asset is based on the probability of a "successful" attack on the asset if an actual attack is attempted. Determining probability is a process of measuring the degree of difficulty that an adversary will have identifying assets' perceived significance and accessing the site, building, or department, as well as the level of resources required to destroy it.

Another component is the ability to determine the security program effectiveness. This is based primarily on the site's security procedures and the ability to deter, detect, and delay adversaries until a response force, such as law enforcement officers, can neutralize the attack. When assessing security system effectiveness, the assessor must consider adversary numbers and capabilities to best determine how the existing security system performs against the full range of threats. Security system effectiveness must also take into account any human and/or technology limitations.

Step 6: Develop recommendation or options to consider (solutions) to best reduce the calculated risk. Several decisions need to be made when considering which solutions should be implemented to protect the organization. Cost is often a huge part of these decisions, along with the effects on the organizational mission. The assessment must take into consideration the composition of the structure or component and the capabilities of any existing security countermeasures to protect against the full range of potential threats. The effectiveness of security measures may directly affect whether an attack will be successful. Even in the event that an attack is unsuccessful, the effects can still have lasting effects on the organization and community.

Having an understanding of the security measures and procedures is critical in protecting lives and other assets. The evaluation of security is not a simple check for features or technology, but rather the integration and interoperability between security processes, human interaction, and technologies. The analysis of security effectiveness must be evaluated against anticipated or real threats and a calculation of the systems ability to provide adequate levels of protection for the facility.

The final step in the assessment process is to determine how best to fix any gaps in the protection scheme. This includes prioritizing the list of recommendations and determining a timeframe to implement the options and performing audits to ensure that the measures are working as intended and verify the threat environment.

Part of preparedness and the mitigation of vulnerabilities requires that the organization establish a means of measuring risk, the effectiveness of the security countermeasures, develop goals for improvement, and audit the security program's progress. They should also review the performance measures of the security system to reduce exposure to risk. Development of a metrics program based on company requirements and any applicable laws and/or regulations should be established. A few metrics for the organization to consider follow:

- Capture baseline risk calculations and the existing protection system effectiveness.
- Develop measurements that can determine the resilience and recovery aspects for the company. The baseline measurements should be documented, along with any data identified during the course of an incident.
- Record all performance measurements and benchmarks for comparison against industry best practices and internal stakeholders.
- Detail measurements for all costs and benefits and returns on investment for the protection system.

Redefining the Risk Formula

The devastating effects on a business, community, first responders, and individuals embroiled in a barbaric active shooter emergency cannot be ignored or discounted by thinking it may never ever happen. The frequency of these ruthless tragedies is not reducing, but increasing enough to be though commonplace by viewers of national news. Many of these viewers are numb to the active shooter emergency, but for the business, the risk is real and cannot be delegitimized; it must be planned for on every level. How does the business realistically reduce the risk of an active shooting?

First, the reader should conceptualize the risk formula risk = threat × vulnerability × consequence. Now look at the formula from the perspective of how risk can be reduced, which is the ultimate goal of both the business and the first responder community. Identifying and reducing risk is a foundational principle of the insurance industry that transcends all business disciplines and offerings. That said, the components in of risk are much more than threat, vulnerability, and consequence, as illustrated in Figure 8–5.

<u>Threat:</u> For the purpose of this book, the threat is an active shooting, which may translate as either an insider or exterior threat.

<u>Vulnerability:</u> For an active shooting, the vulnerability may consist of aspects of the business, its operations, or human involvement. However, vulnerabilities may include some of the conditional elements, but unless the items are highlighted, individually listed, and analyzed, they may be lost in translation based on the experience and understanding of the assessor. That said, practitioners often do not include mitigation, preparedness, response, recovery, or communications under the vulnerability function.

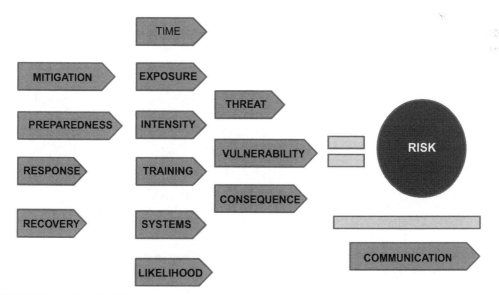

FIGURE 8–5 Redefining the Risk Formula.

<u>Consequence:</u> The consequences of an active shooting mean different things to different entities when considering the perspective of a business, employee, or guest, for each may or may not have a responsibility beyond the attack. The consequence to the target site may mean demolishing the structure, such as the McDonald's restaurant near San Diego, California, in 1984 or the Sandy Hook Elementary massacre in 2012. Customers may boycott the company because of the business's actions, or the business may not know how to effectively allow customers back into the property, such as in the case of the Aurora, Colorado, movie theater shooting in 2012 or be prepared for the number of exceptional employees who will quit the business regardless of the actions of the business in an active shooting emergency.

<u>Intensity:</u> During an active shooting, the intensity of the shooting can be measured in the number of victims and/or shots fired from weapons. If an active shooter focuses specifically on one victim, such as the doctor whom the shooter believes allowed a loved one to die, the only casualty may be the doctor and the shooter if the shooter decides to commit suicide. In other shootings, such as the Virginia Tech shooting or Columbine shooting, the number of victims intensifies the emergency.

<u>Time:</u> The time of day affects the number of potential victims who may be caught in this deadly rampage. If the active shooting occurs late at night or early in the morning, the number of potential victims is reduced merely by the time of the attack.

<u>Exposure:</u> During an active shooting, first responders strive to arrive as soon as possible, because they know the amount of the time the shooter has to select potential victims translates into additional casualties.

<u>Likelihood or probability:</u> A business cannot ignore the likelihood or probability of an active shooter event without considering the insider threat, such as that posed by a disgruntled employee who vows to return and take vengeance against the company, or the quasi-insider threat of an former relative of an employee looking to attack a former lover or ex-spouse, or the outsider threat, such as that posed by a customer who vigorously disdains some aspect of the business or what the business represents.

<u>Training:</u> One of the most valuable elements of reducing risk is training. Without training individual employees in responses, key executives in making timely and effective decisions, and the business in deliberate and rehearsed support to the active shooter response by first responders, and without exercising a reliable and comprehensive companywide business exhaustive effect, the response to an active shooting may be ineffective, unreliable, and fragmented.

<u>Security technology systems:</u> Billions of dollars are spent annually on security technology systems to detect, deter, alert, channel, and deny threats such as active shooters. Technology does play a part in reducing the risk of this type of emergency and in disrupting the active shooter's plan of death and destruction.

<u>Mitigation:</u> The effectiveness of the business in reducing risk can be observed through the mitigation process when focusing on active shooter. If the business or its employees have not emphasized, navigated, and prescribed a coordinated understanding of the potential massacre of unarmed victims by mitigating as many variables as possible before any attack, then

risk effectively will remain the same. Mitigation reduces risk by following and acting on its own definition.

Preparedness: When a company and individuals prepare for an emergency event, they understand the exponentially negative effects on operations and individuals if no preparedness steps are enacted before such an emergency. When preparing for a specific emergency, risk is reduced by removing elements out of danger, empowering individuals through education, and a multitude of formidable and calculated comprehensive actions that are defined by one word: preparedness.

Response: During a fire, an effective and timely response translates into reducing damage to the property. The same holds true for an active shooter emergency. If the response is chaotic and indecisive, marginalized by inaction and inadequacy on all levels, then risk cannot be reduced. However, if an unwavering, committed, and calculated response infuses all business actions when addressing an active shooting before, during, and after an emergency, then risk can be reduced.

Recovery: When does recovery begin for an active shooting? The answer may surprise you: Recovery begins well in advance of any emergency. For a business, time is money, and the longer a business is closed, the greater the loss of revenue, as well as the chance the business will not survive. Thus recovery begins by preparing such documents as the business continuity plan (BCP), a predisaster recovery plan, and answers to questions anticipated from all stakeholders, groups, and entities who may question the business's response or nonresponse during the active shooting.

Communication: The secret sauce that binds and underlines all elements of risk identified above is communication. Regardless of whether the message is written or verbalized before, during, or after the active shooter emergency, communication is key to reducing risk. Think back to any emergency that a business or individual faced: The one aspect consistently identified as a catalyst for problems encountered was communication. This book has devoted an entire chapter, Chapter 6, to communications, as they are the glue that binds an entire Active Shooter program together.

The concept behind this new formula is to bring to the forefront the clearly identified elements of risk for businesses and individuals to effectively argue for, plan for, and document for insurance adjustors, legal staff, the board of directors, and employees how risk can effectively be reduced through reprioritization and strategic-level actionable steps.

Recommendations and Options for Consideration

As security experts, we are often amazed at the lackadaisical attitudes toward security measures and the prevention of crime in some organizations. Threats such as an active shooter are often ignored until they come knocking at the door. The biggest hurdle for any security department is in getting the company to admit that a threat is real. Saying or documenting that a threat does or may exist also means that the company should do something about it. Some security options may be cost-prohibitive to implement or could cause operational hardships and inefficiencies for the organization.

Communications: In an active shooter scenario, the communications aspect is often overlooked. If we consider the school shootings at Columbine and Virginia Tech, it is understandable that many of the students reached for their cell phones to call 911. Our cell phones have become a constant in our lives, and it is often a normal reaction for people to reach for their cell phones as a source of comfort during a crisis. A cell phone may be the only way to communicate during an active shooter event, but this technology is not always perfect. There are often "dead spots" within buildings, which cellular signals cannot penetrate, especially if the building is constructed out of thick, reinforced concrete. Often employees or students will know where the dead spots are within a building—but what if you find yourself hiding in a dead spot during a shooting? In addition to dead spots, a technically savvy attacker may jam cellular signals to prolong the attack and prevent early warnings using cellular communication devices.

In addition to cellular signals, it is important to identify communication vulnerabilities at the site. The identification of primary and secondary communications to the staff, guests, and contractors at the site is a major responsibility of the company. How to rapidly communicate that an active threat is present at the site, as well as where that threat is located and the corresponding actions to take to prevent loss of life and injury, should be well planned out in advance. Recommendations to improve communications should involve the coordination and collaboration of law enforcement and outreach with neighboring businesses and the local community.

Additionally, educating the workforce to report suspicious activity when observed may help to detect and identify specific threats. Having a proper communication plan for every scenario and condition can mitigate some vulnerability at the site.

Special equipment: Organizations that have prepared and assessed this gap in their program may choose to invest in "go bags" or prepositioned equipment. Prepositioning specialized equipment to assist law enforcement responders to get to the active shooter and neutralize the active threat is strongly advisable. Items such as maps, chemical masks, keys or badges, doors stops, bolt cutters, internal motorized carts, and tactical breaching tools might also be part of the specialized equipment, including supporting the medical response by having trauma medical kits with tourniquets, airway tubing, blood clotting bandages and other emergency medical items placed strategically around the site.

Physical security: Physical security measures provide for delays, detection, assessment, access control, and, often, improvement of response function. Security components such as barriers, video surveillance, and intrusion detection should be part of a larger program involving policies, procedures, compliance audits, testing, and periodic updates. The development of a detailed security plan and a rapid response and recovery plan should help augment any physical protective measures at the site and help in the communication function.

Specific options to consider include development of security awareness training programs and procedures, active shooter and workplace violence programs, installation of equipment to provide surveillance and detection of unauthorized activity, and installation of additional protective measures on site, including barriers to limit access for unauthorized personnel.

Physical security countermeasures should be properly analyzed in accordance with the threat level and balance between costs and benefit to determine the best fit for the organization. It is always good to consult a professional if you do not fully understand how procedures, people, and technology can be effectively implemented and incorporated into your organization.

Cybersecurity and social networking: One of the greatest threats to organizations today is the culture of information technology and networking. Both internal and external threats exist and are continuing to grow [5]. Social networks and cyberbullying can cause serious problems for children and adults alike. The ability for organizations to monitor and manage such threats may be paramount to preventing an active shooter. Threats and negative sentiments posted on the Internet are just serious as direct physical threats—perhaps more so. A program to monitor social media and provide anonymous reporting of threats and company violations can assist the organization in combating the escalation of violence resulting from such acts. Additionally, monitoring and securing networks can help prevent other types of criminal and deviant behaviors before they are acted out. Access to special counseling may also be another option to consider for employees who may feel they are being harassed, alienated, or abused via social media.

Acceptable Risk

Some options may drop off the list as the company decides what is best within its budgetary limitations. The organization may choose not to protect an asset or operation because of the tremendous cost to protect it against the greatest credible threat. The active shooter scenario is one risk that many businesses choose to ignore, accepting the risk. This should not be, considering historical evidence of the growing problem of such shootings: These incidents are extremely destructive and devastating to a business as well as a community. No matter how your organization decides to handle this risk, it is important that a documented process be in place detailing the process and the reasoning behind it. Such a process is normally based upon a risk matrix that documents likelihood of occurrence versus the consequences of loss [6].

The reason why the active shooter threat and other types of violence are vital to protect against is because of the amount of loss experienced after these attacks. We are not talking about the theft of services or goods; rather, we are discussing death and serious injuries, multi-million-dollar lawsuits, and people who may never return to school or work.

Audits and Surveys

Performing audits and surveys is an important part of any protection and preparedness scheme. Auditing and surveys take time and resources, but you cannot assess what you have versus what should be. The difference between an audit and survey is that an audit is a periodic evaluation of the existing protective measures and processes to ensure that they are working as designed.

A survey, on the other hand, is the process used to determine who, what, when, where, why, and how. A survey includes protective measures, security procedures, business operations, and the expertise to determine gaps or vulnerabilities in the existing program [7].

The active shooter presents a very unique challenge to most organizations. Performing a proper survey in light of the active shooter threat is very different from, say, a survey looking to prevent theft or vandalism. Although the steps in the process may be the same, the assessor is looking for very different aspects of a protective system to mitigate the active shooter threat.

In additional to the type of operation, the operational aspects of the company must be kept in mind during the process. If the site is a hard target, then it may not be as accessible as a soft target. An example of a hard target would be a nuclear plant; an example of a soft target, a retail store. In this example, it is easy to see the difference in protection measures and accessibility—however, the survey and audit process still follows the same basic formula.

The main difference in the process if we use the nuclear site versus the retail store is the amount of time and resources it takes to perform the audit or survey. A proper survey must consider all protective measures, security procedures, and business operations. In a retail store, this could take a few days to document. At a nuclear site, a thorough survey may take weeks, even months, to properly measure and document because of all the additional security measures, security procedures, and complex business systems and operations in place. Moreover, a nuclear site may have dozens of armed security officers who need to be assessed, as well as shift differentials and environmental considerations not found in a retail store.

Private sector businesses do not normally conduct security, vulnerability, or threat audits unless federal, state, or local laws mandate them. There is a current concern among business executive and legal staff that after a report is written and the audit exposes gaps or weaknesses, the business is obligated to fix the problem regardless of the cost. In addition, if a dangerous event occurs, the organization's liability exposure could be enormous if a known issue was left unresolved. The argument is that if the business chooses cost over the safety and security of its guests and employees, the business has not acted in an appropriate manner.

On the opposing side, after the gaps have been documented, the business must attempt to adjudicate and negate these problems and issues by a clear calculated, structured and feasible approach commensurate with the magnitude of the gap. It should be calculated, embraced, and countered by planning, restructuring, and training adjustments, not by expending large sums of money for technological advances. The most compelling approach to reducing gaps begins with the business's incorporating a formidable response by demonstrating a methodology and business philosophy of resolution and repair, not denial or avoidance.

Budgeting

The cost–benefit aspect of any security countermeasure should be part of the consideration before deciding which measures should be chosen. The cost:benefit ratio is the process of determining whether a company should invest into a measure that provides a return on its investment. The "return" does not necessarily mean only cash savings; often it is safety- or liability-focused, offering a psychological benefit to the organization. This where the security professional can justify their security programs and initiatives using an operational business based model to illustrate the value of security to the company leadership. It is also important to note that the security professional must learn to speak the language that company leadership prefers to use when planning and budgeting. If the request for budget dollars doesn't match the format preferred by senior leadership and the board of directors, chances are that it will be rejected.

There are a few considerations one should evaluate when asking for money or resources to better protect the company:

- Does the measure identify measurable value to the organization in protection of life, dollars, and safety value or brand image?
- Does the measure support other internal departments who can also benefit from implementing the measures?
- Does the measure prevent or hinder the mission of the company or a department?
- Is the measure too costly to implement over the entire life cycle?
- Does the measure support the organizational culture?

The first two questions are readily answered, but often the last three questions can be ignored or lack proper consideration. It has been suggested that if you cannot answer the last three questions in a positive manner, the first two questions may not matter to company leadership.

Often the greatest obstacle to planning, developing, and implementing a good protection program is lack of proper funding.

References

[1] Doss KT, O'Sullivan DA. Physical Security Concepts, 161–182 Davies Sandi, Hertig Chris, editors. The Professional Protection Officer: Practical Security Strategies and Emerging Trends. Boston, MA: Butterworth-Heinemann; 2010.

[2] Jeffery CR. Crime Prevention through Environmental Design. Beverly Hills, CA: Sage Publications; 1971.

[3] ASIS International Facilities Physical Security Measures Guideline. Alexandria, VA: ASIS International; 2009.

[4] ASIS International General Security Risk Assessment Guideline. Alexandria, VA: ASIS International; 2003.

[5] National Institute of Standards and Technology Improving Critical Infrastructure Cybersecurity Executive Order 13636 Cybersecurity Framework. Gaithersburg, MD: National Institute of Standards and Technology; 2013.

[6] Doss KT. Physical Security Professional (PSP) Study Guide, 2nd ed. Alexandria, VA: ASIS International Press; 2011.

[7] Broder J, Tucker E. Risk Analysis and the Security Survey, 4th ed. Boston, MA: Butterworth-Heinemann; 2012.

9

Training, Awareness, Education, and Exercise

As a general rule, the active shooter very rarely takes hostages or attempts to negotiate on any level with the first responder community, because the active shooter is on a mission, and that mission does not involve negotiations or hostages. Rather, the active shooter identifies a killing zone and becomes a hunter within this zone. The shooter may or may not continue seeking new victims as targets of opportunity, which could be individuals who are attempting to escape, or the shooter may continue to seek out specific targets who have eluded the first barrage of bullets. The person who is in charge of the active shooting is the shooter himself or herself—until this ominous fact is altered. One way to break the shooter's cycle is for businesses and first responders to not ignore or discount the concept of an active shooting within the business or community, but rather to train, develop situational awareness, educate employees and responders, and execute a plan.

Training

At the outset of any training course or program, the purpose of the training must be properly defined. The second step in the training process is to determine the type of training, such as whether the training will be educational, directional, informational, or actionable. Traditionally, first responders receive essential actionable training that requires interacting with coworkers and conducting specific actions, such as building entry techniques, life-saving step-by-step procedures, and situational drills. In reality, first responders receive all four types of training, coupled with sequences of actions, interoperable communications, and unity of command. Businesses, on the other hand, look at training from a different perspective, such as whether the training courses are required by law and mandatory. As an example when looking at active shooting training, some businesses will not play the Department of Homeland Security video "Options for Consideration" [1] because the internal human resources department feels the video will unduly scare the employees and them the wrong message—that an active shooting attack is imminent, else the business would not have shown the video. The business sets the philosophy of how it approaches the safety and security of its staff while also considering the same two criteria for guests, contractors, vendors, and volunteers who are on property at any given time. Furthermore, some businesses may consider that the only department that may require active shooting training is the security department. It is unfortunate that many organizations do not consider property wide training cost-effective, so the majority of training is departmentalized or even completely dismissed for philosophical or financial issues. By law, a business is required to provide a safe and secure environment for all individuals on property. How would a court of law, the victim's family, and customers view the business's philosophical or financial persona? Regardless of whether the employee is full-time, part-time, a volunteer, or a contractor, active shooting training should be required in every department and working group for the following reasons:

- How will a business know where and when a tragedy of this magnitude will erupt within the business?
- What if a seemingly trusted employee or family member, infuriated by business decisions or employee discipline or promotion, performs the active shooting?
- Could the shooting be at the hands of complete stranger who has a grudge against the organization?

For a business, training is an essential and necessary activity that can improve business performance, customer service, and employee morale while emphasizing functionality, operations, best practices, and business standards. Training can improve consistency, efficiency, and effectiveness within all (or specific) departments and working groups. Additionally, training can improve product quality and productivity, providing a competitive advantage in employee skills and increasing employee self-worth while also decreasing inefficiencies, workplace accidents, and safety challenges. Training can reinforce business philosophy, image, and brand. Many businesses mistakenly believe that training budgets should be cut to save overhead costs, but in reality, many training methods are free or come with minimal costs and are valued as significant enhancements by employees, communities, contractors, attorneys, and courts.

Training for first responders is an essential job function, duty, and responsibility, but undeniably, it is not equally essential to businesses when it comes to safety and security, as it should be. Appling lessons learned, best practices, and economies of scale are force multipliers in any emergency for first responders, who often review every function or action before any emergency. Training is essential for the safety of the first responders, as well as the success of the response. Safeguarding first responders, defining readiness standards, prioritizing tactical maneuvers, prepositioning resources, and perceiving and negating challenges are all accomplished by the fundamental practices of training, planning, coordination, and interoperability. For first responders, words such as agility, flexibility, diversity, sustainability, and tactical soundness are not punch lines in a joke but rather are a testament to the professionalism and resolve of a professional department.

As the number of active shootings increases across the United States and in other parts of the world, the first responder community has been forced to change its approach and response to the challenges associated with this evolving, dynamic, and formidable emergency. No longer does the strategy of containment and holding until S.W.A.T. arrives effectively stop the instrument of death that continues to take and injure victims trapped in this catastrophic emergency. However, just as with any new tactic or piece of equipment, first responders train on all aspects of the response including actions before, during, and after the shooting.

To be effective, active shooter training cannot be trivial, overly cumbersome, fragmented, or lacking consideration of all aspects of an effective response. Although it is difficult to address every possible scenario as regards the response function, a few items that can be part of the planning and coordination when dealing with multiple agencies, disciplines, and jurisdictions.

According to the Occupational Safety Health Administration (OSHA) discussion of the Incident Command System (ICS) at www.osha.gov./SLTC/etools/ics/what_what_is_ics. html, "ICS is a standardized on-scene incident management concept designed specifically to allow responders to adopt an integrated organizational structure equal to the complexity and demands of any single incident or multiple incidents without being hindered by jurisdictional boundaries [2]."

An active shooting emergency requires a compendium of agencies and disciplines in a coordinated cooperative response before, during, and after threat neutralization. Some people may argue the response to an active shooting is no different than any other emergency that presupposes a multiple agency response. In reality, this human-initiated emergency is a senseless barbaric act that indiscriminately targets the young and old alike, coworker and stranger without hesitation but with maliciousness and forethought toward anyone in the shooter's path. Such a nefarious act cannot be easily predicted by a satellite or seismometer, nor is this emergency an accident that has definitive response actions, such as a natural gas explosion or chemical spill. The active shooter response requires succinct coordination between law enforcement agencies, which are charged with neutralizing the threat and clearing a path to the shooter. Fire and EMS are charged with treating the gunshot victims who are somewhere within the business and who may only have a few precious moments to be transported to nearby hospitals. Preventing the shooter from claiming more victims defines the crossroads between two major response characteristics. Speed is paramount. Safety is a necessity. Confusion, ineffectiveness, inconsistencies, and indecision may all be minimized during an emergency when a coordinated, prescribed, trained, and mutually understood response has been crafted before the active shooting.

Moreover, for training to be effective, it should be realistic and encapsulate all components of the response effort, such as intensified scenarios, use of the exact equipment needed for the response, effective and timely communications, and enactment of the exact command structure. Anything less than a realistic training exercise would jeopardize the success of the real response and devalue the ability of first responders to envision these challenges. Resolving challenges before any emergency empowers first responders, building confidence in their abilities and strategies, while also enriching a cooperative environment between first responding agencies that traditionally operate in their own silo of response. An effective active shooting response takes effort, understanding, and an unwavering commitment of personnel and equipment and provides creditability across a unified front.

As documented over decades of professional service, first responders are experienced in locating victims within an emergency. However, during initial entry into the structure, first responders are now simultaneously looking for the active shooter and any additional shooters, who may be lying in wait for first responders. Just because only one shooter was reported to the dispatcher does not mean that there are not other shooters. To coincide with the entry, first responders are clearing sections of the structure to create safer zones. When these safe zones are identified and established, this will allow medical units to advance and treat the injured victims. This process takes time, coordination, and practice, all honed and perfected through training.

After each first responder has received the proper training and discussed scenarios, options, and challenges for responding to an active shooter, then significant time-wasting measures can be avoided and a commonality of protocols established for each response element regardless of department or agency. Through training, first responders already know to bypass injured people and seek out the shooter to break his or her cycle of control. However, does the training cover the following?

- How to interact and rescue individuals hiding out behind a locked door or stacks of heavy items that create obstructions
- What method of communications will be used to communicate with the people inside who have barricaded offices
- How first responders communicate to people inside the facility that someone, whether friend or foe, is approaching

In an office complex, large shopping mall, or high-rise business tower, communication with the people inside is one aspect that may be carried out hundreds of times. If accomplished consistently, safely, and sensibly by all responding agencies and departments, the response may be considered integrated and transparent across multiple agencies, at least for people who are barricaded or hiding out. If each aspect of the first responder's actions, challenges, and strategies is executed in similar fashion, many of the lingering problems involved in an active shooting may be mitigated. Last, it should be noted that without repeated training and coordination among agencies and departments, the skill sets cannot be considered honed or second nature. Skills are a perishable commodity, and one that loses its advantage with the passing of time; if performed only once, skills may be forgotten at the wrong time.

Statistics have shown that a large percentage of active shooters, after they are done shooting at their initial target or targets, and as soon as they know law enforcement have arrived on property, commit suicide. Thus the sooner armed entry teams can enter the business, the greater potential victims' chance of survival. First responders are practicing entering businesses more quickly, without using the same methodical, tedious, and cautious approach as in the past. New strategies take a lot of practice to minimize the risk to entry teams. No longer do first responders have the luxury of waiting for backup from their own department; they may need to work in unison with multiple agencies, and in the same manner, regarding how to enter into a hostile active shooter environment. Not surprisingly, the victims and public believe that first responders will kick in the door, neutralize the shooter, and save the day.

First responders are not unfamiliar with the chaos associated with emergencies and are equally familiar with violence and man's inhumanity toward fellow man. However, the horrific scenes and carnage found in a massive active shooting parallels a battlefield. Many of the first responders are not military veterans, so mentally and physically preparing them for an active shooting should also be a consideration in the training. If possible military training programs, literature and operational procedures might be shared through a coordinated program between the first responder community and military medical units. Guest lecture presentations by military field doctors and frank discussions of lessons learned can be invaluable tools to effectively minimize the active shooters deadly rampage.

Awareness and Situational Awareness

The foundation of situational awareness does not unfold at the very second when first responders enter the active shooting structure, but rather are enhanced through the following:

- Multi-phase and functional training
- Event-driven realistic scenarios
- Applying the lessons learned from other active shootings
- Planning before an active shooting emergency

Each synchronized element enriches the response and physically and mentally inculcates confidence in responders and reinforces proven skillsets learned over years of professional service. Information and resource sharing are not incremental components that are rationed out as needed, nor are they awareness considerations that may dilute and fracture an active shooter response. Situational awareness is not an item that can provide instant value unless discussed, documented, trained in, and rehearsed. As an example, students may have certain expectations, but when the fire alarm is activated, uncertainty, confusion, and hesitation are all discriminating factors delaying action if this is a student's first fire drill. The military is exceptional at timing actions and identifying steps and procedures to decrease time taken while providing realistic training scenarios that require situational awareness of their surroundings—and injecting variables that might affect every aspect of a response—while identifying a realistic coordinated response time.

To prepare first responders for active shooter emergencies, the training coordinator should consider realistic scenarios based on actual active shootings, multiple variables or challenges, and a variety of business settings that could be experienced during the emergency. Awareness training scenarios are important to prepare first responders to active shooter situations. The following eleven categories provide a basis for scenarios that are important to prepare first responders in an active shooter emergency. As can be surmised from the following, this is only the first step in a realistic active shooter threat training scenario:

- Lone shooter in a mass gathering (concerts, stadium, convention, parades)
- Lone shooter in an open-air environment (streets, multiple exterior locations such as business complexes or neighborhood shopping center, outdoor bazaar, and mobile, either on foot or in vehicle)
- Lone shooter in a manufacturing or chemical facility
- Lone shooter in a refinery
- Lone shooter in a warehouse or storage facility
- Lone shooter in office setting (cubicles, multiple offices)
- Lone shooter in an airport or transportation facility

- Lone shooter in a high-rise building (multiple floors and multiple connecting buildings)
- Lone shooter in a school (elementary, middle school, high school, college, extension campus, night school, private school)
- Lone shooter in a commercial property (mall, restaurant, nightclub, grocery store, theaters, strip mall, hardware store)
- Two shooters in the various environments (Columbine and Las Vegas had two active shooters)

For a business wishing to prescript an active shooting training exercise, it must be noted that the training cannot be ambiguous nor irrelevant to the respective business environment. Businesses do not have time and resources to waste on frivolous or fragmented training and may not be able to conduct exhaustive training exercises. For the business, training must represent realistic scenarios that are feasible and that are significant to the business. The foregoing categories of training mean little to a business unless that model applies to their respective market. Thus the forward-thinking company should ensure that first responders are appropriately trained for their specific business setting and allow them to train at the facility. The company should interact, coordinate, and align key business resources with the very first responders and agencies that will be responding in real life. Do not be dissuaded or comprise in ensuring and cataloguing each expectation and essential action that the business should enact or provide in this life-threatening emergency. Ignoring the steps and coordination efforts will only be counterproductive to the response, whether internally or externally. Proactive and preventive measures implemented by the business enhance and consolidate resources and provide a solid foundation for the emergency.

It is important to determine the number of shooters selected for the training exercise and consider additional aspects of the building or structure, such as number of floors, square footage, entry points, and accessibility identified sites in your respective area. Now consider the unique features and challenges that are not consistent throughout each specific category. For example, there are seven different types of schools, and each level of school provides nuances that may be problematic during the training exercise (as well as in a real life shooting). Thus, for schools, first responders may consider several different training exercises or document what additional response procedures and equipment might be added to the best practices list for that particular level of school. The optimal time to consider equipment enhancements, tactical considerations, communications procedures, and multiple agency coordination for each of the seven different levels of schools is immediately after the training exercise.

To further define the training exercise, consider the variables and upheavals that may be experienced during the active shooting emergency. For example, how effective would a new employee be if he or she showed up to work on the first day with no understanding of the challenges they would face? What standard equipment is needed? What are the boundaries performing the job? The same holds true for training. If an aggregation of likely, predictable, and credible challenges were assembled and incorporated into a single training exercise, then the realistic and unprecedented benefits would outweigh a routine active shooting exercise. Consider the variables and note, if they are not provided or considered in the exercise, how they would be handled during the response. Additionally, consider adjusting the challenges within the scenario from a limited number of challenges in the beginning to a wide variety of variables during the follow-up training exercises. Figure 9-1 identifies some variables and injects that create additional challenges in certain business settings. Consider, too, that a large percentage of the initial emergency calls to 911 are inaccurate. Remember to inject into the scenario some of the changes in Figure 9-1. Because during an active shooting first responders may arrive from numerous state, federal, and local agencies, as well as jurisdictions, please consider the differences in the response and challenges as shown in Figure 9-2.

Challenges

Speed is of the essence, for each second could see another person fall prey to the active shooter. This fact is engrained into each responder and need not be repeated. The faster the response, the greater the chance of saving more lives; but when responders enter a building for the first time, everything is an obstacle course. There are potentially deadly consequences behind each blind hallway or planter—and consider that responders will not recklessly and irresponsibly run through a building as if doing the 100-yard dash. First responders understand that the potential victims want nothing more than to be rescued immediately, but the response cannot be tactically unwise. There are many challenges that may be experienced during an active shooter response, and each must be approached from the perspective of how it will be mitigated. Methods for reducing response time should be developed, discussed, and planned for. Some challenges are either mental or physical distractions to the responders, whereas others require a tactical adjustment by entry teams. The important points of these challenges are to incorporate these variables into the training program so that when encountered the potential effects are significantly reduced, reducing time delays. Remember that if the average shooting duration is twelve minutes and the average response time is three minutes, then the following challenges and the foregoing first responder chart have repercussions for a timely response. The following list documents many considerations that should be accounted for before an incident:

- Fire alarm activated
- Need to wait for equipment before entering or clearing a section
- People running everywhere
- Screaming and yelling
- People injured, some visibly injured and still moving, others sitting or lying on the floor
- Radios not working inside the building
- Never having trained with fire/EMS
- Never having visited the business before, thus having no concept of interior challenges and exposures
- Law enforcement not trained on trauma procedures
- Shooter not found after complete search
- No PA system in the building

Active Shooter(s)

Active shooter(s) may or may not be communicated during initial 911 call; how learned?						
One shooter Male, adult	One shooter Female, adult	One shooter Male, 13–18	One shooter Female, 13–18	Two shooters male (2)	Two shooters Female and male	Two shooters Female (2)
White male	White female	Asian male	Asian female	Black male	Black female	Two the same or different
Active shooter weapons may or may not be communicated during initial 911 call; how learned?						
One handgun	Two handguns	One handgun One shotgun	One handgun One rifle	One handgun Fully automatic rifle	IED Explosives Molotov cocktail	Smoke or gas grenades
Active shooter clothing may or may not be communicated during initial 911 call; how learned?						
Regular clothing	Long coats	Backpacks	Military clothing	Ballistic and tactical vests	Stocking caps	Police-style uniform
Lab coat	Suit	Construction	Employee uniform	Hard hat or baseball cap	Ammo belt	Carry bag
Threat may or may not be communicated during initial 911 call; how learned?						
Insider Current	Insider Former	Outsider Relative of current or former	Outsider Customer	Outsider Random	Outsider cause or anti -company	

First Responders

Law enforcement officers cannot enter until what size force achieved?						
Solo	Two officers Same dept.	Two officers Different dept.	Four officers Same dept.	Four officers Different dept.	Two entry teams	Three entry teams

External law enforcement teams (do not enter; assess for shooter among individuals evacuating)					
Back door	Stairwell exits 2–4	Loading dock	Service corridor	Employee entrance	Guest or main entrance	Parking lot or garage

Equipment and weapons						
Boltcutters	Ballistic shield	Gas masks		Sledgehammers	AR-15	Flashlights	Sniper rifle

Who coordinates with business assets? When and where?					
Surveillance room	Security or control room	Main office	Command center	Emergency evacuation assembly area	Front entrance of building

Business provides or does not provide					
Go bag or go kit	Keys	Floor plan	Radios	Access cards	Employees to show fastest route to shooter
Doorstops	Pictures of employees	Flashlights	Employee roster	Anything discussed during walk through if one done prior	

Response time to the shooting location; what affected response times					
2–5 minutes	5–8 minutes	More than 8 minutes	Heavy traffic	Heavy rain or snow/ icy road conditions	When EMS/firefighters allowed to enter
Arrived, but waited for SWAT	When command center activated		Time of arrival and when shooter neutralized	Need to wait until ____ entry officers ready	

Fire and EMS			
Position vehicles • At facility • Two blocks away • Farther	Allowed to enter building • When called • When section cleared	Who interacts with law enforcement?	Escorted into building Yes No
How communicate with law enforcement?	Establish ICS Yes No	Trained with law enforcement? Yes No	Escorted out of building with injured individuals? Yes No
Issued ballistic vests and helmets? Yes No	Will not enter building until shooter neutralized? Yes No		Allowed to enter when active shooter location unknown? Yes No
Will not enter building when shooter neutralized but still clearing building? Yes No	Will make contact with emergency evacuation assembly area? Yes No		

FIGURE 9–1 Active Shooter Variables and Injects.

Law enforcement officers cannot enter until what size force achieved?						
Solo	Two officers Same dept.	Two officers Different dept.	Four officers Same dept.	Four officers Different dept.	Two entry teams	Three entry teams
External law enforcement teams (do not enter; assess for shooter among individuals evacuating)						
Back door	Stairwell exits 2–4	Loading dock	Service corridor	Employee entrance	Guest or main entrance	Parking lot or garage
Equipment and Weapons						
Boltcutters	Ballistic shield	Gas masks		Sledge hammers	AR-15	Flashlights	Sniper rifle
Who coordinates with business assets? When and where?						
Surveillance room	Security or control room	Main office	Command center	Emergency evacuation assembly area	Front entrance of building	
Business provides or does not provide						
Go bag or go kit	Keys	Floor plan	Radios	Access cards	Employees to show fastest route to shooter	
Doorstops	Pictures of employees	Flashlights	Employee roster	Anything discussed during walk through if one done prior		
Response time to the shooting location; what affected response times						
2–5 minutes	5–8 minutes	More than 8 minutes	Heavy traffic	Heavy rain or snow/ icy road conditions	When EMS/firefighters allowed to enter	
Arrived, but Waited for SWAT	When command center activated		Time of arrival and when shooter neutralized	Need to wait until ___ entry officers ready		
Fire and EMS						
Position vehicles • At facility • Two blocks away • Further	When allowed to enter building? • When called • When section cleared		Who interacts with law enforcement?	Escorted into building? Yes No		
How communicate with law enforcement?	Establish ICS? Yes No		Trained with law enforcement? Yes No	Escorted out of building with injured individuals? Yes No		
Issued ballistic vests and helmets? Yes No	Will not enter building until shooter neutralized? Yes No			Allowed to enter when active shooter location unknown? Yes No		
Will enter building when shooter neutralized, but still clearing building? Yes No			Will make contact with emergency evacuation assembly area? Yes No			

FIGURE 9–2 First Responder Variables and Injects.

- Shooter neutralized, having surrendered and been arrested or shot by first responders, having been killed by a non–law enforcement insider, or having committed suicide
- Best avenue of approach blocked
- Dangerous chemicals found
- People trying to stop the entry team to talk
- Extensive construction encountered
- Shooter doesn't speak English
- People seen hiding behind planters
- People darting out to try to escape when see the entry team, some with hands in air, some not
- Unsure of avenue of approach—no floor plan provided
- Blind hallways
- Glass office walls and wooden door
- During search, people hiding everywhere
- Five people seen wearing same clothing as shooter

- Too few ambulances
- Never having trained with other law enforcement agencies
- Biometrically locked doors
- Surveillance cameras
- Determining location of shooter when no gunshots
- Vehicles unable to park closer than a quarter-mile away
- Smoke and no gas masks
- Determining which agency is in charge
- Vehicles too far away for to carry what equipment needs carried
- IEDs in active shooter's vehicle
- How to get people out of rooms when they are hiding out
- Who interviews witnesses exiting building for updated information
- When the injured are treated
- Searching for a second shooter
- No one from the business assisting
- Lights out in building, requiring need flashlights
- People injured on floor, asking for help
- Unknown number of people inside building
- Small children crying alone in hallway over unconscious female
- Elevators jammed full of people
- Second-floor balcony exposes entry team
- Stairwell jammed with people, some stopped and sitting, down
- Senior citizen in walker moving down the hallway slowly
- Debris all over the floor—papers and equipment turned over
- Shooter reported on two different floors
- Backpack on floor in hallway, possibly the shooter's
- What appears to be an IED found on the floor
- Radio communications spotty and inconsistent
- Long hallways provide no cover
- Access cards needed to enter rooms, departments, and hallways

It is up to the training coordinator to provide a straightforward, relevant, and practical training exercise to maximize the training. It becomes abundantly obvious that the more variables and challenges that can be experienced by entry teams and first responders, the greater the chance of negotiating such obstacles to reduce response times. In reality, each new challenge that is presented to first responders may be problematic and inevitably affects the effectiveness of the response. It is common in life that when a person is prepared for an event and has experienced it, he or she instinctively adjusts to challenges, minimizes indecision and hesitation, and leverages available resources because of his or her situational awareness. A well-organized and disciplined response by both the first responder community and the business is what the employees and the general public expect. A variable that cannot be replicated in the confines of a training exercise is the psychological pressures in both the first responders and business employees during the shooting. These psychological challenges can cause dysfunction, affect confidence, and resonate across every action of the response. To prepare for certain psychological pressures, first responders may use rubber bullets or something similar during the exercise to simulate an actual shooting. If a responder is carelessly in an exposed position, the first responder will know the error immediately. Other departments may use headsets to play prescripted and prerecorded sights and sounds, and the resulting emotional buildup can elevate the first responder's mental platform before entry into the training area. Unfortunately, this aspect of training is often overlooked despite the severity of the psychological pressure on each individual.

For the business that can see the enormity of challenges that the first responder community faces during the active shooting, the actions and assistance the business can provide are crucial to an effective response. The business is not a silent partner or observer, but rather is an essential and collaborative partner in all phases of this emergency. Each aspect of the training exercise should be carefully considered by the business and discussed with the first responder community. The discussion should determine the areas of assistance and mechanisms to reduce these challenges into merely a bump in the process and not a destabilizing hurdle that cannot be negated. The best possible course of action for any business is to invite the first responder community to the property to see each challenge, distraction, and variable first-hand, then mutually identify formidable solutions before any active shooting emergency.

Education

In the private sector, employees are busy with deadlines and completing projects and may work a multitude of different hours in varying locations. These employees may not have the ability to adjust shifts or schedules but may still need training. Training methods today can be administered at an acceptable time for the employee and also allow the employee much latitude in stopping and restarting the training at different times. Look at training from a different perspective—e.g., educational training is not limited to only one form of delivery, but rather includes multiple avenues and platforms. Each training platform or medium identified is realistic and provides timely relevant instructional methods for businesses and first responders alike. Training consists of a cross section of methods and allows individuals to receive valuable information and perspectives at their own pace and during select training times. The length of training and method of delivery is up to management and, in some cases, employees themselves. The training methods and platforms include the following:

- Webinars
- Self-learning tapes
- Working groups
- Conferences
- Seminars
- Classroom or platform instruction both on property or off site
- Independent online study courses
- On-the-job training

- Train-the-trainer sessions
- Corporate or management briefings
- Commercial videos
- In-house academy
- Videos developed by the business
- In-house television network
- Corporate newsletters
- Exercises, including tabletop, orientation, drill, functional, and full-scale

The foregoing training methods apply equally to the private and public sectors. Many of the training methods are free to the public, such as the government active shooter videos and webinars, whereas others may incur a minimal cost. In today's threat environment and the pervasive nature of active shootings, the once rare phenomenon has given way to copycat shooters whose activity may even coincide with anniversaries of previous significant active shootings. What was once believed to be optional training for security departments, employees, and businesses now is mandatory training by all department and working groups. A business cannot ignore the demographics surrounding active shootings, traumatization and devastating effects on employees, or the profound consequences the emergency will have on the business's brand, image, and sustainability. If the business and its employees expect to survive, it is imperative that business resiliency begin well ahead of any perceived or unexpected emergency by anticipating, planning for, training in, and recovering from any event.

It should also be stated that receiving, understanding, and applying critical training learning points is a vital part of the process. Remarkably, a person can be exposed to an entire spectrum of training methods for years but never fully understand or apply any portion of the course material. For training to be effective is should be applied, exercised, revisited several times, and incorporated into everyday as a learned actions. How effective would a business response to any emergency be if the following were true?

- The staff never trained.
- No one understood what he or she could be experiencing during the emergency.
- No one identified employee or business roles or duties.
- No plan guided the response.
- Employees and guests were left to fend for themselves.

Training cannot be discussed without mentioning that some businesses and some departments, such as the human resources and legal departments, believe that training for an active shooter emergency is unrealistic or creates a false sense of panic or stress in employees. These same departments may also surmise that the program may present a training environment in which it is difficult to learn if employees are unaccustomed to the stresses associated with this style of training. It is difficult for a person learn if he or she is frightened and upset throughout the entire training exercise.

An actual active shooter training exercise that uses simulated ammunition and role players as both active shooters and victims is common for first responders, but not for private-sector businesses and employees. If the employees are to participate in the training, special emphasis should be directed toward helping the individual understand and apply actions, while also reassuring the employee that the training is only an exercise. It is common for employees be shown such videos as the Department of Homeland Security's "Options for Consideration" video or the city of Houston's "Run Hide, Fight" video [3] before any active shooter training exercise to ensure that employees understands and mentally prepare for this emergency situation.

Another option is to first physically walk employees through what they may do to protect themselves and others in the room, rather than encouraging the employees to fend for themselves; or the business could provide support during the exercise to assist the staff. One additional option is to monitor as an observer, questioning employees to see whether they would like to quit the exercise. The first responder's role in this process is to learn the business's floor plan, identifying and mitigating any challenges. In addition, the first responders need to practice the proper tactics with the exact equipment needed with the appropriate responding agencies. Last, if the employee did not receive the memo or prior notice of the training, some employees will undoubtedly be disturbed and upset.

Certain individuals and departments may believe that the odds of the business's falling prey to an active shooting or any type of significant workplace violence are miniscule, so any unnecessary emphasis on active shooting would fuel the employee's suspicion that an emergency of this nature is likely. Unlike first responders, businesses rely on revenue generation and the ability of their employees to fulfill deadlines while excelling at all functional tasks and operating in a safe and secure environment. Unfortunately, employees tend to gossip and speculate whenever something new is introduced to the environment. Baby boomers are familiar with fallout shelters and drills, but today's generation is not. Students at all grade levels are familiar with fire drills but less familiar with earthquake drills. Which age group or grade level is familiar with an active shooter drill? With the scale of suffering observed in the victim's families, the shattered and crumbling work environment observed after an active shooting—and the devastating and cancerous effect on each employee regardless of whether on property at the time of the active shooting—the catastrophic effect of the active shooting will be felt well beyond when the last first responding vehicle leaves the property. Employees want a safe and secure environment, and they appreciate a business that anticipates, plans for, and prescripts recovery actions well in advance of any emergency or threat. Ignoring today's threat environment will have repercussions throughout all aspects of the business, possibly for years to come.

Exercise

First responders are imminently familiar with training exercises, but unfortunately the business training programs pale in comparison to what the first responders receive. Unless law mandates such training, or a particular emergency has occurred in the past, the business may not formulate any significant training program that replicates the diversity beyond one or two emergency categories. The Federal Emergency Management Agency, through the Emergency

Management Institute, in the independent online training course "Exercise Design," under IS-139 [4] identified five different exercise programs called "Training, Exercise, and Practice," described as follow:

- **Orientation seminar:** The purpose of an orientation seminar is to familiarize participants with roles, responsibilities, plans, procedures, and equipment. For a business, an orientation seminar is an ideal starting platform. It allows each key employee the opportunity to study his or her actions and discharge responsibilities and duties while contemplating each person within his or her respective department or working group. Discovering and learning options and understanding equipment and communication expectations are paramount to success. Reinforcing emergency evacuation assembly area locations, identifying clear chains of command, and promoting expectations are only a sampling of the integral key elements in the orientation seminar.
- **Drill:** The goal of a drill is to coordinate and supervise all exercise activity, normally to test a single specific operation or function. Possibly the most iconic and mutually understood exercises for a business to perform are drills. A drill can be specific to one department or working group and is indelibly etched on the mind of each employee. This exercise type is not limited to management staff only, for it fosters responsive actions in each employee who may be on the "front lines" of the active shooting and who is personally interacting with panicked guests. From the employee's first day of employment to instilling actions to protect the lives of coworkers and guests, the employee receives a greater benefit from drills than from any other exercise type.
- **Tabletop:** This type of exercise is designed to facilitate the analysis of an emergency event in an informal, stress-free environment. After management personnel understand their roles, duties, and responsibilities in the orientation process, a tabletop exercise will allow key staff the ability to interact with senior management (key decision makers) in the active shooter emergency. This controlled style of exercise will provide participants with an emergency scenario to analyze and increase their awareness of timely and valuable decisions, interactions, and any boundaries of individuals who need to respond to, stabilize, mitigate and aid others, as well as the business, in the recovery process. The tabletop exercise will unilaterally demonstrate the correctness and completeness of the emergency plan while also isolating weaknesses and facilitating mutual understanding among departments and working groups.
- **Functional:** Designed as a fully simulated interactive exercise that tests the capabilities of an organization to respond to the active shooter. For private-sector businesses such as chemical and petroleum refineries, pharmaceutical facilities, ammunition plants, and health care facilities, a functional exercise may seem second nature, but for commercial facilities or any business that relies on walk-in business, a functional exercise may be restricted to a specific department and not the entire business. For a business that maintains a twenty-four hour operation, a functional exercise is unlikely for fear of disrupting customer service, unnecessarily panicking or inconveniencing guests, creating an unfavorable guest experience, and risking business disruptions. If first responders

observe or participate in the exercise, guests may mistakenly question whether they are in a safe environment regardless of whether signage is strategically placed notifying all individuals on property of the exercise.

- **Full-scale:** Designed to simulate a real event as closely as possible, full-scale exercises are the most comprehensive exercise to implement. To date several schools, malls, and hospitals have developed full-scale active shooter scenarios. In these exercises, role players may be an active shooter or a casualty. First responders, dressed in complete tactical gear and deploying any necessary equipment, may also participate in the exercise. Other individuals who may be present are any observers from other facilities or businesses who can gain valuable information from the exercise. In this type of exercise, tactical teams will search preselected areas, and the exercise will continue until the shooter is neutralized and victims treated. Role players follow prewritten scripts while controllers monitor the progress of each participant. From the communications platforms to the command center, each functional area within the business is tested during a predetermined period of time. After completion, the participants assemble for a "hot wash" of the exercise to solicit lessons learned and identify any deficiencies and challenges. Traditionally, during active shooter school exercises, students do not participate, and in hospitals, patients are excluded, as are customers in a commercial business.

Process

To determine the training process, it is wise to consider the active shooting training from the perspective of the organizational culture, including senior management's viewpoint, which may be more unilaterally concerned with revenue margins, employee performance, and the bottom line. These executives are embroiled in a kaleidoscope of challenges that may affect employment levels and high-yield opportunities potentially affecting the business's longevity. That said, when presented with the prospect of propertywide training or specific active shooter training for management, these same key executives may beg off using the following responses:

- Managers and supervisors are too busy to take time out for training.
- Replacements or stand-ins will fulfill any mandated requirement.
- The training is not worth their time.
- Nothing of value can be gained from the training.
- Active shooter training is not relevant to their current job and title.
- The budget isn't stable enough to warrant such training.
- Active shooter training is not mandated by law.
- A shooting won't happen here; the staff is on top of any problem.

As preposterous and insensitive as these responses may appear, the business—or, specifically, the management staff—is responsible for the safety and security of its employees, guests, contractors, volunteers, and vendors who frequent the business. For each of the above declarations, a dozen recriminations can be made. Safety and security for a business and those individuals on property resonates well beyond the bottom line of any accounting document. For an executive to fully grasp his or her responsibility, he or she should personally walk up to any employee and ask: "Do you feel safe here considering the risk of an active shooting?" If they do not, then ask why. If they do, then ask why. To really test the waters on safety and security, one should ask the question of five random customers. But instead of doing so, an executive will begin spewing a complete list of why doing so an unrealistic and unwise question to ask a customer, as well as how doing so might jeopardize the business. But safety and security are more than just words: They include actions and a philosophy visible throughout the business environment. When a customer feels safe and secure, those feelings come from management and from each employee, and they start with training. The aforementioned training areas can enrich any business, so select the platforms best suited for your company's environment.

The two most tragic words in the English language are "if only." If only the business had developed an active shooter plan. If only the company had conducted emergency training and prepared employees for their roles, duties, and responsibilities in the case of an active shooting emergency. If only management had allowed the employees to participate in free online training courses and view free videos on active shooters. Perhaps the results would have been different. No crystal ball will allow a business or its managers, supervisors, or employees to pinpoint whether and when an active shooting will occur, but each customer who crosses the property threshold expects and demands that the company do just that: train in, plan for, prepare for, and anticipate every threats to their families and themselves.

References

[1] Department of Homeland Security "Options for Consideration." <www.dhs.gov/video/options-consideration-active-shooter-preparedness-video/>.

[2] Occupational Safety and Health Administration (2002). <https://www.osha.gov/SLTC/etools/ics/>.

[3] City of Houston, video, "Run, Hide, Fight." <www.readyhoustontx.gov/videos.html>.

[4] Federal Emergency Management Agency, Emergency Management Institute, "Exercise Design," under IS-139. <https://training.fema.gov/is/courseoverview.aspx?code=IS-139>.

10

Recovery

Recovery is identified as the last phase in a disaster or crisis cycle, but it is also the most pertinent phase, invaluable to both the short-term and long-term survival of a business. However, it is the most overlooked and misunderstood phase. Government agencies advise companies to have a recovery plan in place and to have appropriately trained professional staff—possibly through a mixture of internal and external partners—to guide a recovery. But how? Using a technology approach, recovery is referred to as the seamless integration and transformation from disaster to a validated operational sustainment. A business recovery is not the same as a technology recovery, for the emphasis must be directed toward employees, collaborative work environment, business resiliency, and profitability.

When attempting to identify and define recovery, there isn't a single definitive answer to fit all aspects of the process. Each person is different, and because each business is unique, there is no standard recovery definition that will cover all employees, corporations, and business models. For a business, recovery can be financially measured on spreadsheets and other accounting documents showing weaknesses and strengths in the businesses as well as statistically depicting gradual improvements. Financial documents can provide calculated projections for future statistical accomplishments that may be implemented to adjust languishing entries. A business can adjust production, design and develop new marketing strategies, offer product incentives, or increase sales staff. Moreover, the company may be able to identify specific marketing and financial courses of action to implement. However, what is the value of teamwork and an environment that cannot be seen but only felt?

Most Valuable Asset

For an employee after an active shooting emergency, there isn't a method or a spreadsheet to identify, define, and adequately measure recovery. Each employee will process the active shooting incident in his or her own way. All employees, regardless of position with the company, must be considered in the recovery process. Just because an employee wasn't on scene during the incident doesn't mean that he or she will not be significantly affected by the event. The satellite employee may have lost a best friend or a coworker he or she had known for years, or may have been a member of the department who happened to be off property during the shooting. For each employee, it is a personal event that only the individual will be able to determine how to cope with and recover from. Recovery expands well behind the walls of the business as it permeates into employees' homes and families. Many employees may be strong, working side by side with their coworkers during this tragic event, but at home their emotions may overtake their every waking moment. It should be emphasized that the most important

181

asset of any business is its employees. A business cannot recovery easily without strong, competent, and committed employees. Their loyalty, and the bond formed between coworkers and managers, can often be unequaled. These elements configure the environment, saturating and infiltrating every aspect of the customer experience. The business cannot afford to ignore or forfeit a strong employee base or place employees on a second tier of the recovery process.

An area that is often overlooked in an active shooter recovery plan is the loyal customer who has frequented the business for years. Without a strong customer base, which has taken sometimes decades to develop, continued loyalty may be paramount for future business earnings. Think of your favorite restaurant or bar, considering the various aspects of the business that customers find endearing, as well as what separates the establishment from the competition. The customer is there for a reason and will continue to be so as long as his or her needs are fulfilled and the customer experience doesn't change for the worse. What aspects of the business will an active shooting emergency change in the eyes of the customers? Maybe the favorite bartender or customer service manager was a victim of the shooting. Or perhaps the customer will feel unsafe, devastated by the shooting. For a private-sector business, the customer is the catalyst and nucleus of a positive revenue stream. Without cash flow, the business will fail. How will the business reestablish a safe environment and maintain the same feel? What reassurances will the business offer and promote to compensate for this lethal active shooting incident? Unfortunately, each business is a complexity of skillsets, technology, ingenuity, and unyielding desire for success shaped into a proprietary business model. That said, the two common ingredients are employees and customers, who are, and who should be, the focal point of any active shooter recovery plan.

Effects of Decisions

The active shooting emergency will significantly affect the business, both at the time of the shooting and well into the future, regardless of whether individuals are killed. For example, if several employees are injured and some are permanently disabled, the business can be dramatically affected depending on its action or inaction—its response or nonresponse—to issues and concerns. Furthermore, if the business has not prepared responses and answers to basic questions from victims' families, employees, stockholders, law enforcement, lawyers, and the board of directors before the shooting, recovery is extended. **Appendix C** provides a mixture of potential questions that may need to be answered after an active shooting. Hopefully, the prudent executive has anticipated these questions, in advance, to protect business, employees, customers, brand name, and reputation. More than 700 questions are listed Appendix C. Why so many? After each active shooter emergency, people will want answers regarding this horrific emergency. It is not unreasonable for a parent of a loved one—a loved one viciously cut down in the prime of his or her life—to want answers. Law enforcement agencies exhaustively investigate every angle of the shooting to resolve each detail of the incident through their questioning. Employees want prompt answers and want to be reassured that vulnerabilities have been resolved. Customers will want prudent countermeasures to be taken and will want credible answers about why it happened and whether they should return. Stockholders want straightforward answers about how the business will survive and, if there is any disruption, how it was outlined and planned for in the business continuity plan. **Appendix C** consists of overlapping questions from frustrated and traumatized individuals, as well as from agencies who must navigate through a complex emergency in a methodical and impartial manner. The questions at times may appear harsh, insensitive, hysterical, vengeful, or even expressionless, but members of each of the identified categories will want answers unhindered by formality nor minimized in importance. The following different source areas include

- Business decisions
- Human resources
- Communications
- Counseling
- Security
- Financial
- Media and news
- Law enforcement (before and during the incident)
- Law enforcement (investigation)
- Legal
- Business continuity plan
- Trial

Now add to the recovery equation the likelihood of several members of the executive and management staff's experiencing posttraumatic stress disorder (PTSD). This disorder will damage their decision-making ability and the timeliness of their decisions. If the executives are not in a sufficiently stable condition to provide relevant responses and answers to these hard questions, then their emotional condition and decision making process can affect the business on multiple levels for years to come. Additionally, if key executives and managers were victims, activation of the active shooter recovery plan may be delayed or never activated at all, because the surviving employees may not know of its existence. Executives and key employees are essential in guiding and supervising the recovery plan, but only if there is a plan and they are aware of its existence.

Another effect on the business that may change is the workplace environment and internal dynamics of the business. The most important asset of any business is its employees, who are the heart and soul of the business while also reasserting the vision statement of the owners. The employees sacrifice their own personal time, and many consider their coworkers as members of their family. This close family feeling unites employees during compressed deadlines and instills cooperation in all aspects of the business. To these employees, the business is theirs—the matter is very personal. The environment may also be compared to a successful team: In sports, a team comprises specific players who are skilled at a specific function or assignment. When all these talented players are brought together, they form a productive team. But, as we know in sports, the skills of some teams far exceed others. If one of the team is a victim of the shooting or the sheer gravity of the shooting completely disorients the team, such adversity could bring the business to a complete standstill or degrade productivity, regardless of the demands and directives of management.

Business Differences

When comparing the overall damage to image and brand—between the private sector and a government facility—an active shooting is significantly more harmful for a business's image than it is for the government's. A private-sector business relies on revenue to remain open, whereas a government facility is funded by tax dollars and national debt. The type of business can have an enormous impediment on the options and flexibility available to the owners and executive management staff charged to decide the future of the business. A government facility can close an extended period of time, with government services shifted to another location. And taxpayers seemingly tend to move effortlessly to receive their required benefits without the same allegiance and service levels attached to a private-sector business. For example, if a post office is the active shooter location, delivery services can be shifted to another post office. The recovery plan for the government facility, when compared to the private sector, will not consider the options of merging, closing, or selling the facility. But the recovery plan for a government facility will activate measures for employee assistance just as the private-sector planning does.

The recovery plan is designed to weigh and rationalize the nuisances to the business in terms of resiliency and operational requirements. Each type of organization or target location consists of unique and integral elements, compounding the recovery process. Figure 10–1 identifies several business models that may be encountered in the recovery process.

The government sector consists of state, federal, and local government agencies as well as military installations. Quasi-government agencies may include schools, hospitals, and libraries. Franchise businesses may include hotels, restaurants, hardware stores, theaters, food stores, and department stores. Family-owned businesses run the entire gamut of commercial facilities from restaurants, hotels, and animal feed stores to service stations, bowling alleys, and transportation companies. Internet companies provide products, goods, and services over the Internet, making this sector largely unseen by the customer base. Product sales may include door-to-door sales, kiosks, machinery, automobiles, and tenants of shopping malls. Business services may include contractors, insurance agents, consultants, lawyers, accountants, swimming pool services, and dentists. Last, critical infrastructure, as defined by the Department of Homeland Security, is "the assets, systems, and networks, whether physical or virtual, so vital to the

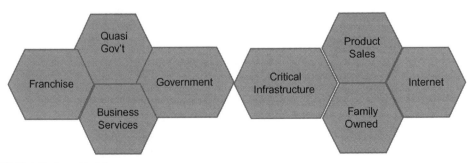

FIGURE 10–1 Business Models.

United States that their incapacitation or destruction would have a debilitating effect on security, national economic security, national public health or safety, or any combination thereof." Critical infrastructure sector categories include the following: chemical, commercial facilities, communication, critical manufacturing, dams, defense industrial base, emergency services, energy, financial services, food and agriculture, government facilities, healthcare and public health, information technology, nuclear reactors/materials/waste, transportation systems, and water and wastewater systems [1]. Even though 85 percent of the critical infrastructure is owned and operated by the private sector, an active shooter crisis will have ramifications within the communities, cities, and townships as well. In most cases the critical infrastructure business is the economic life-blood and major employer, thus these companies cannot sell their properties or cease operations without regionally affecting hundreds, if not thousands, of customers and employees. As you can imagine, the recovery plan for each type of critical infrastructure is complex, and it is imperative that each organization at a minimum develop an active shooter response plan and recovery plan while considering the questions listed in **Appendix C**.

Business Decision and Choice

During and after a shooting, someone will scrutinize every business decision. Employees may take the actions or inaction of management personally, as reflecting the degree to which the organization values its employees. During this extremely critical time, the feelings and emotions of employees, the employee's families, and the community at large will run the entire spectrum of reactions from supportive to angry, hostile, and resentful. The business may be viewed unfavorably if warning signs or complaints were dismissed or ignored by management. How the executive staff managed the entire event will be a topic of discussion for years to come. After the first shot is heard, the executives' decisions and actions will be placed under a microscope. The executive considerations may involve some of the perspectives listed in Figure 10–2 as the business responds to this type of emergency.

Unfortunately, many businesses do not take the time to predetermine their actions and responses during emergency situations. These businesses believe that an active shooter event will never happen to them; essentially, they play the odds against such an emergency ever occurring on their property. These same companies may also consider proper training or planning a waste of time and effort. Moreover, management may believe that such programs are

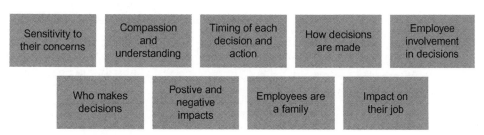

FIGURE 10–2 Business Decision and Choice.

not relevant to the company mission or are not productive in generating revenue. Regardless of whether the emergency resulted from a natural disaster, life safety, terrorism, public health, or an accident, is it possible for a business to be negligent if it never properly planned or trained for these emergencies?

A prudent course of action for any business is to prepare before an emergency situation occurs. Even though many events cannot be prevented, the actions of a business when confronting a disaster, crisis, or emergency or when experiencing controversy, dissention, uncertainty, and a highly emotionally charged atmosphere are conceptually foreseeable. A business can answer basic questions about actions and decisions before an event. The business can also develop credible and insightful responses to actions and decisions when considering questions associated with the event. Each action and decision can be developed in the calmness of a board room rather under the pressure of an actual emergency. The responses should not be developed in a vacuum but rather should be relevant to business components, employee representatives, and key decision makers, contributing to a formidable, credible, and realistic response. Finally, the resulting decisions and answers can be presented to the board of directors and legal staff to ensure corporate unity with an eye toward the company's future. Business success is based on wise and prudent informed decisions, not on hesitation, destabilization, or indecisiveness.

Active Shooter Plan

How would an employee feel about a business if it were not concerned about his or her safety and security? In today's threat matrix, an active shooter emergency does register as a potentially foreseeable issue, regardless of the size or type of the business, number of employees, or business location.

When considering how best to approach the development of the active shooter plan, consider performing a comparison to the company's disaster recovery plan (if available). In essence, these plans are synonymous, for both identify detailed employee actions during and immediately after the incident. The plans provide sequences of action, such as evacuation, sheltering in place, and specific procedures for the protection of life and reduction of damage to the property. Communication platforms and methods should be clearly identified across a wide spectrum of business departments to facilitate reassurance, guidance, and efficiency in performing such actions. Accounting for all employees, visitors, and contractors, caring for the injured, and coordinating a response are all key components in the plan. However, if a business has not experienced a significant disaster or doesn't operate in areas that experience natural disasters commonly, the business may not have developed a disaster recovery plan.

Effective planning for the active shooter plan is extremely important in mitigation, preparedness, and response for the business, and the appropriate actions should be implemented for preservation of life. The active shooter plan is the first constructive plan in the business recovery process, as each step enumerated in the plan, whether mitigation, preparedness, or response, directly affects the recovery function for the business. As an example, risk is often calculated using a formula of threat times vulnerability times consequence ($T \times V \times C$). If the value associated with each element of the formula is altered, it will subsequently affect the value of risk. If a business implements twenty preparedness measures for an active shooter emergency and another similar company does not implement preparedness measures, then the first company has altered the value of risk. Furthermore, if preventive measures are known to the employees and, ultimately, the legal department and insurance carriers, the value-added measures are often felt unilaterally throughout the business. Such types of positive actions provide the foundation for safety, security, and risk reduction for the company.

The active shooter plan is an integrated threat-specific solution for the business and each employee. Let's assume that a business has a very robust active shooter plan that addresses communications, provides a directed and focused response, and clearly identifies employee actions on which employees have been trained. Now let's consider who is working on the property during an active shooter incident. Many businesses use on-site contractors and temporary employment agencies. Other businesses may have volunteers or interns who work at the property during normal business hours. Should the company's active shooter plan be shared with such individuals? A guest may not know the difference between an employee, contractor, temporary employee, volunteer, or intern and may assume that these individuals have been properly trained and understand their duties during an emergency. The active shooter plan should be shared with anyone working on the business property, and it is prudent to have these individuals included in any training exercise. In addition, the supervisor or management team is often responsible for ensuring that these individuals have received the active shooter plan and training. Currently, life safety emergencies are usually addressed during new employee orientation, when these individuals enter the property; so it is a compelling argument to add the active shooter plan to the orientation process.

Some companies will use outside or contract security officers, either as the main security force or to augment existing in-house security staff. The contract security officer company may experience higher turnover in officers, which means that the business may see new contract security employees weekly or even daily. Unless the business decides to share its active shooter plan with these contractors and identifies their areas of responsibility, there is no reason to believe that these individuals will be any more effective than a guest, despite being charged to ensure the safety and security of the site and its assets. Ensuring that the security contractors understand and receive the necessary information to do their job is a critical part of the overall company's security and safety program. Furthermore, it is helpful to consider incorporating into a private security company's contract a requirement that all security contractor employees receive emergency training, planning, and information specific to the property. If the security contractor, whose main mission is to provide a safe and secure environment, disagrees with this business approach, then find another security contractor who places a higher value on the safety and security of the organizations he or she is tasked to protect.

Many companies who have developed an active shooter plan often overlook a specific section on "insider threat." An insider threat is a current or former employee who is keenly aware of all security measures, including the communication platform and codes, employee entrances and exits, the emergency evacuation assembly areas, and the number of security officers, as well as which officers are armed and where employee congregation points are. The insider may possess passkeys, an access card, and biometric access and/or may know key-pad codes to sensitive areas. The Washington Navy Yard shooting on September 16, 2013, in Washington, D.C., left thirteen people dead at the hands of Aaron Alexis, an employee at the site—an example of an insider threat. He was an employee and gained entry into the secure facility not by force, but by using his credentials to enter.

When considering which steps to implement in countering an insider threat, start by presuming that the shooter has access to all areas within the property and knows your active shooter plan. Apply the principle of "looking at both sides of the wire," a tactic often used in the U.S. military during the Vietnam War. The principle starts by installing weapons, equipment, and personnel to prevent entry into a specific defensive position. After all measures have been installed and nothing else needs to be added, then go on the other side of the wire (perimeter) and look at the defensive position from the perspective of the attacker. Any weakness detected should be fortified to prevent or restrict access. Using the same principle, consider what measures or actions can counter what an insider active shooter knows and possesses. As an organization, it is important to review and coordinate all actions with involvement from human resources, legal, security, and executive management before implementing the measure. Possible actions for an active shooter incident may include the following:

- Allow employees to evacuate anywhere they want, except the emergency evacuation assembly area.
- Allow employees to avoid the area of refuge, generally the stairwells, to avoid congregation of potential targets.
- Avoid employee evacuations when the fire alarm is pulled by communicating over the communications platform that there is no fire and providing further instructions regarding the active shooter.
- Deactivate the shooter's access cards, biometric access, and keycodes.
- Use security surveillance cameras to help assess, detect, and identify areas to block off.
- Change the visible security presence, and vary patrol routes, avoiding establishing patterns.
- Increase security inspections of employees at entry and exit points.
- Consider adding additional security technology, such as contraband detectors (metal detectors, etc.).
- Take all threats seriously, and document them all.
- Deactivate computers, biometrics, and card access before terminating an employee or contractor.
- Evaluate the human resources department's procedures concerning difficult employees and threats, as well as how, when, and where employees are terminated.

The foregoing points will start the process of determining how to restrict the access of the insider active shooter and provide some varying methods of detecting an insider who is carrying weapons on property. The evaluation process should be a collaborative effort involving several different departments. This group of departments may be referred to as the insider threat evaluation team. Finally, when developing preventive measures for an open access type business, the security and protection methodology cannot replicate a high-security facility such as a prison or Fort Knox. Remember that it is harder to capture a moving target, so the company should leverage the skills and talents of professionals during the planning phase and empower employees to be part of the solution.

Business Continuity Plan

An active shooter emergency is a manmade event that doesn't have the same historical predictability as a natural disaster, such as hurricane, tornado, or seasonal flooding. The looming catastrophic natural disaster can be tracked by satellites and sensors, with the data then analyzed to provide a warning message and inform all potential victims of the probable destructive powers that may be headed toward them. Conversely, the unsuspecting employee does not have the same luxury or analysis mechanisms during an active shooting. The active shooter emergency cannot be historically predicted by a business, city, community, or targeted victim. The function and primary mission of the business continuity plan (BCP) is still the same—preservation of the lives of the business's employees and customers, as well as damage limitation to the physical structure and operational capabilities.

The purpose of the BCP is to identify, anticipate and document potential pitfalls, then structure a systematic reconstitution approach to continue or resume operations through such actions and concepts as: minimizing downtime, limiting damage to the physical structure, pre-identifying resources and procedures requirements, prepositioning supplies, understanding operational interdependencies, and cross-pollinating duties and functionality. Unfortunately, many businesses do not have a BCP and do not understand the interdependencies between the business's functional requirements and the operational needs. Some businesses believe that writing a BCP is an overpowering and daunting task, one fueled by the complexity of market offerings, shifting customer demands, and the diversity of the business in achieving its strategic revenue goals. Additionally, the executives may not devote sufficient time or effort to developing a BCP because doing so doesn't generate revenue. Even if a BCP exists at the business, incorporating a section on active shooter emergencies is rare.

The BCP is designed to integrate business operations with quality, safety, security, quantitative assessments, environmental, informational security, and interdependency considerations—in both the short and the long terms. A key word for the BCP is "resiliency." Resiliency is specific to operations and functionality. The BCP's chief attributes are consistency, compatibility, and understanding every aspect of the business's market offerings and services. Without a clearly defined and written plan, the negative attributes experienced by a business can result in a significant loss of assets and employees, loss of revenues, decreases in stock values, loss of customers, increased insurance premiums, and delayed recovery.

For many executives, the central focus of the BCP is to return the business back to normal operations as soon as possible. They do not always recognize or accept the short-term or long-term effects a delay can have on employees, investors, and the community at large. The active shooter emergency in many regards has a more significant influence on employees than does a natural disaster. If the active shooter was a current coworker, former coworker, or relative of a coworker, the traumatic effects on employees may last for years. Implementing employee assistance programs and checklists can play a dominant role during and after the emergency.

In addition, it is rare for a BCP to devote a section on employees, even though the primary asset of any business is its employees.

The BCP should be designed to focus on the recovery objectives and help to address the business's return to normal operations. As with any plan, the objectives must be listed and must be clear, concise, and easily understood by all employees, regardless of their position within the business. The objectives may be included as a main section within the document or as a subsection. The objectives should help in maintaining

- Employee confidence and union support
- Customer and client base
- Business reputation, confidence in the business, and brand image
- Timely vendor and supplier support
- Adequate cash flow and consistent revenue
- A safe, secure, and healthful environment
- A positive work environment and teamwork support
- Financial controls, due diligence, compliance, and oversight

In light of employee sensitivities and an undisputed optimal timetable of business and employee expectations, the foregoing objectives are provided only as a starting point in the resumption of business operations. The business cannot relentlessly pursue unachievable objectives hastily developed after the active shooting has occurred. Regardless of whether an employee needs income, the businesses deliberations should also consider that not all employees will desire to resume operations at the earliest moment. Only some employees may want to keep busy at work as part of their healing process. The objectives may also consider a phased resumption of operations, even though this luxury doesn't fit all business models. Any plan to restore the full business functions should be conveyed with an understanding of the implications and challenges involved, including realistic timetables.

When developing and implementing the BCP, it is beneficial to understand and clearly identify the critical functions of every department and working group within the business. If a company consists of sixty-seven departments and has five working groups, the executive staff should be able to immediately list the most crucial market offerings, personnel demands, supplies, and logistics requirements of each area. When the executive staff can recognize such interdependencies and interactions between departments and working groups and can articulate each element's role in the BCP, then the business leadership will comprehend how to restore operations. Downtime cannot be avoided in an active shooting emergency, but minimizing business downtime based on foresight, planning, education, and training is vital. It is imperative that before the words "open for business" are broadcast to the public, the company has formulated fundamentally sound strategic business actions for providing a sustainable recovery.

Command Center

When first responders hear the term "command center," they immediately understand and interact with the command center without hesitation or deliberation. The first responders know its functionality, and the concept is second nature to them. Regrettably, the private sector does not share the same understanding of the importance of a command center during an emergency. After a business has experienced a major natural disaster or an emergency situation, the business usually values the benefits and interactions of the command center across all operational departments and working groups. The business understands the actions taken, including what worked and what didn't. The company can incorporate the critical steps needed to preserve life and limit further damage to the business.

Often businesses do not totally envision the concept or realize the tremendous benefits that a command center brings to the operational integrity and a coordinated response with first responders. Some businesses may have not have previously identified employees for the command center, let alone assigned employees by position, task, duties, or responsibilities. These same businesses may not have invested money into technology, design, and/or communications or may not have invested in proper training for the assigned employees. Last, many businesses do not feel that they have a sufficient employee base to staff operations, or they rely on the same key personnel to resolve all challenges or disasters, their vision of a command center merely the executive conference room or the president's office coupled with employee-issued cell phones. Regardless of the size or operational capability of the command center, the duties, tasks, roles and responsibilities will be scrutinized by anyone the business is charged to protect.

Look at a command center from the perspective of an assistant coach who sits high over the football stadium and watches the defensive team take the field. The assistant coach knows the plays, formations, player abilities, and team limitations and may be able to anticipate the next play. The assistant coach communicates courses of action to his defensive team as quickly as possible to prevent the opposing tea from winning the game. What if an active shooter emergency was occurring at the business right now? How effective would the command center be if key staff employees were never identified and proper training had never occurred? The private sector command center is an important element and must be considered when developing comprehensive response and recovery efforts.

In the height of a disaster, even the most professional employee cannot memorize every action or duty with which he or she is tasked. Without a clearly defined plan that is known and trained in, many adjustments commensurate with the confrontations experienced during a disaster will be detrimental to the plan's effectiveness. The command center is the guiding light during the darkest of hours and exists to prevent a fundamental fault line of indecision and contradiction. Flexibility and transparency from the response role into a human resources recovery embraces the primary asset, employees. Responsibilities also include accounting for and concentrating on all guests, contractors, vendors, and volunteers trapped in an active shooter emergency. Validating the location of employees, confirming injuries, assessing and gauging employees' psychological balance, and assuring all employees that the threat is over are all command center functions. Inevitably, these tasks will be part of an active shooter incident, but they are rarely considered when developing a command center plan and must be expeditiously addressed when they first appear during the emergency.

Notification Structure

Timely and accurate notification is imperative in emergency situations. Knowing the answer to questions in advance distinguishes a business from a mediocre operation to one that values, inspires, and demonstrates confidence in the face of adversity. Not knowing the reporting structure in advance essentially deemphasizes and disrupts a timely response to a disaster. Let's start with three questions:

- Who activates the active shooter plan?
- Who activates the command center?
- Who activates the business continuity plan?

When the response to each question is blank or all the same person, then the business restricts the activation process, especially if the initiator is out of town, unavailable, or a victim of the active shooting emergency. The notification structure should not provide limitations on plan activation when the primary employee is unavailable. However, identifying key employees four or five levels down increases the probability of a timely notification. Consider for a moment how much time and how many lives could possibly be saved by empowering employees to activate the active shooter plan as opposed using to the current notification structure. Businesses routinely instruct employees to the pull the fire alarm during a fire. Is it feasible for the business to expect the same response during an active shooting emergency? This process essentially translates into an employee trusting in his or her own abilities to administer the command center and BCP.

There are different opinions for who activates the active shooter plan. Some businesses believe that only the security department should initiate the plan, whereas other companies rely on supervisors, managers, or team leads. Notwithstanding these two options, some believe that every employee has the right to protect self and coworkers when such an incident arises. What would the proper response be to a telephone call received at the executive office from a front-line employee who stated, "This is John Smith in the accounting department. A man is shooting at employees on the second floor. Two people have been shot. Activate the active shooter plan"? The answer is not always clear or common knowledge to all levels within the company. Eventually this employee's response needs to be discussed throughout all departments and working groups to eliminate any conflicting messages and to help foster trustworthiness through effective leadership.

Emergency Evacuation Assembly Area

Generally employees are aware of the emergency evacuation assembly area as the place to reassemble during or after the disaster. The area was chosen to safeguard employees and visitors. Roll is taken at this location, and daily sign-in sheets are used to check off the employees. Missing employees' names are communicated to the command center, and any injured individuals are redirected to the first responders on scene. However, the emergency evacuation assembly area may not be the ideal location to reassemble and recover when the active shooter is an employee. If the shooter is an insider, the shooter will know where the employees are to meet. The emergency evacuation assembly area is susceptible to greater loss of life if the shooter is an insider threat.

Discussions are warranted when identifying a collection area for employees if the active shooter is a former or current employee. On one side of the discussion, law enforcement and other first responders can provide treatment and armed support to those individuals who are at the assembly area. On the other side, the area may undermine an effective evacuation and can turn the assembly area into a target-rich environment. There is a third side of the discussion. If the business never established an assembly area, neglected to practice evacuation procedures, or thought that an active shooter plan would never be needed, then employees will evacuate in all directions.

Damage Assessment

Unlike a natural disaster such as a flood, earthquake, or hurricane, the physical effects and associated consequences on the business structure are generally more limited in scope during an active shooting emergency. The emergency statistically will not encompass the entire business's footprint. However, if the active shooter carries a improvised explosive device (IED) into the building and detonates the device, the impact and ensuing damage may be substantial. The resulting denotation may include a significant adverse disruption to the building and associated systems, such as electrical, water, and gas lines, ventilation, and any other specialized technologies. Damage may include fire, smoke, water, and natural gas release or simultaneous disruption of multiple systems. An initial damage assessment may not be possible until after key employees are allowed to enter the property. Inside the property, the first damage assessment may only be viewed superficially, using only sight observations for visible damage. Until a trained staff can assess the damage to the physical structure and systems, only observations and comparisons can be made from pre-incident memory.

It should be pointed out that the damage assessment team (DAT) typically only looks at the physical structure, systems, technology, and the infrastructure of the business. The DAT does not pursue or investigate any aspect surrounding the victims, including emotional and/or psychological effects on families or departments affected by the active shooting. Tangible items, inoperability of technology and systems, predictable interdependencies, and quantitative computations are the central focus of the DAT. The team considers comprehensively and thoroughly how visible and invisible damage aspects may compromise company operations. Without the unique skill sets the DAT brings, the company may not fully understand the complexity of the damage.

The DAT is an integral element in the recovery process and must not be dismissed, undervalued or placed on hold. The DAT has a responsibility to review the damaged area impartially and systematically. Before a business can consider resuming either full or partial operations, the executive staff should require a verification process that identifies such areas as what works, what dangers or hazards still exist, estimation of the costs to repair or replace, and estimation of time for completion before the businesses doors can be reopened to the employees and customers. DAT employee expertise should consist of maintenance, information technology, safety, security, risk, utility services, including through the possible use of outside contractors. Depending on the area of the active shooting, specialists may be contracted to assist in the damage assessment process. Additionally, many companies should consider one aspect that is often neglected in the recovery process—performing a building inspection. The property may have undergone all restoration and repairs, but the business can still lose momentum when forced to wait for an occupancy permit or certification. When several businesses are damaged during a natural disaster, it is predictable that the company must wait for such inspections, thus prolonging the recovery process. It is important to have on staff one employee who is a certified building inspector, thus eliminating and superseding the inspection process from an outside agency. The employee possesses the necessary credentials, follows the inspection process impartially, and facilitates the occupancy permit or certification, without unnecessary delay maintenance, information technology, safety, security, risk, utility services, including through the possible use of outside contractors. Depending on the area of the active shooting, specialists may be contracted to assist in the damage assessment process. Additionally, many companies should consider one aspect that is often neglected in the recovery process—performing a building inspection. The property may have undergone all restoration and repairs, but the business can still lose momentum when forced to wait for an occupancy permit or certification. When several businesses are damaged during a natural disaster, it is predictable that the company must wait for such inspections, thus prolonging the recovery process. It is important to have on staff one employee who is a certified building inspector, thus eliminating and superseding the inspection process from an outside agency. The employee possesses the necessary credentials, follows the inspection process impartially, and facilitates the occupancy permit or certification, without unnecessary delay.

When conducting an inspection of the damage, the assessment team cannot speculate on their analysis or be uneducated in the areas of technology functionality, mechanisms, restoration timeframe variances, level of effort requirements, or replacement costs. The process must take into consideration predictable interdependencies, which aspects are attainable versus an accelerated time schedule, and areas that may be problematic based on the level of damage and complexity of the systems. The DAT should consider a straightforward approach to the assessment, such as viewing the damage from the perspective of severity. Under this approach, each item reviewed translates into a category of assessment or a specific value across a wide spectrum of choices. When reviewing items, a "No damage" classification should still be listed to ensure that item is reviewed properly and to remove any doubt about whether it was inspected. Another classification is "Superficial"—which in some cases could mean just applying a new coat of paint, rearranging landscaping rocks, or cleaning up bloodstains, all relatively inexpensive measures. A "Minor damage" classification may include replacing a small section of fencing, replacing drywall to remove bullet holes, or replacing blood-spattered carpeting. When the classification is "Major damage," then there are substantial issues, including some that may require either repair or purchase of new technology. The damage can cascade across multiple systems or areas, with restoration of functionality unable to be achieved in the near term. The "Severe damage" classification may consider reengineering systems, monumental renovations, and the cost of repairs, drawing a sharp line between repairing the problem area or not. When

FIGURE 10–3 DAT Analysis Perspective.

the DAT places a "Total loss or destroyed" classification on an item, it means the damage is permanent and irrefragable. Figure 10-3 illustrates the DAT analysis process. If the system is the lifeblood of the company, the company may have no other option but to close its doors.

Exterior Assessment

Any area or system located outside the walls of the company is considered to be an exterior item under the exterior assessment process. In many active shooting incidents, the exterior of the property is not damaged during the emergency but may be damaged by employees, guests, contractors, and vendors exiting the building to save their lives. When attempting to arrive at the active shooter location as fast as possible it is also not uncommon for first responders to cause exterior damage when they arrive on the property. The exterior assessment analyzes items from an aesthetic and functional aspect, then records the findings in the DAT report, along with any photographs. Consider the following items during an exterior assessment:

- Structures: tents, light poles, patios, fences, gates, courtyard, windows, awnings, sheds
- Furniture: benches, chairs, heaters, tables, trashcans, light fixtures, umbrellas
- Utilities: electrical, natural gas, water, cables
- Landscaping: bushes, trees, flowers, grass
- Transportation: roads, sidewalks, walkover bridges, escalators, elevators
- Hazards: bloodborne pathogens, biohazards, gas line breaks, smoke from fires
- Adjacent properties: any of the foregoing

Interior Assessment

Any area and system located inside the walls of the company is considered to be an interior item subject to an interior assessment. In many active shooting emergencies, the interior of the property is damaged as the shooter moves toward a specific targeted individual(s) or throughout the entire business in an effort to inflict as many casualties as possible. The shooter may shoot indiscriminately at people attempting to flee, into offices of known employees, through office walls and doors, or at law enforcement officers who are responding. The shooter may possess IEDs, gas or smoke canisters, or Molotov cocktails that might be hurled at employees and first responders or strategically placed to disrupt law enforcement tactical teams.

Interior damage may include damage caused by individuals who are attempting to elude and escape the shooter. These individuals may knock over chairs, bookcases, and mail carts to create obstacles for the shooter to negotiate in hopes of allowing additional time for them to escape. Employees "hiding out" from an active shooter may also cause interior damage as they turn over filing cabinets and stack chairs to block entry into the office or conference room. Finally, as the last resort, individuals may choose to fight the active shooter in an effort to save their lives and/or the lives of their coworkers, guests, and friends. These individuals will use any means possible to stop the shooter and may throw any item within their reach to disorient, confuse or injure the active shooter. They will also look for weapons and attempt to use such items as letter openers, scissors and even pencils or pens to stab or poke the shooter in the face.

Consider the following limited interior assessment for the DAT report:

- Structure: windows, doors, walls, ceiling, ventilation system, moulding, carpeting, pillars, elevator doors, railing, light fixtures, toilets, sinks, showers, door handles, locks
- Furniture: chairs, couches, tables, bookcases, pictures, lamps, refrigerators, microwaves, filing cabinets, plants, statutes, end tables, plant stands, dry-erase boards, clocks, shelving, carts
- Office equipment: printers, laptop computers, computer monitors, telephones, fax machines, power tools, radios, paper shredders, televisions, monitors, sound systems, copiers, and specialty equipment
- Utilities: electrical, natural gas lines, water lines, cables
- Hazardous: bloodborne pathogens, biohazards, gas line breaks, fumes, smoke from fires, water damage

Last, regardless of whether the damage assessment is for the exterior to interior of the property, it is foreseeable that not all inconsistencies, operational deficiencies, or abnormalities can be exhausted during the initial damage assessment. Inevitably problems will arise, systems will fail, and unexplainable phenomenon may occur as a normal course of business. The DAT can be tailored to the business's unique features, services, and products.

Restoration Overview

Regardless of the nature of the disaster, the executive staff generally has two major questions that must be resolved before restoring operations. First, how long will the repairs take? It is imperative that the DAT effectively formulate a proposed and defendable timetable for work completion that considers interfacing systems, compressed work schedules, accelerated construction and permits, and stringent oversight by management. The DAT should comprise key employees who will orchestrate repairs, order equipment, locate competent contractors, effectively schedule the work, and assume the role of the project manager to coordinate all aspects of the job. The second question to ask is how much the repairs will cost.

Reunification

Regardless of whether a disaster is manmade or natural, it will significantly affect those individuals caught in its life-threatening path of death and destruction. The business's operational configuration or open architecture may or may not provide the necessary shield of protection in avoiding or deflecting the disaster's full consequences. Because the active shooter emergency has a high probability of inflicting human damage, people may be viewed as a statistic. People who are injured must be considered during the planning phase—e.g., reunification. Irrespective of the individual's position at the business during the emergency, he or she will desire contact with a relative, the employer, or a first responder. Victims tend to find solace and comfort on multiple psychological and sociological levels when they are reunited with a loved one or even a familiar face.

To ensure optimal reunification, coordination between the first responders and the business is advisable. First responders are a tremendous source of assistance in orchestrating and facilitating contacts with relatives and employers. First responders are the appropriate agency to provide death notifications to families, and they should not release the names of victims until the family has been contacted. It should be noted that the business routinely cannot receive information on the medical condition of customers, vendors, contractors, or even volunteers. However, the business can provide information, if known, about which hospital is receiving the victims from the shooting emergency, directing family and friends accordingly.

The business's human resources department is the appropriate department to orchestrate the reunification with employee families, for it typically provides consistent and reliable interactions with employees. In addition, employee files contain important emergency contact information, telephone numbers, and names of relatives who may be contacted in an emergency situation. In an active shooting emergency, the business should not delay reaching out to family members. The business cannot provide the medical conditions of the employee, but the business can provide the hospital where the employee will be treated.

Three Sectors of Recovery

Business recovery comprises three separate and distinct sectors. The principle sectors include the employee, the department, and the business, as shown in Figure 10–4. Each sector may be independently addressed by specific actions, policies, programs, and assessments, or each sector can be drilled down to further isolate individuals, special processes, and procedures. However, only two of these sectors—the department and the business—can be quantitatively be measured by ledgers, journals, and financial documents. Economists may provide

Sectors of recovery		
Employee	Department working group	Business

FIGURE 10–4 Sectors of Recovery.

historical data on recovery or use comparisons with similar businesses, but they cannot provide a specific timeframe for the recovery from an active shooting. Economists and financial planners cannot accurately calculate the effect of the emergency on the employees or the working environment.

For a business and its employees, the recovery process is not a steady or gradual flow upward but rather consists of cyclic and sporadic variances. Not unlike the stock market, variances are noted daily, weekly, monthly, and quarterly. Some of the cycles may be anticipated, such as when the active shooter is scheduled for trial and how the employees will participate in trial preparations. Other times a loud bang outside the employee break room can have traumatic consequences on operations, work environment, and productivity for employees. No simple answer or solution has been identified across any business model that pinpoints all pertinent variables to a successful recovery. Universities, professional business services, and think tanks have for decades attempted to isolate and identify actions, procedures, processes, and policies for successful disaster recovery, but very little has been written on active shooter recovery for any business model. Regardless, the keys to a successful recovery consist of the elements of open communications, effective unwavering leadership, and a dedicated work force.

Three Phases of Recovery

To implement and stimulate recovery, three predictable phases guide and stimulate the recovery. As the company mobilizes the proper resources to make sense of this brutal incident, each fragmented action will contribute to a specific phase of recovery. The value of planning for an active shooter emergency adds clarity and presupposes the employee's timely actions.

- First, realize that there are three phases—immediate, initial, and sustainable. Each phase is unique and blends into the subsequent phase.
- Second, different executive staff employees or managers are the designated leaders for their respective phase. When one person attempts to lead all phases, the recovery may be impeded by time management constraints, stagnation, and mediocre performance as the individual falls prey to stress or is overwhelmed by rapid escalation of demands.
- Third, the sustainable phase converts predetermined actions across short-term and long-term recovery categories.
- Last, recovery is a category by itself and cannot be confused with response, which many people cumulatively lump together without differentiation.

Immediate Recovery

The first step in the recovery process is the immediate recovery actions. These actions demonstrate the preservation of life as the primary priority and are initiated while the active shooting is occurring. After initial shock dissipates, assigned individuals will, it is hoped, begin discharging their duties. The immediate recovery steps are preplanned responses being effectively performed by the employees as well as the business collectively.

Begin to prepare for the immediate recovery process before any disaster or emergency situation through proper training and education and by empowering employees to protect themselves, coworkers, guests, and contractors while also anticipating employee actions during the active shooter incident. The adaptation of the aforementioned actions should translate into the active shooter planning process. Part of the recovery process is to prevent and limit loss of life during an active shooting. Removing potential victims from the shooter's sights encompasses all the attributes of preparedness, mitigation, and response. If a company does not develop and train in an active shooter plan, disseminating it to all employees, delays can and will occur. It is important that the business maintain an open internal and external communication platform and empower employees to consider the best options to protect themselves and others while systematically orchestrating a detailed recovery plan. Without these elements, business recovery may be delayed, especially if the business chooses not to acknowledge any known obstacles to recovery. The corporate philosophy and prioritization of core values set the stage for recovery well in advance of any disaster or emergency.

Employee Actions

Each employee has a responsibility to protect himself or herself, as does the business to provide a safe and secure work environment. Through training and education, the organization's employees transform policies and procedures into valuable actions. The process of safeguarding individuals is not mutually exclusive in the eyes of the employees and the business, but it is communicated in a consciousness-raising method across all facets of the company. If the employee sees an impediment to this process, he or she should understand the process to document and report these issues to management expeditiously. Who is responsible for providing a safe and secure workplace environment? Safety and security are not the sole responsibilities of the security department, because every employee who works in the company should contribute in such efforts. If a guest who visits the property does not feel safe, he or she may go to a competitor silently, without complaining or making a scene. Who is the first individual to notify a business when he or she doesn't feel safe? It is usually an employee. If the employees don't feel safe, how can the business demonstrate any safeguarding measures realistically?

The University of California Santa Cruz [2] and the University of Minnesota Duluth [3] are two of the many sources of the building emergency evacuation plan (BEEP) actions identified in the first column section in Figure 10–5. The actions are most commonly known by individuals who have received mandated training and are aware of the notification process for fires; these actions have proven reliable by first responders in emergency situations.

Building Emergency Evacuation Plan (BEEP) Fire	Practical or Probable During an active shooting
Stay calm, do not rush, and do not panic.	Unfortunately, people cannot always stay calm, do rush and will occasionally panic at the sounds of gunfire or when actually observing the shooter heading towards them. The difference is if the individual see or hear the threat, such as yelling, screaming and gunshots. In a fire alarm, individuals sometimes need confirmation such as smelling smoke, see people running or hear a fire truck. Run, Hide, Fight are each options for the employee or individual to consider when protecting themselves, family members, coworkers and guests. The actions are based on: • the proximity of the shooter to the individual • location of escape routes • individuals ability to move • if the shooter is aware of the individual and location ability to block, lock and barricade the location
Do not ignore alarm	If the alarm is a fire alarm, the shooter may be the individual who pulled the alarm. Caution should be applied before blinding running into the hallway and leaving a concealed position if the individual hears a fire alarm during an active shooter situation. This is a perfect moment to send a message throughout the property how they should respond to the fire alarm.
Leave the building immediately, in an orderly fashion	In an active shooting emergency running or evacuating in the line of fire and sight of the shooter may not be the best course of action and depends upon the location of the shooter and the mental and physical ability of the individual or individuals. Also consider, if there is a chance of being detected or cannot leave the building without assistance, e.g. persons with disabilities before moving. Situational awareness will help the individual determine their proximity to the shooter, the nearest exit, and the mental and physical ability of the individual or individuals who are together. Running or hiding may be options to consider by each individual.
Safely stop your work	Yes and no. Yes individuals should also be aware of machines that may cause physical injury to the users. If the individual is typing a financial document safely saving the document before exiting, then no. Take appropriate actions to protect yourself under all threat conditions. It is commonsense to safely stop work, but when a person is an active shooter it may not be always practical.
Gather your personal belongings if it is safe to do so. (Reminder: take prescription medications out with you if at all possible; it may be hours before you are allowed back in the building.)	People unconsciously take briefcases and bags, while others just leave. Men generally have on their person vital items, such as cell phones, wallets and keys, while women keep these items in their purse which may be left at their workspace. Personal safety is the first priority not personal belongings. Do not take anything that will slow the person down in fleeing the active shooter.
If safe, close your office door and window, but do not lock them.	If a person is running for their life, then closing a door isn't top of the list. When thinking about personal safety, closing a door may alert the shooter to a location. However, closing each door may slow the shooters rampage as he/she searches for targets.
Use the nearest safe stairs and proceed to the nearest safe exit	Locating the nearest safe stairs and safe exit may not be as easy as it sounds. If on the first floor people may choose to exit through a window. The direction of the stairs may be a greater distance than hoped for and potentially exposes the individual to gun fire. Remembering the location of the nearest exit and searching for that exit are two different things. Peering out a door looking for the exit may jeopardize safety if the shooter is close.

FIGURE 10–5 Comparison of individual Actions between a Fire and Active Shooting.

	In the confusion of the first few minutes the shooter may be distracted by individuals who are closer. The choice to run or hide is an option for each individual to consider. Consider any option before moving. Think about your safety and the safety of others.
Do not use the elevator	If there is an elevator that is close the individual may consider that option for escape. However, if the elevator door is slow in closing and the shooter observes the individual entry into the elevator, the person is trapped with no escape. It is always best not to trap yourself without other options. The person cannot run or hide, and the only option is to fight with whatever they have on their person or their fighting skills. As example, the person cannot toss lamps, computers, chairs or vases and cannot use letter openers or scissors found in an office desk to fight the shooter.
Proceed to the designated emergency assembly point for your area.	People will run in every direction to remove themselves from the threat. It may be hours before employees appear at the emergency assembly point if they know it exits. If the active shooter is a current or former employee he or she will know the location of the emergency assembly point which will place a great number of people in harm's way. This is a great company discussion point for the command center staff to consider how they would like to proceed. A second discussion point is whether the assembly point is too close to the shooting and may be moved further away from the building.
Do not re-enter the building or work area until you have been instructed to do so by emergency responders.	Unlike a fire, the office may provide an area that can be barricaded, reinforced and locked to prevent entry. Generally, an active shooter looks for the path of least resistance, unless the shooter is looking for a specific target. If the individual(s) make entry difficult they may move on to the next room or department.
Report to your Work Area Representative at the assembly point to be checked off as having evacuated safely	Unfortunately, many businesses do not have a primary emergency assembly point let alone an alternate assembly point. Employees may not have any prior knowledge of the primary emergency assembly point or who the staff may be. Guests, contractors, vendors and volunteers have no ideal of the location of the assembly point and are not always depicted on evacuation maps.
Other areas of consideration during an Active shooting emergency	
Routinely look for exits and escape routes	Always look for exits and escape routes from any location. This should be standard for every restaurant, hotel, office building, etc.
If possible, use enclosed stairwells in an emergency	An enclosed stairwell offers more protection from falling debris. However, Individuals will use any exit regardless of its primary feature to escape. All people want to do is get out of the area as fast as possible without becoming a victim. An exit is an exit during an active shooting and it doesn't matter if it is enclosed or not. However, if the shooter is targeting people from an elevated position, then cover or concealment should be considered.
Ensure emergency responders are immediately contacted about individuals who are in the building, give location, number of people and the condition of any people remaining in the building.	All important points in every emergency situation. The individual may also be contacted by law enforcement as a witness to the shooting
Individuals cannot return to the building until emergency responders give permission to do so.	In an active shooting and other emergencies when law enforcement says it is safe, then it is safe to reenter, not before. However, many areas of the property will be a crime scene and may be blocked off for days or even weeks.
When the Alarm stops, doesn't mean the emergency is over	In an active shooting and other emergencies when law enforcement says it is safe, then it is safe, not before.

FIGURE 10–5 (Continued)

Initial Recovery

A business and its executive staff are measured, known, and remembered by their actions or inactions, decisions or indecisiveness. Each action, assignment, duty, and area of responsibility should be embedded in every employee—without exception. Unfortunately, many companies do not train their employees well in how to deal with an active shooter or with workplace violence, and the employee is left with only internal resolve, determination, and ingenuity for negotiating the emergency. How effective would a defensive football team be if the team never trained and was never provided with a playbook, if each player had no idea what to do? Then consider how effective a business would be at recovering under the same circumstances, lacking training, planning, and actions. Initial recovery revolves around the three specific categories of importance, as illustrated in Figure 10–6.

The people category includes anyone who is at the business location during the active shooting emergency. Employees, guests, contractors, vendors, volunteers, and others who were on property, as well as anyone who may have been a victim in a neighboring property, injured by a stray bullet, all fall into this area of importance. From identification and observation of stress levels to caring for the injured and assigning cross-trained employees to critical functions consistent actions in the immediate recovery process, how each of these individuals is acknowledged, nurtured, and personally treated may spell the difference between a reassuring positive relationship for the individual and the company—or not. If not treated properly, the affected individuals may create a backlash of negative press through social media, through news outlets, and in the courtroom. Every person who is present during the active shooter crisis is a part of the emergency regardless of whether he or she saw the shooter first-hand, evacuated the building, or was barricaded in an office. People want to be reassured, want answers to their questions, and want help in this time of adversity. People do not want to be ignored nor placed in limbo, nor do they want the company to be insensitive to their needs. People are the glue binding together a sustainable and resilient business and community. How they are treated by the business during this time of crisis will speak volumes about the leadership and professionalism of the organization.

Property is the second category. Each business is unique, and the resumption of business back to normal operational levels is based on unilateral composition of products, goods, or services. Products and goods are typically insured and will inevitably be replaced. Downtime, which may be based on just-in-time inventories or shipping delays, adversely affects the restoration of business operation.

The last category in the initial recovery section is to follow the plan. As we have already discussed, having a plan that fosters recovery is critical in an active shooter scenario. The plan,

FIGURE 10–6 Recovery Categories of Importance.

when coupled with a checklist, brings order to a chaotic situation and helps to reassure every-one involved. The plan should define limitations and leverage the strengths of individuals while providing stability and order to those who are charged with the responsibility of protecting employees and guests. Unfortunately, if the company has no plan, employees may misunderstand their duties during the emergency. Because each business is different, the best place to start in writing the recovery plan is to answer the questions in **Appendix C**. The answers will help to guide the planning process and determine a course of action, as well as stimulating discussion and fostering a collaborative environment.

Sustainable Recovery

According to Merriam-Webster's dictionary, "sustainable" means able to last or continue for a long period [4]. For a business that has suffered an active shooting crisis, the shooting will shake the company to the core, and employees may lose trust in management. The ramifications of the emergency can redefine the business either negatively or positively, depending on the resiliency of the company and its leadership. From the reprioritization and stabilization, the business must select a path to follow during the recovery process that will be financially and ethically sustainable. After an active shooting, a company may decide to restore its operations as fast as possible. People need to work. The employees need an income, and the company, despite the upheaval of the shooting, must open again. But when? When a company can honestly answer these questions without bias and realistically, without compromising its values and business ethics, then the business fundamentally is defining the recovery function. However, all recovery questions should be answered before the emergency, not during the emergency, lest the answers not be thoroughly evaluated or properly assessed by all relevant employees and departments. The business cannot afford inconsistent and fragmented answers based on a kneejerk reaction during a monumental crisis such as that posed by an active shooter.

Additionally, a sustainable recovery also considers both short-term and long-term recovery. A short-term recovery may consist of full or partial operations within the first six months, whereas long-term recovery looks at business operations beyond the six-month mark. The time frame is dictated by the nature and seasonal adjustments of the business. An active shooting at a tourism destination, during the peak of the tourist season, is quite different from one during the off-season months. In addition, revenue forecasts and financial expenditures for inventory purchases may be affected by lending institutions or investors. For a business, a sustainable recovery is based on market demands, the employee workforce, and a flexible, yet unyielding, professional leadership team. If the customer base is skeptical about safety or product delivery deadlines, the business's recovery may not be able to meet such predetermined timelines.

Checklist Process

Why do we use checklists? The answer is simple: so that we won't forget important functions—and to help us properly execute processes in the correct sequence, not relying on memorization to guide every action. Realistically, given sufficient time, an individual may inevitably find a majority of the answers and remember the correct sequences of operation. However, an active shooting event is not calm, nor does the individual have unlimited time to execute the correct steps in the response process. Add into the equation panic, shock, and disbelief, and it is easy to see that a person under pressure will not react as normally. The brain naturally and immediately shifts to self-protection mode and has great difficulty staying focused. When you are in a safe location, can you identify the first fifteen actions to protect the employees, guests, contracts, volunteers and vendors who are currently on property? Would a checklist help?

Many executives and managers believe that they do not need a checklist—not because they dismiss the chance that an active shooting event will occur on their property, but rather because their experience will "kick in" at the right time, as demonstrated throughout their illustrious career. If this is true, then can veteran airline pilots forgo using checklists under every emergency and crisis situation? No. Checklists help *especially* when under pressure. The checklist process allows every employee to function the same regardless of seniority, length of employment, education, or unfamiliarity with the process. Checklists also help people use the proper sequence, which could save lives and neutralize the threat.

Businesses are not unfamiliar with checklists, as exemplified by safety audits, bomb threats, background investigations, and new employee orientation. When considering disasters, crises, and emergency situations, checklists are underused by, even alien to, some in the business world. Safeguarding individuals and the business cannot be limited to redefining and redesigning the response process under every new disaster or when a new executive is assigned. Pre-identification of time-sensitive actions is a powerful tool in ensuring standardization, optimizing resources and skill sets, and providing a comprehensive platform to maximize business leadership in an emergency.

Before any emergency, crisis, or disaster, it is prudent for key executives, management, and the business to translate key operational areas, life safety actions, and a coordinated integration response into checklists for specific needs and functionality. Each business is unique, possessing its own in-house departments or outsourcing business functions and only having a limited number of employees—which may mean that employees are wearing multiple hats. Which brings up a question: Which areas in your business will significantly benefit from a checklist? Some areas to consider may be the following:

- Emergency command renter
- Security surveillance and control room
- Public broadcast exchange (PBX)
- Emergency evacuation assembly area
- Damage assessment

Without covering all five areas, it is appropriate to focus on one area—the emergency evacuation assembly area (EEAA)—to demonstrate the importance of having a checklist and planning before any emergency. The EEAA should be known to all employees, but if the active shooter is a current or former employee, he or she may know the location of the EEAA and navigate toward this area during the attack. Consider security precautions at the EEAA, such as having additional security or armed law enforcement officers securing the EEAA. Law enforcement officers re keenly aware that if the employees and guests meet at the EEAA, there is a risk of the shooter's attacking them there. They are also aware that several of these individuals may be witnesses to the active shooter and must be contacted timely. Insightful, timely information will aid investigative efforts and help the first responders who are entering the building. If the business has properly prepared for an active shooter and collaborated with first responders by inviting them to tour the property and view the active shooter plan, it will reinforce the program. Normally first responders will request a position or post within the EEAA to help with monitoring and protection.

The EEAA is an extremely important component of any emergency evacuation plan. The EEAA is generally located outside the building, in a safe and secure location easily accessible by first responders and emergency personnel. Please note that depending on the magnitude and type of the emergency, the first responder community may not be immediately available to assist at the EEAA. The business should consider sustaining the EEAA operations well beyond the first half-hour of activation and anticipate several hours of functionality before assistance may be provided.

The business is responsible for all guests and employees before, during, and after an emergency. How guests and employees are treated while at the EEAA may resonate into the future—in the form of criticism or accolades—as a result of business preparation, response, actions, planning, communications, and assistance. The EEAA should not be an afterthought but should be equipped and staffed on a scalable level proportionate to the demands placed on the site and the EEAA team. When defining the sections for the checklist, it is important to distinguish all significant areas of responsibility, functions, personnel assignments, tasks, equipment, and special needs for the EEAA. Consider the following:

- Where are the designated locations (primary and secondary)?
- Is the location accessible to disabled and injured individuals (mobility, vision, hearing, endurance, etc.)?
- Preidentify and preassign primary and secondary employees to key positions.
- Train all EEAA employees in their roles, duties, and responsibilities.
- Prestage all necessary equipment and supplies needed to operate the EEAA.
- Be prepared to augment the EEAA staff as the incident escalates in size.
- Determine which communications platform will be used (consider disabled individuals and those in shock).
- What signs will be provided to direct people to the location (how will blind guests locate the EEAA?)?
- Determine how the EEAA will be segmented by
  - Disabled individuals
  - Reunification
  - Injured individuals
  - Law enforcement interviews
  - Equipment staging and supplies

- Documentation and verification
- Communications
- Identify and document which employees have successfully evacuated the building during the active shooting.
- Identify and document which employees are still unaccounted for and who were in the building at the time of the active shooting.
- Document the last known location of employees still in the building, providing the information to first responders.
- Document by name all tenants, guests, and visitors located at the EEAA.
- Document injured individuals who need assistance by name to ensure that they won't be confused as being still inside.
- Communicate the type and severity of injuries of individuals to the first responders, if known. This also includes people in shock. (First responders will prioritize injured needs.)
- Consider a location for the injured closest to first responders, making it easier to provide care, medical support, and protection.
- Consider how the EEAA will be secured to prevent unauthorized people from mingling with injured individuals.
- Document and communicate the known location of and how many individuals are positioned in the areas of refuge or assistance (enclosed stairwells, etc.).
- Instruct all people that they cannot reenter the building under any circumstance
- Instruct employees that they cannot leave the EEAA until permitted to do so by first responders and the company.
- Immediately communicate to first responders if a person desires to reenter the building, including the reason if known and where he or she intends to go.
- Communication methods must be available at the EEAA for all persons, including those who have a disability and those who speak only in foreign languages.
- It is important not to separate persons who have disabilities from family members, friends, or a buddy.
- It is important not to segregate persons who have disabilities by disability (remember that people may have more than one disability).
- Provide updated communication messages verbally and in writing to the EEAA individuals.
- Determine a section within the EEAA for reunification.
- If minor children are located at the EEAA, ensure that only authorized individuals are allowed to remove them after providing proper identification and upon verbal confirmation by the minor.
- Determine a section of the EEAA for law enforcement interviews and investigations.
- Identify individuals who are having emotional instability at the EEAA and direct them toward the human resources counselors or directly to first responders.
- Consider the use of trained human resources counselors and company emergency medical technicians as EEAA staff members, who, if present, should move around the EEAA looking for how to assist people.
- Consider what forms will be needed for each EEAA function.

- Be aware that emotions will be high and will often escalate after employees see injured or dead coworkers or cannot locate coworkers, which will place additional demands on EEAA staff members.
- Ensure that the EEAA is accessible to all individuals, including persons who have disabilities.
- Ensure that the EEAA is shown on the building emergency evacuation maps.
- EEAA equipment may include chairs, wheelchairs, water (to take medicine), food (for people who are diabetic or who have other medical conditions), lights, flashlights, toilets, clipboards, paper, pens/pencils, blankets, portable generator, extra batteries, extra radios, and methods of communication.
- Determine where the EEAA equipment will be kept before the emergency.
- Provide a communications platform for updating guests and employees, including persons who have disabilities and foreign guests.
- Keep news media crews from accessing the EEAA lest they hinder law enforcement investigations.

After all foregoing areas, as well as any new areas identified, have been discussed, with disputed issues resolved by the EEAA team before any emergency, a checklist can be developed. The document should be suitable for use by employees and should be comparable in style, format, and design to other company checklists. It is not impractical for amendments and revisions to the checklist to be made. It is permissible and quite common during training exercises to gauge and confirm the accuracy of the checklist. Because the checklist is a living document, developed for the exclusive use of the business and proprietary to the EEAA, the checklist should improve over time.

References

[1] Department of Homeland Security. <www.dhs.gov/what-critical-infrastructure>.

[2] The University of California–Santa Cruz. <https://facilities.soe.ucsc.edu/emergency>.

[3] University of Minnesota–Duluth. <www.d/umn.edu.ehso/beep/>.

[4] Merriam-Webster Dictionary. <www.merriam-webster.com/dictionary/sustainable>.

Appendix A
Types and Classifications of Murderers

A local news broadcast reports a body found under suspicious circumstances. A viewer watching this program begins the process of analyzing exactly how this death would ultimately be classified. Even though the victim had been shot several times, the news anchor won't say that the individual was murdered. However, the viewer notes the facts provided, then decides that the person was murdered. The next step in this analysis is deciding whether the murder was committed in the first degree, second degree, or third degree or was manslaughter. Is it possible that the victim was not murdered? Perhaps the victim was the attacker and the individual shot the attacker in self-defense? Unless the viewer is in law enforcement, a criminal justice professor, attorney, a judge, or an avid viewer of criminal justice television, it will be difficult to define the differences between first-, second-, and third-degree murder, let alone voluntary manslaughter or involuntary manslaughter. Now add into the definition pool the differences between an active shooter, a mass murderer, and a serial murderer. The following list will help guide the reader in defining various classifications and wordings of murder.

Before looking at the list, it might be interesting to note the source of these definitions. First, local, state, and federal laws clearly define certain levels of murder within a particular jurisdiction. First- and second-degree murder are not identical in all states but are similar in definition. However, not all states recognize the classification or definition of third-degree murder. The second way for definitions to be developed is through medical and psychiatric journals, white papers, and case studies attempting to further classify murders and deaths in a more definable category. After placement in a definable category, efforts can be expended to reduce the categories further, according to the number of cases, and new classifications may be added based on statistical analysis. Third, university and law professors often write research papers attempting to isolate and identify new classifications or further define existing ones. Fourth, a few of the following definitions are not commonly used within the court system or found in legal dictionaries. An example is "autocide," which is not listed in legal dictionaries and is a term not commonly used in the court of law.

Accidental death	USLegal.com defines accidental death as "[a] death resulting from an unusual event that was unanticipated by everyone involved. It should not be intended, expected, or foreseeable. Accidental death further indicates the death cannot be result of suicide, natural causes or murder."
Autocide	Dictionary.com defines autocide as "[s]uicide by crashing the vehicle one is driving." The vehicle can be a truck, van, motorcycle, boat, or airplane. Autocide is a suicide, not a murder.
Aborticide	Freedictionary.com defines aborticide as "[d]estruction of a fetus".

(also known as feticide)	Aborticide can also be defined as the act of killing a fetus in the womb.
Avunculicide	Merriam-Webster's dictionary (www.Merriam-Webster.com) defines avunculicide as "[t]he killing of an uncle by his nephew or niece." History, including the Bible, is full of examples of an uncle's being slain by his nephew or niece.
Amicicide	Freedictionary.com defines amicicide as "the murder of one friend by another." Regardless of the reason, such as withholding drugs, stealing a friend's girlfriend, or an argument over property, the murder of a trusted friend is still a murder.
Androcide	Wikipedia.org defines androcide as "the systematic killing of men for various reasons, usually cultural." Androcide may occur during war or revolution to reduce an enemy's potential army by killing or executing all men or even teenagers in a region or village.
Capital punishment	Merriam-Webster's dictionary defines capital punishment as "[t]he death penalty for a crime." Oxford dictionaries (www.Oxforddictionaries.com/us) defines capital punishment as "the legally authorized killing of someone as punishment for a crime." Thirty-two states exact the death penalty, and most have a minimum age requirement that must be met before carrying out the sentence. Some states are now challenging capital punishment based on the mental capacity of the convicted person to understand the wrongfulness of his or her actions before execution. Eighteen states have either never exacted the death penalty or abolished the death penalty since 1853.
Criminally negligent homicide	The Texas statute for criminally negligent homicide defines it as follows: "A person commits an offense if he caused the death of an individual by criminal negligence." Criminal negligence is defined in Texas statute as follows: "A person acts with criminal negligence, or is criminally negligent, with respect to circumstances surrounding his conduct or the result of his conduct when he ought to be aware of a substantial and unjustifiable risk that the circumstances exist or the result will occur."
Criminally negligent manslaughter	The Texas statute governing criminally negligent homicide defines as follows: "A person commits an offense if he recklessly causes the death of an individual." The difference between manslaughter and homicide is that manslaughter is the unjustifiable, inexcusable, and intentional killing of a person without deliberation, premeditation and malice. Homicide is with deliberation, premeditation, and malice.
Disorganized serial killer	According to Gillian Taber (*Organized and Disorganized Serial Killers*, 2009), disorganized serial killers rarely plan out the deaths of their victims in any way. These killers often leave evidence at the crime scene and display signs of being out of control during the killings. During these serial killings, the people killed just happened to be in the wrong place at the wrong time. These killers generally tend to move to different towns or even states regularly to avoid arrest.
Democide	Freedictionary.com defines democide as "the murder of any person or people by a government, genocide, politicide and mass murder." This type of murder is not done by one individual, but rather under the direction of a government or revolutionary unit. The victims of democide may total thousands and will continue to accumulate until the killing is stopped by a superior power.
Euthanasia (also mercy killing)	Freedictionary.com defines euthanasia as "mercy killing, the deliberate ending of life of a person suffering from an incurable disease." The killer is ending a person's life—in the killer's mind—for compassionate reasons. The killer does not want a loved one or some other suffering person to suffer any longer. The killer wants to remove the person's pain.

Femicide (also gynecide, gynaecide, or gynocide)	The World Health Organization defines femicide as "[v]iolence against women including verbal harassment, emotional abuse, physical and sexual abuse and murder or women." A broader definition of femicide also includes the killing of girls of all ages. Outside of war or revolution, femicide is usually carried out by a partner or ex-partner of the victim.
Felony murder	USLegal.com defines felony murder as "[a] legal doctrine that widens the scope of murder." For example, if a killing happened either accidentally or without specific intent to kill during the commission of a felony, the charge would be murder, not manslaughter.
First-degree murder	Freedictionary.com defines first-degree murder as "a killing which is deliberate and premeditated, in conjunction with felonies such as rape, burglary, arson, involving multiple deaths, and the killing of certain types of people such as a child or a police officer. For first degree murder there must be an intentional murder that is willful and premeditated with malice aforethought. For first degree murder the prosecution must prove beyond a reasonable doubt the following: 1. Unlawfully killed the victim. 2. Killed the victim with malice and aforethought. 3. Killing was premeditated. 4. The victim was killed at a particular location identified in the indictment."
Familicide	Definitions.net has more than one definition of familicide. First, it is a type of murder or murder–suicide in which at least one spouse and one or more children is killed. Second, it may include the killing of a parent or parents as well as possibly other relatives, such as siblings and grandparents.
Family annihilation	Definitions.net defines family annihilation as the "[k]illing of all family members [that] may include a murder–suicide." In some cases, the murderer will kill the entire family and then when it comes to killing himself or herself change his or her mind and flee the scene of the crime.
Filicide	Oxford Dictionaries define filicide as "the killing of one's son or daughter by a parent." A paper in the *Journal of Forensic Science International* in 2014 by Dr. Timothy Mariano, Alpert Medical School of Brown University, indicated that over the last three decades U.S. parents have committed filicide about 500 times every year: Over the course of thirty-two years, more than 15,000 arrests were made in which the victim was either a son or daughter of the murderer.
Fratricide	Merriam-Webster's dictionary defines fratricide as "[o]ne that murders or kills his or her own brother or sister or an individual (as a countryman) having a relationship like that of a brother or sister." The act of fratricide also is considered in a military context such as the death by friendly fire. Because military personnel are considered brothers in arms, the loss of military personnel is like losing a brother or sister, so a friendly fire death can be classified as fratricide.
Geronticide	Lexic.us defines geronticide as the "[k]illing or euthanasia of the elderly." The definition may also include the abandonment of the elderly to die, allowing them to commit suicide or be killed because they cannot protect themselves.
Gendercide	Gendercide.org defines gendercide as "gender-selective mass killing." Gendercide is the systematic killing of members of a specific sex, either males or females, regardless of age.
Genocide	Oxford Dictionaries define genocide as "the deliberate killing of a large group of people, especially those of a particular ethnic group or nation." Genocide may also be the systematic extermination of an entire racial or religious group.
Homicide	Merriam-Webster's dictionary defines homicide as "the act of killing of a person."
Human sacrifice	Wikipedia.org defines human sacrifice as "the act of killing one or more human beings, usually as an offering to a deity, as part of a religious ritual."

Honor-killing	Merriam-Webster's dictionary defines honor killing as "the traditional practice in some countries of killing a family member who is believed to have brought shame on the family." Regardless of the age or sex of the individual who has brought disgrace to the family, he or he will be put to death. Reasons for this type of killing may include committing adultery or seeking divorce, refusing to take part in a prearranged marriage, engaging in homosexuality, changing one's religion, or suffering a sexual assault.
Hedonistic serial killer	CriminalJusticeschoolInfo.com defines a hedonistic serial killer as a "killer driven by the thrill/rush, lust/sexual pleasure or gain brought on by the murder." These killers kill because they enjoy the act of killing and sometimes become sexually aroused during the act of murder. Both women and men can be hedonistic serial killers.
Involuntary manslaughter	U.S. Legal Dictionary (www.definitions.uslegal.com) defines involuntary manslaughter as being when "death is caused during the commission of a non-felony, such as reckless driving[,] and the manslaughter lacks the element of malice." Involuntary manslaughter may also be considered the unlawful killing of another human being without intent.
Infanticide	Merriam-Webster's dictionary defines infanticide as "the killing of an infant." Other definitions may stipulate that the child must be within the first year of its life.
Justifiable homicide	Freedictionary.com defines justifiable homicide as "a homicide that is commanded or authorized by law." As an example, a soldier in war is commanded to kill the enemy without warning the victim ahead of time, and the killing is done aforethought.
Mariticide	Dictionary.com defines mariticide as "the act of killing one's spouse, especially the murder of a husband by his wife."
Matricide	Merriam-Webster's dictionary defines matricide as "the act of murdering your own mother." Matricide also includes murder by the son or daughter of the victim.
Manslaughter	Freedictionary.com defines manslaughter as "the unjustifiable, inexcusable, and intentional killing of a human being without deliberation, premeditation, and malice. Manslaughter is also the unlawful killing of a human being without any deliberation, which may be involuntary, in the commission of a lawful act without due caution and circumspection."
Mass murder	The Federal Bureau of Investigation defines mass murder as "four or more murders occurring during a particular event with no cooling-off period between the murders." A mass murderer may also kill within one location during one continuous period of time, whether a few minutes or a period of days.
Medical serial killer	The Crime Museum describes a medical killer as "a person who has become involved in the medical industry as a way to carry out their nefarious deeds. This type of killer feels they have the perfect cover because it is very common for people in a hospital to pass away. They are usually highly intelligent and know how to carefully and cleverly conceal their murders. As long as it appears that a victim has died a natural death, there will be no reason for anyone to suspect foul play and search for the guilty party. A few doctors in history have managed to kill dozens of people before others began to catch on."
Mission-oriented serial killer	Crime.About.com defines a mission-oriented serial killer as a person who "[t]argets a specific group of people who he believes are unworthy to live and without whom the world would be a better place."
Medicide	Freedictionary.com defines medicide as "a suicide accomplished with the aid of a physician." Medicide may also include a medically assisted suicide by using medication or the absence of medical life-saving equipment.

Murder–suicide	Freedictionary.com defines a murder–suicide as "[a] double act in which a person kills one or more others before killing himself, or at the same time as killing one or more others."
Neonaticide	Freedictionary.com defines neonaticide as "the act of killing an infant within the first twenty-four hours of its life."
Nepoticide	Dictionary.Sensagent.com defines nepoticide as "the killing of a nephew."
Organized serial killer	According to Gillian Taber (*Organized and Disorganized Serial Killers*, 2009), an organized serial killer is likely to plan his or her actions and is extremely careful not to leave any evidence at the crime scene. The organized serial killer is likely to be intelligent, socially skilled, and sexually competent, less likely to live alone, more likely to target complete strangers, and likely to display antisocial and psychopathic personality traits. Typically these serial killers are the most difficult to identify and capture, because they are well organized to the point of being meticulous. They attempt to plan out every detail well in advance and take every precaution to make sure they leave no incriminating evidence behind.
Omnicide	USLegal.com defines omnicide as "[h]uman extinction as a result of human action and most commonly refer[ring] to extinction through nuclear war." Omnicide can also include extinction through means such as global anthropogenic ecological catastrophe.
Populicide	Freedictionary.com defines populicide as "the slaughter of the people."
Parricide (also parenticide)	Merriam-Webster's dictionary defines parricide as "[o]ne that murders his or her father, mother, or a close relative."
Patricide	Merriam-Webster's dictionary defines patricide as "[o]ne who murders his or her own father."
Prolicide	Freedictionary.com defines prolicide as "the crime of destroying one's offspring, either in the womb or after birth."
Second-degree murder	Freedictionary.com defines second-degree murder as "a non-premeditated killing, resulting from an assault in which death of the victim was distinct possibility. In second degree murder the murder was intentional with malice aforethought, but is not planned in advance."
Serial killer	The U.S. Bureau of Justice defines a serial killer as one who commits "[t]he killing of several victims over three or more separate events." A serial killer may also murder three people over a period of thirty days or more, with an inactive period between each murder.
Spree killer	The U.S. Bureau of Justice defines a spree killer as one who commits "[t]he killing at two or more locations with no time break between the murders." A spree murderer will also kill two or more victims, but not all at one location. Even though these murders occur in separate locations, the spree is considered a single incident. Additionally, there is no "cooling-off" or break period between the murders.
Self-immolation	Merriam-Webster's dictionary defines patricide as "a deliberate and willing sacrifice of oneself often by fire"—as history has shown, a form of extreme protest.
Suicide by cop	Wikipedia.org defines suicide by cop as "a suicide method in which a suicidal individual deliberately acts in a threatening way, provoking a lethal response from a law enforcement officer or other legitimately armed individual, such as being shot to death."
Senicide	Freedictionary.com defines senicide as "the killing off of the old men in a tribe." Instead of caring for the elderly, they are killed when they can no longer work or take care for themselves and are becoming a burden.

Sororicide	Oxford Dictionaries defines sororicide as "the killing of one's sister."
Uxoricide	Wikipedia.org defines uxoricide as "the act of killing one's wife by the husband."
Visionary serial killer	Crime.About.com defines a visionary serial murder as follows: "Usually psychotic, the visionary is compelled to murder because he hears voices or sees visions ordering him to kill certain kinds of people."
Voluntary manslaughter	U.S. Legal Dictionary defines voluntary manslaughter as "killing in heat of passion, in self-defense, or while committing a felony." Voluntary manslaughter may also be accompanied by circumstances that mitigate, but that do not excuse, the killing.
Wrongful death	Dictionary Law defines wrongful death as "the death of a human being as the result of a wrongful act of another person: Wrongful acts may include, negligence, an intentional attack, another crime that caused death, manslaughter or even murder."

Appendix B
Psychological Characteristics of Murderers

There is no specific age for an active shooter, so how can an active shooter be classified and categorized by personality and behavioral traits if the age range is from 12 to 88? Can violent video games or movies be the defining factor that causes a shooter to begin his or her deadly rampage? Did the 12-year-old or 88-year-old watch violent movies or play violent video games? Scholars call two or three cases not within the normal range anomalous. Even so, people died, and these cases were classified as active shooters. There is an enormous difference in life experiences, challenges, and variables that affect an individual, including medical treatment.

Researchers and professional organizations have statistically identified a wide variety of ways that murders can be classified, and discussion about the correctness of these classifications has been ongoing for decades. Method of death, thought process, simultaneous murders or extended period of time, location, association with target location and victims are only a few points of consideration when determining classifications. When a category has been identified, researchers will attempt to ensure that the category is correct; if not, a new category may be identified. Furthermore, as new disciplines contribute to the murder classifications, they will use information to approach the topic from a different perspective, for the incident may not be an isolated event, but rather an entirely new category. The new perspective may further verify the traits within the classifications or further expand the indicators to aid professional organizations and law enforcement agencies in developing a new malicious class of murderer.

For any researcher, academic professional, therapist, or investigator who must cope with the horrific effects of an active shooting, allocating precious resources to identify the likely perpetrators in an effort to proactively prevent the scale of suffering is a universal goal. Regardless of the phenomenon known as an "active shooter," there is a new concept associated with the Columbine High School shooting. According to the Oklahoma State Scout, on September 28, 1850, George Pharoah, a 19-year-old student at Rocky Hill Schoolhouse West Chester, Pennsylvania, shot and killed Rachel Sharpless, an 18-year-old schoolteacher. This may have been the first recorded school shooting not associated with Indian raids or war [1]. However, many of the early school shootings focused on one person—not wanton killing of anyone in sight, whether students or teachers. There are many reasons for these shootings:

- Revenge by a parent for excessive punishment by a teacher or administrator
- Misguided love or a love triangle
- A teacher shooting at students for refusing to do work or for other misconduct
- Accidental discharges by students
- Arguments between students
- Disagreement between students and teachers
- Suicide or murder–suicide of a teacher or student

Media coverage accounts of these shootings in newspapers, or even shootings reported to law enforcement, were inconsistent and considered noncontroversial based on the reason for the shooting. Possibly the first mass active shooting in a school, as reported on Sodahead. com, was on May 6, 1940, when ex-principal Vieling Spencer shot and killed five school officials at South Pasadena Junior High School in South Pasadena, California [2]. Perhaps the victims had testified against the ex-principal and this was his method of revenge. The *Huffington Post* listed several school shootings, including possibly the first active shooting with two shooters involved, which occurred on March 12, 1951, at Alexander School in Union Mills, North Carolina. Professor W. E. Sweatt was shot to death by two of his students after what they perceived as an unfair reprimand [3]. Again, revenge appears to have been the obvious motive, and a pattern seems to be developing until, on August 1, 1966, Charles Whitman killed seventeen people and wounded thirty-one at the University of Texas–Austin. The *Texas Monthly* reported the shooting in the article "The UT Tower Shooting [4]." An entirely new active shooter dynamic was developed: shooting randomly at unknown targets having no prior history with the shooter. This new style of shooter had planned, prepared weapons but randomly chose his targets with no feelings, no remorse, and no regard for age, sex, nationality, or race. One has to wonder whether the first responders at that shooting were contemplating whether the active shooter was an anomaly or just the first murderous act that would motivate a chain of imitation shootings. It is abundantly clear that these insensitive, uncompassionate, and fractured individuals require extensive analysis.

New classifications must distinguish unscrupulous murderer(s) from all previous shooters. When attempting to classify active shooters, an underlying and defining question should be asked: Are these individuals synonymous with another classification such as mass murderer, serial killer, or spree or rampage killer? Mass murderers and serial killers have been vigorously analyzed by professional disciplines for decades, supplying a treasure trove of data that will identify commonalities and differences between active shooters and these classifications. A spree or rampage killer is a relatively new category that is not yet fully recognized in the professional community.

Mass Murders

The Federal Bureau of Investigation defines mass murder as "four or more murders occurring during a particular event with no cooling-off period between the murders [5]." A mass murderer may also kill within one location during one continuous period of time, whether a few minutes or over a period of days.

The Mass Murders Table, refer to Figure B–1, identifies the various labels, psychological traits, and indicators of mass murderers as found on the forensicpsych.umwblogs.org website in a section titled, History of Classifications of Serial Killers and Mass Murders [6]. It is important to note that a mass murderer is clearly defined, but the multiple individual aspects and subclassifications of a mass murderer complicate the process of identifying common indicators, psychological traits, and behaviors. Only five common areas were noted, identified by the shaded cells.

Mass Murders					
Source	**Labels, Indicators and Psychological Traits**				
Wille (1974) studied forty subjects and categorized ten different types of murders	**Depressive**	Psychotic	Afflicted with organic brain disorder	Psychopathic	Passive–aggressive
	Alcoholic	Hysterical	**Juvenile**	Mentally retarded	Sex killers
Lee (1988) created labels to differentiate among motives	Profit	Passion	**Hatred**	Power or domination	**Revenge**
	Opportunism	**Fear**	Desperation	Compassion	Ritual killer or contract killer
Holmes and Holmes (2000)	Family slayer	Murder for profit	Murdered for sex	Pseudo-commando	Set and run killer
	Psychotic killer	Disgruntled employee	Discipline type killer	Ideological mass murder	

FIGURE B–1 Mass Murderers.

Serial Murderers

The U.S. Bureau of Justice defines serial killer as "the killing of several victims over three or more separate events [7]." A serial killer may also murder three people over a period of thirty days or more, with an inactive period between each murder.

The Serial Killer table, refer to Figure B–2, identifies various labels, psychological traits and indicators of serial killers as found on the forensicpsych.umwblogs.org website in a section titled, History of Classifications of Serial Killers and Mass Murderers [8]." When compared to Figure B–1, only two common areas were noted, identified by the shaded cells.

As you can see, after decades of reporting, researching, analysis, and extensive interviews, researchers and various professional disciplines do not always agree on what common traits, behaviors, or labels can be applied to the serial killer.

Family Murderers

According to the *USA Today* article "Behind the Bloodshed: The Untold Story of America's Mass Killings [9]," the majority of mass murders (51%) are family-related. The family murderer uses a wide variety of weapons and methods to kill children, spouse, or other relatives not living in the household, including knives, strangulation, vehicles, firearms, and arson. Active shooters consistently use firearms and infrequently use knives or vehicles. Molotov cocktails and other IED-type devices have been deployed in only a small percentage of such killings. The family murderer picks the most ideal time, method of implementing death, and exact location based on the victim's work or school schedule. Family dinners, gatherings, and holidays

Serial Killer				
Source	**Labels, Indicators, and Psychological Traits**			
Guttmacher (1973) Sadistic	Sexual gratification	Established a pattern for killing and selecting victims	Motivated by fantasies	Derive pleasure from dehumanizing victim
Lunde (1976)	Suffers from psychosis	Considered insane		
Danto (1982)	Obsessive–compulsive	Kills in particular style and pattern		
Egger (1984)	No relationship Killer and victim are strangers	Occurs at a different time Compulsive act based on fantasies	No connection to previous murder	Different geographic location
Holmes and DeBurger (1988)	Visionary type obeys commands of voices or visions	Mission-oriented type rids society of certain groups of people	Hedonistic type seeks thrills	Power/control-oriented type exerts power over helpless victim
FBI Behavioral Profile Unit (2013)	Psychological gratification	**Anger**	Thrill	Financial gain
	Attention seeking	Low-average intelligence	Trouble staying employed	Abandoned by father
	Lower- to-middle-class background	Interested in voyeurism	Interested in fetishism	High rates of suicide attempts
	Abused emotionally, physically, or sexually	**Frequently bullied as child**	Involved in petty crimes	Interested in sadomasochistic pornography

FIGURE B–2 Serial Killers.

provide a platform to promote a specific belief or topic that is causing a division in the family. The family murderer may or may not commit suicide after the deadly task has been completed. No known statistics were available concerning family murder–suicides.

The below areas, traits, and behaviors were identified by the Howard Journal of Criminal Justice in the article "Characteristics of Family Killers Revealed by First Taxonomy Study" on August 14, 2013 [10], refer to Figure B–3. The study covered thirty years of case data between 1980 and 2012. The study analyzed seventy-one cases in Great Britain. When compared to Figure B–1, only two common areas were noted, identified in the shaded cells.

Spree or Rampage Killer

The U.S. Bureau of Justice defines spree killing as "[t]he killing at two or more locations with no time break between the murders [11]." A spree murder will also kill two or more victims, but not all at one location. Even though these murders occur in separate locations, their spree is considered a single incident. Additionally, there is no "cooling-off" or break period between the murders.

Family Murderers				
Source	**Labels, Indicators, and Psychological Traits**			
	Few had criminal records	**Male 83%**	Age 30s: 55% 20–10%	Oldest 59 years old
	Attempted suicide 81%	Employed 71%	August 20%	Just under 50% committed on weekends
	Career success prior to murder	Surgeons, police, postmen, marketing executives	Majority of murders took place at home	Most common day Sunday
	Stabbing and carbon monoxide common methods	Family breakup 66%, followed by financial difficulty, honor killing, and mental illness		**Revenge**
Categories	**Types of Family Killers or Annihilators**			
Anomic	Family success or failure is based on economic success. If not successful, family is source of problem.			
Disappointed	If family is not ideal family as the murder envisions it, the family have let him or her down by undermining and destroying values, successes, cultural customs, or religious beliefs.			
Paranoid	The threat to the family is external, such as social services or the legal system. The only person who can really protect the family is the murderer.			
Self-righteous	For example, a man blames his wife the breakup, for his criminal activity, for working and makes more than he does, and for anything that diminishes his status as the head of the house hold			

FIGURE B–3 Family Murderers.

Common Traits of a Rampage Killer			
Mostly murders strangers	Reason for rampage: Divorce or breakup 25% Unexpected employment loss 45%	Public places such as schools, shopping centers, college campuses, malls	**Tends to act alone**
More than 50% history of mental illness	High levels of education	Rarely tries to flee	**Often commits suicide**	Often allows self to be taken into custody
Has military background	**Obtained weapons legally**		

FIGURE B–4 Common Traits of a Rampage Killer.

Since the term spree or rampage killer is a developing category the amount of data is not overwhelming, but may be supported by more theory than concrete indicators. To further complicate the process, if the shooter is killed during his or her attacks or commits suicide, then the pool of similar events is reduced even further.

On PR Web (www.prweb.com), Dr. Michael Nuccitelli discussed rampage killers on July 21, 2012 [12]. He noted the following common traits of a rampage killer, refer to Figure B-4. When compared to Figure B-1, only three common areas were noted, identified in the shaded cells.

One of the most disturbing aspects of attempting to identify common personality traits and behaviors is that even when there are countless warning signs and a long trail of issues observed by nearly everyone who has had contact with the shooter, they are often discarded, never acted on or reported.

- In many cases, these traits and indicators have been present for years with little or no treatment administered to the individual. To begin treatment or counseling, someone must report a concern with the individual.
- In other examples, many individuals instigate threatening communications and issue verbal and written messages—seen by relatives, friends, administrators, and bosses, but ignored or never documented.
- Unfortunately, people don't report questionable individuals. If it's a relative that is acting strange or out of character, the relative will dismiss the emotional or mental display as just a bad day. Rarely do relatives contact law enforcement agencies or mental agencies concerning a family member, unless the pattern of unrest has reached an emotional turning point. The change may be the result of threats of physical violence on a trusted loved one or the relative can no longer defend themselves twenty-four hours a day and cannot feel safe in their own homes.
- Finally, family members often believe that reporting on relatives is disloyal. Even if attackers formulate a plan in treacherous detail, and other family members know about it, this information is often not passed along to the appropriate agency of department to properly mitigate the threat.

There is no demographic profile for an active shooter or any other specific common traits of active shootings. There are significant differences in active shooters' thought processes, target selections, and the reasons behind each attack. Even if every active shooter case has been reviewed in uncompromising detail, not just using a representative sample, maybe active shooter and workplace violence homicides can be classified and categorized. However, if there is a certain profile, then there is a considerable risk of false positives being produced when stereotyping individuals. There is a significant difference between a thought and an action. We can conclude that thousands of students may possess one or all traits and indicators, but thankfully, for many unknown reasons, these individuals never turn those thoughts into actions.

Classifying and categorizing individuals is a significant step in preventing potential deadly actions, in both the short term and the long term. These classifications will help not only the first responders, but our community and society as a whole. The identified individuals may need help in understanding that the path they are headed down is not the correct route and that they may be in need of guidance, seeking medical and clinical treatments to help prevent their thoughts from turning into actions. Articles and studies have attempted to determine the mindset of active shooters in specific settings such as schools, hospitals, and the workplace. These works strive to aid first responders and train workplaces in mitigating and preparing for these events. However, because active shootings can occur in almost any setting, from a crowded mall to the confines of a supervisor's office in a high-rise building, only time will tell whether these articles and studies prove insightful. One underlying fact, which cannot be disputed, is that the active shooter is not a business problem or first responder issue, but rather a community and society problem that must be tackled from all disciplines and professions to find solutions together.

References

[1] <http://oklahomastate.scout.com/forums/2338-general-topics/12932514-oregon-school-shooting>.

[2] <www.sodahead.com/united-states/is-school-shooting-news-popular-because-the-powers-that-be-want-to-ban-guns-look-at-the-list-below/question-4287469/?link=ibaf&q=&esrc=s>.

[3] <www.huffingtonpost.com/chris-rodda/no-mr-huckabee-its-not-be_b_2311607.html?>.

[4] <www.texasmonthly.com/topics/ut-tower-shooting>.

[5] <www.fbi.gov/stats-services/publications/serial-murder/serial-murder-1#two>.

[6] <http://forensicpsych.umwblogs.org/research/criminals/serial-killers-and-mass-murderers/>.

[7] <https://books.google.com/books?id=Sv4zKf8U2nYC&pg=PT51&lpg=PT51&dq=define+spree+killer+Bureau+of+justice&source=bl&ots=yW4N2QKZvF&sig=LYU9LNpGbjVXFiREm932x3Qr9Qs&hl=en&sa=X&ei=ub8aVdMEj96gBLPfgsAP&ved=0CEIQ6AEwBQ#v=onepage&q=define%20spree%20killer%20Bureau%20of%20justice&f=false>.

[8] <http://forensicpsych.umwblogs.org/research/criminals/serial-killers-and-mass-murderers/>.

[9] USA Today. Behind the Bloodshed: The Untold Story of the America's Mass Killings. <http://usatoday30.usatoday.com/news/nation/mass-killings/index.html>, 2014.

[10] <http://www.wiley.com/WileyCDA/PressRelease/pressReleaseId-109344.html>.

[11] <https://books.google.com/books?id=Sv4zKf8U2nYC&pg=PT51&lpg=PT51&dq=define+spree+killer+Bureau+of+justice&source=bl&ots=yW4N2QKZvF&sig=LYU9LNpGbjVXFiREm932x3Qr9Qs&hl=en&sa=X&ei=ub8aVdMEj96gBLPfgsAP&ved=0CEIQ6AEwBQ#v=onepage&q=define%20spree%20killer%20Bureau%20of%20justice&f=false>.

[12] <http://www.prweb.com/releases/ipredator/masskiller/prweb9722127.htm>.

Appendix C
Active Shooting Workplace Violence Recovery Questions

Active shooters can be an uncomfortable and unpleasant conversation to tackle. An active shooter workplace violence question model can help decision makers manage these tragic events and assist in the planning, response, and recovery phases of these tragic events. Provided here are questions that business might face because of an active shooter event. This list is not all-inclusive, and it does not take into account any considerations for which the business model may have already prepared. Because each business is individualized by its market and industry, specific business model, and market offerings, additional questions respective to a specific business may be needed to complete the questionnaire.

Even if a business has an active shooter workplace violence plan, the company will be bombarded by questions from employees, law enforcement officers, first responders, attorneys, insurance companies, families of victims, news media, neighboring businesses, customers, contractors, unions, volunteer organizations, suppliers, and stockholders, among many others. The core questions to any significant recovery may include the following:

- Business decisions
- Human resources
- Communications
- Counseling
- Security
- Financial
- Media and news crews
- Law enforcement
- Trial
- Possible legal action
- Business continuity plan

There are many questions that can help an organization to better plan and prepare for acts of violence in the workplace. Active shooters bring an additional challenge to businesses and the needs to proper identify the needs, vulnerabilities, and available resources are critical in preparing for these incidents. Preparation, in some cases, may be all a business can do. The following tables in Figures C-1 through C-12 can assist the business to better understand some information that is useful to capture during an assessment and should provide a cornerstone to begin with. These lists are not exhaustive and the business should add any questions that are pertinent to their specific company.

Business Decisions			
When an active shooting or workplace violence event occurs, senior management will be thrust into making quick decisions with or without understanding the implications for both the short and long terms. Planning for and anticipating key questions and areas of concern before the emergency will better prepare decision makers. Preparing answers and courses of action before the situation, when decision makers are not under duress or suffering from shock, is a prudent step in protecting the business. Consider the following questions and areas, then add more questions to the list as they are discussed that are specific to your business.			
# **Questions and Areas to Consider**	Yes	No	Comment
1 Should the business be sold?			
2 Should the building be leveled/razed?			
3 Should the business move to a new location or city?			
4 Should the business be merged?			
5 Should the business be closed?			
6 Should the name of the company be changed?			
7 What will it cost to change the company name on all advertising and marketing, etc.?			
8 What will a name change do to government contracts?			
9 What will a name change do to teaming agreements, partnerships, and all existing contracts?			
10 Will a name change negate past performance value on contracts?			
11 What will a name change do to patents, trademarks, and copyrights?			
12 What will a merger do to government contracts?		·	
13 What will a merger do to teaming agreements, partnerships, and leases?			
14 Will a merger negate past performance values on contracts?			
15 Who is assigned to focus on resiliency and the future business?			
16 Which insurance policies will be affected by the shooting?			
17 How much will insurance costs rise?			
18 Will the company allow people to pictures of the business? How will this affect the staff?			
19 Because people will volunteer for help, who is vetting such people to see whether they are allowed to assist?			
20 Who is assigned to contact insurance companies?			
21 Because insurance companies and lawyers will want to visit the business to take pictures, who is assigned to assist them?			
22 How long will the business be closed as a crime scene?			
23 How will the company operate when closed as a crime scene?			
24 Is the business prepared to deal with a sharp drop in stock values caused by investor loss of confidence?			
25 Will the shooting affect sister locations under the same brand name in the same city?			
26 Will the shooting affect sister locations under the same brand name in different cities?			

FIGURE C–1 Business Decisions.

27	What actions will be taken to assist other store locations regardless of state, location, and corporate entity?			
28	Will the shooting affect other locations under the same corporate umbrella in the same city if owner information is provided by news agencies?			
29	Will the shooting affect other locations under the same corporate umbrella in different cities if owner information is provided by news agencies?			
30	Will the incident affect security clearances?			
31	Will the incident affect bank loans?			
32	Will the incident affect future bank loans or lines of credit?			
33	When should employees be allowed to re-enter the building?			
34	When will employees be allowed to remove purses, phones, and other personal belongings left in a hurry?			
35	Should the business allow employees to remove vehicles left in the parking garage if the shooter drove a vehicle to the business?			
36	When should the business reopen? Who decides?			
37	Should holes in walls be plugged before employees are allowed to re-enter?			
38	Should affected areas be remodeled or left the same before employee re-enter?			
39	If one department was affected, should the affected department be outsourced? Does it depend on the number of employees?			
40	Should the business replace all damaged equipment before reopening?			
41	Will employees be allowed to vote about company recovery actions?			
42	Should employees be given more of a voice in what will be done at the company in terms of remodeling?			
43	When family members want to visit the business to view where the loved one was lost, will you honor their request?			
44	Whether the family was or was not allowed to visit, was the decision coordinated with legal?			
45	What effect will rejecting a family visit have on the business when the rejection becomes common knowledge?			
46	When family members want to clean out loved ones' desks and lockers of their personal belonging, will you allow them to do so or prohibit them from doing so, having the business box up their property instead?			
47	How long should a family member visit the property?			
48	How will that message be communicated to the family?			
49	Should there be a memorial at the business, whether temporary or permanent?			
50	How long will temporary memorial flowers remain in front of the business before removed?			
51	Did the business previously determine a location for a secondary or temporary secondary location?			

FIGURE C–1 (Continued).

52	Has an employee been chosen to be in charge of the satellite office and move?			
53	Is the business and management prepared to be second-guessed on everything?			
54	Should the company collect all media coverage of the shooting for use later in court?			
55	Has the business considered using an outside service to collect all news broadcasts and media coverage (radio, news broadcasts, written material)?			
56	Has the business pre-identified the top ten priorities of the business right after the shooting?			
57	Has a company been chosen to provide counseling services?			
58	Has a company been chosen to provide cleanup?			
59	Has a company been chosen to undertake remodeling?			
60	Has a company been chosen to oversee the recovery program, or is it being left to the executive staff and board of directors?			
61	Does the company have a recovery checklist?			
62	Has the company considered the effects of an active shooting on customers, including the chance that competition might make a play for existing clients out of concerns about just-in-time inventory, contract length, and so forth?			
63	If a commercial business relies on walk-in business, has the business considered what actions the business will take to ensure that customers are safe in returning?			
64	Can the business be sued by neighboring business based on the effect the shooting has on their businesses?			
65	Has the company considered the effect of the active shooting on advertisers, sponsors, and marketing companies?			
66	Can sponsors cancel contracts because of the active shooting?			
67	Who will remove killed employees' cars from the company parking lot, their family members or an employee?			
68	How will the active shooting affect and restrict future business?			
69	If the effects on future business can be anticipated, what is the plan to prevent or limit the effects?			
70	How will the active shooting affect current business promotions and marketing?			
71	How will the shooting affect new business promotions and marketing?			
72	What effects will an active shooting have on current union contracts?			
73	What effects will an active shooting event have on future union contracts?			
74	How will increased external demands by lawyers, insurance companies, and law enforcement officers affect sales, profits, business operations, and the employee work environment?			

FIGURE C–1 (Continued).

75	How will the shooting affect production deadlines?			
76	Should volunteers be background-checked?			
77	Is the company prepared for people providing all kinds of goods, services, and assistance in overwhelming quantities?			
78	What effect will rejecting any of the foregoing have on the business if the rejection were made public?			
79	Who is assigned to handle goods, services, and assistance received?			
80	Customers may or may not be supportive over long periods if they are not receiving their shipments, shipments are not received within specified timeframes, orders are confused, or if annual events or promotions are not honored. How will these concerns be addressed?			
81	Be on alert for groups who will use the shooting to support their cause (anti–whatever the business represents)			
82	Who is assigned in the company to contact and interact with lawyers?			
83	If the business does not have a marketing department, should an outside marketing firm be hired?			
84	Should the business consider conducting a business impact study?			
85	When should the command center be activated?			
86	Who can activate the active shooter plan?			
87	Who is responsible for reunification of employees and families?			
88	Where should reunification take place?			
89	Where should employees meet if the active shooter was an insider threat and the shooter knows the location of the emergency evacuation assembly area?			
90	Should a damage assessment be done?			
91	Who is assigned to the damage assessment team?			
92	Does the damage assessment provide degrees of destruction, from none to total loss (physical property only)?			
93	Does the damage assessment look at short-term and long-term effects?			
94	Does the damage assessment look at both internal and external areas?			
95	Does the damage assessment look at IT systems and utilities (considering that some active shooters use IEDs)?			

FIGURE C–1 (Continued).

HUMAN RESOURCES

A business may or may not have a human resources department. Listed here are areas that are key to the business's survival in both the short and the long terms. If the business outsources its human resources functions, then senior management will be required to interact with the outsourced business to ensure that employees needs are addressed uniformly while considering each employee's special needs and conditions. Consider the following questions and areas, then add more questions to the list that are specific to your business.

#	Question and Areas to Consider	Yes	No	Comment
1	Is the business prepared to deal with employees' quitting?			
2	Is the business prepared for employees' having breakdowns at work and at home that may prevent them from coming to work?			
3	Is the business prepared for emotional shifts in employee performance?			
4	How should performance problem employees be handled because of the shooting—the same, or differently?			
5	Should underperforming employees from the same department as the shooting victims, be given more slack than those in other departments?			
6	When can employee parking spaces be reissued that belong to those who were killed?			
7	When can employee offices be reassigned that belong to those who were killed?			
8	When can employee telephone extensions be reassigned that belong to those who were killed?			
9	When should the company directory be changed to remove the names of employees who were killed?			
10	Because the human resources department will see increases in challenges on speech restrictions and in demands from employees, is it prepared to deal with these issues?			
11	The human resources department will see an increase in employees' quitting because of the shooting (flashbacks, shock, work environment, etc.), is HR prepared to deal with this? What identified steps will the business take to salvage these employees?			
12	When and how will the business advertise for employees to fill the positions of employees who were killed?			
13	Is there an HR strategy dealing with how new employees may be accepted by current employees when they fill positions of employees lost during the shooting?			
14	Should management allow employees to make choices when they didn't before, to foster a new cooperative environment?			
15	Should employees vote on decisions and remodeling of the shooting area, even though they have never done so before?			
16	Will this cause more challenges for employees allowed to vote on decisions when their ideas aren't chosen?			
17	What will be done with teddy bears, vases, keepsakes, and the like left outside the building?			
18	Should management hold daily employee meetings? Weekly? For how long?			

FIGURE C–2 Human Resources.

19	Can the company support a victim family memorial fund?			
20	Should the company pay for killed employee's funerals?			
21	Should the human resources department increase staffing levels in anticipation of demands on human resources programs or wait until needed?			
22	Should certain aspects and functions of human resources be outsourced instead of hiring new employees?			
23	During promotions, will there be an advantage or edge be given to employees who experienced the active shooting?			
24	Has the human resources department previously identified processes, steps, and services available to guide HR decisions before an active shooting?			
25	Will any new security procedures and systems be instituted that affect disabled employees (ADA)? If not, is HR addressing accommodations for these employees?			
26	Prepare for employees showing up late to work			
27	Prepare for more employees calling to take off work			
28	Prepare for employees to quit when lawyers and insurance companies are on site			
29	Prepare for more employees requesting to leave early			
30	How long will wreaths be left outside the building?			
31	Prepare for people driving past just to see the location of the active shooting (inquisitive, taking pictures, trying to see the exact spot, trying to enter the property) and their effect on employees			
32	Prepare for people who want to write a book (freelance journalists, etc.)			
33	Prepare for interviews by government agencies on fact finding missions			
34	Prepare for more medical calls on site and the effects of ambulance visible on the property by employees			
35	Should a company representative stay at the hospital with injured employees?			
36	Should a representative stay at the hospital for employees' entire time in the hospital?			
36	Should a representative maintain daily contact with injured employees who are at home?			
37	Should a representative travel with the employee to special surgery outside the state?			
38	Should injured employees be kept on the payroll instead of on workman's comp?			
39	Prepare for employees to quit after every decision			
40	Prepare for senior key employees to quit, not only rank-and-file employees			
41	Should the human resources department include contractors who are working on property in the distribution of HR materials? Does legal agree?			
42	How will the human resources department handle increases in employee family issues and employee family members			

FIGURE C–2 (Continued).

43	Should the human resources department slow down terminations?			
44	Don't terminate around holidays and the annual active shooting day?			
45	Should the yearly employee conference be canceled?			
46	What should the company do about the Christmas party if some victims helped lead the party committee?			
47	Should the human resources department continue, stop, or implement an employee of the month award if, for example, the last employee of the month was killed during the active shooting?			
48	Should employees be allowed to provide input into what they would like to see changed to make them feel safe and want to come to work?			
49	How soon will you allow employees to reenter the workplace?			
50	Should employee committees be created to help with the recovery and healing process, or should that be left to outside counseling services?			
51	If so, what committees should be created? Who should head them?			
52	Who should be included in the committees? How are such employees selected?			
53	How many members, from how many departments, should be included in the committees?			
54	Should you keep a scrapbook of employees who were killed or injured?			
55	If the company does not have an employee newsletter, should the human resources department begin a company newsletter to inform employees of progress on projects?			
56	Employees may bring guns to work for their own protection; will doing so be allowed?			
57	Employees may ask to bring guns to work? Will they be permitted to do so? What will happen if an employee is found carrying without permission?			
58	Prepare for reduced work efforts and emotional problems during the trial and when preparing for the trial			
59	Should the human resources department implement suggestion boxes in each department? How will suggestion boxes be implemented?			
60	How will the human resources department deal with employees relocated off site or to a secondary temporary location who won't return to the building that had the shooting?			
61	Have human resources staff members been trained in how to recognize stress in employees, including PTSD?			
62	Should faith-based groups be allowed on property? If so, where? Which groups or religions will be allowed?			
63	What will be the effect of not allowing faith-based groups to come to the business?			
64	Should a devout employee be appointed as company liaison for all groups?			

FIGURE C–2 (Continued).

65	How will the human resources department monitor the workplace environment, especially if the shooter was a current employee?			
66	Should the human resources department assign an employee to monitor social media sites?			
67	Is the human resources department prepared to teach and broadcast to employees about grief, the stages of grief, and how to deal with grief in themselves and coworkers?			
68	Should teaching about grief to employees be outsourced? How should such information be provided to employees?			
69	Has the human resources department identified what steps it will take to assist employee families who lost a loved one?			
70	Is the human resources department prepared to deal with anger from victims' families?			
71	Will the human resources department deal any differently with a victim's family that files a law suit than it will with a family that doesn't?			
72	What aspects of the human resources functions in dealing with employees and the recovery process should be presented to the legal department before their implementation?			
73	Because guests and individuals will question employees about the shooting and want to their thoughts or feelings, is HR prepared to respond appropriately?			

FIGURE C–2 (Continued).

#	Question and Areas to Consider	Yes	No	Comment
COMMUNICATIONS				
The primary problem that occurs in every emergency situation is communication failure. Using today's communication platforms, no single platform will be able to contact all potential victims—in all locations using all social media sites and regardless of nationality or disability—within the active shooter target site. For a business charged with the safety of guests and employees, difficult questions may be the order of the day. Consider the following questions and areas, then add more questions to the list as they are discussed specific to your business.				
1	During the shooting, what message should be sent over the PA system?			
2	Should there be an all-employee conference? If so, what should be its message?			
3	Who should present at the conference? Counselors? Legal? Upper management? And who should deliver the message?			
4	How many days in a row should there be employee conferences?			
5	What portions of the message presented during the conference will be sensitive to employees? Is the message run by the counselors first?			
6	Who prepares all messages? Who in management approves the messages?			
7	Are all messages approved by legal staff and the board of directors?			
8	How often should messages be provided to employees? At a set time each day, or twice a day? Using what communications platform?			
9	Who should provide messages to employees?			
10	What communications platform or platforms should communicate the message throughout the entire building?			
11	When and what message may be given to contractors, vendors, and volunteers on the property?			
12	What message should be given to stockholders and shareholders? Who prepares the message?			
13	What message should be given to major customers and clients? Who prepares the message?			
14	What identified and primary platform should release the messages to each of the aforementioned groups?			
15	What message do you provide to employees in preparation for the trial?			
16	What message do you provide to employees as law enforcement officers return to the business during the investigation and the business is reopened?			
17	What message do you provide to employees as news media return to the business?			
18	What message do you give to customers who are on property during trial preparation?			
19	Should flyers be provided to customers as they walk into the business, other than sales or marketing promotions?			
20	Should signage be placed indicating why all the police vehicles are on property—i.e. during the investigation and when the business is a crime scene?			

FIGURE C–3 Communications.

21	Prepare for a tremendous increase on PBX calls for quite some time.			
22	Prepare for forwarding and redirecting calls to predetermined offices or individuals based on the nature of the call.			
23	Should you hire extra PBX staff?			
24	What communication message should you provide neighbors?			
25	What communication message should you provide tenants?			
26	Prepare for hundreds of calls from people volunteering to help for free.			
27	What message will be provided to the sales staff about the active shooting in preparation for a sales presentation both in the area and outside the area.			
28	What message will be provided to new hires or job interviewees?			
29	What are the tone and purpose of the message?			
30	Should a letter be provided to any potential customer inquiring about the shooting?			
31	What message should be communicated to employees when insurance companies and lawyers will be on site?			
32	Where are the communications gaps in the building that can be fixed as part of the recovery?			
33	What message about the active shooting should be sent to employee's homes for their families?			
34	Should a message be placed on the company website concerning the active shooting?			
35	Because words can't be taken back, should <u>all</u> messages be approved by the legal department before their release?			
36	How soon should messages be sent to each of the areas mentioned thus far? (Timing is important: Too soon and without enough information could be disastrous. Executives could be in shock, not thinking clearly. But days without a message could affect employee and customer confidence.)			
37	Chart the types of message and the audience (all audiences and all messages) before release.			
38	Do you have a complete list of audience contact information and names, including of customers, key employees, key suppliers, neighbors, employees, contractors, key construction companies, counselors, and so forth? (If not, develop one now)			
39	Should you hire a public relations firm to handle all inquiries and speak for the company?			
40	Because the identity of the message sender is important in the recovery process, should all messages be sent by a PIO or outsourced agency, or by the employees nearest the audience?			
41	If you don't have a public information officer who will be tasked with handling press and media inquiries, should you say anything at all?			

FIGURE C–3 (Continued).

42	Is the business prepared to respond to comments from guests and employees such as "You never told me," "I never knew there was a problem until it happened," and "I asked for help, and you never called me back."			
43	Should you send a message over social media (Facebook, Twitter, etc.)?			
44	If so, what should the message be?			
45	Should you hire an advertising, public relations, or media company to strategize about how to move forward as a company?			
46	Should you sent a message or visit key customers or suppliers in person?			
47	What assurances or positive messages can be provided to dispel the thought that lightening will not strike twice?			
48	Should a company be hired to monitor and record all media sources, instead of using an employee?			
49	When copies of media videos, clippings of newspaper articles and social media negative comments are collected, who should be the primary source of this information?			
50	When should the company give interviews? Who will be allowed to be interviewed?			
51	When should the company give speeches? Should the standard response to questions be "I can't comment on an ongoing investigation"?			
52	Should the company adopt a complete transparency about the event with media, community, and employees?			
53	Because there may be increased personal issues for employees on the home front, what message should be given to employees' families?			
54	Will all new security enhancements and upgrades be discussed with all employees?			
55	Is one of the new security measures a communications system that notifies employees and guests simultaneously across multiple communications platforms?			
56	Did you document all communications and messages sent out during the active shooting, whether by PBX or security dispatch?			
57	What update message will the business send out to employees and guests hiding out from the shooter?			
58	Should you send a message to individuals hiding out inside the business?			
59	What is your message to the entire building when the shooter has been neutralized?			
60	In case of an insider threat, did you send a message to prevent employees from evacuating to emergency evacuation assembly areas?			
61	Did you consider developing active shooter messages before the shooting?			
63	Are your messages sent to legal and the board of directors before release, or just left up to whomever was on scene?			
64	Did you prepare messages in other languages?			
65	Did you prepare messages for disabled individuals, whether guests or employees?			

FIGURE C–3 (Continued).

66	Have you considered sending messages through company computers?			
67	Have you considered scrolling a message across the bottom of video monitors?			
68	Did the company notify first responders about the shooter, including his or her weapon type, clothing, name, employee status, and last known location, as well as the number of shooters, the quickest entry points, and the number of people injured?			
69	Did the company tell first responders about exits, stairs, and elevators in the area of shooting?			
70	Did the company tell first responders how many potential victims were in the area of the shooter?			
71	Did the company tell first responders what the area looks like, whether office cubicle, doored offices, upper-floor visibility, or glass walls, including its size?			
72	Did the company tell first responders about any dangerous chemicals in the area of the shooting?			
73	Did the company tell first responders whether they will need passkeys, biometric locks, or access cards?			
74	Did the company tell first responders whether the security staff is armed?			
75	Did the company tell first responders whether there are surveillance cameras in the area of the shooter?			

FIGURE C–3 (Continued).

COUNSELING			
Traumatic emergency events that occur at a business may affect employees and guests in both the short and long terms. Individuals are different, and so is the level of treatment that employees and guests may receive, but only if the business is prepared to address this issue. Business size and number of employees mean little to individuals who have experienced probably the most shocking event of their life. The business will soon learn that posttraumatic stress disorder (PTSD) is not restricted to the battlefield. Consider the following questions and areas, then add more to the list as they are discussed specific to your business.			

#	Question and Areas to Consider	Yes	No	Comment
1	Is counseling being offered for all employee levels and departments within the company?			
2	Is counseling being offered for part-time employees?			
3	Is counseling being offered for employees at satellite or branch offices?			
4	Was the counseling service selected before the event, or after?			
5	Can counseling service support your entire staff?			
6	Because loud noises may cause panic, instant shock, and flashbacks, is the counseling service prepared for surges in counseling?			
7	Is counseling being offered to employee offices in other states?			
8	Is counseling service prepared for additional counseling requests when lawyers and insurance companies arrive on site?			
9	Because active shooting incident recovery is different from natural disaster recovery in its effects on staff, is the counseling service trained to treat PTSD?			
10	Because loud noises will affect staff, with many employees running and others dropping to the ground, will employees be trained to aid coworkers when this occurs?			
11	Because another shooting, anywhere in the country, may affect the staff in multiple ways, is the company prepared to anticipate emotional ramp-ups after these shootings?			
12	Because the cycle of grief will affect each employee at different times and in different ways, will employees be instructed in the cycle of grief, not just given a pamphlet or handout?			

FIGURE C–4 Counseling.

13	Because employees not physically at the crime scene, such as sales staff on the road or in foreign countries on assignment, can still be affected by the event, is the company prepared to help them as well?			
14	Is counseling being offered to contractors and volunteers working on site at the time of the shooting?			
15	To which department will counselors report?			
16	What information are counselors allowed to release?			

FIGURE C–4 (Continued).

SECURITY
The security department's mission is to preserve the life and safety of all individuals on property regardless of their standing or their reason for being there. The security department is tasked to prepare for, mitigate, and respond to emergency situations. Preparations for a security department include planning, training, identifying best practices, exercising, implementing technology, and education. An effective and timely response by a security department during an emergency situation can save lives. Which department is responsible for assisting guests and employees during an emergency? All of them. Consider the following questions and areas, then add more to the list as they are discussed specific to your business.

#	Question and Areas to Consider	Yes	No	Comment
1	What new security technology should be added to the company?			
2	Can employees determine what new security technology should be added for their own safety and emotional security?			
3	Are you prepared to purchase additional or new security improvements to create a more secure environment:			
4	a. Security cameras?			
5	b. Smart, access, and proximity cards?			
6	c. Panic buttons in offices?			
7	d. Secure surveillance room?			
8	e. Automated building lockdown?			
9	f. Property wide panic buttons?			
10	g. Better communication systems?			
11	h. Rekeyingof entire building?			
12	i. Improved door locks?			
13	j. Safe rooms?			
14	k. Metal detectors?			
15	Will security technology be phased in for cost considerations? If so, in what department order?			
16	Should visible security be added to provide additional reassurance to customers and contractors?			
17	Will additional police presence frighten away business?			

FIGURE C–5 Security.

18	Will security oversee remodeling and cleanup to ensure that items aren't stolen?			
19	Should additional officers be hired? If so, how many? Outsourced, or employees?			
20	Should an outside security, safety, and risk company be contracted to assist in-house security in selecting technologies?			
21	Should a vulnerability assessment be conducted on the property after the event to identify additional weaknesses?			
22	What level of trust will the employees have in the security department because of the shooting?			
23	Should security department personnel be armed now if they weren't before?			
24	What will be the effect if not all employee suggestions about security technology are installed?			
25	Will all new security enhancements and upgrades be discussed with all employees?			
26	If employees are allowed to come to work armed, should the security department know? Should such employees be given a special badge or wristband?			
27	If employees are allowed to come to work armed, should the security department know in which department they work and how the weapons will be secured during work hours?			
28	If employees are allowed to come to work armed, should the security department ensure that the weapons are registered and that the employee has a valid CCW permit?			
29	If employees are allowed to come to work armed, can contractors carry weapons, too?			
30	If employees are allowed to come to work armed and if the security department is armed, should the security department instruct such employees on the use of force policy?			
31	If employees are allowed to come to work armed, should the security department help train these employees?			
32	If employees are allowed to come to work armed, what effect will that have on the security department if its personnel are not armed?			
33	What should the security department do when an employee is found carrying an unauthorized weapon?			

FIGURE C–5 (Continued).

34	If the shooter was a current employee, will that affect the decision to allow employees to carry a weapon?			
35	Should metal detectors be placed at every entrance?			
36	If the business did not have a security staff before the shooting, should it have one now?			
37	Who will be the main contact with law enforcement during the shooting if the company does not have a security staff			
38	Who will be the main contact with law enforcement during the investigation if the company does not have a security staff?			
39	Can security remain inside the business 24–7 to ensure security of the business even during the crime scene shutdown (law enforcement's focus is the investigations and shooting location, not all other areas of the business)?			
40	Should security provide training courses for all new employees on active shooter workplace violence after the event?			
41	Is the security department prepared to handle additional calls from employees who are suspicious of everyone, on a stress rollercoaster, and panicked by every loud noise?			
42	Is the security department prepared to handle additional escorts to the employee parking lot?			
43	Because each employee will expect a different timeframe, is the security department prepared to handle comments when security measures are not installed timely?			
44	Should the security department begin implementing a new emergency communications plan to ensure that all areas of the business can receive emergency messages?			
45	Should the security department identify a lockdown process if one didn't exist before?			
46	Did the employee emergency evacuation assembly area function as intended during the active shooting event?			
47	Did the security department keep the elevators in operation during the shooting?			
48	Was the fire alarm activated on purpose, accidentally, as a planned part of the active shooter plan, or not at all?			
49	Did the security department assist disabled employees or guests during the shooting?			

FIGURE C–5 (Continued).

50	Can the building be locked down in sections to restrict the shooter?			
51	Did the security department escort law enforcement to the shooting location or just point the way?			
52	Was a go bag given to law enforcement officers containing elevator passkeys, hard keys, access cards, maps, doorstops, flashlights, security radio, and the like?			
53	Should the security department develop go bags if it did not before?			
54	Was an officer assigned to keep individuals from re-entering the building during the shooting?			
55	Was a security officer assigned to the emergency evacuation assembly area?			

FIGURE C–5 (Continued).

FINANCIAL				
The most overlooked department during any emergency is the finance department. Finances will play a monumental role in both short- and long-term recovery. Right after the dust settles and the yelling stops, the financial recovery plan should be placed in motion. Unfortunately, many businesses have not considered developing a financial plan specific to emergencies. Consider the following questions and areas, then add more to the list as they are discussed specific to your business.				
#	**Question and Areas to Consider**	**Yes**	**No**	**Comment**
1	Does the company pay funeral costs for employees who cannot afford it?			
2	Should the company pay funeral costs for all employees?			
3	Should the company pay funeral costs for all people killed, including guests, vendors, and contractors?			
4	Should the company establish a memorial fund?			
5	Should the company establish a college trust fund for the children of employees killed?			
6	Because there may not be another significant chance to make a positive statement to employees about their security and safety, how much is the company willing to spend to make employees feel safe?			
7	How will the company handle donations that may be received from the community for the company and employees?			
8	Should the company give money to family members of those who died?			
9	Should the company give money to injured employees?			
10	Because financial effects may significantly affect the business's longevity, how is the financial department preparing for shortfalls and underperformance?			
11	How much is the company willing to spend on security training?			
12	How much will insurance premium rise?			
13	Which insurance policies will be affected?			
14	Will the shooting affect the business's ability to borrow money from any source?			
15	Should the company increase the amount of liquid cash it has available?			

FIGURE C–6 Financial.

16	Does the company have sufficient finances to open a temporary off-site office?			
17	Will the insurance company be able to provide funding in the short term? If so, how much and how soon?			
18	If the office is closed as a crime scene for one week, how will the bills be paid with no access to the building?			
19	Will the company be able to afford the cost of equipment in the temporary off-site location (e.g., computers, security, office materials)?			
20	Can the company obtain a short-term lease with little or nothing down?			
21	Does the company have a finance committee rather than just one finance employee?			
22	Has the financial department previously developed a checklist including anticipated amounts for each entry?			
23	Can the finance department obtain any funding or loans from federal, state, or local government agencies because of the shooting?			
24	If so, how quickly, and in what amounts?			
25	Should the affected company department be closed and outsourced? If so, is doing so financially or psychologically practical for the company?			
26	What financial demands will counseling, insurance premium increases, hiring temporary staff for select positions (HR and PBX), and lost productivity have on finances?			
27	What other financial areas will be affected by the shooting?			

FIGURE C–6 (Continued).

	MEDIA AND NEWS CREWS			
	Every evening, nightly news programs broadcast events from around the world, but this time, your business is the lead story. Many companies consider hiring a public information officer to speak with media outlets on behalf of the company. But very few businesses ever consider the effects that media and news crews will have on the business, employees, and victim families. The business will generally not consider victims who were vendors, contractors, or volunteers, looking only at its own employees. Consider the following questions and areas, then add more to the list as they are discussed specific to your business.
#	Question and Areas to Consider	Yes	No	Comment
1	Is the company prepared to deal with			
2	a. News crews outside the building			
3	b. News crews outside homes of victims			
4	c. News crews outside neighboring businesses, interviewing			
5	d. It all happening all over again during trial			
6	e. It all happening all over again on anniversaries of the active shooting			
7	Prepare for news crews interviewing contractor or vendor companies who were on site during the shooting (depending on whether their contract with you restricts what they can say to the press)			
8	Prepare for news crews who want to do a human interest story about an employee or an employee's family			
9	Should the company allow freelance writers on property or give them access to staff?			
10	Prepare for all prior negative company issues to be brought out again, including file footage about those issues (e.g., XYZ Co. has been the center of several lawsuits . . .)			
11	Because news cameras will create a circus, has the business considered how to help employees who are returning to work pass through news crews?			
12	How long will the news crews be outside the building?			
13	Will the news crews remain on scene throughout the entire crime scene company shutdown?			
14	Should the company hire a company to collect all media sources having to do with the shooting, regardless of media type (newspaper, talk shows, nightly news broadcasts, radio, television, websites, social media)?			

FIGURE C–7 Media and News Crews.

15	Is the company prepared to deal with media sources who trespass on company property to obtain a story?			
16	Are PBX operators instructed in how to deal with media calls			
17	Are employees instructed in how to deal with media contacts?			
18	Will media crews contact the temporary off-site office?			

FIGURE C–7 (Continued).

Trial			
Most companies and first responders forget that approximately 24% of active shooters are arrested and will go to trial. After being arrested, the entire active shooter or workplace violence incident will be relived all over again. Businesses must prepare for the additional attention placed on the business, employees, and victim families, as well as community and stockholder reactions. Businesses must also consider possible drops in revenue associated with the trial. Consider the following questions and areas, then add more to the list as they are discussed specific to your business.			

#	Question and Areas to Consider	Yes	No	Comment
1	How much will a company expect to payout in lawsuits for an AS event if			
2	a. No active shooting plan			
3	b. No training in the active shooting plan			
4	c. Never allowed employees to receive free training			
5	d. Ignored warning signs or dismissed complaints about suspicious incidents or physical and verbal threats			
6	e. Never followed the plan			
7	f. Plan ignored ADA employees and guests			
8	g. First responders not included in planning process			
9	h. Unions not included in planning process			
10	Can the payout be multiplied by the number of victims?			
11	Active shooter goes to trial:			
12	a. Every day of trial is a challenge, bringing counseling demands			
13	b. Should the trial be broadcast in the company lunch room or throughout the entire property?			
14	c. Employees will be witnesses at the trial, bringing counseling demands			
15	d. Employees will miss work preparing for trial and testifying at trial			
16	e. As the trial gets closer, law enforcement officers may visit business to follow up leads, for measurement, and so forth to aid the prosecution. Business functions, meetings, and deadlines may be affected, and employees may be contacted for assistance			
17	f. News crews will be at the business offering live film coverage			

FIGURE C–8 Trial.

18	a. News crews may visit victims' homes			
19	b. Negative comments on social may affect the employee environment			
20	How do you coordinate trial and preparation for trial with contractor or vendors companies who lost employees in the active shooting—or should you?			
21	Because trial will find fault or expose gaps, how will the company address negative findings now also known to employees, customers, stockholders, and competitors?			
22	How will media coverage and trial affect sister properties in the same city and other cities?			
23	Will all news and social media coverage be collected during the trial?			
24	Should the company develop a new marketing and promotion program before the trial?			
25	Will the trial bring closure of the active shooting disaster for the company and all employees?			
26	What message should be provided to customers during and after the trial?			

FIGURE C–8 (Continued).

Law Enforcement Investigative Questions			
An active shooting/workplace violence incident is one of the most terrifying events a business and law enforcement department can ever experience. For those businesses and offices that have lived through such a traumatic event, words can never express the feelings, sensations, and emotional effects the shooting will have from that fateful day forward. Regardless of the number of hours a law enforcement department has trained to deal with active shooting, and unless the law enforcement department has trained at that very business, the shooting site is an obstacle course. In this phase, law enforcement will not stop to answer questions, help the injured, or be delayed in any manner. Their primary mission is to neutralize the threat. Many questions will be directed at the business in rapid succession, but the most important are as follows:			
#	Question and Areas to Consider	Yes	No	Comment
---	---	---	---	---
1	Where is the shooter right now?			
2	What is the shooter wearing (color of clothing, style of clothing, hat, glasses, gas mask)?			
3	What does the shooter look like (sex, race, hair color, facial hair, baldness, height, weight)?			
4	What kind of weapon(s) is the shooter using?			
5	How many shooters?			
6	How many victims?			
7	Is the shooter carrying a bag or backpack?			
8	What is the quickest way to get to the shooter?			
9	How many people are near the shooter?			
10	Are there any cameras in the area?			
11	Where are the exits?			
12	Do you know the shooter (name)?			

FIGURE C–9 Law Enforcement Investigative Questions.

Law Enforcement after Active Shooter Event Ends				
It makes a difference whether the shooter is known to the business. If known, law enforcement officers will ask the business a great many questions in support of the investigation. The Bureau of Labor Statistics has shown that 55% of shooters are familiar with the business or location of the shooting in some way or another. Consider the following questions and areas, then add more to the list as they are discussed specific to your business.				
#	**Question and Areas to Consider**	**Yes**	**No**	**Comment**
1	How long will the company be closed as a crime scene?			
2	Assistance needed in identifying the victims?			
3	Any video footage of the incident required?			
4	Any video footage of any prior incident involving the shooter required?			
5	Law enforcement will ask a great many questions to identify the shooter (s). The shooter may be one of the following:			
6	Former employee:			
7	a. Employee files			
8	b. Human resources files			
9	c. Details on any prior events			
10	d. Problem areas and reason why no longer a current employee			
11	e. Whether there was a progressive discipline process			
12	f. Outline of the progressive discipline process			
13	g. Human resources procedure for handling prior events			
14	h. Relationship, working or private, of shooter to victim(s)			
15	i. Identity of former manager or supervisor			
16	j. Current employees who knew the shooter			
17	k. Former employees who may have known the shooter			
18	Current employee			
19	a. Employee files			
20	b. Human resources files			
21	c. Details on any prior events			

FIGURE C–10 Law Enforcement After Active Shooter Event Ended.

22	a. Problem areas			
23	b. Whether there was a progressive discipline process			
24	c. Outline of the progressive discipline process			
25	d. Human resources procedure for handling prior events			
26	e. Relationship, working or private, of shooter to victim(s)			
27	f. Identity of former manager or supervisor			
28	g. Current employees who knew the shooter			
29	h. Former employees who may have known the shooter			
30	Relative of a current or former employee (still need areas as a current or former employee)			
31	a. Employee files			
32	b. Human resources files			
33	c. Details on any prior events			
34	d. Problem areas			
35	e. Whether there was a progressive discipline process			
36	f. Outline of the progressive discipline process			
37	g. Human resources procedure for handling prior events			
38	h. Relationship, working or private, of shooter to victim(s)			
39	i. Identity of former manager or supervisor			
40	j. Current employees who knew the shooter			
41	k. Former employees who may have known the shooter			
42	Former or current customer			
43	a. Customer files			
44	b. Complaint letters			
45	c. Reasons for complaint			
46	d. How long an issue			
47	e. Which employee interacted with the customer			
48	f. Whether the customer picked the business or used social media to plead cause			

FIGURE C–10 (Continued).

49	g. Contact information for customer			
50	h. Last interaction with customer			
51	i. How many customer called the business			
52	j. Whether customer was removed and 86'd from the business			
53	k. Whether customer harassed employees			
54	l. Any pictures or surveillance footage obtained			
55	m. How many times customer came on the property			
56	n. How each encounter with the customer ended			
57	o. Any settlements made to the customer			
58	p. Whether attorneys were involved			
59	q. Any civil suits brought against either party			
60	r. Whether any matter went to court			
61	s. Copies of court documents and filings			
62	t. Whether any threats were made during conversations with the customer			
63	A crime scene can be closed for days or weeks.			
64	a. Present a case for keeping open certain portions because of their unique features—e.g., systems, lab work, refinery process			
65	b. What systems and departments need to work 24 hours per day that do not affect crime scene?			
66	c. How do you secure the building, cannot turn everything over to the law enforcement, can use in-house security or contract security			
67	d. What employees or departments are required to be present 24 hours per day as identified in your emergency action plan?			
68	e. How will out-of-state shipments already in transit be received?			
69	f. What deliveries will be received at the business?			
70	g. Can IT system be accessed remotely to help move location and business functions off site?			
71	Names of employees, guests, contractors, and vendors who witnessed the shooting			
72	Surveillance camera coverage of the shooting			
73	Any logs providing a timeline of the shooting			
74	Who from the company is assigned to aid law enforcement			

FIGURE C–10 (Continued).

POSSIBLE LEGAL QUESTIONS

Regardless of whether the shooter is arrested, the possibility of legal action is very real. The cost of legal action for a business can be huge and even well beyond any insurance policy resources. The attorneys will want to know everything. No secrets, no hidden files, or carefully misplaced memos or emails—just the truth. If the business did not have an active shooter plan, say so. One point that has always been a stumbling block for a business is providing documents concerning any of the questions listed below. For an attorney, the three most important words are documentation, documentation, documentation. Let me ask a question with a question. How would a judge, jury, and victim's family view a company that cannot provide proof of any one of the questions below? Consider the following questions and areas, then add more to the list as they are discussed specific to your business.

#	Question and Areas to Consider	Yes	No	Comment
1	Do you have an active shooter plan?			
2	Who was in charge of implementing the plan?			
3	Was the plan followed?			
4	If not, why wasn't the plan followed?			
5	Who has access to the plan?			
6	How is the plan accessed?			
7	Who prepared the plan?			
8	Did any outside sources help with plan development?			
9	Did you use a contractor or expert to develop the plan?			
10	Do you have an expert who can testify about the plan?			
11	Did you use a contractor or expert during the event, or was it all done internally?			
12	Did you arrange for counseling before the event or after?			
13	If so, how did you select the counselors?			
14	Who was on the active shooter planning committee?			
15	Did first responders see the active shooter plan?			
16	Were first responders (fire, paramedic, emergency services, law enforcement) invited to tour the business before the shooting?			
17	Were the first responders invited on all operational shifts?			
18	Who is responsible for initiating the active shooter plan?			
19	Are all employees required to read the plan?			
20	Are part-time or on-call employees required to read the plan?			
21	Are contractors and service agencies required to read the plan?			
22	Are volunteers required to read the plan?			
23	Did tenants read the plan?			
24	Did vendors read the plan?			
25	Did employees receive a receipt for reading the plan?			
26	Is there a section on communications in the plan?			
27	What is the primary communications platform for communicating with			
28	a. Employees?			
29	b. Part-time and on-call employees?			
30	c. Contractors?			
31	d. Tenants?			
32	e. Vendors?			

FIGURE C–11 Possible Legal Questions.

33	f. Guests?			
34	g. ADA guests and employees?			
35	What other communications platforms were used?			
36	What was the process for accounting for			
38	a. Part-time and on-call employees?			
39	b. Contractors?			
40	c. Tenants?			
41	d. Vendors?			
42	e. Guests?			
43	f. ADA guests and employees?			
44	How was the plan distributed:			
45	a. New employee human resources orientation?			
46	b. Select portions of plan with tenants, vendors, contractors, volunteers, law enforcement, and first responders?			
47	c. Monthly executive and employee meetings?			
48	d. Employee annual conference?			
49	e. Business newsletter or internal business television network?			
50	f. Department by department presentations by senior management?			
51	g. Five minute preshift briefing review session?			
52	h. Present to part-time employees and volunteers?			
53	Has the active shooter plan been trained on? if so what are the dates for			
54	a. Tabletop?			
55	b. Full-scale?			
56	c. Drills?			
57	d. Functional?			
58	Who attended the training?			
59	How was the training documented?			
60	How many departments participated in the training?			
61	Did any executive, manager, or supervisor ever attend any active shooter training courses, webinars, workshops, online training courses, or training exercises?			
62	Were any memos to the file created to support the lessons learned from the training?			
63	Were any steps are actions taken in response to the training received?			
64	Were all corrective steps and lessons learned implemented?			
65	Were any active shooter training exercises ever held at the business with first responders (law enforcement, fire, emergency services)?			
66	Did any executive, manager, or supervisor ever attend any active shooter training courses, webinars, workshops, online training courses, or training exercises held by first responders or contractors?			
67	Were any memos to the file created to support management training?			
68	Were any corrective steps or actions taken in response to the training received?			

FIGURE C–11 (Continued).

69	Did any employee receive FEMA certification for completing the IS-907 active shooter online training course?			
70	What problems did you encounter during the shooting?			
71	How were these problems corrected?			
72	What message did you communicate to employees and guests when you first learned of the shooting?			
73	What message did you communicate to employees and guess during the shooting?			
74	Do you have a timeline on messages transmitted to guests and employees?			
75	What outside resources did you use to assist your employees?			
76	What outside resources did you use to assist the victim employees families?			
77	When did you contact your insurance company?			
78	When did the insurance company send a representative to assist?			
79	Do you have a timeline of what actions were performed during the active shooting event?			
80	Did you record radio communications during the active shooting?			
81	Where all employees identified in the plan on duty during the shooting?			
82	Do you have active shooting recovery actions?			
83	Who is responsible for the recovery plan?			
84	Is there an active shooting recovery plan team or working group?			
85	Are stockholders and bondholders aware that there is an active shooting recovery plan?			
86	Are stockholders and bondholders aware there is an active shooting recovery planning team?			
87	Are employees aware that there is an active shooting recovery plan?			
88	Are employees aware that there is an active shooting recovery planning team?			
89	What message has been transmitted to stockholders, bondholders, vendors, and contractors?			
90	What message has been transmitted to employees not on the property during the shooting?			
91	What message has been transmitted to satellite offices or offices in another state?			
92	What will new employees be told about the shooting?			
93	Are all communications and statements presented on behalf of the company run by legal first?			
94	Should employees still attend scheduled conferences—e.g., at company booths?			
95	Should employees still present at a major sales event?			
96	What should employees mention about the shooting if they do attend?			
97	Who provided information to law enforcement?			
98	What documents were provided to law enforcement?			

FIGURE C–11 (Continued).

99	What requests were made by law enforcement?			
100	Did management choose not to implement an active shooting program or plan?			
101	Did human resources choose not to implement an active shooting program because it would scare employees?			
102	Did the active shooting plan consider an insider threat?			
103	Did the active shooting plan consider disabled guests and employees?			
104	Does the property have a workplace violence plan?			
105	Did the company ignore previous issues and threats if the active shooter was an employee for former employee:			
106	a. Warning signs?			
107	b. Dismissed prior complaints and notification?			
108	c. Pleas for assistance ignored?			
109	d. Problem person for quite some time?			
110	When should company give interviews? Was this run by legal?			
111	When should company give speeches? Was this run by legal?			

FIGURE C–11 (Continued).

#	Question and Areas to Consider	Yes	No	Comment
	BUSINESS CONTINUITY PLAN			
	A business continuity plan is an identified plan that allows a business to continue operations when facing adverse physical, technological, and emotional conditions. The BCP outlines steps, procedures, and processes while understanding businesses interdependencies, communications platforms, and business model. The BCP takes into considerations all operational departments within the business. The BCP identifies both short-term and long-term actions in preserving the business and its brand, partnerships, contracts, and supply chain, as well as the needs of the employees. Which operational department should be included in the development of the BCP? All of them. Consider the following questions and areas, then add more to the list as they are discussed specific to your business.			
1	Do you have a BCP?			
2	Did the board of directors approve the BCP?			
3	What is the date of the current BCP?			
4	Do you have copies of the current BCP?			
5	Who was in charge of implementing the BCP?			
6	Is the BCP being followed?			
7	If the business does not have a BCP, do the stockholders know there isn't one?			
8	Who has access to the BCP?			
9	How is the BCP accessed?			
10	Who prepared the BCP?			
11	Did any outside source assist with BCP development?			
12	Did you use a contractor or expert to develop the BCP?			
13	Do you have an expert who can testify about the BCP?			
14	Did you use a contractor or expert during the event, or was it all done internally?			
15	Are all your files backed up?			
16	How often did you back up your files?			
17	Do you have a damage assessment team to survey the entire business internally and externally?			
18	Is the damage assessment team consistently monitoring the entire business both during the short term and during the long term?			
19	Does the BCP consider applying for a loan now to cover the gap in revenue and purchasing new security preventive measures?			
20	What is the active shooter event's effect on the entire business?			
21	What is the active shooter event's effect on revenue?			
22	What is the active shooter event's effect on services?			
23	How will the active shooter event affect the business's brand?			
24	Is special emphasis being placed on the IT department and systems?			
25	Does the BCP have recovery objectives for the short and long terms?			
26	Does the business have a resumption of critical business timeline for partial and full operation?			

FIGURE C–12 Business Continuity Plan.

27	Does the business have a resumption of critical business procedure by department and working group?			
28	Is there any new technology that will improve your BCP?			
29	Does the business have a specific IT business continuity and disaster plan?			
30	Does the business have a temporary or secondary location for the IT department?			
31	Does the business have a temporary or secondary location for the entire company?			
32	Does the BCP consider protecting the IT data at the temporary or secondary location?			
33	Does the BCP consider protecting virtual data?			
34	Does the BCP consider outsourcing IT services?			
35	Does the service include			
36	Server and workstation daily backups?			
37	Secondary server replication?			
38	Colocation?			
39	Failover?			
40	Audit?			
41	Security protection?			
42	What departments or working groups can telecommute?			
43	Does the secondary location have access to all main operating systems and data sources?			
44	Does the secondary location have sufficient security systems to protect employees?			
45	Did the BCP consider an insider threat as shooter and how that can affect a business?			
46	What telecommunication system can be used for the secondary location?			
47	If the business uses a PBX operating system, can this function be performed from the secondary location?			
48	How quickly can the telephone company install and change over PBX functions?			
49	What executive is in charge of the secondary location?			
50	Does your BCP consider employees who are victims in the active shooting event and counseling?			
51	Does your BCP consider that employees, including some key employees, will disappear for several days out of shock and fear?			
52	What operational departments were affected by the active shooting event?			
53	Is there a backup plan within the BCP to supplement that department?			
54	What departments are dependent upon the affected department?			
55	At the secondary location, does the BCP consider downtime when necessary systems are not available?			
56	What timeline does the BCP consider for the secondary location to be completely operational?			
57	Does the BCP have a section on unions?			
58	Who is responsible for dealing with the unions?			

FIGURE C–12 (Continued).

59	Does the BCP consider insurance carriers and policies?			
60	Who is responsible for dealing with the insurance companies?			
61	What insurance policies are in effect that cover the active shooting?			
62	Do you have an insurance policy that covers an active shooting event?			
63	Can an active shooter event qualify the business for a disaster loan?			
64	What amount of funding will become available, and when, from insurance companies?			
65	Does the BCP consider outside views and assistance from businesses that have gone through an active shooting incident to provide clarity on challenges?			
66	Does the business model rely on foot traffic?			
67	Does the BCP consider a marketing model to attract more business or to ensure that existing customers will return?			
68	Does the BCP consider using an outside marketing company to help maintain and increase business?			
69	The age of the business will affect the recovery—e.g., an existing company isn't as flexible as a new business, and an existing business's brand, reputation, and history cannot change rapidly. How flexible is the business?			
70	Does the BCP consider a prescripted communication message for all aspects of the shooting, including an all-employee conference, customers, vendors, contractors, neighboring properties, media, stockholders, and so forth?			
71	Does the relocation site contain appropriate security measures to protect the employees?			
72	Does the BCP identify the five most important core areas of the business and in each department and working group that need to be protected?			
73	Does the BCP identify how the company will address these five most important core areas?			
74	Does the BCP identify the ten most important areas of the business that will be affected by the shooting?			
75	Does the BCP identify how the company will address these ten most important areas?			
76	Does the BCP consider all financial effects of a shooting on the business:			
77	a. Cost from victims injured?			
78	b. Cost of insurance premium increase?			
79	c. Cost to bystanders, vendors, and contractors?			
80	d. Cost to the company locally and nationally?			
81	e. Cost to the company brand and image?			
82	f. Cost to stockholders and bondholders?			
83	g. Cost to community relations (what is included in community relations)?			
84	h. Cost of potential lawsuits?			
85	i. Costs multiplied by number of victims?			
86	j. Cost of new part-time and permanent employees (long- and short-term)?			

FIGURE C–12 (Continued).

87	k. Cost to rebuild, remodel, and restore the shooting location?			
88	l. Cost of outsourcing business or department functions?			
89	m. Cost of a secondary location?			
90	n. Lost revenue and downtime while a crime scene, before setting up temporary location, and while replacing key employees killed or injured?			
91	o. Difficulty obtaining loans?			
92	p. Cost of new advertising and promotions?			
93	q. Cost of hiring new employees to replace those that who quit, who were injured, or who were killed?			
94	r. Cost of new security protective measures?			
95	s. Cost of counselors?			
96	Did the business initiate a business impact analysis (BIA)?			
97	Did the BCP consider the damage assessment team and reporting process?			

FIGURE C–12 (Continued).

Appendix D
Active Shooter and Workplace Violence Training Exercise

This section provides three different active shooter workplace violence scenarios. The reader may choose a scenario closest to his or her respective business or may dive into all three scenarios to understand the differences between each. Each scenario looks at the incident from the perspective of first responders and the private sector owner/operators. As the scenario develops, the reader should identify actions relevant to their company and position within the company. The scenarios only look at the incident and do not take into consideration recovery, business continuity planning, or after-event considerations.

To optimize the benefits from these scenarios, it is suggested that the scenario be presented in a group setting. The group should consist of corporate-level executives, managers, supervisors, and front-line employees from different departments. It is advisable to invite a member of the local first responder community to participate in the scenario discussion, for much of the discussion will involve understanding the responders' capabilities and support needs. The questions posed here should help identify any actions and duties. As the answers and responses are developed, ensure that comments, concerns, and actions are clearly identified within your written active shooter workplace violence plan. If you do not have such a plan, prepare one now!

Please consider the following questions in each scenario:

- What preparations should the facility have made to handle this situation?
- What preparations should you take to protect yourself? Coworkers? Guests?
- What actions do you take personally?
- What actions should the supervisor perform in an active shooting?
- What actions should first responders initiate when learning of an active shooter event?
- What actions, decisions, and procedures does the business implement after notification has been made to first responders?
- What are the first five questions and concerns you have concerning the active shooter event?
- What are the business's first five questions and concerns concerning an active shooter event?
- When first responders are on site, how does the business coordinate with them?
- What are the first ten actions the business should perform to assist first responders in neutralizing the threat?

- What are the first ten actions that first responders expect the business to perform to assist them in neutralizing the threat?
- If the active shooter has been neutralized, is the threat over?
- When will EMS be allowed to enter the facility and treat the injured?
- What is the business's process for locating and accounting for employees? Guests? Contractors? Vendors?
- How long do you think the business or location will be a crime scene? Four hours? A day? Three days? One week? Longer?

Scenario #1 Office Complex

For this scenario, look at the active shooting event from four different perspectives and then identify your actions before, during, and after the incident:

- Employees on the first floor
- Tenant properties located within the ten-story building
- Law enforcement officers and first responders
- Employees inside the Smith and Davenport Financial Corporation (a fictitious corporation)

Overview of Middle State Office Complex

- The Middle State Office Complex houses twenty-one tenants
- The complex building is ten stories tall, has no parking garage, and is the tallest building for two square miles.
- The complex contains approximately 350 people, and the largest tenant has 170 employees, located on the third and fourth floors.
- The main entrance has glass revolving doors, and the building outside is primarily a blue glass facade.
- The building is open to the public, with no on-site security.
- Neither the Middle State Office Complex, nor any of its tenants, has been the subject of any comment in the local news media, whether negative or positive.
- The complex is open daily from 7:00 a.m. until 6:00 p.m. and is not open on weekends or holidays.
- The building has electronic access control access after business hours.
- None of the tenants is conducting any laboratory testing or research.
- None of the tenants is a doctors or dentist.
- The complex has an intercom that can be heard on all floors near the elevator lobby.
- Emergency exits are located at the very end of the building, on the east and west side of each floor.
- There is no active shooter plan in place for the complex.
- The complex has no PBX system.
- The Middle State Office Complex has had no threats reported by phone or letter, nor any major issue reported by any tenant.

- The complex is not aware of any significant problems or issues with any tenant.
- The building has surveillance cameras installed only on the front and rear entrances.

Law Enforcement Overview

- City police force (PD):
    - Ten patrol units, one sergeant, and one detective are on duty.
    - Seventy-one sworn officers form the department.
    - Each patrol unit has an M-16, a ballistic vest, a Kevlar helmet, and smoke and gas grenades.
- County sheriff's office (SO):
    - Five patrol units and one sergeant are on duty.
    - Forty-five sworn deputies form the office.
    - Each patrol unit has an M-16, a ballistic vest, a Kevlar helmet, and smoke and gas grenades.
- Neither department possesses the following:
    - Mobile command post
    - Armored vehicles
    - Gas masks
    - Ballistic shields
- Law enforcement has responded to the complex on only one occasion, three years ago. The purpose of the call was to report an intoxicated person who was found in the ground floor women's bathroom.
- Neither the Middle State Office Complex, nor any of the complex's twenty-one tenants, has participated in any of the following law enforcement–sponsored events:
    - Site surveys
    - Vulnerability assessments
    - Training exercises on site
    - Law enforcement conferences, webinars, or community awareness programs
    - Specialized training in terrorism, active shooter, workplace violence, or gangs

Scenario

- Two tenant employees returning from lunch stopped at the elevator lobby, waiting for an elevator, when one of the employees noticed Mr. John Smith, who worked on top floor of the complex. Mr. Smith was carrying a large black bag and wearing a long trench coat. One employee thought this was odd, because Mr. Smith was always well dressed.
- Another tenant employee walking to the elevator noticed Mr. Smith by the planter rummaging through a large bag. He was picking up items out of the bag and appeared to be placing them in his pockets. The employee thought it odd, but not worth a phone call to the police.
- Mr. Smith was still searching in his large black bag by the planter when another tenant employee saw the man pull a large long item out of the bag. To her it appeared to be a gun.

- Mr. Smith headed toward the elevator and waited for the next elevator.
- Several tenant employees entering the building now saw Mr. Smith at the elevator lobby with a shotgun in one hand and the bag in the other.
- One employee said out loud, "I will call the police."
- Mr. Smith looked at the employee and entered the elevator, heading to the top floor of the complex.
- The elevator stopped in front of Mr. Smith's office, and he reached in the large black bag and pulled out a semi-automatic pistol and two magazines. He then placed them in his waist band.
- Ms. Linda Johnson was exiting Mr. Smith's tenant space and stopped when she first saw Mr. Smith.
- Ms. Johnson never heard the three shots that took her life at 1:10 p.m.
- Mr. Smith immediately burst into the tenant office space and began shooting at anyone and everyone.
- Ms. Spencer, the receptionist who was on the phone, was the second person killed.
- Mr. Smith's partner, Mr. Ken Davenport, was the third person killed as he exited his office to see what all the noise was about.
- Mr. Smith began to look about for more employees to shoot.
- The tenant office employed fourteen people.
- Doors were being slammed shut, and the sounds of people yelling could be heard throughout the entire office space.
- 1:11 p.m.: A 911 operator reported receiving this call:

  Caller: Someone is shooting. I've heard five or six shots. People are screaming. There's another shot.
  Operator: What is your location?
  Caller: The Middle State Office Complex.
  Operator: Who is shooting?
  Caller: Someone said it was Mr. Smith.
  Operator: Where inside the complex is the shooting?
  Caller: On the top floor in the Smith and Davenport Financial Corporation.
  Operator: Where are you?
  Caller: I am in Smith and Davenport, hiding in my office.
  Operator: Can you see the shooter?
  Caller: No.

  The phone goes silent.
- 1:12 p.m.: A 911 operator reported another call:

  Caller: My name is Karley Williams and I am at the Middle State Office Complex. I can hear shooting coming from the upper floor of the building.
  Operator: Can you see the shooter?

Caller: No. But it may be Mr. Smith.
Operator: Can you describe Mr. Smith?
Caller: He is wearing a dark long coat, carrying a large black bag, dark hair, average build and maybe 65 years old.

- 1:12 p.m.: A 911 operator reported another call:

Caller: Mr. Smith has a shotgun. Oh my gosh—he just shot someone in the back. This can't be happening. Oh no, he is heading toward me.

The phone goes dead.
- One PD patrol car and one SO patrol car have arrived exactly at 1:15 p.m.
- People are screaming, running everywhere and crying.
- No one appears to be wounded or injured.
- A crowd is forming on the sidewalks and street corners.
- Neither the officer nor the deputy has ever been to the Middle State Office Complex to have any idea what the inside of the building looks like.
- No one came up to the patrol cars to provide information.
- No shooting can be heard.
- Two local news teams have arrived at the building.
- 1:15 p.m.: A 911 operator reported this call.

Caller: Mr. Smith is still inside Smith and Davenport Financial Corporate offices. I can still hear yelling, but no shots right now.
Operator: Where are you located?
Caller: I am across the hall from the corporate offices.
Operator: What did the shots sound like? Shotgun? Pistol? Automatic weapon?
Caller: Very loud, like a shotgun. I heard about ten shots.

- 1:16 p.m.: Police are informed that the shooter is still on the tenth floor.
- Two law enforcement officers enter the elevator and are heading to the tenth floor.
- Sounds of ambulances, police cars, screaming, yelling, people running, noise, and confusion.
- No more shots are heard coming from inside the building.
- 1:17 p.m.: A 911 operator reported this call.

Caller: This is George Hilson, I am at the Middle State Office Complex. I have barricaded myself in my office with my administrative assistant. Mr. Smith has a shotgun and has been shooting people here. I don't know how many he has shot or why. Come quickly.
Operator: Where is Mr. Smith right now?
Caller: I think in the conference room, but I don't know.

- 1:18 p.m.: Someone pulls the fire alarm. Strobe and audible alarm activated.
- Emergency exits are filling up with tenant employees.
- One of the tenant offices is the local ADA assistance center. The office is located on the second floor.
- Tenants begin to lock down all office doors on all floors to prevent the shooting from spreading.
- Tenants are afraid to exit their offices, because they don't know the location of the shooter.
- Because there has been no message communicated over the public address system, many employees have no idea what is happening. They attempt to gain their information from anyone running by.
- Fifteen more PD and SO patrol cars arrive.
- Dispatcher indicates all recent calls are reporting a shooting inside the Smith and Davenport Financial Corporation, on the tenth floor, but no additional details.
- Two fire trucks arrive at the building in response to the fire alarm.
- Two patrol car units set up on both sides of the Middle State Office Complex and watch the emergency exit doors.
- The confusion and noise intensify.
- Two officers are positioned next to the main company elevator when the elevator doors open. People rush out the door. Two people are white males wearing dark jackets.
- Tenant employees are seen running down the emergency stairwells.
- People rush out the emergency exit door. Three people are white males wearing dark jackets.
- A frantic lady runs over to the nearest officer and begins explaining what happened, but she was on the sixth floor. No new intelligence is gained from the conversation.
- The sounds of sirens are growing louder as more and more officers respond from throughout the city.
- Employees are seen hiding behind vehicles, shrubs, trees, and boulders.
- Employees are crying; some are on their cell phones.
- 1:19 p.m.: A total of twenty-five law enforcement officers are at the scene.
- Some of the officers came straight from home and are not in uniform and have no radios.
- Employees are still exiting the building. Most of the employees are confused and have more questions than answers.
- One individual's right leg is covered in blood. He wasn't on the tenth floor and isn't the shooter. The blood was caused from injuries suffered during the evacuation.
- Radio dispatcher broadcasts: The shooter is out of bullets and is stabbing individuals with a large knife.
- Additional police officers enter the company and are heading to the elevators and emergency stairwells. However, the elevators are jammed with guests and employees. Several elevators contain individuals in wheelchairs and using walkers.
- Emergency exits and stairwell are jammed with employees. Some employees are moving; others are sitting on the stairs to catch their breath.

- Each area of refuge that police encounter is jammed with employees and individuals who cannot navigate the stairs.
- The building sprinkler system has been activated and the water is making entry and evacuation more difficult.
- Mr. Smith lit a trashcan on fire and placed the trashcan in a small office close to the smoke detector.
- Screaming is still continuing, but appears to be coming from all corners of the complex.
- Television news crews are positioned in front of the Middle State Office Complex and are trying to interview employees who are exiting the building.
- A news helicopter is circling the building.
- People can be seen waving from almost every window, regardless of floor.
- Mr. Smith cannot be seen from any window inside the Smith and Davenport Financial Corporation.
- Law enforcement officers are stopping each white male wearing a dark jacket and any other white male who fits the shooter's description, regardless of clothing.
- Law enforcement officers are now being confronted by individuals, some stopping to raise their hands and dropping to the ground but others just continuing to run away.
- Employees are exiting the company from emergency exits and the main entrance doors, a total of four different exits.
- Because law enforcement officers are responding from multiple agencies, they all have different radios and dispatchers.
- Off-duty officers arriving at the company do not have police radios, only cell phones.
- Law enforcement officers' cell phones continuously ring as different callers try to make contact because of the radio problem.
- Law enforcement officers have no idea of the locations of other officers.
- Law enforcement officers cannot get through to their dispatch, and there is a serious delay in relaying messages.
- Federal agents are arriving at the Middle State Office Complex. Federal agents also have different radios.
- All entry and access points to the tenth floor have been located and reviewed.
- Screaming can be heard coming from upstairs, but the exact floor cannot be determined.
- The law enforcement departments have been trained on active shooter situations, but not together.
- The PD SWAT team has been notified and is heading to the complex.
- The PD helicopter is circling the building.
- The news helicopter has been ordered to stay clear of the building.
- 1:22 p.m.: Four law enforcement officers arrive on the tenth floor. The officer observes one body lying outside the Smith and davenport Financial Corporation office main entrance.
- 1:22 p.m.: Four officers enter Smith and Davenport Financial Corporation
- 1:22 p.m.: A white male, dark hair, glasses, wearing a dark long coat, believed to be Mr. Smith, is confronted by the four law enforcement officers in the conference room. On the

conference table are a semi-automatic pistol and a shotgun. Mr. Smith is covered in blood. He raises his hands and surrenders.

- Law enforcement officers search the offices. They find six dead bodies and two other employees who have sustained life-threatening wounds. Four other employees are rescued from two separate offices where they had barricaded themselves.

Summary

The shooter may have been arrested, but there are numerous areas and concerns that still need to be addressed by first responders and the Middle State Office Complex. What are they? Did you forget about the mysterious large black bag that could contain an improvised explosive device (IED) or the number of classrooms that are still in lockdown? If you have an active shooter plan, are each of the above points under consideration? Are the challenges clearly identified in your plan?

Scenario #2 Hospital

For this scenario, look at the active shooting event from three different perspectives and then identify your actions before, during, and after the incident:

- Visitor and patients of the hospital
- Law enforcement and first responders
- Employees of the Small City Hospital (a fictitious hospital)

Overview of Hospital

- The hospital has five stories hosting 410 beds with private patient rooms.
- The hospital is 100 percent occupied.
- The hospital is the only Level 1 trauma center in the city.
- The emergency department is open twenty-four hours per day, seven days a week.
- The fifth floor contains long-term patients of different ailments.
- The third and fourth floors are for general patients, with two beds per room.
- The children's medical center and the rehabilitation program is located on the second floor.
- The hospital includes 1,500 employees and 1,350 physicians and nurses on staff.
- The hospital uses approximately twenty-four volunteers, usually senior citizens.
- Small City Hospital sits on forty acres of land, approximately five miles from downtown, in a rural setting with no surrounding buildings.
- Emergency exits are located at the very end of each hallway, on the east and west ends of the floor.
- The nurse's stations are near the elevator lobby, and each lobby contains six elevators.
- Visiting hours are from 8:00 a.m. until 9:00 p.m., and there is no visitors sign-in log nor visitor badge required.
- There are 110 rooms on the fourth floor and 110 rooms on the third floor.

- Primary means of communications is a public address (PA) system that can be heard on each floor and throughout the building, but not outside.
- Telephones are located on floors 3 and above in each room, connecting to the hospital operator and having outside calling capability.
- The entire hospital is surrounded by large parking lots. The hospital does not have a parking garage.
- There have been no recent problems or issues reported by the hospital staff today. However, over the past three weeks, one nurse was stabbed by a patient, a patient punched a doctor, and relatives of patients physically and verbally abused two nurses.
- The hospital has a 25 percent turnover in staff, consistently, for approximately four years.
- There are two in-house hospital security officers per shift, but they are not armed.
- The security office and camera control room is on the first floor, near the general entrance.
- Surveillance cameras are located in each hallway, in guest waiting rooms, in each of the three entrances, in each stairwell exit door, and overlooking the elevator lobby on each floor
- The hospital has no active shooter plan in place but has been thinking about one.
- The hospital has not participated in any active shooter drills or exercises, and hospital executives have not attended any free training courses on active shootings.
- The hospital has not invited first responders to tour the hospital with active shooting scenarios in mind, for first responders frequently visit the emergency room and certain guest floors when guarding prisoners.
- The hospital has received no threats by phone or letter and has not been the subject of major issues reported by news media.
- There are no famous or significant patients currently staying at the hospital and no patients under law enforcement guard.
- The hospital is large but only has three major entrances, which are located at the general hospital, emergency, and outpatient services entrances.

Law Enforcement Overview

- City police department (PD):
  - Thirty patrol units, one sergeant, and five detectives are on duty.
  - 425 sworn officers form the department.
  - Four K-9 units work in the department.
  - Each patrol unit has M-16s, ballistic vests, Kevlar helmets, and smoke and gas grenades.
  - Sergeants' vehicles have gas masks, bolt cutters, battering rams, and cutting torches.
- County sheriff's office (SO):
  - Nine patrol units and one sergeant are on duty.
  - Seventy sworn deputies form the office.
  - Each patrol unit has M-16s, ballistic vests, Kevlar helmets, and smoke and gas grenades.
- The police department possesses the following equipment:
  - Mobile command post

- Two armored vehicles
- Two helicopters
- Gas masks
- Ballistic shields
- Two active SWAT teams
- Eight hostage negotiators
- Bomb detection equipment and robots
- Federal law enforcement:
  - Thirty-five agents (BATF, FBI, USSS, DHS)
- Law enforcement has responded to the hospital on only one occasion, three years ago. The purpose of the call was a murder/suicide. An 82-year-old man killed his wife in the hospital bed, then killed himself with a revolver. She had terminal cancer, and they had been married for forty-nine years.
- The Small City Hospital has <u>not</u> participated in the following events sponsored by law enforcement:
  - Site surveys
  - Vulnerability assessments
  - Training exercises on site
  - Conferences, webinars, or community awareness programs
  - Specialized training in terrorism, active shooter, workplace violence, or gangs

Scenario

- 9:11 p.m.: A 911 operator reported this call:

  Caller: Someone is shooting, I've heard five or six shots. People are screaming. There's another shot.
  Operator: What is your location?
  Caller: The Small City Hospital.
  Operator: Who is shooting?
  Caller: I don't know who is shooting.
  Operator: Where inside the hospital is the shooting?
  Caller: The fifth floor.
  Operator: Where are you?
  Caller: I am in Room 551.
  Operator: Can you see the shooter?
  Caller: No, and I am not going to look either. There's another shot. People are screaming.

- 9:11 p.m.: A 911 operator reported this call:

  Caller: My name is Carol Taylor. I am at the Small City Hospital. A guy has just shot two nurses on the fifth floor of the hospital. Oh, my gosh, he just shot a nurse in the back. I saw her lying on the floor.

Operator: Can you see the shooter?

Caller: "I saw the shooter, but I am hiding now. He is wearing a white coat and looks like a doctor. He has a semi-automatic pistol. This can't be happening.

Operator: What color is his hair? How much does he weigh? How tall is he?

Caller: Gray hair, 250 pounds, maybe six foot two, and maybe 65 years old.

Operator: How many people are shooting?

Caller: I only saw one.

Operator: Where is the shooter now?

Caller: I don't know.

- 9:11 p.m.: A 911 operator reported this call:

  Caller: He just shot the security officer when he came out of the elevator. Oh, no, he is heading toward me.

  The phone goes dead.
- 9:14 p.m.: Two police cars arrive at the hospital.
- Some people are screaming, some are hiding behind vehicles and trees, and some are running anywhere they can, whereas others are in shock or crying.
- Ambulances are arriving at the hospital with patients, unaware of the shooting.
- None of the people exiting the hospital comes up to a patrol car to provide information.
- There are no security nor hospital staff in sight, and the fleeing people aren't stopping for anything.
- 9:14 p.m.: Four more shots are heard inside the hospital, but their location cannot be determined.
- 9:13 p.m.: A 911 operator reported this call:

  Caller: This is security officer Don Johnson from the Small City Hospital. We have an active shooter situation going on right now. My partner ran upstairs, but I haven't heard back from him. There have been over twenty to thirty shots fired on the fifth floor. I don't know who it is. There is a lot of screaming and people running. Please send help quickly.

  Operator: Can you see the shooter on your surveillance cameras?

  Caller: I can only see people running. I don't see him. Wait, he just shot a nurse. He is looking at the camera. He just shot the camera. I don't see anything now.

  Operator: Please describe the shooter.

  Caller: White male, gray hair, glasses, maybe 65, over 200 pounds, and maybe five foot eight.

  Operator: What was he wearing?

  Caller: He has a white jacket on like a doctor, but I don't know him. I have never seen him before.

- 9:14 p.m.: A 911 operator reported this call:

> *Caller: I am at the hospital. I have barricaded myself in a patient room with my dad. There is a man shooting people on the fifth floor. I can still hear him yelling. He is right down the hall from me.*
> *Operator: What is he yelling?*
> *Caller: "You will all pay. You will all pay."*
> *Operator: Stay on the phone for me, please. What is your name?*
> *Caller: "Okay. Nancy.*
> *Operator: Did he say his name or talk with an accent?*
> *Caller: No.*

- 9:15 p.m.: Two officers run into the hospital and are heading toward the emergency stairs, trying to get to the fifth floor.
- 9:15 p.m.: Four more first responders arrive at the Small City Hospital.
- 9:15 p.m.: Two local news television crews arrive at the hospital.
- The elevators are working slowly because of all the people using the elevators to escape the shooter.
- The fire alarm has been pulled. No one knows who pulled the fire alarm. Strobe and audible alarms are activated.
- All the emergency exits are filling up with people.
- Patients who have tried to leave have passed out on the floor or are dragging equipment and tubes behind them.
- Most of the hospital patients cannot move without assistance, because they are too weak or too badly hurt or are on medication and can't move at all.
- The Small City Hospital staff begins to lock down all hospital room doors on all floors below the fifth floor to prevent the shooting from spreading.
- The security officer broadcasts the following message over the PA system: "Stay in your rooms. Lock the door. Help is on the way."
- Hospital staff give directions to go back to rooms, locking and barricading the door.
- 9:16 p.m.: Two law enforcement officers arrive on the fifth floor. The officers see three bodies lying in the hallway floor. They appear to be a nurse, a security officer, and a patient. The shooter is not in sight, and no gunshots are heard.
- Fire trucks are arriving at the hospital in response to the fire alarm.
- Lights are being turned off within hospital patient rooms.
- Patient rooms cannot be locked on any floor except the fifth.
- 9:16 p.m.: Two law enforcement officers see another body of a patient in a wheelchair. The shooter is still not located.
- 9:17 p.m.: The elevator surveillance camera shows a white male in a white coat walking back and forth.
- 9:17 p.m.: A nurse comes out of a patient room. She has been shot in the left arm.
- 9:17 p.m.: Two officers, using hand gestures, try to find out where the shooter is. She doesn't know and walks past the officers.

- Officers contact hospital employees about the shooting and the location of the security control room. An employee only two weeks on the job doesn't know and can't answer questions.
- Officers set up on both sides of the west wing to watch the emergency exit doors.
- Employees and patients are seen waving and yelling from the windows on several different floors.
- More and more officers are entering the hospital. Some officers are looking for the security control room.
- Two officers are by the main hospital elevator when the elevator doors open. People rush out the door. Four of the people on the elevator are white males wearing white jackets.
- People rush out the emergency exit door. Three people are white males wearing white jackets.
- Patients are running over to the officers and are trying to explain what happened. No new intelligence is forthcoming.
- An individual in a fifth-floor window points at a book and throws it to the ground. An officer runs over and picks up the book. Inside are these words: "He is out of bullets and stabbing people with a scalpel. Come quick."
- On the fifth floor, third window from the end, a patient is seen in the window but is thrown out of the window by a white male in a white coat. The victim was an elderly patient.
- 9:18 p.m.: Forty-five law enforcement officers are on scene at the hospital. Some came straight from home and are not in uniform and have no radios.
- Employees and patients are still exiting the building. Many are confused and have more questions than answers.
- Several patients who are exiting the hospital are covered in blood. The blood is from previous injuries and from the shooter.
- Radio dispatcher broadcast: "The shooter is out of bullets and stabbing patients with a scalpel."
- Additional officers enter the hospital. Elevators are jammed with patients, guests, and staff. Several elevators contain patients in hospital beds.
- Emergency exits and stairwells are jammed with people. The individuals, many of them patients, are slowed by their injuries and can barely walk, many sitting on the stairs.
- Stairwells are jammed with medical equipment dropped by evacuating patients.
- Each area of refuge encountered is jammed with patients who cannot navigate the stairs.
- The fire alarm is still sounding.
- Families of patients and hospital employees are arriving at the hospital to help their loved ones.
- 9:18 p.m.: Law enforcement officers move toward the third patient room, using the left or right side of the hallway, but aren't certain whether the shooter is in the room.
- 9:18 p.m.: A white male, with gray hair white and wearing jacket, approximately 65 years old, is sitting in chair in the corner of the left side third window. He is covered in blood.
- 9:18 p.m.: Law enforcement officer directs the man not to move. The officers move quickly toward the man.

- 9:18 p.m.: The man stands up and starts swinging his arm at the officers. In his right hand is a scalpel.
- 9:18 p.m.: Law enforcement officers open fire on the man. The man is shot four times in the chest and falls to the ground but rolls over and gets back up. The man is wearing a ballistic vest.
- 9:18 p.m.: Additional law enforcement offices are running toward the sound of the shooting.
- 9:19 p.m.: The man is the shot again by the law enforcement officers, neutralizing the threat.
- Telephone calls are being received in the PBX at the rate of 200 per minute. The PBX system is completely overwhelmed with calls and has frozen up.
- The hospital manager on duty (MOD) is doing the following:
  - Collecting a list of fifth floor patients.
  - Collecting a list of staff members on duty.
  - Looking for the active shooter plan for the hospital, but believes there may not be one.
  - Contacting PBX to determine what information has not been provided and to see whether she is receiving any communications from people on the fourth floor—but can't get through.
- Hospital employees keep arriving at the security control room, asking:
  - What do you want me to do?
  - What is happening?
  - Where do you want me to help?
  - What do I tell my patients?
  - Should we evacuate the hospital?
- Off-duty hospital employees begin arriving at the hospital to aid the injured.
- 9:19 p.m.: Law enforcement officers are stopping each white male in a white jacket and any other white male who fits the shooter's description, regardless of whether they are wearing a white jacket.
- 9:19 p.m.: EMS personnel have been waiting outside the hospital, treating patients and employees who need assistance, but are asking when they can enter the hospital to help the injured on the fifth floor.
- Law enforcement officers are encountering a large number of people, some stopping to raise their hands and dropping to the ground but others just continuing to walk or run away.
- Individuals are exiting the hospital from the emergency exits and main doors, a total of seven different exits.
- Law enforcement officers have different radios and dispatchers but are teaming or grouping before entering the building.
- Law enforcement officers' cell phones continuously go off as different callers are trying to make contact because radio traffic is terrible and messages are coming too quickly.
- Law enforcement officers are trying to learn each other's positions and to relay messages, there being no common channel and some off duty law enforcement officers being without radios.

- Federal agents and detectives are arriving at the hospital. Federal agents have different radios.
- All law enforcement departments, including federal, state, and local agencies, have been trained on active shooter situations, but not together.
- Both PD and SO SWAT teams have been notified and are heading to the hospital.
- The PD helicopter is circling the hospital.
- The news helicopter has been ordered to stay clear of the hospital.
- The mayor wants a complete update regarding the shooting.

Scenario #3 School

For this scenario, look at the active shooting event from three different perspectives and then identify your actions before, during, and after the incident:

- Employees in the administrative office
- Law enforcement and first responders
- Teachers inside the Old Middle School (a fictitious school)

School Overview

- Old Middle School consists of grades 6–8 with a student enrollment of 1,000, about thirty students to a class.
- Forty-seven staff members are present, including admin (7), teachers (37), maintenance (1), nurse (1), and unarmed security (1).
- Old Middle School:
  - The school was built in 1938.
  - It is a single-story brick building with dropdown wooden windows.
  - The school is locked down during normal school hours.
  - Visitor can only access the school through the administrative office.
  - Classroom doors are wooden with double-paned glass windows.
  - The classroom doors can lock but do not have deadbolts.
  - The campus is gated, with two major entrances (main entrance near the administrative office and a second entrance via a side gate by the athletic field and gymnasium).
  - An eight-foot-high chain link fence completely surrounds the school.
- Old Middle School is the oldest school in the city and is located approximately 1 mile from the city center, which includes the police department and fire department.
- Security features:
  - Public address (PA) system broadcasts throughout the school building and grounds.
  - School staff members wear identification cards featuring a picture of the employee.
  - Surveillance cameras are located in the cafeteria, hallways, gym, and all exterior areas, but not in classrooms. Classroom cameras are budgeted for the next fiscal year.
  - Card access is required for the teacher's lounge and administration records room.

- Each classroom has an intercom and a telephone.
- The two major entrances to the school consist of 2- by 2-inch square steel fabricated fencing and two full standing industrial style turnstiles having exit capabilities only.
- The school does not have an active shooter plan but is scheduled to participate in a full-scale exercise with first responders and law enforcement the following month.
- The school has received no threats, hate mail, nor suspicious telephone calls and has not been the subject of any major criminal activity that anyone can remember.
- The administrative office reports no disciplinary problems or issues with the school staff, and no employees have been fired from the school in over two years.
- The school has been discussed for possible closure in approximately two years, but only dependent on school enrollment.
- The school contains only one large parking lot, located by the main entrance.

Law Enforcement Overview

- Law enforcement recently completed active shooter training at the local high school for the first time.
- The active shooter training was the first exercise that both local and federal law enforcement departments participated in jointly.
- Local law enforcement consists of
  - city police department 45 officers
  - sheriff's office 38 deputies
  - school police department 12 officers
  - city marshal's office 10 officers
  - federal agents 8 agents
  - state police 3 officers
- The local law enforcement active shooter plan has <u>not</u> been finalized nor approved.
- The school police department has one officer assigned to each elementary and high school, but two officers patrol the four middle schools.
- The recent active shooter training exercise produced several areas that need to be improved:
  - No radio channel is common to all responders.
  - There is no consistency in semi-automatic rifles; officers may purchase their own if they wish.
  - Equipment and tactical differences exist between agencies.
  - No law enforcement department have ballistic shields, gas masks, or battering rams.
  - Only supervisors have bolt cutters.
  - Not all agencies participated in the exercise.
  - Senior management did not participate in the exercise.

Scenario

- 8:02 a.m.: A 911 operator received this call:

> *Caller: He is shooting people. Oh, my gosh, he is shooting people.*
> *Operator: Who is shooting?*
> *Caller: A man! He entered our school and he just shot our security guard. He shot him. He's dead. He's dead! He shot him in front of the administrative office.*
> *Operator: What school is it?*
> *Caller: Old Middle School.*
> *Operator: What does he look like?*
> *Caller: White, white, yeah, white. Mid twenties, skinny, maybe 140 pounds, a close haircut, I think brown. I don't know. I don't know. This is terrible.*
> *Operator: What was he wearing?*
> *Caller: Jeans and a white shirt and a black baseball cap.*
> *Operator: What type of gun?*
> *Caller: "A rifle of some type, but he could have more, I don't know. I don't know. It all happened to fast. Oh, yeah—he was carrying a black bag.*
> *Operator: Where is he right now?*
> *Caller: He went into the school, toward the classrooms. I don't know which wing. He shot at me. He pointed the gun at me and shot. I ducked back into the office. I don't know who he is. Come quickly. We need help. We need help now. Save the kids.*
> *Operator: Stay on the line. Help is on the way.*
> *Caller: The security guard isn't moving. This can't be happening. The security guard isn't moving. This can't be happening.*
> *Operator: Help is on its way. Stay calm.*
> *Caller: Okay. Oh no, there's more shooting. The kids are screaming. They need help. Oh, my God, come quickly. We need help now. Right now!*

- Dispatcher: An active shooter call is sent to all law enforcement agencies.
- 8:04 a.m.: A 911 operator receives this call:

> *Caller: I am a seventh grade teacher at Old Middle School. A man with a gun is walking down the school hallway. Is he a policeman? The school administrative office is not answering their phone.*
> *Operator: Can you describe the man?*
> *Caller: He is a white male, a big guy, wearing a white shirt and blue jeans. He was carrying a shotgun, I think. He just entered Room 222.*
> *Operator: Stay on the line, please.*
> *Caller: I hear screaming coming from Classroom 222. Send help now.*
> *Two gun shots are heard over the telephone.*
> *Operator: How many shooters are there?*
> *Caller: Students are running out of the classroom into the hallway. There is another shot and another shot. Send help now. Why aren't the police here?*

- The Old Middle School executes its lockdown procedures.
- Two of the classrooms have substitute teachers, who do not know the lockdown procedures.

- The police helicopter has left the airport and is heading toward the school.
- 8:06 a.m.: Three patrol cars arrive at school.
- 8:06 a.m.: A 911 operator receives another call:

Caller: Oh, my gosh, one of the students has just been shot in the hallway. I can see the shooter dragging a teacher on the floor by her hair.

- The shooter fires two more shots at students who are running to get away. One student falls to the ground.
- The administrative office is calling each classroom near Room 222 to determine whether there are any injuries and to instruct them to lock down.
- Some students are using their cell phones to call their parents.
- Other students are receiving text messages from their parents.
- Teachers are trying to keep their students quiet by using hand gestures.
- Teachers are moving students away from doors and grouping students together behind anything they can find.
- Teachers are receiving cell phone calls and text messages from students' parents.
- Teachers are using cell phones to communicate with other teachers within the school to see what they know and to try and to out where the shooter is.
- Some teachers are afraid to answer their cell phones, or have turned off their phones' ringers.
- Students are very frightened, want the shooting to stop, and want to leave.
- Students are crying; some are in shock and are afraid to move.
- Students are afraid to say anything or make any noise for fear of being killed.
- Teachers and students are listening to every sound, constantly watching doors and looking out windows for the police.
- 8:06 a.m.: First responders are beginning to arrive at the school.
- First responders will not enter the building until instructed to do so by their supervisors.
- Students from other classrooms are seen frantically waving for help.
- Some students are seen jumping out of the windows of one classroom.
- 8:07 a.m.: Four more patrol cars arrive at the school.
- 8:07 a.m.: Three officers are in the school, working their way to Classroom 222. The officers are from two different departments.
- 8:07 a.m.: Two unmarked law enforcement vehicles arrive on scene.
- A detective and federal agents enter the school and head toward the administrative office to view the surveillance cameras.
- 8:08 a.m.: The parents of students who live nearby are arriving at the school and want to get their kids right away. One of the parents is very upset and is threatening to enter the school on his own unless his son is brought to him.
- 8:08 a.m.: Three offices are outside Room 222. The door is closed, and no noise is heard inside the classroom.
- 8:08 a.m.: Two officers are outside the building, looking into Classroom 222. The shooter is not seen.

- 8:09 a.m.: three officers enter Classroom 222. The shooter is not in the room. Four students have been shot, and approximately 15 students are huddled in the corner of the classroom.
- 8:09 a.m.: Police officers inside the administrative office play back surveillance tapes to see where the shooter has gone.
- 8:09 a.m.: The surveillance camera shows the shooter walk over to the wall and pull the fire alarm.
- The administrative office, over the PA system, tells all classrooms to ignore the fire alarm and stay in lockdown.
- 8:09 a.m.: The shooter enters Classroom 233 after shooting the door open, then points his rifle at the teacher and shoots her twice. The shooter points his rifle down the hallway. The shooter is seen yelling, but there is no one in the hallway.
- 8:09 a.m.: More law enforcement officers are entering the school from three different directions.
- 8:10 a.m.: The shooter begins shooting at the three officers exiting Room 222. One officer is wounded in the leg.
- Students in Classroom 233 begin to panic and start jumping from the windows. Several of the students injure themselves on broken glass even though the building is only a one story building. The students are running in no particular direction. Other students are frozen in place or in shock.
- The shooter moves to classroom 235 and attempts to open it, but it is locked.
- Teachers continue to call the administrative office for updates while still receiving text messages and cell phone calls.
- 8:11 a.m.: The surveillance camera shows the shooter entering Classroom 237, after which he throws a black bag into the hallway. A review of surveillance tapes shows the shooter looking through the black bag and picking up several different items, then placing them back into the bag.
- 8:11 a.m.: Police officers exchange gunfire with the shooter.
- The administrative office notifies the detective and federal agents that Classroom 237 is vacant. No students are visible, and both exit doors to the classroom are accessible from the hallway.
- Law enforcement officers are now monitoring all school surveillance cameras.
- First responders are directing students who jumped out of the windows to come toward their position.
- First responders are beginning to assist injured students.
- Law enforcement officers are guarding all school exits and are closely checking each person evacuating the school to ensure that shooter is among them.
- School maps on room locations and exits/entrances are provided to law enforcement officers.
- The school administrative office phones are overwhelmed. The administrative office is trying only to answer phones from teachers in lockdown.
- The school administrative office reviews its checklist of emergency contact notifications, but unfortunately not all the contact names and numbers are accurate.

- The school administrators' consider evacuating classrooms that are not in the active shooter's area.
- The administrative office is busy locating the student daily attendance rosters for students in the affected classrooms.
- The administrative office is locating files on all teachers in the affected classrooms.
- More and more parents are arriving at the school to pick up their children.
- First responders block the streets; some responders must park more than three blocks away.
- Television news crews are beginning to arrive at the scene.
- A news helicopter is now flying over the school.
- The governor's office is calling for updates.
- Ambulances are arriving but can't get close to the school to help the students.
- First responders are contacting the parents of students who are at the school to see whether they have received calls from their kids located inside school. First responders are also trying to determine student locations, the location of the shooter, and information about the shooter, such as his name, the number and types of his weapons, what is inside the black bag, and what he has said or asked.
- First responders are maintaining contact with all first responders to work effectively in this active shooter incident, including through interior, exterior, and camera surveillance; crowd control; coordination; and communication.
- 8:12 a.m.: SWAT arrives at the school. Members are not dressed in tactical gear but have their equipment and weapons.
- The bomb squad is called because of a black bag thrown into hallway. It could contain an IED or other weapons such as gas or smoke.
- 10:13 a.m.: The shooter again shoots at officers, around the doorframe without aiming, then tosses a dark object into the hallway. A few seconds later, a white smoke grenade explodes, filling the hallway with thick white smoke.
- 10:13 a.m.: The shooter begins firing out the windows toward the first responders and bystanders.
- 10:13 a.m.: The school's surveillance cameras show only the lower half of the shooter, who is seen in the hallway trying to enter Classroom 240—but the door is locked.
- Screaming is heard coming from Classroom 240.
- The shooter's position is radioed to all first responders.
- 10:13 a.m.: A second team of officers enters from the emergency exit and approaches to approximately sixty feet from Classroom 240 and the shooter.
- 10:13 a.m.: The shooter is neutralized by the first responders.

Summary

The shooter may have been neutralized, but numerous areas and concerns still need addressing by first responders and the Old Middle School staff and administrators. What are they? Did you forget about the mysterious large black bag that could contain an improvised explosive device (IED) or the number of classrooms still in lockdown? If you have an active shooter plan, are each of the above points under consideration? Are the challenges clearly identified in your plan?

Appendix E
Case Studies

Active shooter and workplace violence case studies may provide a double perspective for the reader, specifically from the different observations and viewpoints of first responders and private sector owners/operators. After each case study, questions will draw out key learning points to reinforce actions before, during, or after the event.

Case Study #1: Jerad Miller and Amanda Miller

Business Setting

Shooting location #1: Cici's Pizza is located on the east side of Las Vegas, almost four miles away from the Las Vegas Strip. The restaurant is situated in a shopping plaza near the south end of the building, close to a side street.

Shooting location #2: Walmart is located approximately 100 yards away from Cici's Pizza, just south on the same side of the street and just across the side street. Walmart is the anchor store of the adjacent shopping plaza.

Introduce the Active Shooting Incident

On June 8, 2014, a Sunday, at approximately 11:22 a.m., Las Vegas Metropolitan Police Department (LVMPD) officers Alyn Beck and Igor Soldo were casually eating lunch at Cici's Pizza. Both officers were sitting in a booth facing the main entrance. The restaurant was half full of customers when Jerad Miller and Amanda Miller entered. The LVMPD black-and-white marked police cruisers were sitting just outside the main door in the parking lot.

Without acknowledging the officers, and without any dialogue, Jerad Miller shot Officer Soldo in the back of the head with a handgun. Officer Beck tried to engage the Millers but was shot in the throat. Neither officer was able to return fire at the Millers. Officer Beck was shot several more times while on the floor by the Millers after Officer Beck was pulled from the booth. The Miller's then covered Officer Beck with a Gadsden Flag bearing the words "Don't tread on Me," a yellow banner featuring a coiled snake originally used in the American Revolution. After Officer Soldo's body was pulled from the booth, the Millers pinned a swastika pin on Officer Soldo that read: "The beginning of a revolution."

The Millers took both officers' sidearms and extra magazines and left the pizza parlor without saying anything. The Millers ran approximately 100 yards away and entered the Walmart. Jerad Miller walked toward the cash registers and fired one shot from a handgun into the ceiling, then yelled, "The revolution has started. The cops are coming. Get out!" Amanda Miller walked over to grab a shopping cart and headed toward Jerad Miller. Customers ran out of the store in every direction.

Joseph Robert Wilcox was a customer at Walmart when he and his friend heard the shot fired by Jerad Miller. Mr. Wilcox had a carrying a concealed weapons (CCW) permit and was carrying his weapon that day. Mr. Wilcox headed toward Jerad Miller to do something about the shooting inside Walmart. Unfortunately, Mr. Wilcox did not know Amanda Miller was with Jerad as he approached him. Amanda shot Joseph Robert Wilcox in the back without warning, killing him.

The Millers moved away from the main Walmart entrance toward the back of the store. Along the way, they used a baseball bat to smash the ammunition locker and grab more ammunition for their weapons. The Millers were not running away, but rather appeared to be preparing to ambush more law enforcement officers. Amanda Miller fired several shots at an unaccompanied officer who had entered Walmart. The officer fired several shots at Amanda, hitting her in the right shoulder. Both were shooting at close range.

A four-officer tactical unit entered the store and headed toward the location the first officer reported. Law enforcement units blocked the rear exits of Walmart with their cars to prevent the Millers from exiting. The Millers retreated into the automotive department and began to take items from the shelves to protect themselves. Officer tried to negotiate with the Millers, but Jerad yelled back at the officers: "Stand down. You have failed. I'm in charge now." The Millers exchanged gunfire with the law enforcement officers for about fifteen minutes. During the firefight, Jerad Miller received a fatal wound that would soon end his life. The Millers fired thirty-six rounds, and the officers sixteen rounds, during the gun battle.

While the Millers lay on the floor, bleeding and trapped by law enforcement officers, Amanda Miller attempted to shoot Jerad Miller with her handgun. She turned the handgun on herself, firing one shot into her head. She died at the hospital.

Investigation

For more than six years, Jerad Miller had held radical anti-government views and often spoke of an awakening of the people. He called for action to abolish what was wrong. He believed that if anyone got in his way, they would be slaughtered—and that if he were killed, it would only make him a martyr.

Jerad and Amanda Miller left Las Vegas to join Cliven Bundy in his standoff with the Bureau of Land Management to prevent the BLM from removing livestock from the Bundy ranch, 80 miles northeast of Las Vegas, Nevada. The Millers left everything to join the cause against the government. However, the Millers were asked to leave because of Jerad's felony conviction. Amanda followed Jerad wherever he went.

The Millers were at a neighbor's apartment, at approximately 4:30 a.m. on Sunday, June 8, 2014, when they indicated that they would murder police officers. Because of their views and past statements, the neighbors did not take the threat seriously.

Law enforcement investigators found documents from the Millers in an apartment that suggested that the shooting of the two LVMPD officers was not an isolated planned attack. The documents disclosed a detailed plan to attack and take over a courthouse in Las Vegas while also executing as many public officials as possible.

Jerad Miller could not possess or own any guns because of his felony conviction. Amanda Miller purchased the gun Jerad used in the attack in Indiana. The source of the other weapons is unknown, but neither one of the handguns was registered in Clark County, Nevada.

Social Media

Active shooters are not unfamiliar with social media and the media's potential to share views, thoughts, and inner feelings. Some use these sites to solicit support for their cause, whereas others express hatred, anger, and the motives behind their deadly rampages to justify their actions. Not every active shooter broadcasts his or her views in advance, and not everyone who broadcasts his or her views in vivid detail will become an active shooter. An active shooter cannot be predicted by what is placed on social media sites, but it is important to listen to such words in determining mitigation, preparedness, and response strategies.

Jerad Miller and Amanda Miller took advantage of these sites to broadcast their ideals, intentions, beliefs, and warnings. In many ways, they believed themselves revolutionaries against a fascist and tyrannical American government. From Satan running our government to comparing America to the former World War II Nazi Germany, Jerad Miller voiced his views and opinions for years. But why, after so many years, did his words turn into action?

The following was posted on Jerad Miller's Facebook page on June 2:

We can hope for peace. We must, however, prepare for war. We face an enemy that is not only well funded, but who believe they fight for freedom and justice. Those of us who know the truth and dare speak it, know that the enemy we face are indeed our brothers. Even though they share the same masters as we all do. They fail to recognize the chains that bind them. To stop this oppression, I fear, can only be accomplished with bloodshed. May the best men of our beloved nation stand and fight tyranny, without fear and without regret. May we stand proud as free men instead of kneeling as slaves. May we offer our children a free and just world with our blood, sweat and tears as payment. Let our wives and lovers take vengeance upon our enemies in our absence. We cannot fail in this endeavor of Liberty, if we do we risk leaving our orphaned children to the will of tyrants. We, cannot with good conscience leave this fight to our children, because the longer we wait, our enemies become better equipped and recruit more mercenaries of death, willing to do a tyrants bidding without question. I know you are fearful, as am I. We certainly stand before a great and powerful enemy. I, however would rather die fighting for freedom, than live on my knees as a slave. Let it be known to our children's children that free men stood fast before a tyrants wrath and were found victorious because we stood together. That we all cast aside our petty differences and unite under the banner of Liberty and Truth. May future generations look back upon this time in history with awe and gratitude, for our courage to face tyranny, so that they could live happy and free [1].

In early May 2014, Jerad Miller posted the following:

There is no greater cause to die for than liberty. To die for that cause is easy, to live for it is another matter. I will willingly die for liberty. Death, in a sense is freedom from tyranny. Death, is the easy way out. Most notably is the "suicide by cop" routine. Yes, standing before despots is dangerous and most likely does not end well for you. I know this, my wife knows this. Soon they will come for us, because they don't like what we think, and what we say. They don't like the fact that we, simply will not submit to fascist rule. We don't have much, but we are willing to sacrifice everything......for you, for your freedoms. Even if you wouldn't let us have ours. We know who we are and what we stand for, do you? [2]

On June 7, 2014, Jerad Miller posted the following at 4 a.m. (The shooting rampage in Las Vegas began at 11:22 a.m. on Sunday):

The dawn of a new day. May all of our coming sacrifice be worth it [3].

SUMMARY OF DATA AFTER THE SHOOTING

Date of shooting	June 8, 2014
Time of shooting	11:22 a.m.
Day of the week	Sunday
Suspect(s)	Jared Miller
	Amanda Woodruff Miller
Suspect(s) description	White male
	White female
Suspects' clothing	Jared Miller: short-sleeved light-colored shirt, black tennis shoes, white socks, light-colored camouflage pants; later added dark tactical vest
	Amanda Miller: short-sleeved light-colored shirt, black tennis shoes, white socks.
	No hats, glasses, ballistic vests, or gloves noted
Suspects' special equipment	Bag containing a shotgun, the officers' two handguns, two other handguns, 200 rounds of ammunition, knives, first-aid supplies, camouflage clothing, and MRE-style food. Tactical vest containing shotgun ammunition
Suspect's home	Moved to Las Vegas, Nevada, in January 2014
Suspects' relationship	Married September 2012, in Indiana
Location of shooting	Las Vegas, Nevada, two locations, across the street from each other:
	Cici's Pizza, 309 N. Nellis Blvd, Las Vegas, Nevada
	Walmart, 201 N. Nellis Blvd, Las Vegas, Nevada
Distance between locations	100 yards
Distance from shooters residence	Approximately 4 miles
Reason for shooting	Exact reason unknown; anti-government views and postings noted
Type of shooting	Mobile shooting, two shooting locations, barricaded inside a storage room, no hostages
Vehicles	Unknown
IEDs	None

How targets selected	Random government target—police officers
Law enforcement response time	Approximately 2 minutes
Duration of shooting	Approximately 25 minutes
Shooters' weapons	Smith & Wesson M&P 9mm handgun
	Ruger .38 caliber revolver
	Winchester 12-gauge pump shotgun with pistol grip
Weapons per shooter	One each per shooter, with shotgun in bag; added two weapons from slain law enforcement officers
Shooters' prior experience with weapons	None noted
Military experience	No military experience
Age of shooters	Jared Miller 31
	Amanda Woodruff Miller 22
Casualties	Three victims killed at two separate locations
	One law enforcement wounded (shrapnel)
	One shooter killed by police: Jared Miller
	One shooter suicide: Amanda Miller
Age of victims	Alyn Beck 41
	Igor Soldo 31
	Joseph Wilcox 31
Prior history of shooters with victims	No prior association
Prior history of shooters with location	No prior association
Criminal history	Jerad Miller had a criminal history in the states of Washington and Indiana. He had arrests and charges on his record, including misdemeanor battery, felony drug trafficking, arrest on a strangulation battery charge, obstruction of a public officer, DUI, as well as convictions for third-degree malicious mischief, third-degree theft, harassment, and taking a motor vehicle without permission.
	Amanda Miller had no known criminal record.
Shooter's prior experiences with law enforcement	January 2014 interviewed by law enforcement concerning a threat to "shoot up" a Bureau of Motor Vehicles Office in Indiana.
	April 2014 interviewed by law enforcement concerning a neighbor's domestic violence case.
	May 2014 interviewed by law enforcement concerning an acquaintance's sexual assault.
Health/mental issues of shooter(s)	No documented or known psychiatric record for either Jared Miller or Amanda Miller.
Employment of shooter(s)	Amanda worked at Hobby Lobby.
	Jerad dressed up as a comic book character, Joker, to pose with tourists for tips on the Las Vegas Strip and Fremont Street.
Prior video and social media presence	Very active on YouTube and Facebook
Incident resolution	Jared Miller: death by gunshot wounds fired by law enforcement during the gun battle in Walmart
	Amanda Miller: shot in the shoulder by law enforcement, but committed suicide by a single gunshot to her head

Case Study #2: Michael Zehaf-Bibeau

Business Setting

Shooting location #1: National War Memorial
Shooting location #2: Centre Block Parliament Building

Introduce the Active Shooter Incident

On October 22, 2014, shortly before 10:00 a.m. E.D.T., Corporal Nathan Cirillo of the Argyll and Sutherland Highlanders of Canada was one of three sentries from the ceremonial guard posted at the Canadian Tomb of the Unknown Solider. Only minutes before the end of the sentries' shift, witnesses saw Zehaf-Bibeau arrive at the Canadian National Memorial carrying a rifle. He was dressed in blue jeans and a black jacket, with a keffiyeh scarf covering the lower half of his face [4].

Zehaf-Bibeau shot Nathan Cirillo twice in the back at close range, fatally wounding him. Cpl. Kyle Button and Cpl. Brandon Stevenson, two other soldiers on sentry duty, attempted to stop Zehaf-Bibeau, but they were fired on and forced to flee to the other side of the memorial. Zehaf-Bibeau then pulled down his scarf, held his rifle one-handed over his head, and yelled "For Iraq!"

Cpl. Wiseman, who was nearby, then attempted to stop Zehaf-Bibeau, but Zehaf-Bibeau made an attempt to run him over in a small gray Toyota car. The three soldiers, along with several bystanders, attended to Cirillo as they could before the paramedics arrived and took Cirillo to the hospital.

Zehaf-Bibeau then began to drive his car west along Wellington, only a short distance to Parliament Hill. He abandoned his vehicle and ran through an open gate in the fence surrounding the Parliament Hill precinct and carjacked a parliamentary vehicle assigned to ministers of the Crown, which he then drove to the Centre Block Parliament Building.

Samearn Son was one of two security guards on duty when Zehaf-Bibeau entered the Centre Block Parliament Building through the main entrance (which was unlocked) under the Peace Tower [5]. Son saw the rifle in Zehaf-Bibeau hands, grabbed it, and pulled it toward the floor, yelling, "Gun! Gun! Gun!" Son was shot in the foot and had to let go of the attacker. Son limped out of the building and calmly told a CBC reporter outside, "I will survive." Inside the Centre Block, Zehaf-Bibeau exchanged gunfire with security personnel and was wounded.

Zehaf-Bibeau then ran toward the Library of Parliament along the Hall of Honour corridor, pursued by Royal Canadian Mounted Police (RCMP) officers. During the shooting, a single bullet penetrated the outer doors to the New Democratic Party (NDP) caucus room. Inside the room, NDP Members of Parliament (MPs) tried to find good cover to hide. At the same time, across the hall, Conservative MPs erected a makeshift barricade at the doors to their room by piling chairs and using flagpoles as rudimentary spears [6].

Zehaf-Bibeau reached an alcove near the Library of Parliament entrance, then hid himself out of sight of RCMP officers. Fortunately, the alcove was near Sergeant-at-Arms Kevin Vickers. Mr. Vickers was a distinguished policeman with the RCMP before he joined the staff of the House of Commons in 2005. Vickers retrieved a 9mm handgun from a security-box, then entered the hall near Zehaf-Bibeau. The security team then yelled to Vickers that the suspect was hiding in the alcove near him. Vickers then moved behind a nearby column, then sprang past the column while firing at Zehaf-Bibeau, thereby incapacitating him. The security team moved toward Zehaf-Bibeau and fired as well. More than thirty shots were fired in the final gunfight. Television footage of the shootout showed a team of RCMP officers converging in the vicinity of the alcove when two loud gunshots rang out, followed by numerous gunshots in rapid succession. Then everything went silent.

Investigation

Zehaf-Bibeau, according to court documents, was born Joseph Paul Micheal Bibeau, but in 1995, after his conversion to Islam, his parents legally changed his name to Joseph Paul Michael Abdallah Bulgasem Zehaf-Bibeau to better reflect the other half of his heritage.

A habitual offender, Zehaf-Bibeau had an extensive criminal record for several types of criminal offences, including larceny and drug possession, along with several parole violations [7]. He received several criminal convictions, at least one of which resulted in a custodial sentence of sixty days' prison incarceration. Zehaf-Bibeau had recently been deemed a "high-risk traveler " by the Canadian government and had his passport seized.

A day before the attack, while Zehaf-Bibeau was waiting to register his purchase of the Toyota vehicle used in the shooting, multiple witnesses saw Zehaf-Bibeau engaged in a "heated discussion" with another man. According to a witness, Zehaf-Bibeau said, "If soldiers bombed your family, wouldn't you want to kill them?"

The exact manner in which Zehaf-Bibeau obtained his gun has not yet been determined. Zehaf-Bibeau was legally prohibited from possessing or acquiring firearms because his history of illegal drug use, lack of a permanent address, and previous criminal charges and convictions prevented him from obtaining a Canadian firearms license.

Social Media

Active shooters are not unfamiliar with how social media works and how the various media allow them to share viewpoints, thoughts, and feelings openly. Some use social media sites to solicit support for their cause, whereas others merely express hatred, anger, and the motive behind their beliefs to justify their actions. Not every active shooter will broadcast his or her views in advance of a shooting, and not everyone who podcasts his or her views in vivid detail will become an active shooter. An active shooter cannot be easily predicted by what is placed on social media sites, but it is important to listen to such words watch, on video, accompanying body language to determine how best to mitigate, prepare for, and respond to potential threats.

Zehaf-Bibeau made a video before the attack in which he expressed religious motives and ideological conflict with the Canada's foreign policy in the Middle East [8].

SUMMARY OF DATA AFTER SHOOTING

Date of shooting	Oct 22, 2014
Time of shooting	9:52 a.m.–9:55 a.m. EDT
Suspect	Zehaf-Bibeau
Suspect's description	32-year-old Canadian
Suspect's clothing	Blue jeans, black jacket, keffiyeh scarf
Suspect's special equipment	.30–30 Winchester Model 94 rifle
Suspect's home	Ottawa mission shelter
Location of shooting	Parliament Hill, Canada, two locations:
	Centre Block Parliament Building
	Peace Tower
Reason for shooting	Exact reason unknown; anti-government sentiment noted
Type of shooting	Multiple shootings, two locations
Vehicles	Small grey Toyota car
IEDs	None
How targets selected	Random government target—guards
Shooter's weapons	.30–30 Winchester Model 94 rifle
Casualties	Two dead, including shooter; three nonfatal injuries
Age of victim	Cirillo, 24
Shooter's criminal history	Extensive criminal record
Prior video and social media presence	Video made before attack

References

[1] <www.motherjones.com/politics/2014/06/jerad-amanda-miller-las-vegas-shooting-cliven-bundy-anti-government>.

[2] <www.thedailybeast.com/articles/2014/06/09/hatriot-politics-created-the-las-vegas-killers.html>.

[3] <www.ibtimes.com/who-are-jerad-amanda-miller-las-vegas-shooting-suspects-spoke-doing-next-columbine-photo-1596298>.

[4] <http://news.nationalpost.com/2014/10/22/canadian-soldier-shot-outside-of-parliament-hill-timeline-of-events/#__federated=1>.

[5] <www.reuters.com/article/2014/10/22/us-canada-attacks-shooting-idUSKCN0IB1PY20141022>.

[6] <http://en.wikipedia.org/wiki/2014_shootings_at_Parliament_Hill>, Ottawa.

[7] <www.cnn.com/2014/10/22/world/americas/canada-ottawa-shooting/>.

[8] <www.nbcnews.com/storyline/canadian-parliament-shooting/michael-zehaf-bibeau-parliament-hill-shooter-made-video-attack-n318661>.

Index

Note: Page numbers followed by "*b*" and "*f*" refer to boxes and figures, respectively.

Made in the USA
Columbia, SC
17 February 2019